The Elements of Instruction

The Elements of Instruction provides a common vocabulary and conceptual schema of teaching and learning that is fully applicable to all forms of instruction in our digital-centric era. This critical examination of educational technology's contemporary semantics and constructs fills a major gap in the logical foundations of instruction, with special attention to the patterns of communication among facilitators, learners, and resources. The book proposes a new framework for organizing research and theory, clear concepts and definitions for its basic elements, and a new typology of teaching-learning arrangements to simplify the selection of optimal conditions for a variety of learning goals. As trends in media, technology, and methodology continue to evolve, these historically contextual, back-to-basics pedagogical tools will be invaluable to all instructional designers and educational researchers.

Michael H. Molenda is Associate Professor Emeritus in the Department of Instructional Systems Technology in the School of Education at Indiana University Bloomington, USA.

Deepak Prem Subramony is Associate Professor and Coordinator of Educational Technology Graduate Programs in the Department of Curriculum and Instruction in the College of Education at Kansas State University, USA.

The Elements of Instruction

A Framework for the Age of Emerging Technologies

MICHAEL H. MOLENDA
DEEPAK PREM SUBRAMONY

NEW YORK AND LONDON

First published 2021
by Routledge
52 Vanderbilt Avenue, New York, NY 10017

and by Routledge
2 Park Square, Milton Park, Abingdon, Oxon, OX14 4RN

Routledge is an imprint of the Taylor & Francis Group, an informa business

© 2021 Taylor & Francis

The right of Michael H. Molenda and Deepak Prem Subramony to be identified as authors of this work has been asserted by them in accordance with sections 77 and 78 of the Copyright, Designs and Patents Act 1988.

All rights reserved. No part of this book may be reprinted or reproduced or utilised in any form or by any electronic, mechanical, or other means, now known or hereafter invented, including photocopying and recording, or in any information storage or retrieval system, without permission in writing from the publishers.

Trademark notice: Product or corporate names may be trademarks or registered trademarks, and are used only for identification and explanation without intent to infringe.

Library of Congress Cataloging-in-Publication Data
A catalog record for this title has been requested

ISBN: 978-1-138-72102-9 (hbk)
ISBN: 978-1-138-72107-4 (pbk)
ISBN: 978-1-315-19472-1 (ebk)

Typeset in Bembo and Avenir
by Deanta Global Publishing Services, Chennai, India

To two scholarly giants, no longer with us, who meant a lot to us personally and did so much to establish the bona fides of the field of educational technology

- Larry Lipsitz, editor and publisher of *Educational Technology*, from its first issue to its last—1966 to 2017. Also, his publishing house—Educational Technology Publications—brought to print scores of valuable scholarly works that he personally championed

- Robert Heinich, editor of *AV Communication Review* (*AVCR*), which under his 13-year stewardship evolved into *Educational Communication and Technology Journal* (*ECTJ*), one of the most respected scholarly journals in its field

M.H.M.

D.P.S.

Contents

List of Figures   ix
Acknowledgments   x
About the Authors   xii
Preface   xiv

1 Status and Directions   1

2 A Framework for the Instructed Learning Process   31

3 Learning, Instruction, and the Elements of Instruction   81

4 Communication Configurations and Methods   108

5 Presentation   143

6 Demonstration   173

7 Discussion   187

8 Tutorial   212

9 Repetition   229

10 Study   266

11 Expression	281
12 Summary and Conclusions	298
Epilogue	311
Glossary	314
Index	324

Figures

2.1	Molenda–Subramony Framework of the Forces Affecting Instructed Learning	32
2.2	Adaptation of Walberg's (1984) "Causal Influences on Student Learning"	36
2.3	A hypothetical depiction of the implications of Hattie's (2009)	37
2.4	Huitt's (2009) Systems-Based Framework	38
2.5	Proximal Factors Directly Affecting Instructed Learning	39
2.6	First-Level Distal Factors Indirectly Affecting Instructed Learning	44
2.7	Second-Level Distal Factors Indirectly Affecting Instructed Learning	59
4.1	The Presentation Communication Configuration	118
4.2	The Demonstration Communication Configuration	119
4.3	The Whole-Class Discussion Communication Configuration	120
4.4	The Small-Group Discussion Communication Configuration	121
4.5	The Tutorial Communication Configuration	122
4.6	The Repetition Communication Configuration	123
4.7	The Study Communication Configuration	125
4.8	The Expression Communication Configuration	126
5.1	The Presentation Communication Configuration	144
6.1	The Demonstration Communication Configuration	174
7.1	The Whole-Class Discussion Communication Configuration	188
7.2	The Small-Group Discussion Communication Configuration	188
8.1	The Tutorial Communication Configuration	213
9.1	The Repetition Communication Configuration	230
10.1	The Study Communication Configuration	267
11.1	The Expression Communication Configuration	282
12.1	Molenda–Subramony Framework of the Forces That Impact Instructed Learning	302

Acknowledgments

I would not have persisted in pursuing this arduous process without the encouragement of a number of colleagues over the years. My first colleague, Mary Frances Johnson, at the University of North Carolina at Greensboro, was a paragon of professional comportment. I am still striving to live up to her example and that of Donald P. Ely, my mentor at Syracuse University and later a colleague, friend, and collaborator. For this project, I profited immensely from vigorous exchanges of opinions with Charles Reigeluth and Theodore Frick, friends and colleagues at Indiana University, and Richard E. Clark of the University of Southern California. Another Indiana colleague, Ivor K. Davies, was working along parallel lines in the 1970s; his writings confirmed that I was onto an idea worth pursuing. Fortunately for me, he was also available and willing to serve as a sounding board in the formative stage of preparing this manuscript. The original versions of the "configuration" illustrations were drawn by Prof. Elizabeth Boling, another Indiana colleague, a talented visual designer who helped me think through the symbolic representation of the communication configurations.

Most of all, I thank my wife, Janet Stavropoulos, for her constant encouragement and highly honed talents as an editor. It really helps to have an English professor and manuscript editor in the family!

Michael H. Molenda

Having worked with Michael Molenda to successfully produce a significant contribution to the pedagogy literature—an *Educational Technology* special issue comprehensively describing and systematically dismantling the near-impregnable fortress of prescriptive pseudoscience that had built up over the decades around Edgar Dale's "Cone of Experience"—back in 2014, I did not hesitate for a moment when Mike graciously invited me to collaborate with him on this project. Previously I had studied with Mike (2001–2005) while pursuing my doctorate at Indiana

University Bloomington, during which time he also served on my program advisory committee. While our cultural backgrounds and ideological perspectives are admittedly different, I would not be exaggerating if I were to say that I have learned more about pedagogy from Mike than I have from any other individual I can think of. Hence, I must acknowledge him before all else.

I would also like to recognize Todd Goodson—my Department Chair at Kansas State University—for his constant inspiration, encouragement, and support with regard to this project. And last, but most definitely not the least, I would like to acknowledge my loving spouse Sławomir Dobrzański. None of this would make any sense whatsoever if he weren't a part of my life.

Deepak Prem Subramony

About the Authors

Michael H. Molenda is Associate Professor Emeritus in the Department of Instructional Systems Technology at Indiana University Bloomington, Indiana, USA, where he taught from 1972 to 2005. He is coauthor of the first five editions of *Instructional Media and the New Technologies of Instruction* and coeditor of the Association for Educational Communications and Technology (AECT)'s 2008 definition book, *Educational Technology: A Definition with Commentary* (as well as being author or coauthor of five chapters in the book). He served as founding editor of *Asia-Pacific Cybereducation Journal*, 2003–2005. He has documented the history of educational technology and of instructional systems design in AECT's *Handbook of Research on Educational Communications and Technology*, 3rd ed. (2008) and in ISPI's *Handbook of Improving Performance in the Workplace*, vol. 1, *Instructional Design and Training Delivery* (2009). He has contributed numerous encyclopedia articles on educational technology topics, including for AECT's 2013 *Encyclopedia of Terminology for Educational Communications and Technology*.

Deepak Prem Subramony is Associate Professor and Coordinator of the Educational Technology Graduate Programs in the Department of Curriculum and Instruction in the College of Education at Kansas State University, Kansas, USA. He holds an MA in Mass Communication (2001) from the University of Minnesota–Twin Cities and a PhD in Instructional Systems Technology (2005) from Indiana University Bloomington. Prior to arriving at Kansas State, he held faculty positions at Utah State University and Grand Valley State University. His primary scholarly interests revolve around the issues of (a) equitable access to the emancipatory potential of Information Age educational and communications technologies (ECT), and (b) the complex relationship between ECT and stakeholders from historically underrepresented, underserved, and marginalized groups. In

2014 he coauthored (with Michael Molenda and others) a special issue—"The Mythical Retention Chart and the Corruption of Dale's Cone of Experience"—of *Educational Technology*, a journal on whose editorial board he also served for several years. He is currently serving as president of the Association for Educational Communications and Technology (AECT)'s Division of Culture, Learning, and Technology.

Preface

As coauthors, we entered this project with rather contrasting perspectives—with one being grounded in a classical Western liberal-arts tradition, and the other in a postcolonial, critical movement focusing on cultural diversity, power disparities, access, equity, privilege, and intersectionality. We also represent different, almost mutually exclusive generations—one began teaching in 1968 and was personally acquainted with some of the pioneers of the visual education movement dating back to the 1920s, while the other happened to commence his faculty career the very year (2005) the former retired! This unique intergenerational collaboration has allowed us to tap into an unparalleled breadth of experience—stretching from the Jet Age to the Information Age—a span that neatly coincides with virtually the entire lifespan of educational technology, the field with which the two of us have been primarily affiliated.

We both agree that, throughout our combined 67 years in pedagogy, some fundamental things have remained unchanged. Through this book we seek to foreground and highlight those fundamentals, raising them above the distracting cacophony of noisy bandwagons centering on various "emerging technologies." We have a handful of major objectives in writing this book:

1. To critically examine some of the major constructs in educational technology—and in pedagogy generally—with a view to pointing out how enduring misunderstandings and miscommunications surrounding the very meanings of key terms have hobbled fruitful theoretical discussion and the meaningful conceptualization of inquiry; see Chapter 1.
2. To provide a framework for research and theory in pedagogy; see Chapter 2.
3. To position our framework within the universe of learning theories and current neuroscientific findings; see Chapter 3.

4. To provide a typology of teaching–learning arrangements, variously referred to by pedagogues over the decades as "methods," "strategies," "modes," "formats," etc. This became the typology of communication configurations, spelled out in Chapter 4.
5. To elaborate on the meanings and implications of the communication configurations described in Chapter 4; see Chapters 5 through 11.

We consider the ideas in this book as hypotheses. We eagerly look forward to seeing them tested and revised, for the betterment of research and theory in pedagogy.

Michael H. Molenda
Bloomington, Indiana, USA

Deepak Prem Subramony
Manhattan, Kansas, USA
March 28, 2020

Status and Directions 1

We stand at the beginning of the third decade of the twenty-first century, gazing in wonder at the bounty promised to education by new and emerging digital technologies. Advocates of emerging technologies, such as artificial intelligence, virtual and augmented reality, MOOCs, blockchain technology, and similar developments, envision a transformation of education and training the likes of which mankind has never before experienced.

Indeed, they envision a transformation of human capabilities, coming generations of "digital natives" who think and feel in ways qualitatively different from their ancestors. These visions raise the question that appeared as the title of an article in 2013: "Are 20th-Century Methods of Teaching Applicable in the 21st Century?" (Bassendowski and Petrucka 2013). This book aims to answer that question. What has changed in today's world of teaching and learning, and what remains the same? Our basic position is that a great deal more is asserted about "what's new" than is proven, and a great deal that has been proven is being ignored.

Aims of this Book

We intend, first, in this chapter, to critically examine some semantic issues that hinder clear communication about the phenomena we study in the field of pedagogy, particularly terms related to the use of technology in education. Constructs such as *media, multimedia, distance education, MOOCs, educational technology, emerging technologies,* and *social media* have frequently been used as independent variables with a wide variety of different phenomena deployed as the actual operational definition of each, leading to results that are largely uninterpretable. Later in this chapter we will attempt to cast some light on the meanings of these constructs.

Second, in Chapter 2 we propose a new framework for organizing research and theory on instruction to fill a major gap in the logical foundations of the field.

Third, in Chapter 3 we propose new, clearer concepts and definitions for the basic elements that constitute instruction, which requires a closer look at the theories of learning that underpin instruction. One outcome of that closer look is the suggestion for a new term—*instructed learning*—to describe the outcome of instructional interventions.

Fourth, in Chapter 4 we introduce a new typology of teaching–learning arrangements, a tool to simplify the process of selecting the optimal conditions for different sorts of learning goals. The typology is based on the patterns of communication among facilitators, learners, and resources; these patterns fall into eight categories, which we call *communication configurations*. We also introduce a new precising definition for *method* and provide examples of instructional methods, which are explored in depth in each of the following chapters (5 through 11).

Most of the remainder of the book, Chapters 5 through 11, is devoted principally to a category-by-category examination of the communication configurations introduced in Chapter 4. For each category—Presentation, Demonstration, Whole-Class Discussion, Small-Group Discussion, Tutorial, Repetition, Study, and Expression—we define the construct, list the formats in which each configuration typically occurs, explore the origins of each configuration, discuss "best practices" for gaining the maximum learning benefits from each, and show how each configuration plays a role in different instructional methods. We conclude, in Chapter 12, by recapitulating the major claims made in this book and the points supporting those claims, and by pointing out an issue that may deserve greater attention than is being paid by educators to date.

Talking Past Each Other

We agree with the many scholars who claim that fundamental work remains to be done in the scholarship of pedagogy. Educators, trainers, and instructional designers lack a common vocabulary and a common conceptual schema for the most basic tools they work with. Educational researchers lack operational definitions for many of the treatments they study. This definitional gap is a conceptual problem, but it has both theoretical and practical consequences. Among the most prominent advocates for taking a fresh look at the foundations is M. David "Dave" Merrill, who has contributed many evidence-based ideas for designing instruction to meet his standard of "e^3," i.e., to be effective, efficient, and engaging (Merrill 2013). To lay a foundation for his design principles, Merrill proposes a systematic approach, beginning with rigorous definitions of basic terms, such as *instructional event*, *instructional interaction*, *content element*, and *component skill* (2013, 48–53).

Another contemporary theorist who deals with these basic issues is Theodore "Ted" Frick, whose perspective is rooted in the philosophical framework of semiotics, related to general systems theory. He proposes that the study of educational processes be labeled as *educology*, and that this field of organized knowledge should be based on a glossary of standard terms, including *educational system*, *intentional system, learning, teacher, student, content, context,* and *system environment* (Frick, 2019).

We agree with Merrill, Frick, and other recent critics, especially such as Reigeluth and Carr-Chellman (2009), who point out the shortcomings in the conceptual framework and terminology in the field of pedagogy; further, we agree with their basic approach, which is to attempt to be as systematic as possible in choosing and using our "terms of art." Two of our major purposes in this book are to propose our own conceptual framework (see Chapter 2) and our own set of basic terms (see Chapter 3) for the field of instruction. In those discussions, we point out where we agree and disagree with Merrill's and Frick's choices of labels and definitions. We extend this argument in Chapter 4, where we propose a new way of looking at teaching–learning arrangements—*communication configurations*. We hope that these proposals may help lay a new foundation for better professional communication.

A Note about Creating Constructs and Definitions

Throughout this book, we attempt to be transparent about designating new or revised constructs and also about providing definitions for both new and familiar constructs. In this we are guided by the advice of Dusek (2006) regarding the traits of different types of definitions. He differentiates among three common types of definitions—in addition to the dictionary definition—encountered in academic works: *reportative, stipulative,* and *precising*. *Reportative* definitions simply report how words are used in everyday conversation. Lexical definitions—those that appear in dictionaries—are usually claimed to be reportative. The dictionary's lexicographers typically claim that they are offering definitions that are descriptive of how words are generally used, not prescriptive—judging between "correct" and "incorrect" usage. However, dictionaries necessarily play a somewhat normative role, since they do draw boundaries around meanings. *Reportative* definitions are adequate for day-to-day human communications; we want our words to signify the same thing to our listeners as they do to us, otherwise conversation becomes unintelligible. On the other hand, reportative definitions are often too fuzzy to serve the purpose of scholarly discussion.

Stipulative definitions are concocted by scholars to conclusively establish the meanings of key terms for purposes of logical discussion; their critical attributes and boundaries are stipulated by the writer. Stipulative definitions are imperative for discourse in fields such as logic and mathematics. In general, they facilitate discourse as long as all parties adhere to the artificially concocted definition. However, as Dusek (2006, 28) points out, there is always the danger that one or more parties will unconsciously start using a defined term according to its lexical, rather than its stipulated, meaning. At that point, clear communication breaks down.

Precising definitions begin with the lexical meaning and then add additional criteria that narrow down the boundaries of what is included and what is excluded. Precising definitions are common in legal discourse; for example, how many convictions, of what sort, make a person a "habitual offender?" Or who qualifies as a "parent?" What we intend to offer in this chapter and subsequent chapters are precising definitions. We strive to stay within the commonly understood, or reportative, meanings, while specifying critical attributes and setting boundaries that reduce the likelihood of misunderstanding. For example, in common usage, the term *game* is often used to describe activities that may more accurately be labeled as puzzles, contests, simulations, or simulation games. Each of these has quite different instructional implications, so important distinctions are missed when all are aggregated under one label.

Problematic Constructs

Media

Until the twentieth century, the term *medium* (plural *media*) was used primarily in the sense of an environment, a substance surrounding an object, separating it from outside forces—such as using agar as a growth *medium* in a petri dish (*Oxford English Dictionary*, 2nd edition 1989). In the early decades of the twentieth century, with the advent of industrial-level newspaper and book printing and distribution—and later, radio broadcasting—the concept of *mass media* was born. These "emerging technologies" seemed to create enveloping environments into which readers and listeners could immerse themselves.

"Magical" Media

When television joined radio in the mid-twentieth century, these technologies allowed the broad dissemination of entertainment and information at a speed and a cost that other mass media—such as newspapers, magazines, books, theater, and cinema—could not compete with. Electrical signals flying at nearly the speed of light could produce sounds and pictures out of thin air. It seemed magical. And the people who appeared on radio and television basked in the glow of this magical force; they took on credibility and enjoyed prestige beyond that of other entertainers and journalists. Pioneers in communication research, Paul F. Lazarsfeld and Robert K. Merton, termed it the "status conferral function" of the mass media (Lazarsfeld and Merton 1948, 235–236).

It was entirely foreseeable that educators would seek to capitalize on these new technologies for their own purposes, entranced as they were by the halo of excitement surrounding broadcast media and other revolutionary innovations of the day. For example, in the late 1920s, early in the era of commercial air travel, a teacher and a class of elementary students flew aboard a converted commercial aircraft for "aerial geography" lessons (Cuban 1986, 8). Similarly, in 1984 NASA launched its

Teacher in Space Project, aimed at carrying teachers into space to beam lessons from the Space Shuttle back to Earth and later to return to their classrooms to share the experience with students. It is unclear how the pedagogical impact of such treatments was expected to be enhanced by their being conducted inside an airplane or beamed from outer space. The "active ingredient" of such treatments appears to be the mystique—the status conferral—of being associated with a popular and very modern high-tech innovation.

More realistically, educators started "schools of the air" to broadcast lessons to elementary, secondary, and college students in their regular classrooms. The original rationale was to standardize the presentation of material, employing talented presenters and writers and skillful audiovisual production staffs to provide lessons of higher quality than everyday classroom teachers could prepare. In the 1950s, with a booming postwar population, the motivation was more economic: Television could fill the gap in supply of qualified teachers for all the new schools being built. The unspoken rationale was that the "magic" of broadcasting gave televised lessons an impact so much greater than just the words and images being transmitted, that they could replace some of the most important functions of live teachers.

Many of these efforts later foundered as tele-educators struggled with the mundane concerns, such as providing content that fit the curricula of different school districts at the same time and furnishing the classroom management and instructional support that only a live, trained facilitator could provide. In the 1960s, in the era of school desegregation in the United States, at least one major school district attempted to use televised lessons to provide white teachers for predominantly African American classrooms and African American teachers for predominantly white classrooms. A cynic observed that now that they had used television to solve the problem of desegregation by showing Black and White children, maybe they could solve the problems of hunger and poverty by showing pictures of food and money. The saga of schools' endeavors with broadcast radio and television are well recounted in Cuban (1986) and Saettler (1990).

It was not only broadcasting that cast a spell. Even before the turn of the twentieth century, audiences flocked to travelogues and other public entertainments featuring "magic lantern" slides. Early in the new century, Edison's motion picture projector provided an even more compelling visual experience—real-life people and places shown in realistic motion. Educators were quick to perceive the possible benefits for classroom instruction and strove to acquire the needed hardware and software.

> Educators could find many types of films to use—theatrical films edited for special purposes, industrial films, government films, and a smaller number of films produced specifically for the classroom. Schools that wanted to be viewed as progressive rushed to build collections of films.
>
> *(Molenda 2008, 6)*

The attraction was understandable. There is a certain kind of magic in viewing a bright, enlarged—bigger than life-size—image in a darkened room. But the "magic" pertains to the "gaining attention" step in the process of perception, learning, and retention, and to the emotional factors linked to cognitive processes discussed further in Chapter 3. As we understand today, whether the image will be incorporated into the viewer's mental repertoire depends on the extent to which the image is accompanied by instructional activities that support the cognitive organization and future activation of the knowledge (Merrill 2013, 172).

The "No Significant Difference Phenomenon"

The idea that took root in those early days—that the "new media" radiated some sort of mysterious power—has continued through the era of television and into the eras of the computer and the mobile device. Hundreds, if not thousands, of research studies have been conducted to compare the outcomes of "media" treatments with "conventional" treatments. However, periodic efforts to summarize the findings of this research have typically come up empty. An early, representative summary found that:

> It is an indictment of our present state of knowledge that we know neither how to describe the psychological effects of…technologies nor how to adapt them to the purposes of education. The impact of technologies both ancient and modern on children's learning is either negligible or unknown.
> *(Olson 1974, 6)*

The recurrence of this sort of summary conclusion led Thomas Russell to dub it "The No Significant Difference Phenomenon." He compiled and maintained a list of hundreds of so-called media comparison studies that discovered "no significant difference" between treatments, eventually publishing the list in book form (Russell 1999). His goal was to discourage further investment in "media comparison" studies, not to disparage the potentially positive applications of technology to instruction. He acknowledged that when lessons and courses were redesigned to integrate media resources, the extra attention to pedagogical design often led to the adoption of more powerful *methods* of instruction. On this important point Russell was reflecting the argument made by Richard E. Clark more than a decade earlier, as discussed below.

Do Media Affect Learning?

In 1983 Clark published a major research review ("Reconsidering Research on Learning from Media") criticizing the proposition that *media* have direct causative influence on specific types of learning. It touched off a controversy that continued for a decade, with point-counterpoint articles between Clark and various critics, especially Robert Kozma (1991), in professional journals and panel discussions at academic conferences. Clark's basic claim was that:

> The best current evidence is that media are mere vehicles that deliver instruction but do not influence student achievement any more than the truck that delivers our groceries causes changes in our nutrition.
>
> *(Clark 1983, 445)*

Later, in a review of research on computer-based instruction (1985), Clark suggested that the use of superior pedagogical *methods* explained the success of some "media" treatments rather than the media component itself. Hence the label applied to this exchange of views—the media-methods debate. The "methods" part of this issue will be explored at greater length in Chapter 4.

Conflating Channels with Messages

We agree with Clark that there have been conceptual problems hindering our appraisal of the possible uses of auditory and visual resources in education and training. The first problem is that many authors—including those involved in the media-methods debate—fail to clearly define how they are using the term *media*. We accept Clark's "vehicle" analogy (1983, 445), which is also supported by the dictionary's contemporary definition of the term *media* (plural of *medium*) as: "newspapers, radio, television, etc., collectively, as vehicles of mass communication" (*Oxford English Dictionary*, 2nd edition 1989). Unfortunately, in educational research the concept of media is too often conflated with the messages transmitted through those channels. For example, if an evaluation study showed that preschool children's numeracy skills improved after watching three particular segments of *Sesame Street*, someone might say it demonstrated that "children can learn from television." However, it was not "television" that was effective, it was those three specific audiovisual experiences. This issue was neatly summarized by Wilbur Schramm's claim that "learning seems to be affected more by what is delivered than by the delivery system" (Schramm 1977, 273). That is, listeners may hear essentially the same voices, music, and sounds regardless of whether those signals travel through the air, through wires, are relayed by satellites in geosynchronous orbit, or are recorded and played back through a speaker. Therefore, our discussion focuses on the sounds and images that are taken in by the sensory systems of learners. To avoid possible misunderstanding, we use the term *resources* to refer to materials themselves, as is discussed at greater length in Chapter 3.

Media Do Matter, Logistically

Having made the point that the term *media* should be limited to identifying technological delivery channels, we are quick to acknowledge that those "mere vehicles" have enormous practical significance. While the Internet is more than the sum of its parts, the electronic transmission part has earthshaking consequences. For an individual anywhere in the world to be able to communicate, cheaply and quickly, with billions of other people creates whole new worlds of human possibility. In their day, radio and television had similar revolutionary impacts, regardless of the content that was being transmitted. The expansion of human reach was itself life changing.

Media distribution systems may vary greatly in their capacity and the breadth of their reach. One system may allow a higher resolution image or sound than another. For example, an animated illustration of the process of mitosis may lose its illustrative power if shown on a small, low-resolution cellphone screen rather than a full-size TV monitor.

From an institutional perspective, the choice of media distribution system may have significant logistical—time and cost—consequences. For example, if an institution's educational program consists mainly of lectures, it might be economically advantageous to use broadcasting to expand the audience more affordably than hiring many halls and sending out many lecturers. If an institution's educational program consists mainly of printed information, such as correspondence study, it might be advantageous to use a website to distribute the information rather than mailing printed material. So different media distribution systems can have differential cost advantages. Televised instruction has often been used as the most cost-effective way to reach isolated student populations across sparsely populated expanses such as the Great Plains, Desert Southwest, Australian Outback, Canadian North, and Alaska. As recently as the early 2000s—when one of the authors (Subramony) was performing fieldwork in the Alaskan arctic—high-school-level students residing in the roadless Alaskan interior were taking advanced placement courses via interactive television; in the years since, this has mostly been replaced by online instruction.

Media delivery systems may also offer time advantages. Consider the case of a new drug treatment for opioid overdose. It might be cost-beneficial to have one trained team of health educators travel around a region teaching groups of medical professionals how to administer the treatment. In the months needed to complete the live training sessions, hundreds more victims may die. An alternative might be to arrange a live video conference attended simultaneously by medics around the region, with follow-up conferences as needed—a time trade-off of a few days versus a few months.

Multimedia

The issues of conflated meanings and hyperbolic expectations that we are raising are not limited to controversies of the 1980s; it continues with the newer media forms of today, particularly the concept of "multimedia" effects. This is another case in which a term with a connotation of glamour has been attached to a completely mundane phenomenon with the expectation that the label carried with it some special instructional power.

Mind-Blowing "Multimedia"

The term *multimedia* as used in contemporary educational research has a far different meaning than when it was coined in the 1960s to refer to psychedelic sound-and-light shows presented at discotheques, as in this early observation in show-business newspaper, *Variety*: "Brainchild of songscribe-comic Bob ('Washington Square') Goldstein, the 'Lightworks' is the latest multi-media music-cum-visuals to debut as discothèque fare" (Albarino 1966). *Multimedia* was turned into a popular culture sensation by the flood of multiscreen, multisensory slide and film exhibitions experienced by over 50 million people at the World's Fair in Montreal in 1967.

Multimedia at Expo 67

Among the many exhibition halls and pavilions at Expo 67 were a cluster of specially designed theaters showing state-of-the-art experimental audiovisual experiences that were exploring new ground in immersing viewers in a juxtaposition of multiple sounds and images meant to jar the senses into new and different levels of perception—a sort of surrogate for hallucinogenic drugs. For example, *We Are Young!* was a six-screen, 3,000-square-foot immersion into the emerging youth culture of the 1960s, from go-go dancers to alienated urbanites (Gagnon and Marchessault 2014, 119). *A Place to Stand*, shown on one gigantic screen with six-channel stereo surround sound, projected multiple images of different sizes to celebrate the province of Ontario (168). More abstract was *Kaleidoscope*, "a psychedelic, abstract sound-and-image play over mirrored surfaces, using sculpted light, film, and slide projections" accompanied by an electronic music score (55). Viewers stood inside a "tower of light" and watched a fantasia of ever-changing cascades of colors and images.

Labyrinth entailed a journey through three chambers, representing humanity's journey through mythic time by means of ambiguous, often disorienting, combinations of allegorical film images synchronized to electronic music. Chamber 2, for example, was:

> an M-shaped chamber formed by three semi-mirrored prisms that house hundreds of tiny lights winking on and off, reflections against a black infinity. Some people...say they felt weightless, some say serene, suspended between worlds...against a primitive pattern of sound (jungle noises, hyenas, drums) into abstract electronic sound.
>
> *(Gagnon and Marchessault 2014, 40–41)*

Not only at *Kaleidoscope* and *Labyrinth*, but throughout the multimedia exhibitions, music was an intrinsic part of the show rather than a mere accompaniment to the images (21). The producers were reaching for total, immersive, and provocative experiences. This is what *multimedia* meant at its inception. People who used the term in those days used it in its everyday meaning, or its reportative definition—an immersive experience involving disorienting application of a wide range of sights and sounds simultaneously.

Evolution of Interest in Multimedia in the 1960s through the 1980s

While it was impractical to reproduce the multimedia extravaganzas outside the venue of a World's Fair, popular and scholarly fascination with multimedia continued. Audiovisual educators experimented with multiscreen slide projections, exploring possible synergistic effects of displaying complementary or contrasting images synchronized with soundtracks incorporating the human voice, music, and sound effects. This interest is reflected in the annual conference programs of the Department of Audio-Visual Instruction (DAVI)—known as the Association for Educational Communications and Technology (AECT) after 1971—then the largest professional association for educational media. In 1967 and 1968, there was a smattering of research reports on "multi-media" (or "multimedia") programs, for example, "Encoding and Decoding Verbal and Pictorial Stimuli." DAVI's 1969 convention program featured a "Multimage (borrowing the French usage from Montreal) Festival," described as "visual essays in the cognitive and affective domains using multiple image projection." About a dozen multiscreen presentations were shown and repeated over three afternoons. The research reports tended to reflect more interest in synergistic effects: "Recognition Learning from Single- and Multiple-Channel Presentations within the Audio Sensory Domain" and "Efficiency of Learning when Both Incidental and Intentional Learning Occur Simultaneously" (DAVI 1964–1970).

At DAVI's 1970 convention, the Multimage Festival—now running in two venues, repeated over three days, featuring dozens of presentations—was joined by three nights of Underground Movies and an Environmental Theater—"an inflatable facility designed to be used for sensitivity training. The audience is surrounded by 360° sound and pictures" (DAVI 1964–1970). Research reports reflected a hint of critical analysis, for example, "Structural Coherence in Verbal and Pictorial Displays" and "Some Multi-Media Classrooms Revisited: What's Working and What Isn't." By the mid-1970s, interest was at its peak, with the Multi-Image (dropping the French usage) Festival at AECT's 1977 convention featuring three dozen presentations, joined by a Multi-Image Symposium with another dozen exemplars, a Multi-Image Workshop, and The Best of Multi-Image. Furthermore, AECT now incorporated an affiliated organization, the Association for Multi-Image. Research reports continued to trend toward critical analysis, for example, "Recognition Memory for Pictures Presented in a Rapidly Changing Array under Differentiated Display Conditions." Increasingly, convention sessions devoted to multimedia and examples shown were more in the domain of advertising and public relations (e.g., *The Spirit of South Carolina!*) than in the domain of instruction.

Interest tapered off in the next few years; by the time AECT's 1980 convention came along, the Multi-Image Festival was absent from its program, and the number of sessions devoted to multimedia had dwindled to a few (AECT 1974–1981). At this point, *multimedia* still retained its reportative definition—sight and sound sensory immersion.

The Constructivism Movement and a Shifting Definition

Beginning in the late 1980s, the Constructivism movement in educational psychology supplied the theoretical impetus to reawaken interest in learning environments that allowed learners to pursue problems under realistic conditions—"authentic" and "holistic" experiences that allowed the maximum freedom for learner control and exploration (Bransford, Brown and Cocking 2002). With the growing power of computers to simulate real-life settings, educators began creating realistic simulations, narrated video modules, and other sight-and-sound products under the guise of "constructivist learning environments." In conjunction with this renewed interest in realistic and immersive experiences, the label of *multimedia* began to reappear in pedagogical discourse, only now with the meaning of "any combination of text, graphic art, sound, animation, and video that is delivered by computer" (Vaughan 1993, 3). At that point, it still carried the connotation of complex, reproducible programs that involved not only multiple senses but also multiple neural processing systems—pictorial images, graphic images, moving images, musical sounds, natural sounds, and words spoken and printed.

However, when Richard E. Mayer, Richard E. Anderson, and other cognitive psychologists began to use the term *multimedia* in their research (Mayer and Anderson 1992), their operational definition boiled down to any instructional event—not necessarily even a reproducible product—in which both verbal information and visual information were used. Since that time, in educational research, the concept of *multimedia learning* has been defined as simply "learning from words (e.g., spoken or printed text) and pictures (e.g., illustrations, photos, maps, graphs, animation, or video)" (Mayer 2014, ix). As Mayer goes on to say, these conditions are met when a lecturer draws a diagram on a chalkboard or when a student reads a textbook with illustrations (Mayer 2014, 2–3), thus including the most common everyday teaching–learning arrangements—no electricity required. Mayer's stipulative definition stretches the concept of *multiple*—which means several or many (more than two) elements—and distorts the concept of *media*, whose primary meaning is a technological means of communication. Thus, not only is *multimedia* stripped of its original reportative definition—a synergistic combination of voice, music, and multiple still and moving images—but also of its basic denotations. Hence, *multimedia learning* seems to us to be a misnomer. Since seeing (words and pictures) and hearing (words, natural sounds, music) are the two sensory modes involved, perhaps *bimodal learning* would be a more apt term. And if this learning happens as a result of deliberate instruction, we would call it *bimodal instructed learning.* This wording would be more technically accurate, and it would avoid the emotive bias carried by the term *multimedia*. The complexities involved in bimodal instructed learning will be explored at greater length in Chapter 5.

Distance Education

Let us first understand that "distance education" is not a delivery system, a new medium, or a new type of learning; it is rather the name given to a particular sort of educational *program*. As we will discuss later in this chapter, for such a program to be considered legitimate according to US federal standards, it must provide bona fide interactive learning opportunities to participants—codified as "regular and substantive interaction between the students and the instructor." This qualification is necessary because of a long history of abuse of various iterations of the construct of distance education.

Early Correspondence Study

The idea of offering university credit for nonresidential study first gained serious traction in the mid-nineteenth century when an "external programme" was chartered at the University of London. This model was emulated at the University of Chicago and, later, Columbia University and the University of Wisconsin in the United States late in the nineteenth century under the label of *correspondence study*. People who were unable to attend formal educational institutions could enroll in a correspondence school, from which they received printed lessons through the mail. They completed written assignments, which were checked by knowledgeable readers, who then mailed evaluative feedback to the learner along with the next lesson—a form of tutorial instruction.

Indeed, correspondence study by mail was one of the pillars in the establishment of the University of Chicago in the late 1890s. Founder William Rainey Harper was committed to the wide dissemination of knowledge beyond the walls of the university, to members of the general public who could never expect to attend a residential college. Although these courses proved to yield learning gains comparable to on-campus courses, they faced constant skepticism from the faculty of the "University Proper." What led to the slow decline of Chicago's correspondence study program in the 1920s and eventual demise in the 1960s, though, was competition from for-profit ventures. Hundreds of vendors sprouted up, luring unwary customers into expensive courses that failed to deliver on their promises. The national scandal over these abuses ruined the reputation of correspondence study and forced the prominent universities to back away from correspondence study, or, at best, to make it a quiet backwater, well insulated from the "University Proper" (Pittman 2008; Hampel 2010).

The problem of fraudulent for-profit operations ballooned after World War II and the Korean War, when veterans were allowed to use their federal educational benefits for correspondence courses, and again in the 1970s when federally guaranteed student loan funds were allowed to be used for correspondence study. A government investigation of veteran participation in correspondence courses in 1972 found that "three-fourths never graduated and just 6 percent found work in their fields of study" (Whitman 2018). The US Congress finally took action to address this problem a good two decades later, by attempting in 1992 to redefine what programs could be supported by the troubled federal student loan program. The main impetus for this reform was a 1992 US Government Accountability Office report that found modern correspondence schools to have twice the student loan default rates of other colleges/universities. The sobering findings of this report prompted Congress to decree that to be eligible for federal aid institutions had to show that they offered students "regular and substantive interaction" (RSI) with faculty at least half of the time, or for at least half of students. At the time, such interaction was only feasible within face-to-face programs, and so correspondence schools were effectively blocked from receiving any federal student loan funds.

Electronically Mediated Distance Education

The correspondence-study model was upgraded technologically in the 1970s, thanks mainly to the exemplary undertakings of Britain's Open University (OU). The OU used broadcast radio and television supplemented by print and audiotape materials as the main presentation formats. Students interacted with tutors, either at local learning centers or via telephone, to work through the material and complete assignments. Course credit was granted based on performance on coursework and examinations. A good deal of the success of this model could be attributed to the serious effort to staff local learning centers and telephone call centers with well qualified tutors who could guide distant learners through the material. The OU model came to be emulated by many other open universities that sprang up in the next decades, although not always with the same academic rigor and commitment to expert learner guidance.

Distance Education Goes Online

A further technological revolution started around the latter half of the 1990s when personal computers became ubiquitous and the World Wide Web made communication over distance rapid and inexpensive. The advent of online learning made it possible for the earlier correspondence or OU models to evolve into more multifaceted forms, especially in the hands of capable instructional design professionals. Unfortunately, what happened far more often was that the same old, noninteractive correspondence study models were repackaged for online delivery with precious few alterations made to their underlying instructional design or strategies. The slang employed within industry circles for such courses back in the day—when one of the authors worked as an instructional designer in Asia— was "shovel-ware," as in, you simply "shovel" your paper-based instructional materials online, verbatim, and call it an online course.

Government Intervention in Distance Education

Both legitimate, nonprofit educational entities as well as for-profit fraudsters were guilty of producing such low-quality online instruction, and both benefited tremendously from the fact that their online programs were eligible to receive federal student loan funds. Incidentally, when the "dot.com bubble" burst in the early 2000s, many for-profit ventures collapsed as quickly as they had arisen (Molenda and Sullivan 2003); those that survived the crash—like University of Phoenix Online—primarily did so by serving students carrying government-backed student loans, loans on which the latter frequently ended up defaulting due to either dropping out of their programs or failing to find suitable employment after graduating from them. The university itself saw its once-massive enrollments gradually decline, especially after investigations revealed its abysmal graduation rate. On the other hand, online distance-education programs offered by traditional universities have continued to grow, although that growth is increasingly driven by more online courses being taken by regular residential students rather than by attracting larger numbers of nontraditional learners.

The pressing instructional quality issues plaguing many online courses and programs—and the consequent federal student loan default crises—led Congress to intervene again, in 2008, which they did by formulating a formal definition of distance education that explicitly included the RSI requirement, thus creating a concrete federal aid policy distinction between correspondence and distance education programs (Toppo 2018). According to the 2019 edition of the Code of Federal Regulations (CFR), Part 600.2 of Title 34 officially defines distance education as follows:

> Distance education means education that uses one or more of the technologies listed in paragraphs (1) through (4) of this definition to deliver instruction to students who are separated from the instructor and to support regular and substantive interaction between the students and the instructor, either synchronously or asynchronously. The technologies may include—
>
> (1) The Internet;
> (2) One-way and two-way transmissions through open broadcast, closed circuit, cable, microwave, broadband lines, fiber optics, satellite, or wireless communications devices;

(3) Audio conferencing; or
(4) Video cassettes, DVDs, and CD-ROMs, if the cassettes, DVDs, or CD-ROMs are used in a course in conjunction with any of the technologies listed in paragraphs (1) through (3) of this definition.

To reiterate the importance of RSI within the context of bona fide online programs that *are* eligible to receive federal student loan funds—as opposed to correspondence courses that are *not*—the CFR explicitly characterizes correspondence courses as *not* featuring RSI:

Correspondence course:

(1) A course provided by an institution under which the institution provides instructional materials, by mail or electronic transmission, including examinations on the materials, to students who are separated from the instructor. Interaction between the instructor and student is limited, is not regular and substantive, and is primarily initiated by the student. Correspondence courses are typically self-paced.
(2) If a course is part correspondence and part residential training, the Secretary considers the course to be a correspondence course.
(3) A correspondence course is not distance education.

This 2008 policy change saw its first instance of active enforcement in 2012, when the US Department of Education (ED) audited Saint Mary-of-the-Woods College and determined that the latter did not maintain RSI between students and faculty (Kronk 2019). ED consequently recommended that the college be asked to return $42 million in federal financial aid. The next high-profile case emerged in September 2017, when an ED audit determined that most of the courses offered by the Western Governors University failed to meet their RSI standard and called for the latter to pay back at least $713 million in federal aid (Toppo 2018).

On the other hand, as distance education continues to rapidly grow and evolve, critics have been assailing the US government's conceptualization and enforcement of RSI standards thus:

(a) ED never fully defined RSI, so each stakeholder has understood it differently; besides, each ED audit shifted expectations in this regard; and when reasonably concrete criteria were eventually provided, these were applied through the lens that F2F instruction is the standard to which all other modalities need to conform (Poulin 2019).
(b) Online education proponents see RSI as an anachronistic impediment to innovation in an era where one-third of students study at least partially online as rapidly evolving technology changes how students and faculty engage, and unworkable within contemporary distance education where successful models featuring little or no live instruction exist (Toppo 2018).

A Definition of Distance Education

Unfortunately, aside from the legal problems associated with the label, the term *distance education* has often been used rather loosely, encompassing incidental activities such as high school students interviewing a famous author via telephone, and informal arrangements such as a series of YouTube videos being offered under the title of an "academy" or "university." We propose a precising definition to denote a formal program with specific educational intentions:

> *Distance Education*: a program of some duration with specific learning goals, leading to formal recognition of achievement (such as course credit or professional certification), in which the learner is separated from the instructor and in which communication technologies facilitate frequent and substantive dialogue between the remote student(s) and the instructor and possibly among the students themselves.

Note that the "separation" discussed above may include separation from other students and that it exists for the majority of what would be the "classroom" portion of the program. This clarification is necessary because even in residential courses students are at many times separated from their instructors and other students.

The distance education applications of each of the different communication configurations will be discussed in their respective chapters (Chapters 5 to 11).

MOOCs

Massive Open Online Courses (MOOCs) are a development within the concept of distance education that emerged from the open educational resources (OER) movement. The original conception in 2011 was to "provide unlimited participation in an educational experience via the Web, typically for free" (Bonk et al. 2018, 250). The ideal was to offer high-quality, enriched learning resources—not just video lectures prepared by professors at prestigious universities but also discussion forums, collaborative projects, resource sharing, and community-building technologies. The initial courses offered by the University of Illinois at Springfield, Stanford University, and a few others—which reached tens of thousands of users at a time—were followed within two years by offerings from 150 universities, involving over a thousand instructors (Shah 2017), all eager to stake a claim to this newly opened territory, leading a *New York Times Education* writer to dub 2012 "The Year of the MOOC"—an accolade echoed by Martin Weller (2018). Early on, observers speculated that this service of "free higher education" on a global basis would disrupt the existing system of residential universities.

The growth curve of new offerings rose steadily through the rest of the decade, with providers seeking ways to generate revenue to cover the considerable financial and manpower costs of developing high-quality electronically delivered courses serving massive numbers of participants. However, it quickly became clear that simply having well-organized presentations and some provisions for learner interaction was a necessary, but not sufficient, condition for effective instruction. As Konnikova (2014) observed, MOOC completion and passing rates were abysmal. With hundreds of thousands of students populating some MOOCs, it was easy to get lost in them. Students received little personal acknowledgment or contact to hold them to account, and thus tended to drop out the second they were unhappy, frustrated, or overwhelmed. Besides having abysmal completion rates, early MOOCs also exhibited precious few traits of well-designed instruction (Margaryan, Bianco and Littlejohn 2015).

The MOOC enterprise has followed a trajectory similar to the "boom and bust" story of correspondence study in the early twentieth century and for-profit online universities in the dot.com bubble era—which were attempting to accomplish very much the same thing as MOOCs. That is, aggressive for-profit competition and financial and pedagogical challenges, including skepticism of regular university faculty, have tended to erode the support of these ventures by universities. Meanwhile, MOOCs were finding a niche market away from the university—addressing the needs of corporate training, particularly in high-tech job skills. Subjects that are more dependent on discussion and reflection, where there is not one correct answer, are not easily reduced to computer-scored exercises and tests. In MOOCs with global reach, discussion forums can become chaotic, accommodating learners with vastly varying entry skills, languages, cultures, and ages.

By 2019 two niche markets were dominating the MOOC scene: corporate training in high-tech skills and university master's degree courses and whole programs, typically in computer science or business. The key to success in both cases is finding a profitable "price point." Corporations subscribe to the services of the major MOOC providers, such as Coursera, edX, or Udacity, when it is more cost-beneficial than developing and conducting their own training courses. Coursera (with 37 million registered users), for example, was offering a certificate at successful course completion for about US$50 per course, plus an "audit" option that allowed users to watch the video lectures but not take exercises or tests (Campus Technology 2018).

Traditional universities had been a declining factor in the MOOC movement until 2019, when several universities formed partnerships with for-profit MOOC platforms, like Coursera, to develop online degree-granting programs—such as Georgia Tech's online master's degree in computer science. These degree-granting programs cost about one-third as much as a comparable residential program. Thus, as the MOOC enterprise has evolved, it has moved away from some of the features that were expected to be its defining traits—broad education for the masses, open to all, and free of cost. Ray Schroeder, one of the "founding fathers" of MOOCs, claims that the latter have matured in scale and sophistication in recent years. While many are no longer truly free and without prerequisites, they remain less expensive than on-campus offerings, and represent a fully functional degree platform that is serving millions of learners globally on a daily basis (2019).

Educational Technology

Just as the terms *media* and *multimedia* have suffered from construct identity problems, so also has the term *educational technology* been similarly misconstrued. Educators who consider themselves part of that domain consistently use the term *educational technology* as the name of a field of theory and practice, as indicated by definitional projects undertaken by AECT in 1977 (AECT Task Force on Definition and Terminology 1977) and 2008 (Januszewski and Molenda 2008). Nevertheless, scholars from outside the field frequently use the term to encompass all sorts of interventions purported to improve learning. Whether it is a school providing e-books to replace textbooks, a teacher using videoconferencing to link her students with another classroom, or a college student using a YouTube video clip for creative writing ideas—some would say each case is "applying educational technology." The problem of labeling two or more different phenomena with the same name has been recognized since the earliest days of educational psychology. More recently, it has been referred to as the "jingle" fallacy (different phenomena under the same name), paired with the "jangle" fallacy (two or more names for the same phenomenon). This construct identity confusion easily leads to thinking of *educational technology* as a specific intervention, or as a treatment in a research study.

Indeed, numerous meta-analyses have been conducted in which a broad array of technological applications are grouped together under the umbrella of *educational technology*; see Tamim et al. (2011) as a recent example. By ignoring the great differences in types of actual interventions and the great differences in instructional design within them, it is no wonder that analysts are unable to reach any clear conclusions about the benefits of "technology"—again, the "no significant differences phenomenon." This specific critique was made by Ross, Morrison, and Lowther: "Educational technology is not a homogeneous 'intervention' but a broad variety of modalities, tools, and strategies for learning. Its effectiveness, therefore, depends on how well it helps teachers and students achieve the desired instructional goals" (2010, 19).

A slightly different alternative is to consider *educational technology* to be, not an intervention, but a mere distribution vehicle—as Clark treated "media." But the jingle fallacy still applies. Just as not all instructional methods that incorporate technology are equal, not all technological delivery systems are equal. Audio modules, such as podcasts, have very different information-carrying potentialities than video modules, such as YouTube instructional videos (often mistakenly labeled as "tutorials"). A computer-based drill-and-practice program for arithmetic would have little in common with a computer-based physics simulation that allows users to manipulate, for example, the length of a pendulum in order to see the results. We propose using *educational technology* only to refer to a field of study and practice.

More recently, the problematic constructs of *media*, *multimedia*, and *educational technology* are receiving less attention as the new frontier of interest, being overshadowed by the construct of *emerging technologies*, a label suggesting a set of developments so diverse and fast-changing that they are best described not by their physical features but simply as being emergent. Individually, these developments each have potential for contributing to the advancement of the mission of education, but, treating them as a single construct leads once more into the jingle fallacy.

Emerging Technologies

The term *emerging technologies* has long been emerging (irony unintended) within the educational technology field's discourse over the recent decades. This is in keeping with the very nature of the concept itself, since emergence is a transient state of being that is temporally and spatially relative. As Veletsianos (2016) explains, technologies and associated teaching, learning, and scholarship practices are rendered emergent by sociocultural factors—by the environments and contexts in which they operate. The term *emerging technologies* thus refers to different phenomena across time and space; technologies and practices that are emerging in one place or time may be established in another. Anderson (2016) observes how currently emerging technologies are often applied to the same challenges that inspired educators working with older, currently established, technologies that were themselves emerging at the time. We empathize with Pacansky-Brock's (2013, viii) quip that writing a print-based book about emerging technologies can seem like a "contradiction"; any static book, book chapter, or article that espouses a primarily tools/hardware/software-focused—as opposed to a more enduring concepts-and-principles-focused—approach to the subject of emerging technologies essentially becomes dated from the very moment of its publication.

Emerging Technologies—Not Necessarily New?

Pacansky-Brock (2013, viii) defines emerging technologies as "tools that are making an impact in teaching and learning but are not yet adopted in mainstream teaching practices." Veletsianos (2016) describes emerging technologies and practices as featuring four key characteristics: (a) they are not necessarily defined by newness, i.e., they may or may not be new; (b) they nevertheless represent evolving entities that are continuously being refined or developed; (c) we are as yet unable to fully understand their teaching and learning implications, since researchers have not yet been able to thoroughly research them; and (d) they promise significant teaching and learning impact, which is mostly unfulfilled at the present time. It is clear from both authors' conceptualizations that any definition of emerging technologies explicitly refers to and is contextualized within a particular moment in time.

Emerging Technologies—Necessarily New?

Veletsianos (2016) emphasizes that both "emerging technologies" as well as "emerging practices" constitute "emerging phenomena in education." A team of scholars from Universidad Internacional de La Rioja in Spain listed the following as being key "emerging phenomena" as of 2013: (a) Web 2.0-based tools and systems, (b) ubiquitous computing, (c) augmented reality, (d) access-to-content related technologies, (e) human–computer interaction, (f) learning analytics, (g) games and virtual worlds, (h) collaborative environments and technologies, (i) semantic-aware systems, and (j) personalized, adaptive technologies (de-la-Fuente-Valentin et al. 2013).

Emerging Technologies—New This Year?

Meanwhile, on the other side of the English Channel, British open education expert Martin Weller (2018) listed the following "emerging phenomena" in chronological order as having caused annual excitement within the educational technology community over the 20-year period from 1998 through 2017:

- 1998: Wikis—embodying the optimistic spirit and philosophy of the open Web
- 1999: E-learning—as a framework for technology, standards, and approaches
- 2000: Learning objects—reusable digitized entities that could be referenced during learning
- 2001: E-learning standards—IMS and SCORM in particular
- 2002: Open educational resources (OER)—fueled by the open-source movement
- 2003: Blogs—democratizing online content creation and expression
- 2004: Learning management systems (LMS)—today's central e-learning technology
- 2005: Streaming video—further democratizing online content creation and expression
- 2006: Web 2.0—umbrella terms encompassing all user-generated Web content services
- 2007: Online virtual worlds—including the infamous Second Life
- 2008: E-portfolios—portable electronic showcases for individuals' learning and skills
- 2009: Social media—platforms like Twitter that allow users to make global connections
- 2010: Connectivism—claimed to be the first Internet-native learning theory
- 2011: Personal learning environments (PLE)—personalized sets of learning resources
- 2012: Massive open online courses (MOOCs)—trying to massively disrupt higher education
- 2013: Open textbooks—fostering equitable access via openly licensed electronic textbooks

- 2014: Learning analytics—collecting and analyzing data related to learners' behavior online
- 2015: Digital badges—awareness and legitimacy of these continue to remain challenges
- 2016: Artificial intelligence (AI)—reviving a concept that was all the rage in the 1980s–1990s
- 2017: Blockchain—the technology currently underpinning cryptocurrencies like Bitcoin.

What we are attempting to demonstrate here is that the construct of *emerging technologies* lacks a consensual definition. Indeed, as Weller proposes, its essence changes as frequently as once a year—that is, it refers to whatever technological innovation is being promoted in the world at large. Advocates simply assume that whatever novel concept is affecting the digital marketplace will or should eventually impact education, although the connection is seldom clearly drawn. Needless to say, we assert that this infinitely broad conceptualization is untenable for scholarly exploration. To treat *emerging technologies* as a single construct invokes the jingle fallacy. On the other hand, the various phenomena discussed under the umbrella of *emerging technologies* do represent potentially useful, even transformative, ideas. We include the umbrella term in our title in order to acknowledge the context of the conversation into which we are entering. We want to discuss the potentialities of innovative, technology-leveraged instructional strategies, but on our own terms, not on the terms of the techno-enthusiasts. Good pedagogy must supersede technological tinkering.

Social Media

The final problematic construct to be discussed here and in subsequent chapters is *social media*, designated by Weller (above) as *the* "emerging technology" of 2009. Computer applications that allowed users to share content and build social networks emerged in the late 1990s, but the ones that gained mass adoption—such as Facebook, YouTube, and Twitter—came along in the mid-2000s. In the years since then, these phenomena have only grown more pervasive, both in public attention and in educational experimentation.

Defining Social Media

Taken together, *social media* represent the chief, emblematic manifestation of the "Web 2.0" era—the fundamental shift in how people use the Internet, a shift toward a more social, collaborative, interactive, and responsive Web (Nations 2019). In the simplest sense, the term *social media* refers to the many easy-to-use services for interacting with other people online (Neal 2012). A frequently cited formal definition, given by Kaplan and Haenlein (2010), portrays *social media* as "a group of Internet-based applications that build on the ideological and technological foundations of Web 2.0, and that allow the creation and exchange of User Generated Content" (61). Putting this into a larger context, Kietzmann et al. describe *social media* as employing mobile and Web-based technologies to create highly interactive platforms through which individuals and communities share, cocreate, discuss, and modify user-generated content, placing human societies in the midst of an altogether new communication landscape (2011). Under this label are included such different applications as blogs, discussion forums, photo and video sharing, personal messaging, product and service reviewing, and social gaming. The common properties among these phenomena are: (a) Web 2.0-based applications, (b) carrying user-generated content, and (c) designed and maintained to facilitate the forging of social networks.

The "social" part of the term is not problematic; clearly, these phenomena facilitate social interaction. The "media" part of the term is not so straightforward. The label arose in popular culture as a way of contrasting these social computer applications with the previous notion of *mass media*. People were increasingly finding their entertainment, not in watching commercial television but in creating, uploading, and sharing textual and audiovisual content. The *social media* label created an easy parallelism for discussion. But the computer applications that comprise social media do not actually constitute new and different *media*. They employ the same communication channels as other computer applications: data transmitted through wired or wireless pathways, received—viewed and heard—by means of displays on monitors or smartphone screens accompanied by speaker systems. Thus, the "media" part of the term is a bit of a misnomer. Nevertheless, the term *social media*—defined as a set of Web-based applications that enable users to conveniently create and share information with other users—has some utility as an umbrella term, but with the minor caveat that it, too, is prone to the construct identity problem. It does not represent a single construct that can be treated as an independent variable in research or as the subject of a meta-analysis.

Social Media and Education

From an educational standpoint, although the computer applications that comprise "social media" are relatively new, the functions they offer have a considerable history. Learners have always been able to "generate new content" and share that content with others in written form—with pen or typewriter and paper. Those texts could be shared by exchanging paper documents, which could also be duplicated and circulated beyond just two people. Learners could also share oral messages—through face-to-face discussions, telephony, or audio recordings. Visual messages could be shared through circulating drawings, photos, or video recordings. What is new with social media is that these bundles of computer applications integrate existing communication channels—"old media"—with user interfaces that are relatively intuitive to employ, affording relatively easy and quick generation and interchange of information. Further, some applications have the potential for content posted there to spread virally over social networks; they give users tools to share and reshare content, such as Twitter's retweet button, Facebook's share icon, or Tumblr's reblog function. This means that a student's blog post could "go viral," giving them an audience of hundreds or thousands of other members of that social network, a sort of celebrity that formerly required laboriously working through a number of gatekeepers before achieving publication status.

Please note that we use the term *social media* hesitantly and would like to emphasize that this loosely defined construct actually consists of a variety of different digital applications, each offering markedly different functionalities. Hence, each has different implications for different parts of the instructional process—user generation of content, interaction among members of a community, presentation and storage of information, skill practice through games and simulations, and so forth. Rather than viewing *social media* as a single, discrete treatment, we view them as a cluster of software applications that together can have a cumulative impact.

Social Media's Sociocultural Impact

Social media are now becoming essentially ubiquitous and all-pervasive in all but the least socioeconomically developed human societies, especially among the Millennial and Generation-Z demographics. Schrader (2015) notes that 83 percent of Millennials—who ranked "technology use" as the trait most characteristic of them as a generation—reported sleeping with their smartphones. As Acar (2014) observes, whenever the way people communicate or exchange messages changes, many other things change. This notion was first proposed by Harold Innis as "the bias of communication." In his survey of the forces that shaped Western civilization, he noticed that when the primary means of communication change—from oral to written to printed to broadcast—the way we view the world changes, ushering in new forms of political and social organization (Innis 1951). Acar (2014) suggests that the sociocultural impacts of social media need to be assessed in terms of short-term vs. long-term effects and direct vs. indirect effects. Short-term effects of social media exposure include reduced self-control and higher propensity to give up on challenging tasks; the long-term effects are still to be determined, although we already observe a fragmenting of audiences around preferred social networks, leading to a more "tribal" mentality.

Regarding direct and indirect effects on people, Acar contrasts the effects of social media versus traditional mass media. As he explains, in a world without social media (which was reality until relatively recently in human history), traditional mass media mostly tended to affect those who are directly exposed to their messages, with indirect effects—i.e., on individuals not directly exposed to the aforementioned messages but informed by those who were—occurring much more rarely, since there was no interactivity between media sources and message recipients. In contrast, since social media have pervaded human society, indirect effects have increased exponentially. An opinion leader, one of those fabled "social media influencers," acquires or adopts something—possibly after seeing it on mass media—and soon afterward her followers follow suit after seeing her display or talk about it on social media. More important, Acar emphasizes, in today's socially mediated world not only opinion leaders but also average users can drive the indirect effects of messages.

A dramatic example of the power of social media to shape public affairs was the manipulation of American voting behavior in the 2016 presidential election. The Internet Research Agency (IRA), based in St. Petersburg, Russia, conducted an information warfare campaign through social media platforms:

> Masquerading as Americans, these operatives used targeted advertisements, intentionally falsified new articles, self-generated content, and social media platform tools to interact with and attempt to deceive tens of millions of social media users in the United States. This campaign sought to polarize Americans on the basis of societal, ideological, and racial differences, provoked real world events, and was part of a foreign government's covert support of Russia's favored candidate in the U.S. presidential election.
>
> *(Select Committee on Intelligence 2019, 3)*

With regard to sociocultural and political impact, there could hardly be a more electrifying demonstration of the power of a media conglomeration.

The potential impacts of social media specifically on the processes of instructed learning are discussed in Chapter 2.

The Technocentric Bias

One reason that it is difficult to have a reasoned discussion about the improvement of instruction is that American educationists, not only those engaged in the field of educational technology, have often been prone to a technocentric bias, a belief in the innate superiority and infallibility of technology-based interventions. For example, as early as 1911, after inventing the motion picture projector, Thomas Edison had launched a series of educational films, and he confidently predicted that films would soon replace textbooks in schools. Technocentrists are wont to uncritically advocate technology-heavy interventions to solve literally every educational, social, or moral problem faced by humanity. Weller (2018, 46) describes their attitude as an "evangelist's zeal," in which persuading other educators to adopt a given technology is in itself the end goal, as opposed to finding an appropriate solution to a specific problem.

Larry Cuban, former president of the American Educational Research Association (AERA), famously described in the 1980s how the introduction of any new technology into teaching and learning follows a predictable cyclical pattern of "a solution in search of a problem." It begins with enthusiasm and extravagant promises, followed by failure to achieve expectations and speculations on where to assign blame, and finally criticism of the technology itself as ineffective and costly, leading to disillusionment and a negligible impact (Cuban 1986). He saw the cycle repeat itself since the 1920s, from film, to radio, to television, to programmed teaching machines, to early desktop computers. Many emerging technologies remain emerging, often for years or even decades, becoming cardinal examples of the triumph of hope over experience; their inherent seductiveness keeps people's hopes up in spite of the fact that the former is vastly outweighed by the impracticalities that arise during their actual implementation into teaching and learning contexts. A prime illustration of this phenomenon is virtual reality (VR). Along with its sibling, augmented reality (AR), VR has long been held up as a force that could potentially revolutionize how humans teach and learn. As Kavanagh et al. (2017) explain, the widespread adoption of VR has yet to occur even though it has been promoted for educational adoption for over half a century—due to its technical limitations and the costs and logistics involved in its deployment. As a result, it continues to remain a niche player, with a small number of educational areas accounting for the vast majority of VR implementations.

Apart from the uncritical cheerleading for technological solutions that technocentrism engenders, another factor responsible for educators' constant scramble to keep current with everything new and "emerging" within the technological sphere is the pace of change within that sphere. In the current Information Age, technological innovation is occurring at a rate so unprecedented in human history that keeping up with it requires obsessive attention. Educational researchers find themselves caught in an unenviable position; they seek to scientifically study the role and impact of technology-based interventions with regard to teaching and learning, but with technology evolving so rapidly, the scientific method and the scholarly peer-review and knowledge dissemination processes are unable to keep up. By the time the role and impact of a given technology-based intervention are scientifically studied, the technology driving said intervention may have already obsolesced.

Consequent to its breathless attempts to keep abreast of ever-accelerating new developments in technology, the field is "remarkably poor at recording its own history or reflecting critically on its (own) development" (Weller 2018). The result is a literature full of bandwagons and buzzwords as fungible and ephemeral as the technological innovations that provoke them. It is also a literature that consists of endless reinventions of the wheel; Weller describes how "tired concepts," well-known to the older generation are often recycled as new discoveries. He attributes this phenomenon to the field of educational technology being one "to which people come from other disciplines, so there is no shared set of concepts or history" (2018, 34). A similar anomaly afflicts the field of corporate training and development. Successful line workers or salespersons may be recruited to pass their expertise along to novices; thus, they may find themselves in the training profession as merely one stage in their corporate career. As a consequence, the literature of training and development has been slow to become professionalized. An early review of literature (Campbell 1971) found it to be "voluminous, non-empirical, non-theoretical, poorly written, and dull. As noted elsewhere, it is fadish [*sic*] to an extreme" (565). The base of research and theory have grown since then, but faddishness is still a trademark, as it is in education.

Our General Approach

We hope to avoid the bias of technocentrism and the vice of faddishness, while seeking out those aspects of instruction that can be enhanced and expedited through wise use of audiovisual, digital, and psychological technologies. Our focus is on those fundamental features of the teaching–learning enterprise that have the most direct impact of the quality of instructed learning. In this pursuit, we do not depend on any particular theory of learning or instruction.

We reject "isms" and find value in an eclectic approach. The new constructs we propose, such as *instructional events, communication configurations*, and *methods* are not new theoretical abstractions, but labels for observable activities that are there to be seen whether we give them names or not. They do not derive from any preconceived theoretical platform. In suggesting new definitions, we begin with ordinary lexical definitions, make their critical attributes explicit, and draw boundaries in order to avoid overlap with other closely related terms. We make these distinctions to help pedagogical discourse become more precise. We aim to promote terminology that can be shared across disciplines and subdisciplines. We hope to reach all who work in education and training, formal and nonformal, not just educational technology or instructional design specialists. Hence, our approach is that of "back to basics" as we attempt to understand "what works" and "how it works" in the realm of educational innovations.

Our intent is to be descriptive, not prescriptive. The framework we propose in Chapter 2 simply describes the relationships that have emerged from research; it is a map, and we make no claims about how to use the map. The typology of communication configurations outlined in Chapter 4 (and elaborated in Chapters 5–11) simply describes the categories into which instructional activities can be clustered; the typology implies no hierarchy among the categories, nor does it suggest how to use these building blocks in instructional design. We do discuss the strengths and limitations of each communication configuration, but again, these are merely descriptions of the physical characteristics and pedagogical affordances of each configuration. We venture into prescription only in suggesting, in Chapters 5–11, "best practices" for employing each configuration—rules of thumb for allowing activities done in that configuration to reach their full potential. We are not proposing "instructional principles" or "guidelines for instructional design." We are merely describing the tools available. It is our hope that these descriptions promote better communication within the field of pedagogy.

Finally, we aim to position our ideas in historical context, acknowledging that all ideas, however apparently novel, have historical antecedents. Too often, scholars have felt compelled to proclaim their insights as revolutionary breaks from the past, just in order to get a wide hearing. We see more continuity than disruption in the flow of scholarly thought. Even groundbreaking discoveries in allied fields, such as neuroscience, more often than not merely confirm earlier speculations based on behavioral observations. And glamorous new "emerging technologies," although they may disrupt established businesses, seldom offer education functionalities that were previously unattainable.

Chapter Summary

Are twentieth-century methods of teaching applicable in the twenty-first century? At heart, that is a key question that this book attempts to answer. Are there general understandings of learning and instruction that transcend the comings and goings of new forms of technology? We claim that there are a number of misunderstandings that hinder any pursuit of an answer to this question. It begins with lack of shared meanings for the most basic elements of the teaching–learning enterprise, which will be elaborated in Chapter 3. Clear thinking about these issues is also hindered by definitional murkiness and hyperbole surrounding the concepts of *media, multimedia, distance education, MOOCs, educational technology, emerging technologies,* and *social media*. We side with the educationists who define *media* as information delivery channels and recommend focusing instead on *resources*—the words, sounds, and still or moving images perceived by learners—as the entities responsible for stimulating learner interest and understanding. Thus, we focus not on the shiny new hardware or innovative software but rather on how those tools are used to provide the resources that help learners perceive, understand, remember, and apply new knowledge and skills. We aim to avoid technocentrism and faddishness, following a "back to basics" approach to finding commonsense solutions to perennial concerns of education and training. We also aim to position our propositions in historical context, acknowledging that all of our ideas have historical antecedents.

In the next two chapters, we identify and define the basic "terms of art" that are central to discussion of the processes of instruction, and we propose a verbal-visual framework to represent the key factors in the instructional process. In Chapter 4, we offer some new tools to use in selecting or designing more effective instructional solutions, including a typology of communication configurations and a new precising definition for "methods." The largest part of this book is devoted to exploring the eight configurations outlined in Chapter 4: Presentation, Demonstration, Whole-Class Discussion, Small-Group Discussion, Tutorial, Repetition, Study, and Expression.

Works Cited

Acar, Adam. 2014. *Culture and Social Media: An Elementary Textbook.* Newcastle upon Tyne: Cambridge Scholars Publishing.

AECT. 1974–1981. *National Convention Programs.* Conference Program, Washington, DC: AECT.

AECT Task Force on Definition and Terminology. 1977. *The Definition of Educational Technology.* Washington, DC: Association for Educational Communications and Technology (AECT).

Albarino, Richard. 1966. "Goldstein's Lightworks at Southampton." *Variety*, August 10.

Anderson, Terry. 2016. "Theories for Learning with Emerging Technologies." Chap. 3 in *Emergence and Innovation in Digital Learning: Foundations and Applications*, edited by George Veletsianos, 35–50. Edmonton, Alberta, Canada: Athabasca University Press.

Bassendowski, Sandra Leigh, and Pammla Petrucka. 2013. "Are 20th-Century Methods of Teaching Applicable in the 21st Century?" *British Journal of Educational Technology* 44 (4): 665–667.

Bonk, Curtis J., Mimi Miyoung Lee, Thomas C. Reeves, and Thomas H. Reynolds. 2018. "The Emergence and Design of Massive Open Online Courses." In *Trends and Issues in Instructional Design and Technology*, 4th ed., edited by Robert A. Reiser and John V. Dempsey, 250–258. New York: Pearson.

Bransford, John D., Ann L. Brown, and Rodney R. Cocking. 2002. *How People Learn: Brain, Mind, Experience, and School.* Washington, DC: National Academy Press.

Campbell, John P. 1971. "Personnel Training and Development." *Annual Review of Psychology* 22: 565–602.

Campus Technology. 2018. "Coursera's CEO on the Evolving Meaning of 'MOOC'." *Campus Technology*, September 18. Accessed January 25, 2020. https://campustechnology.com/articles/2018/09/12/courseras-ceo-on-the-evolving-meaning-of-mooc.aspx.

Clark, Richard E. 1983. "Reconsidering Research on Learning from Media." *Review of Educational Research* 53 (4): 445–459.

Clark, Richard E. 1985. "Evidence for Confounding in Computer-Based Instruction Studies: Analyzing the Meta-Analysis." *Educational Media and Technology Journal* 33 (4): 249–262.

Cuban, Larry. 1986. *Teachers and Machines: The Classroom Use of Technology Since 1920.* New York: Teachers College Press.

DAVI. 1964–1970. *National Convention Programs.* Conference Program, Washington, DC: DAVI.

de-la-Fuente-Valentin, Luis, Aurora Carrasco, Kinga Konya, and Daniel Burgos. 2013. "Emerging Technologies Landscape on Education. A Review." *International Journal of Artificial Intelligence and Interactive Multimedia* 2 (3): 55–70.

Dusek, Val. 2006. "What is Technology? Defining or Characterizing Technology." Chap. 2 in *Philosophy of Technology: An Introduction*, edited by Val Dusek, 26–36. Malden, MA: Oxford Blackwell.

Frick, Theodore W. 2019. "Importance of Educology for Improving Educational Systems." In *Learning, Design, and Technology: An International Compendium of Theory, Research, Practice and Policy: Systems Thinking and Change*, edited by J. Michael Spector, Barbara B. Lockee and Marc D. Childress. New York: Springer International Publishing.

Gagnon, Monika Kin, and Janine Marchessault. 2014. *Reimagining Cinema: Film at Expo 67.* Montreal, QC: McGill-Queen's University Press.

Hampel, Robert L. 2010. "The Business of Education: Home Study at Columbia University and the University of Wisconsin in the 1920s and 1930s." *Teachers College Record* 119 (9): 2496–2571.

Innis, Harold. 1951. *The Bias of Communication*. Toronto, ON: University of Toronto Press.

Januszewski, Alan, and Michael Molenda. 2008. *Educational Technology: A Definition with Commentary*. New York: Lawrence Erlbaum Associates.

Kaplan, Andreas M., and Michael Haenlein. 2010. "Users of the World, Unite! The Challenges and Opportunities of Social Media." *Business Horizons* 53 (1): 59–68.

Kavanagh, Sam, Andrew Luxton-Reilly, Burkhard Wuensche, and Beryl Plimmer. 2017. "A Systematic Review of Virtual Reality in Education." *Themes in Science and Technology Education* 10 (2): 85–119.

Kietzmann, Jan H., Kristopher Hermkens, Ian P. McCarthy, and Bruno S. Silvestre. 2011. "Social Media? Get Serious! Understanding the Functional Building Blocks of Social Media ." *Business Horizons* 54 (3): 241–251.

Konnikova, Maria. 2014. "Will MOOCs Be Flukes?" *The New Yorker*, November 7. Accessed January 26, 2020. https://www.newyorker.com/science/maria-konnikova/moocs-failure-solutions.

Kozma, Robert B. 1991. "Learning with Media." *Review of Educational Research* 61 (2): 179–211.

Kronk, Henry. 2019. "What is Regular and Substantive Interaction? The Term that Has Defined Online Learning Still Lacks Clear Definition." *ElearningInside*, March 8. Accessed January 26, 2020. https://news.elearninginside.com/what-is-regular-and-substantive-interaction-the-term-that-has-defined-online-learning-still-lacks-clear-definition/.

Lazarsfeld, Paul F., and Robert K. Merton. 1948. "Mass Communication, Popular Taste, and Organized Social Action." In *The Communication of Ideas*, edited by Lyman Bryson, 95–118. New York: Harper.

Margaryan, Anoush, Manuela Bianco, and Allison Littlejohn. 2015. "Instructional Quality of Massive Open Online Courses (MOOCs)." *Computers and Education* 80: 77–83.

Mayer, Richard E., ed. 2014. *The Cambridge Handbook of Multimedia Learning*. 2nd ed. New York: Cambridge University Press.

Mayer, Richard E., and Richard B. Anderson. 1992. "The Instructive Animation: Helping Students Build Connections Between Words and Pictures in Multimedia Learning." *Journal of Educational Psychology* 84 (4): 444–452.

Merrill, M. David. 2013. *First Principles of Instruction*. San Francisco, CA: Pfeiffer.

Molenda, Michael. 2008. "Historical Foundations." Chap. 1 in *Handbook of Research on Educational Communications and Technology*, edited by J. Michael Spector, M. David Merrill, Jeroen van Merriënboer, and Marcy P. Driscoll, 3–28. New York: Lawrence Erlbaum Associates.

Molenda, Michael, and Michael Sullivan. 2003. "Issues and Trends in Instructional Technology: Treading Water." In *Educational Media and Technology Yearbook 2003*, edited by Mary Ann Fitzgerald, Michael Orey, and Robert Maribe Branch, 3–20. Englewood, CO: Libraries Unlimited.

Nations, Daniel. 2019. "What Does 'Web 2.0' Even Mean? How Web 2.0 Completely Changed Society." *Lifewire*, June 24. Accessed November 2, 2019. https://www.lifewire.com/what-is-web-2-0-p2-3486624.

Neal, Diane Rasmussen. 2012. "Introduction." In *Social Media for Academics: A Practical Guide*, edited by Diane Rasmussen Neal, xxiii–xxviii. Oxford, UK: Elsevier Science & Technology.

Olson, David R. 1974. "Introduction." In *Media and Symbols: The Forms of Expression, Communication, and Education. The Seventy-Third Yearbook for the National Society for the Study of Education*, edited by David R. Olson, 1–8. Chicago, IL: University of Chicago Press.

Pacansky-Brock, Michelle. 2013. *Best Practices for Teaching with Emerging Technologies*. New York: Routledge.

Pittman, Von. 2008. "An Alien Presence: The Long, Sad History of Correspondence Study at The University of Chicago." *American Educational History Journal* 35 (1): 169–183.

Poulin, Russ. 2019. "Negotiated Rulemaking: The Complexity of "Regular and Substantive Interaction"." *WCET Frontiers*, April 26. Accessed January 26, 2020. https://wcetfrontiers.org/2019/04/26/negreg-regular-and-substantive-interaction/.

Reigeluth, Charles M., and Alison A. Carr-Chellman, eds. 2009. *Instructional-Design Theories and Models: Building a Common Knowledge Base*. Vol. 3. New York: Routledge.

Ross, Steven M., Gary R. Morrison, and Deborah L. Lowther. 2010. "Educational Technology Research Past and Present: Balancing Rigor and Relevance to Impact School Learning." *Contemporary Educational Technology* 1 (1): 17–35.

Russell, Thomas L. 1999. *The No Significant Difference Phenomenon as Reported in 355 Research Reports, Summaries and Papers*. Raleigh, NC: North Carolina State University.

Saettler, Paul. 1990. *The Evolution of American Educational Technology*. Englewood, CO: Libraries Unlimited.

Schrader, Dawn E. 2015. "Constructivism and Learning in the Age of Social Media: Changing Minds and Learning Communities." *New Directions for Teaching and Learning* 144: 23–35.

Schramm, Wilbur. 1977. *Big Media, Little Media*. Beverly Hills, CA: Sage.

Schroeder, Ray. 2019. "The Maturing MOOC." *Inside Higher Ed*, March 6. Accessed January 26, 2020. https://www.insidehighered.com/digital-learning/blogs/online-trending-now/maturing-mooc.

Select Committee on Intelligence, U.S. Senate. 2019. "S. Rep. on Russian Active Measures Campaigns and Interference in the 2016 U.S. Election, Vol. 2: Russia's Use of Social Media with Additional Views." Rep. No. 116-XX.

Shah, Dhawal. 2017. *MOOCs Find Their Audience: Professional Learners and Universities*, July 24. Accessed January 25, 2020. www.classcentral.com/report/moocs-find-audience-professional-learners-universities/.

Tamim, Rana M., Robert M. Bernard, Eugene Borokhovski, Philip C. Abrami, and Richard F. Schmid. 2011. "What Forty Years of Research Says About the Impact of Technology on Learning: A Second-Order Meta-Analysis and Validation Study." *Review of Educational Research* 81 (1): 4–28.

Toppo, Greg. 2018. "Defining 'Regular and Substantive' Interaction in the Online Era." *Inside Higher Ed*, August 8. Accessed January 26, 2020. https://www.insidehighered.com/digital-learning/article/2018/08/08/new-debate-regular-and-substantive-interaction-between.

Vaughan, Tay. 1993. *Multimedia: Making It Work*. Berkeley, CA: Osborne McGraw-Hill.

Veletsianos, George. 2016. "The Defining Characteristics of Emerging Technologies and Emerging Practices in Digital Education." Chap. 1 in *Emergence and Innovation in Digital Learning: Foundations and Applications*, edited by George Veletsianos, 3–14. Edmonton, Alberta, Canada: Athabasca University Press.

Weller, Martin. 2018. "Twenty Years of Edtech." *EDUCAUSE Review* 53(4): 34–48.

Whitman, David. 2018. *The Cautionary Tale of Correspondence Schools*. December 11. Accessed January 26, 2020. https://www.newamerica.org/education-policy/reports/cautionary-tale-correspondence-schools/.

A Framework for the Instructed Learning Process

2

Making Sense of the Complexity of Learning

Instruction, whether it takes place in a school, a college, a corporate training center, a military post, or some other context, involves learners, facilitators, resources, and settings that differ on many dimensions. The teaching–learning arrangements and the organizational structures for each context can vary quite drastically, including the richness of resources available. Each context has different audiences, with widely varying aptitudes, interests, and motivations. The social and organizational surroundings of education have always been complex and dynamic, but in recent times—driven by rapid changes in technology and instability in social and political spheres—those surroundings have become increasingly unsettled. And each of these variables has been shown by research to have some effect on the quantity and quality of learning that takes place.

Does this complexity mean that we are doomed to wallow in a morass of competing influences, large and small, that churn around each teaching–learning encounter? No, of course not. Viewing the research on instructed learning through a systemic lens allows us to sort through the multiple layers of influences and find the underlying order.

In this chapter, we present a verbal-visual framework derived from an evidence-based analysis of the most salient factors that influence learners' achievement of instructional objectives. The process of learning under instructional conditions—guided by a facilitator or pedagogical device and directed toward specified learning goals—we refer to as *instructed learning*, a term borrowed from neuroscience and second-language acquisition, as explained in greater detail in Chapter 3. In virtually the whole of the literature on educational research, the outcome of teaching–learning activities is referred to simply as *learning*. As is explained in Chapter 3, this term is inadequate, given our present understanding that the learnings resulting from

32 A Framework for the Instructed Learning Process

planned instruction are qualitatively different—neurologically speaking—from learnings induced by firsthand, real-world experience. As we will demonstrate in this chapter, the forces that affect instructed learning can be viewed in layers. Some of the factors identified in research, the first layer, directly affect that nucleus; they are the proximal causes of increases in learning effectiveness. Other factors, the second and third layers—distal causes—do not directly affect learning outcomes but affect the factors that do determine learning effectiveness.

The Framework

Due to the multiplicity of variables involved in instructed learning, plus the complicated connections among them, it is especially important to have a road map to orient our discussion. We propose Figure 2.1 as a conceptual framework for understanding the forces that affect instructed learning. A conceptual framework is simply a high-level picture of the concepts involved in a process and the possible connections among them. More formally, it can be defined as a visual or written product that "explains, either graphically or in narrative form, the main things to be studied—the key factors, concepts, or variables—and the presumed relationships among them" (Miles and Huberman 1994, 18).

Our framework is a structural framework rather than a process model. It intends to portray the hierarchy of factors that influence instructed learning,

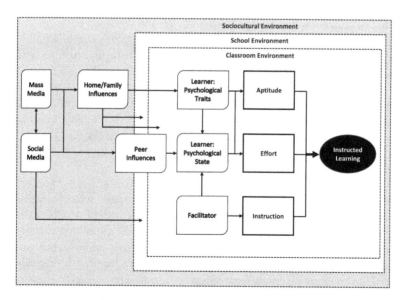

Figure 2.1 Molenda–Subramony Framework of the Forces Affecting Instructed Learning.

as opposed to showing how a system operates and changes over time, which is the point of a model. This framework is based primarily on the results of meta-analyses of educational research studies in which different treatments are compared in terms of outcomes (usually defined as learner performance on tests). Thus, it is limited to findings of research on instructed learning, learning occurring under instructional conditions. It is also limited to performance on planned assessments—tests. Students undoubtedly learn many things during their time in school, college, or training program, and many important learnings, such as social and interpersonal skills, are not measured on end-of-course examinations. Our focus is on learnings that are measured as described in each research report—usually student performance on some sort of test.

Limitations of the Framework

For purposes of visual simplification, certain factors are purposely omitted from the framework. First, the diagram does not depict all the high-impact variables that are contained within the boxes in the diagram. For example, the "Aptitude" box contains the important sub-factors of intelligence, past academic achievement, and mastery of prerequisite skills. All these important sub-factors are discussed in the narrative text accompanying each diagram.

Also not shown are the *frame factors* that surround the instructed learning process. These are the forces that give limits to all of the factors that are visualized. They act as affordances or constraints on Instruction, Facilitators, Peer Influences, etc. For example, time is a major frame factor, determining the amount, frequency, and duration of instructional activities; the learner can expend effort and the instruction can be implemented only to the extent that time is allotted to the task. The physical surroundings are another frame factor. Facilitators can only implement the types of instruction that are allowed by the room size, furnishings, and material resources available. In any instructional setting, the tools and instructional strategies available to Facilitators are constrained by class size, allocation of teachers, allocation of space, student discipline, and the like. Frame factors are discussed in more detail near the end of this chapter.

The framework presented here (Figure 2.1) is specifically descriptive of the conditions in formal education at the elementary and secondary level. Frameworks for higher education or corporate training would entail different frame factors, and somewhat different distal factors—the boundary conditions, including economic, political, and legal forces—that are two or more steps removed from the teaching-learning interaction. The proximal factors, the factors that directly affect the achievement of learning, such as the learner's attributes and interaction between learner, facilitator, and subject matter, are probably quite similar for learners in schools, universities, or corporate or military training contexts.

One major organizational-structure difference between formal education and corporate education is that the former has as its end the education of the learner while the latter has as its end the improved operation of the organization doing the training. A consequence of this difference is that the framework for corporate education would be larger, extending beyond instructed learning to include *transfer* of learned skills to the job and the effect of that improved individual performance on team and organizational success. Rather than focusing on instructional events, the corporate framework would take an explicitly systemic form, focusing on factors before, during, *and after* training (Salas et al. 2012, 77–79).

Claims about the Framework

This framework was developed out of necessity, to help the authors understand and explain how the pieces of our topic fit together. We would happily have adopted an existing framework, preferably one that had been agreed upon consensually by scholars in our field. Surprisingly, no suitable "big picture" framework has come to our attention. The literature of education does include many attempts to depict in verbal-visual form the relationships among various factors involved in learning and instruction, but none is comprehensive, logically sound, and convincingly derived from research. One early attempt by Cooley and Lohnes (1976) included six components, all of which are included in our framework: (a) "initial ability," which includes maturational level, intelligence, and prerequisite skills; (b) "opportunity," which refers to curricular emphases; (c) "motivation"; (d) "structure and placement," which refers to the organization of instructional activities and materials; (e) "instructional events," the specific teaching–learning activities; and (f) "criterion ability," or learning as measured by performance tests. If the components were arranged into a causal chain, the Cooley–Lohnes model could serve as a solid starting point for a comprehensive framework.

A number of other attempts, usually referred to as "models"—including those by Carroll, Proctor, Cruickshank, and Gage and Berliner—are presented and compared by the William G. Huitt team (McIlrath and Huitt 1995), whose work is discussed below. Each of the proposed "models" is found to account for only a small number of the variables found to be critical in subsequent research. Hence, Huitt and his colleagues developed a more complete "model," shown in their 1995 paper and further elaborated into a full "framework" (as they label it) in 2009—described in more detail below.

Above, we referred to the dearth of adequate frameworks as "surprising"; that is because clear conceptual frameworks are considered essential to research in both the physical and social sciences. They provide a road map for planning research and a context for interpreting research findings, which is precisely what Cooley and Lohnes were proposing. The failure to develop, in the succeeding decades, comprehensive frameworks more fully elaborated than Cooley and Lohnes' may help explain the frequent criticisms of lack of coordination among various "islands" of research in education.

Sources of the Framework

Meta-Analysis by Walberg

The initial source used to identify the key elements of our framework was a meta-analysis by Herbert J. Walberg and associates at University of Illinois at Chicago (Walberg 1984). For several years prior to this publication, Walberg's team had been sifting through a vast store of earlier educational research as well as conducting their own studies in a quest for a theory of educational productivity. His team of investigators conducted quantitative syntheses of nearly 3,000 studies of productive factors, and they probed the significance of these factors in large sets of US national data on learning achievement (such as the National Assessment of Educational Progress). The 1984 article reported a major synthesis of this research and provided a flow diagram of causative factors that inspired the first version of our framework. Walberg's synthesis drew immediate praise from the eminent Ralph W. Tyler (1902–1994), often referred to as "the father of educational evaluation and assessment":

> Herbert Walberg has done a superior interpretation of one of the most massive collections of data on school learning. [H]e recognizes the complexity of much human learning and does not try to reduce it to a simplistic model,... he seeks to explain interactions among variables in common-sense terms.
> *(Tyler 1984, 27)*

Walberg's research group continued to publish reports on educational productivity (Fraser et al. 1987; Monk, Walberg and Wang 2001) but did not alter the verbal-visual model presented in 1984, shown in Figure 2.2.

Meta-Analyses by the National Research Council

The National Research Council supported two major efforts to synthesize research on human learning: *How People Learn* (National Research Council 2000) and *How People Learn II* (National Academies of Sciences 2018). Both studies addressed natural learning outside of school, as well as instructed learning, but did not distinguish between the two processes. The latter volume updated our understanding of cognitive processes for acquiring, organizing, and integrating new knowledge based on recent research in neurology and cognitive science. Neither study offered a model or framework of the instructed learning process, but both described the role of motivation and teaching–learning strategies on effective learning, and both acknowledged that learning was affected by the culture that surrounded it, especially *How People Learn II* (henceforth abbreviated as *HPLII*). Taking into account the *HPLII* emphasis on the sociocultural dimension

36 A Framework for the Instructed Learning Process

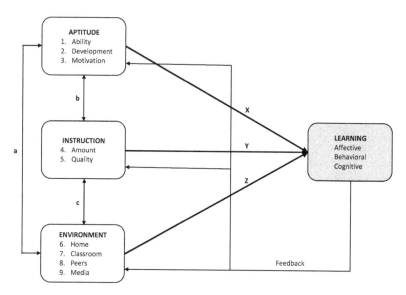

Figure 2.2 Adaptation of Walberg's (1984) "Causal Influences on Student Learning." Walberg's illustration has been redrawn to clarify some of the linkages. The thick arrows—X, Y, and Z—indicate the direct causal effect of Aptitude, Instruction, and Environment. These three factors also affect each other, as shown by arrows a, b, and c. These factors are, in turn, affected by Feedback (dotted line) regarding success of ongoing Instruction.

required giving it a prominent place in our own framework (see "Sociocultural Environment" in Figure 2.1).

Mega-Analysis by Hattie

The most recent and significant syntheses of research on the teaching–learning processes have been those of John A. C. Hattie of New Zealand (2009, 2012). He and his collaborators conducted a "mega-analysis," a meta-analysis of meta-analyses, synthesizing the findings of some 52,000 research studies that had been gathered into over 800 meta-analyses. Their methods were similar to those of Walberg mentioned earlier, examining the effects of all sorts of treatments on student learning outcomes, defined as test results, and converting those results into effect sizes. Hattie's team identified 138 factors as correlated with successful learning. He did not attempt to diagram causal chains that would show connections among proximal and distal factors; he merely listed all 138 factors, ranked according to effect size, although he did cluster those factors into six groups, which will appear in the discussion to follow.

A Framework for the Instructed Learning Process

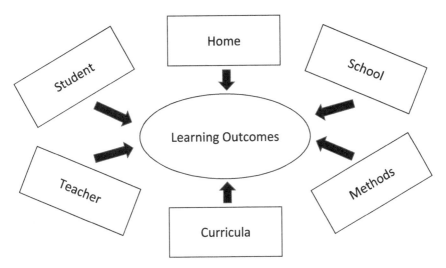

Figure 2.3 A hypothetical depiction of the implications of Hattie's (2009) mega-analysis: six clusters of factors, each presumably directly affecting Learning Outcomes.

It is surprising that neither the *HPLII* synthesis nor the Hattie mega-analysis attempted to portray their findings as a verbal-visual model or framework, a feature that would be most valuable for guiding future research. If these two groups were to diagram their conclusions as they represent them in their publications, the resulting diagram would look something like Figure 2.3—six clusters of variables, each presumably affecting learning directly.

Those six factors, explicitly identified by Hattie and implicitly supported by *HPLII* are: Student, Home, School, Teacher, Curricula, and Methods. Those factors are all accommodated in our framework, but they are arranged in a way that is more logically appropriate—each affecting other variables at varying distance—proximal to or distal from—the core function of instructed learning.

Research Synthesis by Huitt

While *HPLII* and Hattie fail to acknowledge the complex connections among these factors, implying that all are proximal, a 2009 research synthesis by William G. Huitt and his research team (Huitt et al. 2009) situate Hattie's major factors (those with effect size above 0.40) within a system-based framework. The Huitt framework, shown in Figure 2.4, arranges the Hattie variables according to whether they fit at the level of home, school building, or classroom level, thus acknowledging that different factors arise at different echelons within the domain of instructed learning.

38 A Framework for the Instructed Learning Process

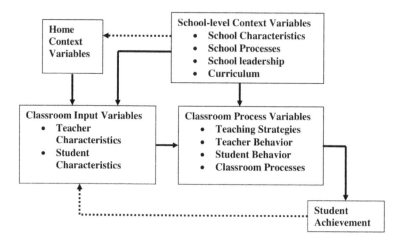

Figure 2.4 Huitt's (2009) Systems-Based Framework.

This classification of influences by systemic level is represented in our Figure 2.1 by the box "Home and Family Influences" and the areas labeled "School Environment" and "Classroom Environment." We take this systemic analysis one step further, distinguishing factors that directly affect the interaction of learners with instructional activities from those that are increasingly distant from this central interaction—the proximal and the more and more distal. We are able to hypothesize about the positioning of these causal linkages thanks to the discerning conclusions of the Walberg research group, discussed above, and the analyses by the Huitt group of Hattie's mega-analyses (Huitt et al. 2009).

Factors Directly Affecting Instructed Learning: Proximal Factors

The framework in Figure 2.1 is constructed from the inside out: near the learner to distant from the learner (right to left in the diagram). We will examine each step outward, focusing on successive pieces of the overall framework, shown as Figures 2.5, 2.6, and 2.7.

The primary system level is the learning-experience level. The key entity is the learner; the primary function of this whole system is the facilitation of instructed learning, shown in Figure 2.5 as the goal of the system.

Thus, the core of the framework shows three influences that directly affect instructed learning, the proximal factors. They are derived primarily from Walberg's overall conclusion that "the major causal influences flow from aptitudes, instruction, and the psychological environment to learning" (1984, 21). They are

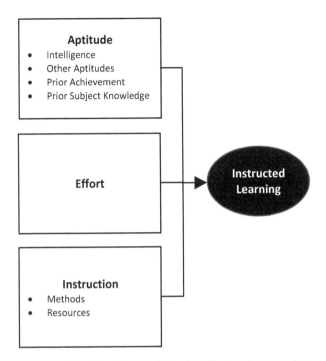

Figure 2.5 Proximal Factors Directly Affecting Instructed Learning.

depicted in Walberg's verbal-visual model (Figure 2.2) as Aptitude, Instruction, and Environment; Effort is not visually depicted, but Motivation is included under Aptitude (not really appropriate, since motivation is a temporary psychological state, not a permanent psychological trait). In a later version of Walberg's model (Fraser et al. 1987, 192) "Disposition to Learn" is shown as one of four proximal factors. These proximal causal factors are represented in Figure 2.5 as Aptitude, Effort, and Instruction. The arrows leading to Instructed Learning can be interpreted as implying that learners, given the necessary aptitude (both general intelligence and specific prior knowledge) and the necessary effort, combined with appropriate instructional activities, can attain successful instructed learning.

Aptitude

Aptitude refers to the innate capacity—mental, physical, or emotional—for learning. There are myriad factors that comprise aptitude, but three emerge as salient in the research meta-analyses: intelligence, prior academic achievement, and prior content knowledge.

Intelligence

"Intelligence" is a much-contested concept, with debate as to whether there is such a thing as general intelligence, and, if not, how many kinds of intelligence there are. Howard Gardner, for example, famously argues for seven separate types of intelligence (Gardner 1983). Psychometricians, like Willingham (2004), counter that these factors are not independent, but actually quite highly intercorrelated; and, further, that they are better viewed as talents or abilities, as they have been recognized historically. Willingham argues that the term *intelligence* is better reserved to refer to the sorts of thinking skills that are required for academic success. In this view, intelligence is viewed as hierarchical in nature, with some sort of general intelligence underlying mathematical and verbal intelligence, the two notable subsets of general intelligence of interest in formal education.

Recent research on the neural networks involved in cognitive activities indicates that "networks with modules that can change readily turn up in individuals who have greater executive function and learning capacity, " which the authors claim "correlates with better cognitive function" (Bertolero and Bassett 2019, 32). More specifically, Bertolero et al. (2018) find that

> there is a general optimal network structure for cognitive performance—individuals with diversely connected hubs and consequent modular brain networks exhibit increased cognitive performance, regardless of the task
> (765).

These findings tend to support the notion of "general intelligence," consisting of executive function and learning capacity. For our purposes, we accept the term *intelligence* at face value, in its commonly understood meaning—the innate capacity for cognitive learning, reasoning, understanding, and similar forms of mental activity.

As another indication of the robustness of the conventional notion of general intelligence, recent research indicates that intelligence, as measured by IQ tests and school success, has a strong inherited component. One study comparing identical twins raised apart showed a correlation of 0.74 on IQ tests taken as adults, while those same twins compared with their adoptive siblings have a zero correlation (Bouchard 1998). Recent studies in the United Kingdom have also shown that at the secondary school level (Smith-Woolley, Pingault and Selzam 2018) and the university level (Smith-Wolley et al. 2018), academic achievement is highly correlated with genetic endowment.

Other Aptitudes

Learners vary with regard to physical aptitude as well as intellectual aptitude; many elite athletes could be said to be "physical geniuses." Again, there is a notable tendency toward the inheritance of physical ability, a tendency that is visible to the public in terms of elite professional athletes who follow in their parents' footsteps. Sometimes the resemblance is uncanny. In American baseball, for example, Bobby Bonds and his son Barry were both powerful hitters (over 300 career home runs) and fast base runners (over 400 stolen bases). Cecil Fielder and son Prince were both exceptionally powerful sluggers, each hitting exactly 319 home runs in their careers. In basketball, Wardell "Dell" Curry retired as his team's all-time scoring and three-point shooting leader, while his son Stephen has set new professional league records for scoring and three-point shooting (Curry's younger son, Seth, also plays in the highest professional basketball league in the United States.) In American football, Archie Manning played quarterback and finished his career high on the list of most passes completed; his sons Eli and Peyton both had even more stellar careers playing quarterback, each winning the national professional championship twice.

Similar family stories could be told for musical talent, business acumen, and political finesse—and other domains aside from the cognitive domain. For the purposes of the framework, the term *aptitude* is considered to include innate capacities for social, musical, and physical prowess as well as intellectual prowess.

Prior Achievement

Concerning cognitive ability, in the absence of an IQ score or other measure of intelligence, prior academic achievement can serve as a surrogate, as students who do well at one grade level tend to score higher on tests at more advanced educational levels.

Prior Subject Knowledge

The third component of Aptitude, prior subject knowledge, can be summarized in the aphorism, "Start where the learner is." As self-evident as that advice seems, it is too often disregarded, since it is certainly not easy to find out where each individual is when faced with classes of scores or hundreds of learners. This is one of the motivations to develop systems of individualized instruction.

In the cognitive domain, remembering new information and understanding new concepts depend on whether the instruction connects with the learner's existing mental model of the world (Merrill 2013, 13). For more procedural or how-to learning, there are typically underlying facts and principles that need to be understood before the learner can knit them together into a sequential series of actions that lead to the desired outcome. These prior learnings are referred to as prerequisite skills. A frequent cause of learning failure is putting learners into an instructional activity for which they lack the prerequisite skills.

Conversely, one of the largest sources of wasted time and money in corporate training is to require training on skills that have already been mastered. Mager (1977) cited numerous case studies of businesses that had reduced training costs dramatically merely by ceasing to put employees through training programs for knowledge and skills they already possessed. In both cases—instruction based on a faulty foundation or instruction that duplicated existing skills, the failure could be avoided by pretests to determine whether the learners possess the prerequisite skills…or have already mastered the target skills.

Effort

When learners are "motivated" to learn or "interested" in pursuing some new topic these feelings have consequences only when those feelings are manifested in terms of the *effort* learners then expend on the learning task. The concept of *effort* is defined in the *Encyclopedia of Education* as "whether a student tries hard, asks for help, and/or participates in class" (Renninger 2003, 704). Bandura (1977) explored the factors that determine whether learners will invest sustained effort in learning tasks. Salomon (1981) provided a label for this construct: *amount of invested mental effort* (AIME). Better retention and deeper processing happen when learners expend mental energy to relate the new knowledge to prior knowledge, analyze it, and rehearse it mentally or physically. In its guide to "what works" in classroom instruction, the Association for Supervision and Curriculum Development (ASCD) included "reinforcing effort" as one of its nine recommended strategies (Dean et al. 2012). Hence, we include Effort, paired with appropriate learning activities, as one of the proximal causes of instructed learning.

If Aptitude accounts for the largest share of success in instructed learning, Effort most likely would be second in terms of effect. Learners who are bright and motivated to pursue their learning goals diligently will find a way regardless of the quality and quantity of Instruction they receive.

John Dewey would add a caveat. In his book *Interest and Effort in Education* (1913), he asserted that when learner effort was elicited through coercion, rather than true interest, the instructed learning would be retained, if at all, as inert knowledge. To have worth—and to be applied to real-world problems—learning must be personally meaningful, motivated by one's own needs and interests. In the next section, we discuss the causal connection between the factors of Learner: Psychological State (the learner's temporary conditions, including situational interest) and Effort.

Instruction

This proximal factor consists of the quality and amount of teaching–learning activities in which the learner participates. It should not be surprising that quality of instruction has a direct effect on learning outcomes; perhaps it would be surprising to some that it is only one of the three major influences. After all, a generation of critics have insisted on the need to hold teachers accountable for the quality of instruction they provide. Far fewer critics acknowledge that Aptitude and Effort play a major role. We would argue that they actually play a larger role than Instruction. William James (1842–1910), "the father of American psychology" proposed this notion over a century ago in *Talks to Teachers*:

> Psychology can state your problem in these terms, but you see how impotent she is to furnish the elements of its practical solution. When all is said and done, and your best efforts are made, it will probably remain true that the result will depend more on a certain native tone or temper in the pupil's psychological constitution than on anything else.
>
> *(James 1899, 183–184)*

In other words, even when teachers do their best regarding Instruction, the outcome still depends more on how the learner's Psychological Traits and Psychological State affect their Aptitude and Effort.

Instruction includes providing the learner with *resources* that afford the sorts of mental and physical practice needed to master the specified knowledge or skill (discussed in Chapter 3) and selecting *methods* of instruction that are appropriate for the specified objectives (discussed in Chapter 4). It does not include the traits possessed by teachers; that is a more distal influence—Facilitator—to be discussed below. Here, what counts is what the teacher *does* in terms of selecting and implementing appropriate resources and methods. Because resources, methods, and the other elements of Instruction are the subject of the rest of this book, they will not be elaborated further in this chapter.

As mentioned earlier, time is considered a frame factor, so the amount of instruction is not visually depicted in our framework. Suffice it to say, research indicates that *time-on-task*, or preferably, *academic learning time*—the amount of time spent engaged with instruction—is correlated with extent of successful learning outcomes. See, for example, Anderson (1984) and McIlrath and Huitt (1995, 7–8).

First-Level Distal Factors

Many of the forces that consistently show a causal relationship to learning actually affect learners indirectly; that is, they affect Aptitude, Effort, or Instruction rather than affecting Instructed Learning directly. These first-level distal factors—Learner: Psychological Traits, Learner: Psychological State, and Facilitator—are shown in Figure 2.6.

44 A Framework for the Instructed Learning Process

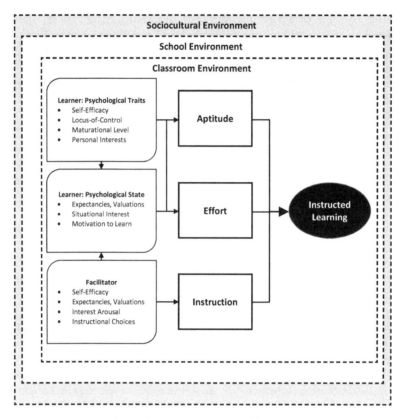

Figure 2.6 First-Level Distal Factors Indirectly Affecting Instructed Learning.

Psychological Traits

This factor consists of several sub-factors that together represent the quasi-permanent psychological attributes that people carry with them throughout life. This includes aspects of personality such as self-efficacy and locus-of-control, which have been identified as salient in meta-analyses of research on instructed learning.

Self-Efficacy

Self-efficacy is defined as a person's judgment about their ability to accomplish a given task. A person might have a high level of self-efficacy about driving a car but a lower one about solving a quadratic equation. There is ample research evidence regarding the connection of self-efficacy to motivation to learn; self-efficacious students participate more readily, work harder, and persist longer on learning tasks (Bandura 1997). One large-scale study of high school students found that "perceived academic competence" had a larger effect on student achievement than did teacher expectations or high-quality pedagogical methods (Akey 2006).

Locus-of-Control

Locus-of-control is a psychological concept referring to a person's beliefs about how much control they have over their daily experiences (Rotter 1966). In education, locus-of-control refers to how students perceive the causes of their academic success or failure. Students with an *internal* locus-of-control tend to feel that their success or failure is a result of how hard they work and how much effort they invest in learning. Students with an *external* locus-of-control tend to believe that their outcomes result from external factors beyond their control, such as stressful circumstances, injustice, or teachers who are biased or unskilled. Research has shown that learners with internal locus-of-control tend to be more proactive and effective during the learning process, while those with external locus-of-control tend to be more reactive and passive.

Maturational Level

Humans change, grow, and develop throughout life, both physically and cognitively. Maturational level refers to the stage of physical or cognitive development that has been reached by a given learner at a given time. The sequence of development is biologically determined and does not depend on the experiencing of specific external stimuli. New capabilities may be attained by maturation or by learning, most commonly by a combination of both. For example, children learn to talk only when they have reached a certain developmental stage, but the language they learn depends on what they hear.

Instruction can have an impact only if the learner has reached the maturational stage needed for that type of learning. The sensory, motor, and nervous system structures have to be ready. For example, an infant cannot be taught to run, simply because the required psychomotor structures are not yet in place. This is well recognized for motor skills and cognitive skills, but undoubtedly is just as true for affective and interpersonal skill learning. The well-known pedagogical theories of Jean Piaget and Maria Montessori are fundamentally based on their understanding of the biological maturational processes that underlie all types of learning.

Of course, as aging progresses some faculties decline. In late adulthood, people may struggle with losses in sensory inputs and outputs as well as memory difficulties. In formal education, it is unusual to have to deal with learners in the late stages of adulthood, but in corporate training it is not unusual. In the corporate training domain, this population can be problematic. That is, research indicates that older adults tend to achieve less mastery of training material while completing the training tasks more slowly and taking longer to complete the training program (Kubek et al. 1996).

Personal Interests

Effort tends to increase when learners have personal interest in the material (e.g., "I really want to know more about prehistoric climates because I'm fascinated with dinosaurs"). Personal interests derive from the person's past experiences, which are affected by their home environment, peers, and information emanating from social media and mass media. This factor is considered a disposition that learners carry with them over time, from day to day and task to task (Harackiewicz and Hulleman 2010). Also referred to as *individual interest*, it is viewed as "a relatively enduring preference for certain topics, subject areas, or activities" (Schiefele 1991, 302). Hidi and Renninger would differentiate between "an emerging individual interest" and "a well-developed individual interest," the latter defined essentially like Schiefele's "individual interest" (Hidi and Renninger 2006). In any event, Schiefele's research indicates that students with high individual interest in a subject "engage in a more intensive and meaning-oriented processing of a text" (306–307), thus lending support to John Dewey's position, described above under Effort.

Taken together, self-efficacy, locus-of-control, maturational level, and personal interests constitute the most salient more-or-less permanent Psychological Traits that influence Effort.

Learner: Psychological State

Psychological state is a construct to describe the transitory feelings and thoughts a person has at a given time. Educational research has revealed that several specific aspects of learners' mental state have a significant effect on whether the person is ready and eager to learn. Expectancies and valuations, situational interest, and motivation to learn can serve as powerful prompts to Effort. The same factors have been found to matter in corporate training as well (Salas et al. 2012, 84–85).

Expectancies and Valuations

According to expectancy-value theory (Eccles 1983), students' leanings toward or avoidance of learning tasks are most proximally determined by two factors: expectancies for success and perceived task value. Expectancy is the belief that one's effort will result in attainment of a desired performance goal, in this case, learning. Learners' expectancies are primarily based on their past experiences ("have I been successful at this in the past?"), the perceived difficulty of the task, and their feelings of self-efficacy (discussed under Psychological Traits).

Task values refer to how important or useful the task is perceived to be. Expectancies and valuations interact to predict how eagerly learners engage in and persist in learning tasks. This factor is particularly prone to influence from learners' cultural capital and habitus, self-identity, privilege, and intersectionality, as discussed below.

Situational Interest

Researchers have identified two types of interest: *situational* interest, which is spontaneous, transitory, and environmentally activated, and *personal* interest (discussed above under the heading of Psychological Traits), which is based on enduring personal values and is activated internally. Situational interest appears to be especially important in catching students' attention, whereas personal interest may be more important in holding it. Research suggests that situational interest can be increased through strategies such as: (a) offering students meaningful choices, (b) providing engaging presentations and resources, and (c) encouraging learners to draw connections with prior knowledge (Schraw, Flowerday and Lehman 2001).

Motivation to Learn

Motivation to learn appears as one of the nine factors found by Walberg to be most highly correlated with achievement; likewise, *HPLII* places it high on the list of crucial factors. Hattie treats "motivation" differently, viewing it more as a stable trait rather than as a transitory state and even conflating it with other factors, such as interest. *HPLII* takes pains to define *motivation to learn* quite precisely, claiming that it is "distinguishable from states related to it, such as engagement, interest, goal orientation, grit, and tenacity, all of which have different antecedents and different implications for learning and achievement" (National Academies of Sciences 2018, 109). Research in the corporate domain indicates that *motivation to learn* is just as critical to stimulating Effort as in formal education, and it is a function of Psychological Traits, the work environment, and the methods selected by the Facilitator (Salas et al. 2012, 84), just as in formal education.

Humans are curious by nature but not necessarily about the topic being taught as part of an externally imposed curriculum. Indeed, natural curiosity tends to fade as the amount of compulsory schooling increases (Gottfried, Fleming and Gottfried 2001). Traditionally, educational institutions have adopted external controls such as tests, grades, and artificial rewards ("honor student," "dean's list," and the like) to encourage academic achievement by replacing curiosity with rewards and punishments. Contemporary research focuses on the distinction between *extrinsic* (performing to earn a reward or avoid punishment) and *intrinsic* motivation (doing an activity for its inherent satisfaction). Richard M. Ryan and Edward L. Deci have led this area of research for decades, in the process developing a theory of motivation, self-determination theory (SDT), that proposes that humans have fundamental needs for competence and autonomy (Ryan and Deci 2016). In general, giving students choices and allowing a degree of self-direction allows intrinsic motivation to work. On the other hand, many forms of extrinsic control—threats, deadlines, and competitive pressure—tend to depress motivation. However, Ryan and Deci (2000) find that there is a spectrum of extrinsic motivation, and that some forms can be effective; students who feel accepted into a group can "buy into" the pursuit of goals that are presented as related to the values of the group.

The effects of curiosity, or intrinsic motivation, on learning have been investigated through functional magnetic resonance imaging (fMRI); the researchers found that "participants showed improved memory for information that they were curious about" (Gruber, Gelman and Ranganath 2014, 486). Classroom-tested and research-based techniques for piquing learner curiosity include evoking controversy, pointing out incongruities, encouraging prediction of an outcome, eliciting personal experiences, and the like (Goodwin et al. 2019)

John M. Keller proposes a practical framework for designing motivational instruction that combines elements from different categories: media message design, psychological traits, and psychological states. The "ARCS model" focuses on Attention, Relevance, Confidence, and Satisfaction (Keller 2010). Attracting the learner's attention is accomplished through the design of the resources they are given (as is recommended by Schraw et al. above). Making the material relevant to the learner entails heightening the valuation of the goal. Giving confidence translates as boosting learners' sense of self-efficacy. Providing satisfaction entails using extrinsic and intrinsic motivators effectively.

Another practical framework, the Belief-Expectancy-Control (BEC) framework (Clark and Saxberg 2018), accepts that expectancies, valuations, situational interest, and motivation to learn are separable variables, but proposes treating them as an interrelated cluster, what one might call a "motivation problematique." They define this motivational conglomerate as "a cognitive and affective process influencing whether people start a learning task, persist at it once started, and invest adequate mental effort to succeed" (Clark and Saxberg 2018, 2). They propose that the stages of starting, continuing, and completing a learning task each involve a different hurdle from the list of factors that constitute Psychological State. For example, getting started on a task primarily involves the issue of valuation, while continuing to persist involves the issue of self-efficacy, and completion of the task may be affected by negative emotions. Breaking the problematique of motivation into stages, they suggest, offers the prospect of practical solutions in a step-by-step fashion.

Effect of Classroom Environment on Psychological Traits and State

The classroom social environment is identified by Walberg as one of the nine key factors affecting instructed learning (Figure 2.2), defining it as "the cohesiveness, satisfaction, goal direction, and related social-psychological properties or climate of the classroom group perceived by students" (Walberg 1984, 24). He later elaborated on this point: "Good morale means that the class members like one another, that they have a clear idea of the classroom goals, and that the lessons are matched to their abilities and interests" (Walberg 2006, 110). Hattie's mega-analysis ranks one Classroom Environment factor—classroom cohesion—among the top 50 positive factors (2009, 103), citing meta-analyses that support cohesiveness among students and cooperation among adults as being associated with academic success.

The authors of *HPLII* view the classroom as a social setting with its own culture, which includes the physical appearance of the room, the furniture and resources available, the rules that guide behavior, and how accepting the atmosphere may be. They view academic success as dependent on a climate that welcomes and feels familiar to all (National Academies of Sciences 2018, 136–143).

Ryan and Deci (2016), in their synthesis of research on motivational factors, propose that motivation to learn is enhanced when the classroom climate is supportive of student autonomy—"namely, listening, creating time for students' independent work, allowing students to talk…[etc.]" (108). But it is not just teacher behavior that sets the tone; all the sorts of peer influence discussed above play a major role in constituting the climate of the classroom.

Facilitators strive to establish a climate of tolerance and risk-taking by assuring learners that they will not be criticized if they make a mistake. By their behavior, they convey a relaxed attitude where the teacher and learners do not feel that they have to take themselves too seriously. An aspect of this is the adroit use of humor, especially self-deprecating humor, to create a relaxed but energetic atmosphere. In their review of research on the use of humor in educational settings, Banas, Dunbar, Rodriguez, and Liu (2011) found one clear generalization:

> The use of positive, non-aggressive humor has been associated with a more interesting and relaxed learning environment…[and] greater perceived motivation to learn…
>
> *(137)*

Effect of School Environment on Learners, Facilitators, and Instruction

In addition to the social factors that make a difference at the classroom level, there are factors that arise at the level of the school (in the case of corporate training these would be issues at the organization level, an echelon above the training program itself). Individual classroom teachers or individual corporate trainers have no control over policies put in place by higher authorities. The overall organizational structure determines a great deal of what is taught and how it is taught. As Larry Cuban (1992, 36) observes, conventional age-graded schools "have self-contained classrooms that separate teachers from one another, a curriculum distributed grade by grade to students, and a time schedule that brings students and teachers together for brief moments to work." He sees these structures profoundly influencing "*how teachers teach, how students learn, and the relationships between the adults and children in each classroom*" (36, emphasis added).

In addition to the restrictions posed by school organization, specific school-wide policies can affect the school environment. Examples of such policies would be admission standards, curriculum choices, mainstreaming of special needs students, ability grouping, and the like.

Admission or selection policies, besides determining the Aptitude level of the population of the school, can also affect learners' motivation to learn. Students admitted to "selective" high schools and universities enter with a heightened sense of self-efficacy and expectation of succeeding. They also have a better chance of falling into cliques composed of academically competitive peers. In corporate training programs, employees tend to respond more positively to training if they believe they have been selected for training for the right reasons and if their supervisors are supportive. Training that is advertised as mandatory tends to be viewed as more important, heightening employee expectancies (Salas et al. 2012, 83).

The curriculum—the subjects chosen to be taught—defines the boundaries of instructed learning outcomes. What objectives are pursued in the classroom are limited by curriculum choices at the school level. As an extreme example, see the French educational policy for their colonies in Africa; in the 1800s and well into the 1900s, "Their curriculum was a practical one based on manual labor and vocational training" (Clignet and Foster 1964, 193). Further, the school may also mandate what instructional approaches should be used to pursue those objectives, such as the phonics approach to reading, or problem-based approach to science, or Learning for Mastery as an overall approach. The school may also specify how students should be grouped within classrooms, for example, mainstreaming of special needs students or ability grouping for gifted students.

Decisions made at the echelon above the classroom thus have major implications for what objectives will be pursued and how facilitators will pursue them. They also affect social relationships among students. The choice of language of instruction, for example, can create an in-group of language-majority students versus an outgroup of language-minority students. Even innovations that generally have a positive effect on learner motivation, such as cooperative learning groups, can generate heightened intergroup tensions if done without attention to alleviating the unequal status of ethnic minority students (Cohen and Lotan 2014). Another intervention—ability grouping—although intended to help all students get the most appropriate instructional treatments at the appropriate time, contributes to the stratification of the school into groups about whom teachers and administrators—and the students themselves, who quickly figure out where they fit in the achievement hierarchy—have different expectations. Unfortunately, these expectations tend to be self-fulfilling, with the "high ability" students succeeding and the "low ability" students failing (Weinstein 2002).

Effect of Sociocultural Environment on Psychological Traits and State

The sociocultural environment within which learners are born, raised, and live affects their self-efficacy, locus-of-control, maturational level, personal interests, expectancies and valuations, situational interest, and motivation to learn. These Psychological Traits and States of the learner (which subsequently determine the Effort they put into learning) are strongly influenced by their own cultural capital and habitus, self-identity, privilege, and intersectionality. This important influence is represented in Figure 2.6 by the shaded rectangle surrounding all of the factors discussed so far.

Cultural Capital

As the eminent French sociologist Pierre Bourdieu (1990) explains, learners with higher socioeconomic status (SES) origins inherit significantly different *cultural capital*—cultural background, knowledge, disposition, and skills—than those with lower SES origins. Learners growing up in environments where culturally valued activities like reading, travel, museum visits, and concert- and theatergoing are frequently practiced get socialized into the dominant culture that the educational system requires for academic achievement. Schools—where most instructed learning takes place—value and reward the cultural capital of the dominant classes, facilitating their easy translation into superior academic credentials. We will talk more about this aspect when discussing School Environment.

Habitus

Learners also acquire a distinct *habitus*—"a subjective but not individual system of internalized structures, schemes of perception, conception, and action common to all members of the same group or class"—along with their cultural capital (Bourdieu 1990, 86). Functioning constantly as a matrix of perceptions, appreciations, and actions—as a system of lasting, deeply internalized, and transposable attitudes, beliefs, values, and dispositions integrating past experiences—a learner's habitus affects their perceptions regarding self-efficacy and locus-of-control, as well as their interests, expectancies, valuations, and motivation. The learner's habitus engenders their aspirations—internalizations of objective probabilities that reflect the learner's view of their chances of success. Lower-SES learners raised in environments where success is rare are less likely to develop strong ambitions than upper-SES learners inhabiting environments where the connection between effort and reward is infinitely clearer.

Privilege and Intersectionality

Meanwhile, learners' cultural capital and habitus are closely linked to their privilege and intersectionality—both important sociological concepts that must be comprehended in order for us to better understand where our learners are coming from and how they relate to instructed learning. In her seminal paper (McIntosh 1988), American feminist scholar Peggy McIntosh outlined her influential concept of a "knapsack" of privilege, which she formulated as a direct repudiation of the myth of meritocracy that constitutes a basis of modern capitalist society. She characterized privilege—conferred through one's belonging to a "dominant" group based on any given criterion such as race, gender, sexual orientation, culture, citizenship, etc.—as "an invisible weightless knapsack of special provisions, assurances, tools, maps, guides, codebooks, passports, visas, clothes, compass, emergency gear, and blank checks" (1988, 1–2) about which its possessor is meant to remain oblivious and ignorant of his obliviousness. Furthermore, the existence of a matrix of privileges enjoyed by the dominant groups invariably engenders a corresponding matrix of oppressions experienced by the subjugated groups; some take "active forms which we can see" and others take "embedded forms which as a member of the dominant group one is taught not to see" (17).

Logically extending McIntosh's arguments related to privilege and oppression, American critical race theorist Kimberlé Williams Crenshaw coined the term *intersectionality* to describe how different forms of discrimination can interact and overlap, and to emphasize the need to account for multiple grounds of identity when considering how the social world is constructed (Crenshaw 1991, 1245). While originally employed to explain how race and gender intersect and compound each other as forms of oppression in the lived experiences of women of color, the concept of *intersectionality* has since broadened to encompass the entire gamut of pertinent social variables including sexual orientation, nationality, socioeconomic class, disability, etc. (Emba 2015). Intersectionality reminds us that our identities based on race, gender, class, and sexuality accompany us in every social interaction (Collins 1993)—including instructional activities. It helps us understand that human beings are complex beings who experience oppression in ways that are deeply intersected, in ways that cannot be disassembled and their parts analyzed separately; their myriad aforementioned sociocultural identities are thus profoundly interconnected with all other parts of their experiences and identities (Richards and Barker 2015)—once again including educational experiences. An intersectional perspective allows us to see that we cannot begin to understand the contexts, experiences, issues, and needs of learners if we ignore and fail to take into account some very important parts of their identity and experience as human beings, parts that are inextricably interlinked with every other part thereof.

Digital Divide

Since the dawn of the current Information Age, a persistent and deeply impactful symptom of socioeconomic inequalities among learners has been the so-called

Digital Divide—the widening and increasingly calamitous gulf between those who are appropriately positioned to effectively harness the puissant emancipatory potential of the myriad media technologies—including the "emerging" technologies we refer to in this book—that are key to socioeconomic success and upward mobility within Information Age societies and those who are not. Borrowing McIntosh's theoretical lens, Subramony (2014, 7) proposed that the individuals belonging to those social/economic/cultural groups that are located on the "right" side of the Digital Divide could be seen as the largely oblivious beneficiaries of a vast matrix of privileges, unconscious possessors of a significant knapsack of gifts, when it comes to their relationship with media technologies. Evoking Crenshaw's concept of intersectionality, Subramony described these individuals as occupying "happy intersections" of demographic, economic, political, social, and cultural factors that make it possible for them to harness the full emancipatory potential of these technologies to get even further ahead within today's Information Age socioeconomic framework. In contrast, those on the opposite side of the tracks vis-à-vis the Digital Divide do not possess said knapsack, but instead remain trapped under multiple layers of oppressions.

Self-Identity

The learner's Psychological Traits and States are substantially influenced by their self-identity vis-à-vis the dominant class/cultural/economic systems that they construct based on their lived experiences within those systems. British social scientist Paul Willis (1977) saw learners as social agents who view, inhabit, and construct their own world. Some construct self-identities that aspire to upward socioeconomic mobility and comply with dominant rules and norms. Others construct oppositional self-identities—based on their profound insights into the economic condition of their social class—that reject the dominant achievement ideology; they become subversive nonconformists, believing that their chances for upward mobility are so remote under the current socioeconomic power structure as to render any attempts at good behavior and conformity pointless. Henry Giroux—one of the founding theorists of critical pedagogy in the United States—presented his theory of student resistance (1983), explaining how students' opposition and nonconformity toward the educational system were responses rooted in their moral and political indignation and critique of school-constructed ideologies and relations of domination rather than any sort of psychological dysfunction.

Finally, the effect of the learner's sociocultural environment extends to their prior achievement and subject knowledge (factors of their Aptitude), since prior achievement and mastery of prerequisite skills—including literacy and numeracy—depend on their access to learning resources and ability to extract the benefits of said resources, which again are a function of their cultural capital and habitus, self-identity, privilege, and intersectionality.

Facilitator

As described in Chapter 3, we use the term *facilitator* to designate the person who propels instructional events, selecting the objectives and guiding the learner through the instructional activities. In elementary and secondary education this role is most often played by people called *teachers*, but not always, by any means. Paraprofessionals often assist individuals or small groups in their work, as do community volunteers and even fellow students, in the case of peer tutoring or peer instruction. All of these are playing the role of *facilitator*.

In the popular mind, elementary and secondary schoolteachers are not only the most important, but virtually the sole cause of student success or failure in school. Politicians periodically pass legislation aimed at "holding teachers accountable" by examining their students' scores on standardized tests. Similar arguments have been advanced regarding college professors. But the fact is that teachers, professors, and other facilitators have little to no control over what Aptitudes their students have nor what Psychological Traits those students possess. They do, however, have influence on their students' Psychological State—those factors that affect their motivation to learn—and do make choices about what sorts of Instruction to implement.

Teachers' Self-Efficacy

We have discussed above the importance of learners' sense of self-efficacy, as first proposed by Bandura (1977). As it happens, teachers' behavior is also affected by their sense of self-efficacy (Berman and McLaughlin 1977). As expressed in a report of the National Association of Elementary School Principals,

> teachers who believe they can teach all children in ways that enable them to meet these high standards are more likely to exhibit teaching behaviors that support this goal.
>
> *(Protheroe 2008, 45).*

That is, teachers who believe they can reach all students tend to choose instructional methods and resources that do reach all students.

Teachers' Expectations and Valuations

Hattie's mega-analysis identifies teacher expectations as one of the factors with a positive, if "moderate" effect on instructed learning (Hattie 2009, 121–124). At the same time, Hattie acknowledges that the construct of *teacher expectations* is a contested one, citing Weinstein's observation: "Expectancy processes do not reside solely 'in the minds of teachers' but instead are built into the very fabric of our institutions and our society" (2002, 290). Weinstein discusses the sorts of institutional practices that create a stratified school culture, which, in turn has negative effects on student achievement. These include ability-based grouping and tracking; less-than-challenging curricula; normal-curve notions about ability; motivational systems that promote performance goals (vs. mastery goals), extrinsic reinforcement, and competition; and the climate of relationships in the school and with parents (Weinstein 2002, 207).

Regarding valuations, students can detect when teachers are enthusiastic about the subjects they teach. Students perceive a learning task as valuable when teachers demonstrate the importance or usefulness of the new knowledge. Csikszentmihalyi and McCormack (1986) found that

> adolescents respond to teachers who communicate a sense of excitement, a contagious intellectual thrill. When excitement is present, learning becomes a pleasure instead of a chore.
>
> *(418)*

Stimulating Situational Interest

Situational interest, the transitory interest that catches the learner's attention during an instructional event, is largely within the control of facilitators. They can create face-to-face lectures or recorded presentations that feature, for example, provocative visuals, personal storytelling, or probing questions. They can explicitly draw connections between the current topic and material that learners already know. They can offer students meaningful choices for follow-up activities. Strategies such as these can spark engagement in the moment. Students claim they learn more from instructors who show empathy, display passion for their subject, and provide behavioral models for how to think about their subject.

Making Instructional Choices

The one factor over which facilitators have considerable control is Instruction, one of the three proximal causes of instructed learning. Even at that, there are constraints on choice of instructional method imposed by frame factors, such as physical facilities, resources available, class size, curricular mandates, and supervisors' expectations. Despite all these limitations, choices made by facilitators do make a difference and facilitators still have the responsibility of following "best practices" as far as those constraints will allow. Facilitators, whatever domain in which they work, tend to be more successful when they have better mastery of the subject matter and more highly developed pedagogical skills (Loeb 2001, 102).

Elementary-Secondary Education

Walberg's 1984 research synthesis does not treat the facilitator as a causative factor in his model; instructional quality and quantity are leading factors, but the facilitator implementing them is not visible in his verbal-visual model (Figure 2.2). Like Walberg, the authors of *HPLII* do not focus directly on teachers themselves but rather on the effects produced by the tactics and strategies they employ. However, a large-scale longitudinal analysis of elementary-secondary student achievement in the state of Tennessee concluded that "teacher effects are dominant factors affecting student academic gain" while heterogeneity of students and class size have little influence (Wright, Horn and Sanders 1997).

Hattie, aggregating many meta-analyses, also establishes the teacher as a causative variable and identifies several teacher factors as highly correlated with student success:

> It is teachers *using particular teaching methods*, teachers *with high expectations for all students*, and teachers *who have created positive student–teacher relationships* that are more likely to have the above average effects on student achievement.
> (Hattie 2009, 126, author's emphasis)

Higher Education

While the effect of the teacher on student achievement is possible to infer from ample databases of standardized test data in elementary and secondary education, such data are not available for other contexts, such as higher education or corporate education programs. Indeed, for higher education it is clear that other factors—such as the values and expectancies of one's peer group and the amount of time spent studying alone (Astin 1992)—matter as much as or more than the instructor. Unlike schoolteachers and corporate trainers, college professors have job demands for research and service that compete for their energy. As expectations for research productivity continue to rise, the time and energy available for teaching declines. Indeed, Kuh (2003) suggests, as have many before him, that professors are incentivized to enter into a sort of "disengagement compact" with their students: "I'll leave you alone if you leave me alone" (28). Consequently, the student's own drive to engage in learning plays a larger role than in other contexts, as do other institutional factors that support student engagement, such as opportunities for research, internship, service-learning, and overseas study.

Corporate Training and Education

Research on factors driving success in corporate training tend to identify, not the Facilitator per se, but the methods and resources used in instruction.

For example, Salas, Tannenbaum, Kraiger, and Smith-Jentsch (2012, 85–88) list "instructional strategies and principles" among the factors "that matter" in training, emphasizing the importance of engaging learners in activities, such as simulations and behavior modeling, that allow practice-and-feedback on target skills.

It would be fair to conclude that instructor enthusiasm is always a positive factor in promoting learning motivation and interest. The evidence is clearest in elementary and secondary education, while in higher education and corporate training—because of the maturational level of the learners, their workplace needs, and the organizational factors surrounding them—other factors weigh more heavily in the motivational equation.

Effect of Sociocultural Environment on Facilitators

Facilitators' own cultural capital and habitus, self-identity, privilege, and intersectionality—along with certain fundamental cultural and educational beliefs/assumptions they hold—influence how they perceive and characterize their own role, the learner, and the teaching–learning process; this in turn affects the instructional methods and resources they employ.

Mismatch between Facilitators' and Learners' Cultural Status

When facilitators possessing socioeconomically more valued cultural capital and more effective habitus are put in contact with learners from socioeconomically marginalized backgrounds, this throws up potential opportunities and pitfalls. Consequently, the facilitator must navigate adroitly and skillfully, figuring out how to nudge learners along pathways to emancipation and empowerment without making them feel devalued or disrespected. This requires the facilitator to check some of their tacit/explicit assumptions with regard to teaching and learning. Two common assumptions among professional educators are that the current ideological, structural, and media/technological frameworks within which most instructed learning takes place are (a) morally and ethically well intentioned, and (b) culturally neutral.

Critical scholars argue, however, that neither of these assumptions is warranted, and that they both reflect the obliviousness that characterizes privilege. For those unfamiliar with the label, critical scholars interpret the acts and the symbols of society to understand how various social groups are oppressed, believing that understanding the ways human being are oppressed enables one to take action to change oppressive forces. These scholars align themselves with the interests of those opposed to the dominant order of society and explore how competing interests clash and how conflicts are resolved in favor of particular groups (Seiler 2006).

A specific group of critical scholars—whom one may call "social reproductionists"—argue that modern schools are set up and operate in a way that perpetuates the intergenerational reproduction of socioeconomic inequalities, rather than promoting the empowerment and upward mobility of learners from socioeconomically marginalized backgrounds by providing them with appropriate pathways to meaningfully harness the emancipatory potential of instructed learning.

Cultural Biases of Technology

Meanwhile, and this is ever more germane given the increasing time, effort, and material resources accorded to the integration of media technologies—including the "emerging" technologies we refer to in this book—into teaching and learning, many professional educators persist in believing that instructional methods and technologies are ideologically objective and culturally neutral. However, noted environmentalist and education scholar Chet Bowers—see Bowers, Vasquez, and Roaf (2000)—reminds us of the "multibillion dollar reasons" (184) that the vendors of media technologies have for maintaining the myth that these technologies are culturally neutral. Said technologies in fact encode Western ideals of individualism and a rootless form of existence (Howe 1988). As Bowers et al. (2000) explain, the myth of the cultural neutrality of technology was important in hiding the forms of cultural transformation that needed to take place in order to enable the spread of the Industrial Revolution; and technology-mediated learning is currently reinforcing the same modern, Western pattern of individual-centered relations and forms of consciousness—equating greater individual autonomy, consumerism, and technological development with progress—during what is essentially the Industrial Revolution's digital phase.

That neither of the two sets of issues introduced in the preceding two paragraphs have historically attracted much attention or interest among the dominant, mainstream voices within professional educator communities—especially educational technologists (Subramony 2004, 2017)—speak to the privilege enjoyed by the latter. As David Gaider—a gender, sex and sexuality activist within the US computer gaming industry—famously put it, privilege "is when you think that something's not a problem because it's not a problem for you personally" (Gaider 2013). The intergenerational reproduction of socioeconomic class inequalities—and the role of schools in perpetuating it—will naturally not be pressing, foregrounded issues for a given individual if they and their family currently enjoy a high SES and actually look forward to its intergenerational reproduction. Similarly, the cultural non-neutrality of technology will not be negatively consequential for a given individual if the cultural values embedded in the former are compatible with their own cultural values.

Second-Level Distal Factors

Two other factors—Home and Family Influences and Peer Influences—identified as critical by Walberg, Hattie, and *HPLII*—are represented in Figure 2.7 as second-level influences; that is, they do not influence instructed learning directly but rather underlie the first-level factors.

Home and Family Influences

Awareness of the contribution of the home to academic success escalated after publication of the famous Coleman Report (Coleman 1966), whose overall conclusion was that the socioeconomic background of students' families was more highly correlated with academic achievement than any differences in schools, such as facilities or staffing. This raises the question of what is it that differs between high-SES homes and low-SES homes that can have educational consequences.

Home Environment

The original Walberg research synthesis (1984) reflects the first wave of research in the years since the Coleman Report. That research led the Walberg team to

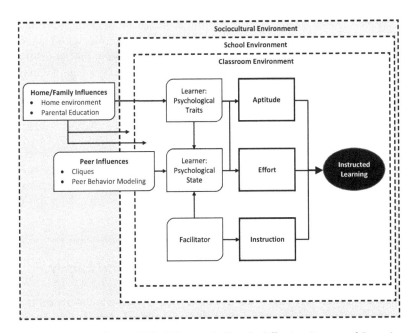

Figure 2.7 Second-Level Distal Factors Indirectly Affecting Instructed Learning.

classify *Home Environment* as one of the nine factors most closely associated with academic achievement. Walberg cited some specific sources of that correlation, including supervised homework, reduced time watching television, and the "curriculum of the home" (Walberg 1984, 25). The latter refers to daily features of life in supportive homes, including informed parent–child conversations about school, encouraging leisure reading, deferring immediate gratifications in favor of longer-term goals, expressions of affection and interest in the child's activities, and other intangible psychological supports—which would include *cultural capital* and *habitus*, discussed earlier. Thus, Figure 2.7 shows that Home and Family Influences directly affect learners' Psychological Traits. Connell and Wellborn (1990) indicate that parents play a key role in providing their children with motivational resources, including self-esteem, agency, and self-control. Some families also support school achievement by instilling high expectations and good work habits in their offspring (Entwisle and Alexander 1996). These are the sorts of Psychological Traits that provide impetus for the investment of Effort in the learning process.

Parental Educational Attainment

More recent research has cast more light on the specific aspects of higher SES homes that matter for instructed learning. Egalite (2016) identifies several variables that can be shown to have a causal connection with academic achievement. First, higher SES families tend to have higher parental educational attainment. Consequently, they read to their children, get involved in school affairs, and inculcate their children into a social network of people who value educational attainment (again, *cultural capital*). Second, higher-SES parents can afford to live in communities with higher-quality schools and to invest in access to extracurricular activities, thus enriching the school experience and giving their children incentive to stay in school. Third, higher SES households are more likely to have a stable, two-parent foundation, meaning more time to get involved in school activities and providing role models for their children. Having an absent father leads to an increase in truancy and grade repetition, especially among boys.

The child-rearing practices described above also contribute to the learner's Aptitude, especially language fluency and cultural knowledge that underlies various subjects in the curriculum. Finally, homes with greater financial means tend to have more choices in choosing schools with better resources, more highly qualified teachers, and therefore higher quality of instruction.

Effect of Sociocultural Environment on Home and Family

Home and Family values are largely determined by the ways in which learners and their parents or relatives are shaped by their SES and cultural identity. Everything we discussed with respect to the effect of the sociocultural environment on learners earlier in this chapter logically applies to their family members as well. Learners acquire a significant portion of their cultural capital from their families, with high-SES children inheriting substantially different, and more valued, cultural capital than low-SES children, whose families are often immigrants, ethnic minorities, and/or language minorities (Bourdieu 1990). Learners also acquire much of their habitus (Bourdieu 1990) from their families. Family background hugely informs an individual learner's socioeconomic and cultural privilege (McIntosh 1988)—or lack thereof—and is a crucial element of their intersectionality (Crenshaw 1991).

Peer Influences

Whether in school, college, or workplace training, as social beings, humans are affected by the attitudes, values, and behaviors of the people around them. Walberg's meta-analyses show "peer group" as one of the nine factors determined to be necessary for productive learning; Hattie includes "peer influences" among the 50 factors most highly associated with successful learning. Neither research group attempts to show where peer influences fit in the chain of causation. In our framework, as shown in Figure 2.7, Peer Influences are depicted as straddling all three environmental levels: outside the school, inside the school, and inside the classroom. As is explained in greater detail below, peer relationships can have a direct effect on learners' expectancies, values, and motivations—the constituent elements of Psychological State. Peer relationships also play a role in creating a positive or negative climate for learning within a school, thus becoming part of the School Environment. Likewise, peer relationships can have a moment-to-moment impact within the classroom, influencing whether students will expect to learn and will expend the effort needed to learn—thus forming part of the Classroom Environment. The mechanisms for these peer influences are detailed in the following sections.

Cliques

Friendship circles, cliques, and other sorts of "peer groups" are notable features of any organization, especially schools, and especially schools populated by adolescents. However, the study of the effects of peer groups on academic achievement is fairly recent. Kindermann's review of literature (2016) finds a high correlation between students' peer group memberships and their engagement in the classroom; for example, students in the "Brains" cliques have more academically oriented friends and have the highest level of academic achievement. This is not surprising, as students tend to self-select into peer groups with similar motivational orientation (Wentzel and Meunks 2016, 16).

Peer Behavior Modeling

At the higher education level, a major meta-analysis of research on student success in college found that the peer group emerged as "the single most potent source of influence on growth and development during the undergraduate years" (Astin 1992, 398). In another recent review of elementary-secondary school research, Wentzel and Muenks (2016) add the notion of students' modeling academic values and feelings of self-efficacy. Elementary school children, as well as older students, have been observed tackling challenging academic goals after seeing peers do so. Thus, through face-to-face communications and behavior modeling, peers activate the expectancies, values, and motivation to learn that produce the Effort to succeed.

Effect of Sociocultural Environment on Peer Influences

Relationships with peers also greatly hinge on the self-identity constructed by the individual learner vis-à-vis the educational system that represents the dominant class/cultural/economic system (Willis 1977; Giroux 1983), as well as the respective self-identities constructed by their peers both within and outside the learner's own socioeconomic class and cultural group. These relationships are also determined by the learner's—and their peers'—relative privilege (McIntosh 1988) and intersectionality (Crenshaw 1991). Learners also acquire varying degrees of cultural capital and habitus (Bourdieu 1990) from their peers.

Effect of Sociocultural Environment on School and Classroom Environment

The School Environment is, at its most basic level, a consequence of (a) how schools are fundamentally conceptualized and structured, and (b) the kind of cultural capital they are set up to reward—both of which are functions of the complex socioeconomic and cultural forces that created the educational system. Sociologists Samuel Bowles and Herbert Gintis (1976, 2002) have long upheld a social reproductionist view of schooling; they have maintained that modern public school systems are set up to reflect the interests of capitalist business owners rather than any democratic or pedagogical ideal. In their view, schools (a) primarily serve to socialize future employees to work uncomplainingly within hierarchical corporate structures—by structuring social interactions and individual rewards in ways that mirror workplace environments, while (b) doing precious little to stop the intergenerational reproduction of social inequality, i.e., to break the cycle of low socioeconomic status (SES) children growing up to be low-SES adults.

Bourdieu (1990), in contrast, focuses more on cultural processes as opposed to structural determinism to explain how schools work to foster the intergenerational reproduction of social inequality. According to him, schools embody the interests of dominant classes by acting to reward the cultural capital of said classes while simultaneously acting to systematically devalue that of marginalized classes. Schools thus become the marketplace where the cultural capital of dominant classes is exchanged for the currency of academic credentials, which is subsequently converted back into economic capital via entry into highly remunerated professions—representing a perfectly legitimized cycle of social reproduction. Giroux puts a finer point on it when he explains that schools reproduce existing power relations "via the production and distribution of a dominant culture that tacitly confirms what it means to be educated" (1983, 87).

Third-Level Distal Factors

Some of the other factors identified by Walberg, Hattie, and *HPLII* as critical—mass media and social media—are represented in Figure 2.1 as third-level influences; that is, they do not influence instructed learning directly but rather underlie the second-level factors, which affect the first-level factors, which directly influence Effort or Instruction.

Mass Media

Walberg's original synthesis (1984) identified mass media as one of the nine factors indicated by research as critical to achievement. This was based primarily on his finding that the amount of out-of-school television watching was significantly negatively correlated with academic achievement. Researchers have investigated several different potential causes for this negative effect. One popular theory is termed "displacement," proposing that the time spent consuming entertainment television displaces time spent reading, playing, or doing homework. Other theories look to changes in Psychological Traits attributable to media consumption. A well-designed longitudinal study in New Zealand followed 1,037 children from ages 5 to 15. It found that higher television consumption at an early age was linked to attention problems in adolescence, even controlling for gender, cognitive ability, and socioeconomic status (Landhuis et al. 2007).

Now that computer-based media have eclipsed broadcast television as the main competitor for children's viewing time, many of the same types of investigations are re-asking the same questions about Web and social media influences. Not surprisingly, the answers follow the pattern found earlier with television.

Mass media—including computer-based forms—can also be viewed as a cultural force, both helping to shape the larger culture and mirroring that larger culture, as indicated by the two-headed arrow in Figure 2.1. Media messages may support or inhibit the pro-social attitudes and behaviors that comprise School Climate, as well as the attitudes held by parents and student peers.

Social Media

As discussed in Chapter 1, we are accepting the popular term *social media* to refer to the set of Web-based applications that enable users to conveniently create and exchange information with other users. These tools are used, first and foremost, by everyday people for everyday communication and entertainment. For example, in 2018, nearly 70 percent of US adults used Facebook and over 70 percent used YouTube—with most of them doing so on a daily basis. Among young people, those percentages are even higher, and the range of platforms used is even broader (e.g., WhatsApp, Instagram, Snapchat, and TikTok). So, we will first discuss the influence of this out-of-school social media usage on the distal factors that have an indirect effect on instructed learning. Following that, we will discuss the influences of in-school use of social media—their effect on the classroom environment and their usage as instructional tools.

Social Media and Peer Influences

Schrader (2015) and others (Kietzmann et al. 2011) extol the role of social media in transcending classroom boundaries, claiming that social media use creates new and larger communities of learners, and allows for reaching a broader spectrum and more diverse collaborators in the learning process, potentially including those with physical and cognitive disabilities and a range of personalities and interaction styles. The effect, then, is to expand the pool of peers with whom learners can interact.

As Schrader explains, in traditional classrooms care must be taken to attend to those who traditionally are the nonparticipants and excluded others—those less outspoken, bullied, shy, less popular, or less socially integrated. Interpersonal skills that are important components of learning and sociocultural adaptation—such as social compliance, cooperation, and the development of positive, effective relationships—can be appropriated via social media use. Social media thus enables broader classrooms featuring more equalized participation. Schrader goes on to explain how—contingent on equitable access to technology, of course—social media can empower diverse learners by countering the effects on their classroom performance of pernicious expectancies based on their demographic features, thus enabling them to be judged on the content of their contributions rather than on their race, gender, class, etc.

When those peers are able to communicate easily among themselves through social media they are more likely to reveal more of their identities—age, gender, profession, personal interests, etc.—than might occur in a classroom setting (Kietzmann et al. 2011). This expands the opportunities for the personal connections that power peers' influence amongst themselves. Further, as they exchange more subject-matter related information, learners have more chances for peer behavior modeling, as they make judgments about who might be opinion leaders on various issues.

Social Media and Classroom Environment

As discussed earlier in this chapter, Classroom Environment has a proven connection to instructed learning outcomes, particularly when the members like each other, have high morale, and are cohesive as a group. Taylor (2015) and Junco (2014) point out that social media can contribute to this atmosphere in several ways. For example, social media tools allow the instructor to remind students frequently about due dates and expectations, thus contributing to a feeling of a well-organized class that offers positive expectations for all. And when participants engage in civil discourse, giving and receiving praise and support, cohesiveness deepens.

Social Media and Learners' Psychological State

As pointed out earlier in this chapter, the learner's expectancies for success and valuation of active participation in learning activities can enhance their Effort, one of the three key ingredients of successful outcomes. While the use of social media does not per se communicate high expectations, the instructor's use of those tools to establish high expectations, along with messages and supports that make those expectations attainable, translates to positive academic expectancies (Junco 2014, 176). If, in addition, peers show buy-in through their communications and their valuation of diverse ways of learning, the effect is magnified.

Social Media and Instruction

Up to this point, we have discussed the potential effects of social media usage on factors that indirectly affect instructed learning; the effects are "trickle-down." However, there are also claims about effects on Instruction, which directly facilitates instructed learning. Several of these claims are summarized by Junco (2014):

- "*Active learning.* Using social media to continue class discussions allows students to be active participants in the learning process—extending what they learn in the classroom to personal or professional settings." (175–176)
- "*Prompt feedback.* One of the major benefits of using social media in the classroom is that students can receive prompt feedback from each other as well as from their instructors, allowing them to focus their learning more appropriately." (176)
- "*Time on task.* Another affordance of using social media in courses is that when planned appropriately, they can increase the time students spend interacting with course content. This leads not only to content-level knowledge but to further engagement." (176)

When students spend more time processing the subject matter through online discussion forums, chats, and collaborative group work, the chances of comprehension and retention increase (Taylor 2015). In addition, these discussions help learners personalize and contextualize the material—proven strategies for long-term retention.

When students generate new material, *publish* it through social media platforms, and receive feedback from other participants—what some refer to as engaging in "the read-write Web"—they are practicing the processes of critical thinking (Taylor 2015; Allison and Kendrick 2015, 113).

Emancipatory Learning and Social Constructivism

These processes of peer collaboration across geographical and cultural divides and critical thinking honed by peer interaction lead learners, according to Tadros (2011), toward the emancipatory potential of social media; potentially subverting the traditional pedagogical model of the knowledgeable teacher depositing knowledge upon the ignorant student (84). This is a theme that Paulo Freire (2000) elaborated in his seminal *Pedagogy of the Oppressed*: engaging students in the learning process, getting them to relate what they have learned to their real lives, and encouraging critical thinking and nurturing self-motivation.

Schrader (2015) sees both the cognitive and sociocultural constructivist theoretical perspectives blending seamlessly with the technological affordances provided by social media for learning, knowledge development, meaning making, and mind changing. From a cognitive angle, she sees social media providing "interactions that *create opportunities* for the…cognitive equilibration processes of *assimilation and accommodation* of new experiences to one's knowing system" (84). Meanwhile, through the sociocultural lens, Schrader sees social media providing opportunities "for the sociocultural *appropriation* of new skills," with knowledge construction occurring "through community engagement, dialogue, and communication *in a community of shared activity*" (84). In such a community, students "learn to both think and explore within and outside of their own perspective or mindset [and] to take perspectives of others in important ways that influence social-emotional learning" (84).

Sociocultural Environment: A Summary

It will be clearly noticeable from our preceding discussion of the multiple distal factors influencing instructed learning that all of these factors are underlain and affected by the sociocultural environment within which they are situated. In fact, all of the elements that must come together in order to make instructed learning possible —viz., learners, facilitators, resources, settings, teaching–learning arrangements, and organizational structures—are embedded and operate within a given sociocultural environment.

It is in light of this that we depict Sociocultural Environment in Figure 2.1 as a large, shaded field underlying all of the boxes denoting the distal factors that influence instructed learning. Our perspective here is congruent with that of the authors of *HPLII*, who also approach the whole subject of human learning from a sociocultural perspective, pointing out that learning cannot be separated from the culture in which it takes place (National Academies of Sciences 2018, 22). "Culture" is defined here in its sociological sense: as a way of life of a group of people—the behaviors, beliefs, values, and symbols that they accept, generally without thinking about them, and that are passed along from one generation to the next.

Frame Factors

The term *frame factor* is used to refer to those features of a setting that serve as resources or constraints for actors in that setting. In our framework, as depicted in Figure 2.1, it might be assumed that Facilitators have all the qualifications they could need and that all possible means of instruction are available—whatever methods or resources needed are at hand. But, of course, in reality, time and money are not infinitely available, thus limiting the options available to all the actors. A school may not have well-qualified staff; the space and furniture may not allow flexibility in using different grouping methods; the media resources may be meager to nonexistent. Thus, we want to acknowledge the existence of real-world constraints, in the form of frame factors.

Among the factors that expand or limit the activities of teachers and learners are, for example, laws and governmental regulations, funding, moral and ethical norms, professional standards of teachers and administrators, amount of time available, physical environment, and student health and well-being. By and large, these types of factors do not appear among the variables unearthed in the sorts of educational research studies compiled in the meta-analyses discussed in this chapter, yet they must be acknowledged as significant facts of life for those engaged in teaching and learning. We have discussed in the immediately preceding sections of this chapter just how powerful an effect sociocultural and economic factors can have on the lives of facilitators and learners in the school setting. Next, we will briefly consider some of the obvious frame factors that constrain all activities within the system.

Laws and Governmental Regulations

Public educational institutions are established by governments in order to provide some level of general education to the population. In many countries, laws and policies governing public (and often private) education are laid down at the national level. There are many exceptions: In the United States and Germany, for example, educational policies are controlled by the states; in some European countries, various provinces are granted autonomy over local issues, including education, in deference to the claims of cultural minorities. Such laws and regulations establish the "floor" for delivery of educational opportunities to the communities they oversee.

In the United States, during the nineteenth century, colleges and universities voluntarily agreed to define high school degrees according to the "Carnegie unit"—essentially how many hours spent in the presence of a certified teacher—and college degrees according to "Student hours"—again, defined as time spent with a qualified instructor. These definitions have often been enshrined in state law or regulations. The benefit of these definitions has been to give institutions the capacity to standardize functions such as admission and graduation standards and to enable comparisons across institutions. A drawback has been to constrain institutions from exploring more cost-effective ways to conduct education, such as the use of non-licensed paraprofessionals or to substitute distance education experiences for face-to-face classroom experiences. An example of the significance of changing a legal definition occurred in 1998 around the issue of distance education. The California Community College Board of Governors changed the requirement for personal contact from "regular *personal* contact" to "regular *effective* contact" (Burnett 2020). This one-word change allowed online courses to proceed without the necessity of an on-campus discussion session. Within a few years, hundreds of thousands of California community college students were enrolling in online courses, a number that has grown each year, reaching over a quarter of all student-hours by 2017 (California Community Colleges Chancellor's Office 2017). Another example related to distance education is reported in Chapter 1, in which a change in the definition of distance education in US federal regulations (requiring "regular and substantive interaction") effectively ended subsidization of correspondence study programs.

Funding

The amount of money devoted to educational activities unquestionably enhances or constrains what can be accomplished within the system. Governing bodies of educational institutions and corporate training programs decide how much money to expend on those institutions and programs. Rational decision-makers are interested in deriving the greatest possible benefits from the least investment. Indeed, some educational research programs, such as Walberg's at the University of Illinois at Chicago, cited earlier, attempt to calculate the contribution of various causal factors to successful achievement outcomes in order to measure the overall economic productivity of different combinations of factors. An early meta-analysis of studies of school funding and achievement failed to find a "strong or systematic relationship between school expenditures and student performance" (Hanushek 1986). Later studies of the same data using higher-quality selection criteria and more discriminating statistical treatments found the opposite, that "resource variables such as PPE [per-pupil expenditure] show strong and consistent relations with achievement" (Greenwald, Hedges and Laine 1996).

Studies since then have confirmed the positive relationship between financial inputs and student achievement (Baker 2017). Of course, no one is proposing that more money spent, willy-nilly, leads to better outcomes. Rather, fine-grained economic impact studies show that the payoff comes when the additional funds are invested in attracting more highly qualified teachers, reducing class size, and providing teachers with professional development support to enable them to use more powerful instructional methods (Baker 2017, 2). That is, if the funds are focused on the factors of Facilitator and Instruction, they can have an impact on improving instructed learning.

Moral and Ethical Norms

Laws are not sufficient for specifying all the things educators should do or refrain from doing for the benefit of learners. All cultures have norms of morality that speak in general to fair treatment and safety of learners in classrooms. Educators typically belong to professional associations that promulgate specific codes of ethics to cover the situations encountered in various specialty areas. For example, the code of ethics of the Association for Educational Communications and Technology (AECT) speaks to learners' rights of access to materials that present varying points of view and of equitable access to all appropriate educational programs. While adherence to such norms does not necessarily affect learning outcomes, it does at least reduce possible harm to the learners in the system, giving them a chance to perform up to their ability.

Professional Standards

Educators, through their professional associations, subscribe to professional standards that "communicate expectations to practitioners, supporting institutions, professional associations, policy makers and the public about the work, qualities and values of effective educational leaders" (NPBEA 2015, 4). Such standards constrain professional performance regarding interactions with other staff, with students, with parents and community members, and regarding decisions about curriculum and instruction. Such standards provide "guard rails" to deter substandard instructional practices, assuming they are well promulgated and well enforced.

Time

Time is the one irreplaceable resource for all human endeavors. For learners, "time on task" has always shown a high correlation with academic achievement. Walberg's (2006) summary of research places "amount of time students engage in learning" as one of the nine factors most highly correlated with productivity in learning (108–109).

This includes such measures as amount of school attendance, length of school year, amount of attention to lessons, and amount of time devoted to homework.

In one of the earliest attempted models of critical factors for school learning, John B. Carroll (1963) asserted that the single most important variable was the *time* given to master new knowledge or skills. He later modified this claim to add the notions of *effort* and persistence; the learner has to be willing to *use* the time given to continue to grapple with the learning task (thereby aligning his model more closely to our model in Figure 2.1).

Berliner traces the history of educationists' concern for learner time (1990) and the many different ways of measuring this concept, pointing out that time has always been viewed as one of the most important frame factors. Allocation of time to different subjects or different learning goals is widely used by curriculum planners as a means to guide teachers' attention to what is important. But researchers agree that it is not merely the time the learner is exposed to information that matters, but rather the time learners spend engaged with the material.

On the other side of the coin, "time to teach" has long been a concern among teachers. They have always had too many demands placed on their time, with too little regard for protecting the time needed to prepare and implement their lessons. Hence "time to teach" is a perennial advocacy issue for professional associations such as the National Education Association.

Physical Environment

Anyone who has tried to maintain attention during a lecture in a stifling hot room knows how critical room temperature and air movement are. Light control is a constant concern, in terms of having enough light to read and write and being able to selectively dim the light when trying to project a legible image on a large screen. Ambient noise can hamper the ability to hear what is going on. In the 1960s, when "open classrooms" were an emergent trend it was quickly discovered that large open spaces with multiple learning groups chattering simultaneously did not work. Teachers competed to make themselves heard above the ambient noise. Before long, they were erecting bookcases and other sound barriers to allow students to hear each other or to read books.

The constraints posed by different physical environments are discussed further in Chapter 3 under the heading of Setting.

Student Health and Well-Being

Hundreds of studies published in journals of nutrition, pediatrics, and child psychology document the importance of good health and psychological well-being to academic success. Hunger and food insecurity depress children's academic performance and behavior in school. Hungry children have lower test scores, and they are more likely to repeat a grade, come to school late, or miss it entirely. Psychological suffering, such as from abuse or homelessness, affects students' psychological traits, such as self-esteem, and psychological state, such as valuation of school, expectancy of success, and relationships with peers and teachers.

The constraints of two or more frame factors can cascade, forcing students to struggle against the odds to attain success. An example of interacting and cascading frame factors is told in a vivid narrative written by Yolanda Ingle after spending a year in the field, observing students who attended middle schools in El Salvador that were beginning to receive televised lessons in core subjects (Ingle 1973). The television programs were a vehicle for implementing a new curriculum. Ingle follows two students from their homes, one in a poor village, the other in an urban neighborhood. They leave on foot before dawn without breakfast and they walk miles to their schoolhouses. Not only do the students arrive tired and hungry, but they have to struggle for a place to sit or stand in overcrowded classrooms, which grow hot and stuffy as the day goes on. Classes end at noon because the schools—and the same teachers—serve two shifts. On some days the television signal is fuzzy or the television receiver is malfunctioning, or the teacher simply decides not to turn on the television set. If the poorly paid and minimally trained teacher doesn't have a backup plan, they simply miss those lessons for those days. Even when the TV lessons proceed, some students cannot see the screen and some chat and move about, making a distracting environment. Some teachers conduct follow-up activities after the TV lessons, others do not. School supplies are always lacking; some students do not even have pens or paper. This may not be a representative sample of schools in the United States, but it illustrates how frame factors such as poverty, shortage of resources, and unreliable teaching practices can interact to impede learning.

Implications of the Framework

The purpose of the framework in Figure 2.1 is to lay out a map of the factors most closely associated with success or failure in instructed learning. The factors closest to the final box, Instructed Learning, are those indicated by research to be proximal causes: Aptitude, Effort, and Instruction; each of which, in turn, has more distal causes. With the framework in front of us it is easier to understand judgments such as, "as important as the home and family environment is to academic success, it exerts influence only through mediating factors such as Psychological State and Aptitude."

Giving Context to Prior Research Syntheses

The research syntheses by Hattie and *HPLII* do not attempt to show the interconnections among factors; they simply assert that each of these identified factors somehow seems to influence instructed learning success or failure. By failing to show the causal chains, these reports are subject to interpretation as either *oversimplifying* the case—there are a small number of factors, each of which has a direct effect on learning, or *over-complicating* the case—there are a multitude of very different factors acting simultaneously, offering little hope for a place to start to seek improvement.

Framing the Contents of this Book

While the central concern of this book is Instruction, we do not wish to create the impression that Instruction is the only—or the most important—factor in the classroom. It is, however, as this analysis shows, the one factor that is most under the control of teachers, professors, trainers, and all those who plan and implement instructional events. It is therefore worthy of close and deep analysis.

What Does <u>Not</u> Affect Academic Outcomes?

In view of the multiplicity of factors that have been identified as feeding into successful academic achievement, one might well ask: What *doesn't* affect academic outcomes? The easiest generalization would be: those things that the general public argues about! Student achievement is not directly—or even indirectly—affected by most of the "educational reform" panaceas offered by political leaders. The issues that parents and taxpayers argue about most vociferously are cosmetic changes that appeal to the eye but have little to do with academic performance. Four examples that illustrate this point are school uniforms, merit pay for teachers, class size, and the replacement of public schools by private or charter schools.

School Uniforms

Many claims can be made for and against the mandate to wear a certain type of uniform in elementary or secondary school. While there may be psychological benefits for some students in some cases, there are also drawbacks, especially in the eyes of students themselves. At the end, though, do school uniforms affect outcomes? From his synthesis of data from two large American databases, David Brunsma (2004) found no significant effect on achievement at the elementary level and a significant negative effect at the high school level. He concluded:

> There is no evidence from this set of analyses that dress codes or uniforms positively affect the school or its students in discernible ways, nor do they influence the very processes that do affect schools and students (i.e., climate, pro-school attitudes, etc.).

(142)

Another study, by Ryan Yeung, using large data sets and econometric analyses of American schools, concludes that "the results do not suggest any significant association between school uniform policies and achievement" (2009, 847).

Merit Pay

Given the meritocratic bias in the American self-image, it is not surprising that political leaders periodically propose to assess teachers' performance by their students' test performance and to reward those teachers whose students do best, known as "merit pay." Gius's findings (2012) are typical of research on this topic: Using district-level data from two large national data sets, "the results of this study suggest that merit pay is not positively related to student academic attainment" (Gius 2012, 93). This should not be surprising since—as we have shown—there are so many factors at play that outweigh the value of some putative teacher motivation based on a small pay increment.

Class Size

An issue that perennially arises when teachers negotiate with administrators over their working conditions is class size. Teachers feel that smaller classes allow more individual attention and enable more engaging instructional activities. Administrators resist because smaller classes require more teachers, thereby driving up costs. Hattie's mega-analysis finds a very low correlation between class size and student achievement (2009, 86). He and many other analysts have concluded that although smaller class size theoretically enables better instructional practices, in reality, teachers tend not to change their teaching practices, even when class size changes. To improve learner achievement requires either more motivated or better instructed students; both of these variables require a change in teacher behavior. It appears that such a change in behavior is unlikely to happen without in-service training, enlightened supervision, and additional incentives.

Charter Schools

One of the most popular panaceas in contemporary times in the United States is to replace public schools with private or charter schools. In the 1950s, this issue was framed in terms of allowing tax monies to be used to support religious schools. It was a major issue in the 1960 presidential election as Catholics were anticipating the election of a Catholic president, John F. Kennedy, who would presumably be sympathetic to this proposition. In more recent times, "religious freedom" is often used as argument in favor of private schools, but this claim is frequently subsumed under the claim that nonpublic schools simply provide a higher quality learning environment. Hundreds of district-by-district evaluations have been done, generally showing either no significant difference or a small difference in favor of public schools. One particularly well-designed longitudinal study (Pianta and Ansari 2018) followed a representative sample of American children for ten years, assessing their academic, social, psychological, and attainment outcomes at age 15. When the data were examined without adjusting for sociodemographic characteristics, private schools showed better results. However, when family socioeconomic status (previously well established as highly correlated with school success by Hattie among others) was taken into account, all the advantages for private schools evaporated. Bottom line: "There was also no evidence to suggest that low-income children or children enrolled in urban schools benefited more from private school enrollment" (Pianta and Ansari 2018, 419). Hattie's mega-analysis agrees:

> Not surprisingly, given the close to zero effect, there is a mixture of positive and negative effects, and there is much variation across the states. The hype and promise is much greater than the effects on student achievement.
>
> *(2009, 76)*

The point of this discussion of "what doesn't work" is that when one is looking for ways to improve instructed learning, one must ask whether the proposed improvement can reasonably be expected to have an effect on Effort or the quality or quantity of Instruction. If the factors that most directly cause learning are not affected by an innovation, there is little chance that student achievement will suddenly soar.

Chapter Summary

The verbal-visual framework proposed in this chapter was created by the authors, based on several large-scale summaries of research on the factors that influence Instructed Learning. It was necessary to create our own framework, since a suitably comprehensive, evidence-based framework seems to be absent from the major discussions of research and theory in education and training.

The framework depicts the flow of influence from those furthest from the "front lines" of Aptitude, Effort, and Instruction and progressing toward factors more closely related to Instructed Learning. This framework can provide a road map for future research and theorizing. It allows scholars to locate their hypotheses in relation to the big picture. Our hope is that future research will allow others to amend the map, to make it fit the data better, or to adapt it to specific environments. For example, we would expect a framework for Instructed Learning in the realm of corporate training to have somewhat different contours, even different factors at play. For present purposes, the framework offers placeholders for the elements of instruction that are the subject of the rest of this book. We want readers to be cognizant of where each topic fits in terms of the big picture.

Works Cited

Akey, Theresa M. 2006. *School Context, Student Attitudes and Behavior, and Academic Achievement: An Exploratory Analysis.* New York: MDRC.

Allison, Mark, and Lynn Marie Kendrick. 2015. "Toward Education 3.0: Pedagogical Affordances and Implication of Social Software and the Semantic Web." *New Directions in Teaching and Learning* 144: 109–119.

Anderson, Lorin. 1984. "Instruction and Time-on-Task: A Review." Chap. 7 in *Time and School Learning: Theory, Research and Practice*, edited by Lorin Anderson, 143–166. London: Routledge.

Astin, Alexander W. 1992. *What Matters in College: Four Critical Years Revisited.* San Francisco, CA: Jossey-Bass.

Baker, Bruce D. 2017. *How Money Matters in Schools.* Palo Alto, CA/Washington, DC: Learning Policy Institute, 21. Accessed October 23, 2019. https://learningpolicyinstitute.org/sites/default/files/product-files/How:Money_Matters_REPORT.pdf.

Banas, John A., Norah Dunbar, Dariela Rodriguez, and Shr-Jie Liu. 2011. "A Review of Humor in Educational Settings: Four Decades of Research." *Communication Education* 60 (1): 115–144.

Bandura, Albert. 1977. "Self Efficacy: Toward a Unifying Theory of Behavioral Change." *Psychological Review* 84: 191–215.

Bandura, Albert. 1997. *Self-Efficacy: The Exercise of Control.* New York: Freeman.

Berliner, David C. 1990. "What's All the Fuss About Instructional Time?" In *The Nature of Time in Schools: Theoretical Concepts, Practitioner Perceptions*, edited by Miriam Ben-Peretz and Rainer Bromme, 3–35. New York: Teachers College Press.

Berman, Paul, and Milbrey Wallin McLaughlin. 1977. *Federal Programs Supporting Educational Change.* Vol. 7, *Factors Affecting Implementation and Continuation.* Santa Monica, CA: Rand Corp.

Bertolero, Maxwell A., and Danielle S. Bassett. 2019. "How Matter Becomes Mind." *Scientific American* 321 (1): 26–33.

Bertolero, Maxwell A., B. T. Thomas Yeo, Danielle A. Bassett, and Mark D'Esposito. 2018. "A Mechanistic Model of Connector Hubs, Modularity and Cognition." *Nature Human Behavior* 2: 765–777.

Bouchard, Thomas J., Jr. 1998. "Genetic and Environmental Influences on Adult Intelligence and Special Mental Abilities." *Human Biology* 70 (2): 257–279.

Bourdieu, Pierre. 1990. *The Logic of Practice.* Cambridge: Polity Press.

Bowers, C. A., Miguel Vasquez, and Mary Roaf. 2000. "Native People and the Challenge of Computers: Reservation Schools, Individualism, and Consumerism." *American Indian Quarterly* 24 (2): 182–199.

Bowles, Samuel, and Herbert Gintis. 1976. *Schooling in Capitalist America: Educational Reform and the Contradictions of Economic Life.* New York: Basic Books.

Bowles, Samuel, and Herbert Gintis. 2002. "Schooling in Capitalist America Revisited." *Sociology of Education* 75 (1): 1–18.

Brunsma, David L. 2004. *The School Uniform Movement and What It Tells Us About American Education: A Symbolic Crusade.* Lanham, MD: Scarecrow Education.
Burnett, Henry. 2020. Interview by Michael Molenda. (February 3).
California Community Colleges Chancellor's Office. 2017. *Distance Education Report.* Sacramento, CA: California Community Colleges Chancellor's Office.
Carroll, John B. 1963. "A Model of School Learning." *Teachers College Record* 64: 723–733.
Clark, Richard E., and Bror Saxberg. 2018. "Engineering Motivation Using the Belief-Expectancy-Control Framework." *Interdisciplinary Education and Psychology* 2 (1): 1–26.
Clignet, Remi P., and Philip J. Foster. 1964. "French and British Colonial Education in Africa." *Comparative Education Review* 8 (2): 191–198.
Cohen, Elizabeth G., and Rachel A. Lotan. 2014. *Designing Groupwork: Strategies for the Heterogeneous Classroom.* 3rd ed. New York: Teachers College Press.
Coleman, James S. 1966. *Equality of Educational Opportunity.* Office of Education; U.S. Department of Health, Education, and Welfare, Washington, DC: U.S. Government Printing Office.
Collins, Patricia Hill. 1993. "Toward a New Vision: Race, Class, and Gender as Categories of Analysis and Connection." *Race, Sex, and Class* 1 (1): 25–45.
Connell, James P., and James G. Wellborn. 1990. *Competence, Autonomy, and Relatedness: A Motivational Analysis of Self-System Analyses.* In *Self-Process and Development. The Minnesota Symposia on Child Psychology*, edited by M. R. Gunnar and L. A. Sroufe, 23:43–77. Hillsdale, NJ: Lawrence Erlbaum.
Cooley, William W., and Paul R. Lohnes. 1976. *Evaluation Research in Education.* New York: Irvington Publishers.
Crenshaw, Kimberlé. 1991. "Mapping the Margins: Intersectionality, Identity Politics, and Violence Against Women of Color." *Stanford Law Review* 43 (6): 1241–1299.
Csikszentmihalyi, Mihaly, and Jane McCormack. 1986. "The Influence of Teachers." *Phi Delta Kappan* 67 (6): 415–419.
Cuban, Larry. 1992. "Computers Meet Classroom; Classroom Wins." *Education Week*, November 11: 27, 36.
Dean, Ceri B., Elizabeth Ross Hubbell, Howard Pitler, and Bj Stone. 2012. *Classroom Instruction That Works.* 2nd ed. Alexandria, VA: ASCD.
Dewey, John. 1913. *Interest and Effort in Education.* Boston, MA: Houghton-Mifflin.
Eccles, Jacquelynne S. 1983. "Expectancies, Values, and Academic Behaviors." In *Achievement and Achievement Motives: Psychological and Sociological Approaches*, edited by Janet Taylor Spence, 75–146. San Francisco, CA: W. H. Freeman.
Egalite, Anna J. 2016. "How Family Background Influences Student Achievement." *Education Next* 16 (2). Accessed February 5, 2019. https://www.educationnext.org/how-family-background-influences-student-achievement/.
Emba, Christine. 2015. *Intersectionality.* September 21. Accessed September 11, 2019. https://www.washingtonpost.com/news/in-theory/wp/2015/09/21/intersectionality-a-primer/.
Entwisle, Doris R., and Karl L. Alexander. 1996. "Family Type and Children's Growth in Reading and Math Over the Primary Grades." *Journal of Marriage and Family* 58 (2): 341–355.
Fraser, Barry J., Herbert J. Walberg, Wayne W. Welch, and John A. C. Hattie. 1987. "Syntheses of Educational Productivity Research." *International Journal of Educational Research* 11 (2): 145–252.
Freire, Paulo. 2000. *Pedagogy of the Oppressed.* New York: Continuum.

Gaider, David. 2013. "Sex in Video Games." *GDC Vault*, March 28. Accessed September 11, 2019. https://www.gdcvault.com/play/1017796/Sex-in-Video.

Gardner, Howard. 1983. *Frames of Mind: The Theory of Multiple Intelligences*. New York: Basic Books.

Giroux, Henry A. 1983. "Theories of Reproduction and Resistance in the New Sociology of Education." *Harvard Educational Review* 53: 257–293.

Gius, Mark. 2012. "The Effects of Teacher Merit Pay on Academic Attainment: An Analysis Using District-Level Data." *Journal of Economics and Economic Education Research* 13 (3): 93–108.

Goodwin, Bryan, Harvey F. Silver, Susan Kreisman, and Matthew J. Perini. 2019. *Tools for Igniting Curiosity*. Denver, CO: McREL International.

Gottfried, Adele Eskeles, James S. Fleming, and Allen W. Gottfried. 2001. "Continuity of Academic Intrinsic Motivation from Childhood through Late Adolescence: A Longitudinal Study." *Journal of Educational Psychology* 93 (1): 3–13.

Greenwald, Rob, Larry V. Hedges, and Richard D. Laine. 1996. "The Effect of School Resources on Student Achievement." *Review of Educational Research* 66 (3): 361–396.

Gruber, Matthias J., Bernard D. Gelman, and Charan Ranganath. 2014. "States of Curiosity Modulate Hippocampus-Dependent Learning via the Dopaminergic Circuit." *Neuron* 84: 486–496.

Hanushek, Eric A. 1986. "Economics of Schooling: Production and Efficiency in Public Schools." *Journal of Economic Literature* 24 (3): 1141–1177.

Harackiewicz, Judith M., and Chris S. Hulleman. 2010. "The Importance of Interest: The Role of Achievement Goals and Task Values in Promoting the Development of Interest." *Social and Personality Psychology Compass* 4 (1): 42–52.

Hattie, John A. C. 2009. *Visible Learning: A Synthesis of over 800 Meta-Analyses Relating to Achievement*. New York: Routledge.

Hattie, John A. C. 2012. *Visible Learning for Teachers: Maximizing Impact on Learning*. Abingdon: Routledge.

Hidi, Suzanne, and K. Ann Renninger. 2006. "The Four-Phase Model of Interest Development." *Educational Psychologist* 41 (2): 111–127.

Howe, Craig. 1988. "Cyberspace is No Place for Tribalism." *Wicazo sa Review* 13 (2): 17–27.

Huitt, William G., Marsha A. Huitt, David M. Monetti, and John H. Hummel. 2009. "A Systems-Based Synthesis of Research Related to Improving Students' Academic Performance." *Educational Psychology Interactive*, October 16–19. Accessed October 8, 2019. http://www.edpsycinteractive.org/papers/improving-school-achievement.pdf.

Ingle, Yolanda R. 1973. "An Observation Study of Two Classrooms." In *Television and Educational Reform in El Salvador*, edited by Henry T. Ingle et al., 64–103. Washington, DC: Information Center on Instructional Technology, Academy for Educational Development.

James, William. 1899. *Talks to Teachers on Psychology; and to Students on Some of Life's Ideals*. New York: Henry Holt and Company.

Junco, Reynol. 2014. *Engaging Students Through Social Media: Evidence-Based Practices for Use in Student Affairs*. San Francisco, CA: Jossey-Bass.

Keller, John M. 2010. *Motivational Design for Learning and Performance: The ARCS Model Approach*. New York: Springer Science + Business Media.

Kietzmann, Jan H., Kristopher Hermkens, Ian P. McCarthy, and Bruno S. Silvestre. 2011. "Social Media? Get Serious! Understanding the Functional Building Blocks of Social Media." *Business Horizons* 54 (3): 241–251.

Kindermann, Thomas A. 2016. "Peer Group Influences on Students' Academic Achievement." In *Handbook of Social Influences in School Contexts: Social-Emotional, Motivation, and Cognitive Outcomes*, edited by Kathryn R. Wentzel and Geetha B. Ramani, 31–47. New York: Routledge.

Kubek, Jean E., Norma D. Delp, Tammy K. Haslett, and Michael A. McDaniel. 1996. "Does Job-Related Training Performance Decline with Age?" *Psychology and Aging* 11 (1): 92–107.

Kuh, George D. 2003. "What We're Learning About Student Engagement for NSSE: Benchmarks for Effective Educational Practices." *Change* 35 (2): 24–32.

Landhuis, Carl Erik, Richie Poulton, David Welch, and Robert John Hancox. 2007. "Does Childhood Television Viewing Lead to Attention Problems in Adolescence? Results from a Prospective Longitudinal Study." *Pediatrics* 120: 532–537.

Loeb, Susanna. 2001. "Teacher Quality: Its Enhancement and Potential for Improving Pupil Achievement." Chap. 6 in *Improving Educational Productivity*, edited by David H. Monk and Herbert J. Walberg, 99–114. Greenwich, CT: Information Age Publishing.

Mager, Robert F. 1977. "The 'Winds of Change'." *Training and Development Journal* (October): 12–20.

McIlrath, Deborah A., and William G. Huitt. 1995. "The Teaching-Learning Process: A Discussion of Models." *Educational Psychology Interactive*, December. Accessed October 3, 2019. http://edpsycinteractive.org/papers/modelch.html.

McIntosh, Peggy. 1988. *White Privilege and Male Privilege: A Personal Account of Coming to See Correspondences Through Work in Women's Studies*. Wellesley, MA: Center for Research on Women, Wellesley College.

Merrill, M. David. 2013. *First Principles of Instruction*. San Francisco, CA: Pfeiffer.

Miles, Matthew B., and A. Michael Huberman. 1994. *Qualitative Data Analysis*. 2nd ed. Thousand Oaks, CA: Sage Publications.

Monk, David H., Herbert J. Walberg, and Margaret C. Wang, eds. 2001. *Improving Educational Productivity*. Greenwich, CT: Information Age.

National Academies of Sciences, Engineering, and Medicine. 2018. *How People Learn II: Learners, Contexts, and Cultures*. Washington, DC: The National Academies Press.

National Research Council. 2000. *How People Learn: Brain, Mind, Experience, and School*. Expanded Edition. Washington, DC: The National Academy Press.

NPBEA. 2015. *Professional Standards for Educational Leaders*. Policy Paper, Reston, VA: National Policy Board for Educational Administration.

Pianta, Robert C., and Arya Ansari. 2018. "Does Attendance in Private Schools Predict Student Outcomes at Age 15? Evidence from a Longitudinal Study." *Educational Researcher* 47 (7): 419–434.

Protheroe, Nancy. 2008. "Teacher Efficacy: What Is It and Does It Matter?" *Principal*, May/June: 42–45.

Renninger, K. Ann. 2003. "Effort and Interest." In *Encyclopedia of Education*, edited by James W. Guthrie, 704–707. New York: Macmillan Reference USA.

Richards, Christina, and Meg-John Barker, eds. 2015. *The Palgrave Handbook of the Psychology of Sexuality and Gender*. New York: Palgrave Macmillan.

Rotter, Julian B. 1966. "Generalized Expectancies for Internal Versus External Control of Reinforcement." *Psychological Monographs: General and Applied* 80 (1): 1–28.

Ryan, Richard M., and Edward L. Deci. 2000. "Intrinsic and Extrinsic Motivations: Classic Definitions and New Directions." *Contemporary Educational Psychology* 25 (1): 54–67.

Ryan, Richard M., and Edward L. Deci. 2016. "Facilitating and Hindering Motivation, Learning, and Well-Being in Schools: Research and Observations from Self-Determination Theory." In *Handbook of Motivation at School*, 2nd ed., edited by Kathryn R. Wentzel and David B. Miele, 96–119. New York: Taylor & Francis.

Salas, Eduardo, Scott I. Tannenbaum, Kurt Kraiger, and Kimberly A. Smith-Jentsch. 2012. "The Science of Training and Development in Organizations: What Matters in Practice." *Psychological Science in the Public Interest* 13 (2): 74–101.

Salomon, Gavriel. 1981. "Introducing AIME: The Assessment of Children's Mental Involvement with Television." In *New Directions for Child Development: Viewing Children through Television*, edited by Hope Kelly and Howard Gardner, 89–101. San Francisco, CA: Jossey-Bass.

Schiefele, Ulrich. 1991. "Interest, Learning, and Motivation." *Educational Psychologist* 26 (3–4): 299–323.

Schrader, Dawn E. 2015. "Constructivism and Learning in the Age of Social Media: Changing Minds and Learning Communities." *New Directions for Teaching and Learning* (144): 23–35.

Schraw, Gregory, Terri Flowerday, and Stephen Lehman. 2001. "Increasing Situational Interest in the Classroom." *Educational Psychology Review* 13: 211–224.

Seiler, Robert M. 2006. *Human Communication in the Critical Theory Tradition*. Accessed September 24, 2019. http://people.ucalgary.ca/~rseiler/critical.htm.

Smith-Wolley, Emily, Ziada Ayorech, S. Dale Philip, Sophie von Stumm, and Robert Plomin. 2018. "The Genetics of University Success." *Scientific Reports* 8 (Article number 14579): 1–9.

Smith-Woolley, Emily, Jean-Baptiste Pingault, and Saskia Selzam. 2018. "Differences in Exam Performance Between Pupils Attending Selective and Non-selective Schools Mirror the Genetic Differences Between Them." *npj Science of Learning* 3 (1): 1–7.

Subramony, Deepak Prem. 2004. "Instructional Technologists' Inattention to Issues of Cultural Diversity Among Learners." *Educational Technology* 44 (4): 19–24.

Subramony, Deepak Prem. 2014. "Revisiting the Digital Divide in the Context of a 'Flattening' World." *Educational Technology* 54 (2): 3–9.

Subramony, Deepak Prem. 2017. "Revisiting Instructional Technologists' Inattention to Issues of Cultural Diversity Among Stakeholders." In *Culture, Learning and Technology: Research and Practice*, edited by Roberto Joseph and Joi L. Moore, 28–43. New York: Routledge.

Tadros, Marlyn. 2011. "A Social Media Approach to Higher Education." In *Educating Educators with Social Media*, edited by Charles Wankel, 83–105. Bingley, UK: Emerald Publishing Limited.

Taylor, Mark. 2015. "Leveraging Social Media for Instructional Goals: Status, Possibilities, and Concerns." *New Directions for Teaching and Learning* 2015 (144): 37–46.

Tyler, Ralph W. 1984. "A Guide to Educational Trouble-Shooting." *Educational Leadership* 41 (8): 27–30.

Walberg, Herbert J. 1984. "Improving the Productivity of America's Schools." *Educational Leadership* 41 (8): 19–27.

Walberg, Herbert J. 2006. "Improving Educational Productivity: An Assessment of Extant Research." Chap. 10 in *The Scientific Basis of Educational Productivity*, edited by Rena F. Subotnik and Herbert J. Walberg, 103–159. Greenwich, CT: Information Age Publishing.

Weinstein, Rhona S. 2002. *Reaching Higher: The Power of Expectations in Schooling*. Cambridge, MA: Harvard University Press.

Wentzel, Kathryn R., and Katherine Muenks. 2016. "Peer Influence on Students' Motivation, Academic Achievement, and Social Behavior." In *Handbook of Social Influences in School Contexts: Social-Emotional, Motivation, and Cognitive Outcomes*, edited by Kathryn R. Wentzel and Geetha B. Ramani, 13–30. New York: Routledge.

Willingham, Daniel T. 2004. "Reframing the Mind." *Education Next* 4 (3): 19–24.

Willis, Paul. 1977. *Learning to Labor: How Working Class Kids Get Working Class Jobs*. New York: Columbia University Press.

Wright, S. Paul, Sandra P. Horn, and William M. Sanders. 1997. "Teacher and Classroom Context Effects on Student Achievement: Implications for Teacher Evaluation." *Journal of Personnel Evaluation in Education* 11: 57–67.

Yeung, Ryan. 2009. "Are School Uniforms a Good Fit? Results from the ECLS-K and the NELS." *Educational Policy* 23: 847–874.

Learning, Instruction, and the Elements of Instruction 3

Chapter Overview

The framework presented in Chapter 2 illustrates the place of Instruction in the overall process of promoting instructed learning. It is not the only factor at play, and it may not always be the most important factor, but it is one factor over which planners and facilitators have a great deal of control. They have no control over the innate physical and mental abilities of their learners; they have limited control over the factors that play into the learners' drive to invest effort in the learning task; so they need to make the most of what they do control—the conditions of the teaching–learning encounter.

Our goal here is to help educators think and talk about the basic issues of instruction more clearly, using a common set of terms. The need for such a unifying effort was recognized by Reigeluth and Carr-Chellman (2009a):

> we became increasingly concerned about the extent to which instructional theorists seemed to be working in relative isolation from each other, building their own view of instruction with little regard to building on what knowledge already exists and what terminology already exists and what terminology has already been used for constructs they also describe.
>
> (xi)

To have a fresh start, we must begin by stating our assumptions about the processes of human learning, since the whole purpose of instruction is to support learning through consciously selected interventions.

We begin with a brief overview of human learning, focusing on those types of learning that occur more or less effortlessly and those that require conscious effort and, usually, the assistance of a third party—another way of saying *instruction*. The latter type of learning, the type that requires assistance, we refer to as *instructed learning*—that is, learning shaped by instruction.

Next, we discuss the distinction between learning and instruction and provide definitions for the most basic elements that comprise instructional events—the elements that are visible whenever instruction is taking place—learner, facilitator, and resources, in some setting, and the patterns of communication among them. The scope of this chapter can be summarized as the answers to three questions:

What is learning?
What is instruction?
What are the basic elements of instruction?

What is Learning?

Learning is studied under the auspices of neuroscience, psychology, and many specializations within those fields, including educational psychology. Each field imposes its own frame and its own terminology to define learning. Most of the theories of learning proposed by psychologists were developed before there were robust methods of observing the actual functioning of human brains, thus those theories dealt with regularities that could be observed by watching humans perform or by asking them to talk about or make choices about problems presented to them. As the methods of science have progressed, the biological processes underlying those observations have become clearer and, in general, have tended to confirm the validity of psychologists' hypotheses—at least within the boundaries of each researcher's framework (e.g., true for the animals studied or the problems studied but not necessarily generalizable to other animals or other problems).

Neuroscience Perspective

Neuroscience focuses on the biological processes underlying learning and memory; or as phrased by Eric R. Kandel in his Nobel Prize lecture: "What changes in the brain when we learn? And, once something is learned, how is that information retained in the brain?" (Kandel 2004, 477). Thus, neuroscience defines learning and memory in terms of changes in the strength of synaptic connections between precisely connected cells. This is the path—the search for mechanistic explanations for the phenomena of learning—followed by Kandel and his colleagues at New York University and Columbia University from the 1970s through the 1990s.

Since the time of Kandel's research, advances in functional magnetic resonance imaging (fMRI) and supercomputing have allowed researchers to understand how the specialized regions of the brain are interconnected and, especially, how they are coordinated to carry out complex cognitive functions. This new field of network neuroscience proposes that brains perform as "massive orchestras of neurons that fire together in quite specific patterns" (Bertolero and Bassett 2019, 28). Just as an orchestra has different sections, the brain consists of a number of modules, each a local network. Some modules are devoted to attention, memory, and introspection, others to hearing, vision, and motor movement (2019, 29). The "frontoparietal control module," for example, functions in a way analogous to an orchestra conductor, coordinating processes such as the learning of complex cognitive tasks (2019, 29).

As will be discussed below, recent advances in neuroscience have provided some physical science support for principles proposed by psychologists based on their observations of human learning, although these understandings at the molecular, cellular, and neural network levels are still in their infancy. What we do know is that human learning is a complicated matter, involving activity in multiple parts of the brain and nervous system for even the most commonplace sorts of learning. It is the task of psychologists to search for patterns within the complexity. Behavioral psychologists and cognitive psychologists attempt to infer inner mental processes by observing outward behavior. These fields are more likely to discover relationships of immediate practical value for those engaged in promoting learning in humans—educators.

It is also important to note that *instructed learning* seems to be distinguishable from natural learning in terms of the neural pathways by which it is processed, stored, and retrieved (Kandel 2006, 132; Phelps 2006, 31–33). This must be kept in mind when reviewing the several theories of learning discussed below, some of which were derived from observations of natural learning.

Behaviorist Perspective

The branch of psychology with the longest and broadest history is *behaviorism*. Behaviorists attempt to draw inferences based on external observation of the behavior of organisms. Brought to a high level of sophistication by Ivan Pavlov (1849–1936), the principles of behaviorism were reinterpreted in the 1950s under the label of "radical behaviorism" by B. F. Skinner (1904–1990) in works such as *Science and Human Behavior* (Skinner 1953). He drew a distinction between the sorts of reflex behavior studied by Pavlov, governed by the principles of what Skinner termed *classical conditioning*, and the larger category of voluntary responses exhibited by humans in everyday life, governed by the principles of what Skinner termed *operant conditioning*—reinforcing a behavior in the presence of a particular stimulus.

Neuroscience research has discovered the physiological basis of this sort of learning—that synaptic connections can be strengthened or weakened through the simplest sorts of learning processes—habituation, sensitization, and classical conditioning (Kandel 2006, 204). Kandel calls this sort of learning process *implicit* learning, which leads to implicit memory (2006, 132). It has an unconscious, automatic, reflexive quality and underlies classical conditioning as well as perceptual and motor skills in general.

This very basic process is shared among many species, from fruit flies to chimpanzees. The question arises as to whether the molecular and cellular mechanisms of learning and memory discovered in simple animals can be generalized to humans. Kandel notes the many commonalities found in the physiological process of learning in simple animals and humans and concludes that they "represent a family of processes that share a common logic and some key components but vary in the details of their molecular mechanisms" (2006, 422).

Research in neurophysiology has identified a second type of learning process. It deals with conscious behaviors—such as recall of people, places, facts, and events. These types of learning typically can be expressed in words or pictures. Kandel (2006) refers to this type as *explicit* learning, which leads to explicit memory (also called declarative memory). These sorts of learning tasks require physically more complex neural circuitry than implicit learnings, involving connections between the hippocampus and medial temporal lobe, with many more possible storage sites than implicit learnings (Kandel 2006, 280). Having multiple storage locations is not surprising, considering that a single memory has multiple facets—each event contains images, sounds, smells, bodily sensations, and so forth. This finding lends support to the cognitivist claim that a different set of principles governs certain aspects of human learning, including those dealing with verbal information and abstract concepts. On the other hand, the behaviorist focus on the power of rewards to shape learned responses has also found support in neuroscience research. That is, some forms of conscious, explicit learning—other than the reflex type of learning—have been shown to be enhanced when coupled with rewards. To simplify somewhat, the promise of a reward focuses the brain's control processes, improving attention to "task-relevant information coded and maintained in frontoparietal brain regions" (Etzel et al. 2016).

When behaviorism was the ascendant theory of learning, critics questioned whether principles established through observations of rats and pigeons could be directly generalized to human learning, and especially if those principles were adequate to explain the acquisition of skills that humans possessed and simpler animals did not, such as language. As indicated above, behaviorist theory has proven robust for explaining implicit learning in humans and for explaining some forms of explicit learning. However, cognitive science research and more recent neuroscience research has shown that other theories account more parsimoniously for other more complex types of learning, especially those mediated by language. While behaviorism has continued to play a prominent role in psychology, particularly in the form of behavior therapy—techniques for altering maladaptive behaviors—within the field of education, it has come to share the stage with other perspectives that focus more closely on the mental processes that are seen as essentially human and central to education.

Cognitivist Perspective

Cognitive psychologists rely on both behavioral experiments and verbal reports to draw inferences about the learner's mental processes. Jerome Bruner (1915–2016) carried out behavioral experiments in the 1940s that led him to begin studying the internal interpretations that humans made along with their externally observable responses. He became one of the founders of the nascent field of cognitive psychology with the publication of *A Study of Thinking* (Bruner, Goodnow and Austin 1956). At first, the computer offered a useful metaphor for those internal processes, but by 1990 Bruner had come to reject the computer model, advocating a more holistic understanding of the human mind as an instrument for creating meanings (Bruner 1998).

A basic concern of cognitive psychology from its inception has been understanding how information moves from perception to working memory to long-term memory and how mental structures are built up as people strive to impose meaning on the stimuli around them (Neisser 1967). These references to working memory and long-term memory remind us that learning is a process with a number of stages, including acquiring new knowledge or behaviors, storing that material in memory, and retrieving the stored information or reproducing the learned behavior. Long-term storage and later retrieval depend greatly on how well the new information is integrated into the learner's mental structure. This has been appreciated since the earliest days of educational psychology, as evidenced by the advice given by William James in his *Talks to Teachers* in 1899:

> The art of remembering is the art of *thinking*....when we wish to fix a new thing in either our own mind or a pupil's our conscious effort should not be so much to *impress* and *retain* it as to *connect* it [italics in original] with something else already there. The connecting is the thinking; and, if we attend clearly to the connection, the connected thing will certainly be likely to remain within recall.
>
> *(1899, 143)*

One of the significant early findings of cognitive research is that visual and auditory information appear to be processed in working memory, and later stored, through different neural channels. This phenomenon was dubbed "dual-coding theory" by Paivio (1971). It seems that visual information is processed and stored as spatial or analog data, while verbal information is processed as linear or digital data. Experiments have shown that people tend to remember visual images better than verbal information, but different types of visuals are remembered at different rates. For example, faces with different features are remembered better than snowflakes with different features (Goldstein and Chance 1970). As with verbal information, visuals are also remembered better if the viewer is able to make a meaningful interpretation of the image or if the image is distinctive or striking in some way. Although dual-coding theory is still debated among cognitive scientists, neuroscience experiments with fMRI have given support to its claims. These findings have huge implications for our understanding of learning from audiovisual media, as discussed in Chapter 5.

Cognitive Load Theory

At the working memory stage, where conscious thought takes place, capacity is very limited, such that only three to five "chunks" of information can be manipulated at one time. These capacity issues have led to a line of research on the problems of overloading the processing capacities of learners—cognitive load theory. Paas and Sweller (2014) distinguish among three types of cognitive load: intrinsic, which refers to the inherent complexity of the material being studied; extraneous, meaning distracting information, such as music playing in the background or confusing layouts of texts or images; and germane, information that is relevant to the learning task. As will be discussed later, one of the challenges faced by instructional designers is avoiding extraneous cognitive load and keeping germane cognitive load within the processing capacities of the learner.

From the standpoint of the learner, it is advantageous to practice basic skills to the point of automatization in order to free cognitive capacity for higher-order thinking—for example, to develop the skill of touch-typing so that one can write a paragraph focusing entirely on forming the right words into sentences rather than having to thoughtfully seek out the correct keys to press for each character. The value of automatization has been recognized since the dawn of psychology, as indicated in William James's observation: "The more of the details of our daily life we can hand over to the effortless custody of automatism, the more our higher powers of mind will be set free for their own proper work" (1899, 67).

Constructivism

A variation of the cognitivist perspective known as *constructivism* emerged in the 1990s. It arose from a more radically subjectivist philosophy, insisting that each person's internal construction of reality, while idiosyncratic, was equally valid as any other person's construction. A mutually acceptable interpretation of reality could be achieved through social negotiation with other people. There never has been a canonical conception of constructivism, but the schools of thought under that umbrella agree that appropriate conditions for learning include complex, realistic problem environments, social negotiation of meanings, encouragement of multiple perspectives, and mindful reflection (Driscoll 2004, 391).

The cognitivist and constructivist perspectives converge under the umbrella of *learner-centered education*. This concept has been endorsed by the American Psychological Association (APA) in the form of a set of principles, including: "The learning of complex subject matter is most effective when it is an intentional process of constructing meaning from information and experience" (APA Task Force on Psychology in Education 1993). These principles have been subsequently reconfirmed and applied to *digital* forms of instruction by Barbara L. McCombs and Donna Vakili (2005).

Emotion and Cognition

Because early models of cognitive learning were based on an information-processing model, the role of the emotions in learning tended to be overlooked. But generations of human experience have taught us that vivid, emotional experiences tend to be remembered better, longer, and in more detail than more mundane experiences. And, indeed, neuroscience research revealed that the hippocampus, the part of the brain most associated with long-term memory, "has strong reciprocating connections to the amygdala and other modules in the limbic area which are involved in the generation of emotions" (Geake 2009, 115). Child psychologist Stanley Greenspan (1941–2010), best known for his treatment of children with autism spectrum disorder (ASD), developed a theory of how human mental structures evolve from birth through infancy and into adulthood. His most distinctive claim is that "in fact, emotions, not cognitive stimulation, serve as the mind's primary architect" (Greenspan and Benderly 1997). Specifically, Greenspan and Benderly propose that:

> Each sensory perception therefore forms part of a dual code. We label it both by its physical properties (bright, big, loud, smooth, and the like) and by the emotional qualities we connect with it (we might experience it as soothing or jarring, or it might make us feel happy or tense). This double coding allows the child to 'cross-reference' each memory experience in a mental catalogue of phenomena and feelings and to reconstruct it when needed.
> *(1997, 21)*

This theory is as yet not clearly verified or refuted by basic neuroscience research. The Phelps Lab at Harvard University is a leader in investigating the intersection of human learning and emotion. Their tentative conclusion is, first, that the concept of emotion may be as complex as that of cognition, with the learning process of each divided into several stages (Phelps 2006, 46). And, second, that "emotion and cognition interact at all stages of information processing, from early perception to higher reasoning" (Stanley, Ferneyhough and Phelps 2009, 836). Their work does support the general notion that human learning cannot be fully appreciated without considering the roles of both emotion and cognition. This inextricable relationship becomes relevant when we turn to the role of emotional factors—such as arousal, curiosity, motivation, and interest—in designing and implementing instructional interventions. Ideally, of course, all instruction should be attractive, eye-opening, and meaningful so that it is attended to, comprehended, and integrated into the learner's repertoire.

Social Learning Perspective

A third major perspective, *social learning theory*, addresses a gap not covered adequately by behaviorist or cognitivist theories: How do humans rapidly acquire novel skills that are more complex than just knowledge of facts? And how do they do so without any noticeable practice of component skills or reinforcement of "successive approximations" (the term used by behaviorists to refer to the gradual development of a new skill through trial and error practice)?

Albert Bandura (b. 1925) became interested in imitation, vicarious learning, and behavior modeling while studying adolescent aggression in the 1950s. His research demonstrated that humans frequently acquired new skills, skills which might involve quite complex procedures, by merely observing another person (or a video recording of another person) performing the target behavior…or even just being told how to do it (Bandura 1977). He went so far as to assert that "most human behavior is learned observationally through modeling: from observing others, one forms an idea of how new behaviors are performed, and on later occasions this coded information serves as a guide for action" (1977, 22). This became the basis of Bandura's *social learning theory*, a theory that was later extended by Bandura (1986) and renamed as *social cognitive theory*—which posits that individuals can learn directly through observations of the behavior of others made in the context of social interactions.

Independently, neuroscience researchers discovered *mirror neurons*, neurons that fire both when an organism acts and when that organism observes the same action being performed by another (Rizzolatti and Sinigaglia 2008). By this means, birds and various primates have been shown to be able to learn directly by imitation, without prompting, practice, or reinforcement. Although the extension of the theory of mirror neurons to the human brain is still somewhat speculative, some sort of mirroring system consistent with mirror neurons has been established. Although the details of how the brain accomplishes this sort of implicit learning are unclear, the notion of mirror neurons lends support to Bandura's theory.

Note that the research with primates and with humans stipulates that this sort of imitative learning is not merely an automatic response; rather, it is a social act. The learner must have a social relationship with the model—for example, viewing the model as someone worthy of emulation—and must feel that the behavior being modeled will lead to a good outcome.

Note also that learning through behavior modeling also assumes that the learner possesses the prerequisite skills to perform the target skill. The sports fan sitting at home watching a football game on television could not replicate the performance of a quarterback, no matter how many times they watched video replays; they lack both the cognitive and motor prerequisite skills. Experiments done even with skills that appeared to be easily attainable—such as throwing darts or juggling bowling pins—demonstrated not only that mere observation was insufficient for skill acquisition (for which prerequisites were lacking) but also that viewing of video demonstrations led participants to vastly overestimate their actual ability to perform such skills (Kardas and O'Brien 2018).

An Eclectic View of Learning

There are, of course, many other theories of learning, each intended by its author to be a comprehensive explanation of human learning, but each is better seen as a different perspective on the broad question of how people learn. We are assuming that each of these theories has validity within the context specified by its authors: Neuroscientists are focused on what is happening at the cellular level; behavioral psychologists are focused on the organism's observable behavior; cognitive psychologists are probing the internal mental processes. These theories do not contradict each other, they merely view human learning from different perspectives. A useful analogy would be that of an alien observer looking into the same human dwelling through different windows. Someone looking in through the kitchen window might hypothesize that human beings mainly prepare and eat food. An observer looking through the bedroom window might hypothesize that humans mainly copulate and sleep. An observer looking through the family room window might conclude that humans mainly do a lot of leisurely play and media watching—and so on. All these inferences are partly correct, but each one captures only a part of the whole. Putting these perspectives together would yield an eclectic view that comes closer to the truth. Some readers might be familiar with another similar analogy, namely, the traditional Indian fable of "The Six Blind Men and the Elephant."

Thus, we adopt a broad, eclectic view; first, defining *natural learning* as the acquisition of new—or the modification of existing—knowledge, skills, or attitudes resulting from the individual's interaction with the environment, and, second, defining *instructed learning* as the acquisition of new—or the modification of existing—knowledge, skills, or attitudes resulting from the individual's participation in instructional events.

Crossing the Bridge from Learning to Instruction

This brief survey of learning processes has established that humans learn through several quite different neurological pathways—at least three are well researched: implicit, explicit, and imitative processes. Of course, many learned skills entail a combination of implicit, explicit, and imitative processes. For example, driving a car assembles a host of automatic reflexes regarding steering, shifting, signaling, and braking. At the same time, driving requires conscious explicit skills, such as following a map, deciding when to change lanes, and determining how far to drive before refueling. The driver's posture, attentiveness, and road etiquette may have been acquired through imitation, perhaps by observing a parent's driving.

The point is that the multiplicity of learning processes and the complexity of many human capabilities argues for a varied and complex set of tools for helping people learn these capabilities. We can begin by recognizing two broad classes of human capabilities. First, from birth to death, as we go about our daily lives, we learn naturally through our encounters with the world around us. David C. Geary (2008) advocates an evolutionary perspective on human learning, which is strongly supported by the work of neuroscience researchers such as Kandel, cited above. Geary and other educational psychologists, including Paas and Sweller (2014, 28), refer to these naturally occurring processes of learning as biologically *primary* learning; this category includes such implicit skills as reflexive motor skills, reading human emotion in faces, listening to and speaking a mother tongue, and performing basic problem-solving. We acquire such skills quickly and easily, without conscious effort.

By contrast, biologically *secondary* learnings include knowledge and skills that are needed for successful navigation of the cultural environment but are not an inborn part of neurological development. As Geake (2009, 53) puts it, "school learning relies on appropriating brain functions which originally evolved for other purposes." That is to say, the brain did not evolve as an instrument for thinking; it evolved as an instrument for survival. This helps account for the special role that fear plays in the learning process. Organisms that did not learn quickly—the first time—to flee from dangerous situations did not live to pass along their genes to future generations.

Much of school learning would follow the pathways of *explicit* learning and memory, to use Kandel's distinction. Importantly, these include reading and writing, since written languages are codes constructed by humans to symbolize the sounds of the spoken language. As such, they are artificial, arbitrary codes. Again, understanding and speaking one's native language is learned naturally, without conscious effort. But to learn to decode written language—to read—and then to encode—to write—requires considerable guidance and practice. The same is true of mathematics, another arbitrary, human-constructed symbol system. To master the code requires effort and, usually, the assistance of a knowledgeable tutor. We refer to these sorts of learning as *instructed learning*, discussed at greater length below. To meet the need for knowledgeable guidance and supervised practice in order to acquire these *instructed learning* skills, the art and science of instruction was developed.

The Cultural Invention of Instruction

Within the hunter-gatherer and early agricultural societies, instruction to acquire secondary learnings occurred within the ambit of home and family, largely through imitative processes. Bruner reported on observations done in the 1960s of the !Kung people, an isolated group living on the western edge of the Kalahari Desert and living the hunter-gatherer lifestyle:

> Most of what we would call instruction is through showing. And there is no practice or drill as such, save in the form of play modeled directly on adult

models—play hunting, play bossing, play exchanging, play baby tending, play house making.

(1966, 151)

But as agricultural surplus allowed the growth of cities, a more complex social system evolved. The need to keep records of trade exchanges led to the development of alphabets and numeral systems, that is, mathematical notation. Scribes and accountants were now required, in addition to agricultural labor, builders, military forces, religious clerics, and administrators. Societies that succeeded in the competitive strife of early city-states and empires were ones that found ways to institutionalize the instruction needed to hone the skills required by these occupations.

Embedding Instruction in Educational Institutions

In the Europe of medieval times, increasing specialization of labor required aspiring carpenters, masons, farriers, locksmiths, glassmakers, and a hundred other trades to master a range of technical skills. In those times, such skills could be attained through apprenticeship in a guild, a process that varied greatly from place to place and over time, but essentially involved learning through tutorial guidance. The earliest universities carried over the guildhall tradition by offering tutoring to the sons of the elite. Meanwhile, churches and cathedrals organized schools for less privileged children and adolescents, mainly to learn the skills of literacy and numeracy—reading, 'riting, and 'rithmetic, the three Rs—needed for the smooth functioning of church, state, and commerce.

The history of education since medieval times can be viewed as a long, arduous struggle to extend educational opportunities to more people and to devise means of helping those people learn more effectively, efficiently, and humanely. Over the centuries, community leaders came to understand that biologically secondary learning requires activities that learners cannot easily manage by themselves—gathering expert knowledge, tutoring, productive discussion, focused reading of text, and thoughtful construction of written, spoken, or artistic expressions. Schools and colleges were created to be places where those structured educational activities could be carried out on a continuing basis. Formal education offers a scaffold for such focused activities—curricula, schedules, grades, and other corrective feedback, convenient spaces for learning and experimenting, and so on.

Educational Institutions Are Not Always Benign

That is not to say that educational institutions have always focused solely on benevolent purposes. The social systems that schools were created to support themselves have had both noble and ignoble goals over the centuries, and the schools reflected those biases. For example, colonial overlords often offered education to their colonized people in a selective, strategic manner aimed at maintaining their control over local natural and human resources. Schools and colleges established to promote particular religious doctrines often put proselytizing above truly liberating studies. Where business interests control the curriculum, students might be treated more as future employees to be trained for the jobs available rather than as individuals with vast potential whose education was aimed at unleashing that potential. Nevertheless, the overall purpose of organized education and training is to help learners master those biologically secondary skills that only rarely would be mastered if people were left to their own devices.

Instruction Is Not Always the Answer

It must be noted that in the workplace and other "real-world" settings there are occasions when performance shortfalls need to be addressed by some sort of training—an instructional intervention. However, there are many more occasions when other sorts of interventions are more appropriate. The field of human performance improvement has identified at least half a dozen categories of interventions to improve performance *other than instruction*: organizational systems change, incentives, cognitive support, better tools, improved physical environment, and selection of personnel who have the inherent ability (e.g., strength, temperament, creativity) to do specific jobs (Wile 1996). Particularly abundant are occasions when cognitive support is sufficient; people can do the job if merely given some information at the time it is needed—often referred to as a job aid. Examples include assembly directions that accompany unfinished furniture, drop-down menus on computer software, and color-coded templates for piano keys to aid the novice pianist. In academic settings, such as schools and colleges, instruction is considered the main business, and other performance-improvement interventions are usually conceived of as aids to instruction, not substitutes for it.

What Is Instruction?

We preface this discussion with a note about terminology. For our purposes, the term *education* has a broader and more amorphous meaning than the term *instruction*. We use *educational* to refer to institutions, such as schools, colleges, libraries, and museums—and resources, such as books, recorded media, and artifacts—that generally provide access to knowledge and self-improvement. Some of the resources and activities within *educational* institutions may be *instructional*—such as textbooks and class attendance—but many are not. For example, living in a dormitory is not an *instructional* activity, but it does contribute to one's overall social development. As is discussed fully below, we use *instructional* to refer to activities and resources that are specially designed and used to achieve prespecified learning objectives.

A dictionary definition of *instruction* is insufficient for scholarly discourse. A technical definition can help distinguish among such related terms as teaching, training, education, schooling, and informing. We are seeking terminology broad enough to encompass all sorts of efforts to help others learn but narrow enough to separate our concept from others that carry extra baggage, such as the regimentation connoted by *training*, the triviality of *informing*, or the formal, professional role implied by *teaching*.

Merrill's landmark attempt to codify a technical vocabulary for the field of instructional design specifies several critical attributes for the concept of *instruction*; they can be paraphrased as:

- a conscious effort
- to create a learning environment
- for learners
- to acquire specified knowledge or skills. (Merrill 2013, 6)

These attributes are also found in the definition of *instruction* provided by Marcy Driscoll in her highly regarded survey of learning and instruction (Driscoll 2004): "the deliberate arrangement of learning conditions to promote the attainment of some intended goal" (352–353). A definitional task force of the Association for Educational Communications and Technology (AECT) specified two critical attributes that are also strongly implied or explicitly stated in Merrill's and Driscoll's definitions—that the process be *controlled* and that it be *purposive* (AECT Task Force on Definition and Terminology 1977). By *controlled* is meant that a third party guides the learner along an anticipated path; by *purposive* is meant that the process is directed toward a more-or-less explicit learning goal.

Merrill further adds the notion that it is the purpose of instruction to promote learning that is "effective, efficient, and engaging" (Merrill 2013, 6). We accept effectiveness and efficiency as hallmarks of success, although *engaging* is more of a means to effectiveness than an end in itself. These terms, plus *humane*, are included in order to recognize that instruction, since it aims to manipulate human behavior, must also meet an ethical test. First, the means used for instruction must be humane; they should not inflict suffering, physical or mental, upon learners. Second, learners have the right to expect that the instruction in which they invest effort will yield good results (*effective*) and, third, that it will do so with the least waste of time and other resources (*efficient*). The notion of efficiency that we have in mind is described in colorful terms in a nineteenth-century railroad engineering text:

> It would be well if engineering were less generally thought of, and even defined, as the art of constructing. In a certain important sense it is rather the art of *not* constructing: or, to define it rudely, but not inaptly, it is the art of doing well with one dollar that which any bungler can do with two, after a fashion.
>
> *(Wellington 1887, 1)*

Thus, we define *instruction* much as Driscoll does, as a deliberate effort to provide learners with conditions suitable for achieving specified learning objectives. Further, to be considered successful, instruction should be humane, effective, and efficient.

The notion of "suitable conditions" in our definition derives originally from the work of Robert Gagné, who titled his first book *The Conditions of Learning* (1965), claiming: "This book is about the *conditions of learning* [emphasis in original]. It attempts to consider the sets of circumstances that obtain when learning occurs" (1965, 5). The title emphasizes his core argument that different learning objectives require: (a) different *external* conditions—arrangements of instructional elements; and (b) different *internal* conditions—the learner's aptitudes, motivations, and prior knowledge. For example, one sort of learning objective might require only the simple presentation of a fact; another might require repeated practice with constant feedback; while another might require reflective thought and expressions of one's own interpretation, based on a great quantity of personal experiences and prior learning. Each of these arrangements represents different *conditions*, external and internal. Gagné's approach was further explored in his own later editions of *The Conditions of Learning* and in subsequent works. By the late 1980s, he was able to provide a list of the sorts of conditions that were required for learning in the different domains (Gagné and Glaser 1987). For example, for the Intellectual Skills domain, the necessary conditions include retrieval of subordinate skills, guidance by verbal or other means, demonstrated application by student with precise feedback, and spaced reviews (1987, 64). Gagné also referred to these *conditions* as *requirements*. Later, under the label of *requirements*, others—such as David Merrill in *First Principles of Instruction* (2013) and Charles Reigeluth in "Situational Principles of Instruction" (Reigeluth and Carr-Chellman 2009b) —followed with more fully elaborated prescriptions for various types of learning tasks.

Instructed Learning: Learning under Instructional Conditions

The scope of this book is limited to the sorts of learning that take place under the umbrella of instructional interventions. We use the adjective *instructed* to refer to learning that is undertaken within instructional settings. It differentiates between the natural learning that is the subject of most theories of learning and the artificially stimulated learning that is nurtured in classrooms, laboratories, and training centers. The term *instructed learning* came into common use in the 1990s in the field of second language learning (see, e.g., Ellis 1990). Ellis's book title has become the contemporary label for that field, exemplified by the name of the journal, *Instructed Second Language Acquisition*. The term *instructed learning* has also become an accepted technical term in neuroscience. It is used in the Phelps Lab at New York University, which focuses on the intersection of emotion and human learning. They use *instructed learning* to refer to learning prompted by symbolic communications rather than direct experience, for example, learning to fear a neighbor's dog by being told that it is vicious rather than by being bitten (Phelps 2006, 31). The Cole Neurocognition Lab at Rutgers University has adapted the term in naming the object of their study—"rapid *instructed* task *learning* (RITL)." Like the Phelps team, the Cole team is focused on learning prompted by communication rather than by reinforcement (Cole, Laurent and Stocco 2013). Thus, in both second language learning and neuroscience, the term is used to distinguish natural learning that takes place without outside assistance from learning under the guidance of another person or pedagogical device. In both fields, it is established that the two classes of learning follow different neural pathways and, hence, form differently in the human brain.

Thus, we define *instructed learning* as human learning that is mediated symbolically in planned interactions between facilitators and learners.

Incidentally, the term *instructed* in *instructed learning* is not meant to privilege any particular teaching–learning strategies. Whether the methods being used purport to be "learner-centered" or "teacher-centered," the intended outcome is still instructed learning.

Basic Elements of Instruction

A primary claim in this book is that clear communication about the process of instruction must begin with that which is visible and tangible. We want to build a foundation for understanding instruction with concrete building blocks, not abstract concepts that might be interpreted in different ways by different readers. We begin with the learner(s) and a facilitator, who may be joined by resources, all situated in some sort of setting and engaged in some pattern of communication. The possible combinations of interactions among these elements are numerous but not infinite! We aim to introduce ways of categorizing the many combinations into manageable chunks, to make the task of designing effective instruction easier, not more difficult. We begin with the instructional event, the time and place at which instructed learning takes place.

Instructional Event

Merrill, attempting to provide a technically precise set of terms, defines an instructional event as "the combination of an instructional mode and a content element" (2013, 53, 71). By *instructional mode* he means any interaction between instructor and learner and by *content element* he means specific bits of the targeted subject matter. Frick, who, like Merrill, is trying to establish a standard glossary of terms in the field of education, does not use the term *instructional event*. Instead, Frick's basic unit of instruction is an *education system*, which he defines as "an intentional system consisting of at least one teacher and one student in a context" (Frick 2019); he explains that *intentional* refers to "intending to guide student learning."

By the way, our definition of *instructional event* differs greatly from the terminology used by Robert Gagné when he advocated the notion of "events of instruction" (Gagné, Briggs and Wager 1992), by which he meant the major steps or phases in the typical lesson structure. For example, in his "nine events of instruction," the third event is "stimulate recall of prior learning." Thus, he is using the label *event of instruction* to describe specific tactics undertaken at specific stages during a lesson—a very different concept than we are discussing here.

The definitions of Merrill and Frick yield several critical attributes for an instructional event:

- a controlled interaction between instructor and learner
- an interaction that is also purposive—"intending to guide student learning"
- containing some subject matter
- in some context.

These attributes are also reflected in Marcy Driscoll's "four components" of instruction: learner, learning task, learning environment, and context or frame of reference (Driscoll 2004, 353). We choose to focus on *instructional events* as the basic unit of any teaching–learning encounter, and we define this unit as a physically observable occurrence (as Merrill advocates), not as some ongoing relationship (as Frick advocates). Thus, an *instructional event* is any occasion during which one or more learners engage in purposive and controlled learning in some setting. A facilitator is usually either physically present or lurking in the background, but instructional events can take place without a facilitator being visible—for example, a student alone preparing an outline for an essay. Likewise, instructional events usually include some sort of resources but not always. A tutor could merely be holding a conversation with a tutee. Subject matter, or "a content element," as Merrill phrases it, is certainly involved in the process, but "content" is not visible (until it is embedded in some resource) so is not mentioned in our definition. We accept Frick's "context" as a critical attribute, which we refer to as a *setting*; the event must take place someplace and that someplace would be visible to an observer.

So, an elementary school class watching a video projection of a butterfly emerging from its cocoon would be an instructional event, as would a college class listening to a lecture on economics. A high school student working at home on geometry problems from a textbook would be participating in an instructional event, as would a business employee engaging in an online simulation of a sales problem. The event could be as brief as a student reviewing a list of vocabulary words on the way to Spanish class. During that class, the students might listen to a short lecture, then break into pairs to practice conversation, then finish the class with five minutes of written reflection notes. Each of these episodes would constitute a separate instructional event. A new event begins when the type of activity changes.

To have an instructional event, the only absolutely necessary elements are a learner who is directly or indirectly under the influence of a facilitator and the setting in which the learning takes place. As stated earlier, to be instructional—or *instructed*—the situation must be purposive and controlled, guided directly or indirectly by a third party. Even when no facilitator is present, such as a student reading a textbook at home or writing a term paper in a library, typically a facilitator prompted that activity and will evaluate whether the activity was successful. In the rare case in which an individual purposefully pursues a learning goal totally on their own initiative, it could still be classified as an instructional event, with the learner acting also as facilitator.

Learner

We have been using the term *learner* to refer to the subject of instructional efforts. Frick prefers the term *student*, defined as "a person who intends to learn content with a teacher" (2019, 19). We accept the definition but prefer a different label. *Student*, like *teacher*, has the connotation of membership in a formal education institution, whereas we want to consider all people in all sorts of settings, formal and informal. Therefore, we define a *learner* as anyone who voluntarily enters into an instructional setting and participates in teaching–learning activities. Educational institutions are filled with students, but those students are not always learners. They spend a lot of their time in noninstructional settings—cafeteria, dormitory, lounge, sporting events, extracurricular clubs, and so on. They are counted as learners whenever they are engaged in structured activities with learning goals. The classroom is the most common venue for learning, but it could also be the library where a student is writing a term paper or the playing field where a student is refining an athletic skill. It could also be at a debate team practice, crafting argumentation skills. At a residential institution, the residence hall can become an instructional setting when, for example, students are engaged in a wellness program to support their physical fitness, nutrition, and stress management.

Just as not all students are learners, not all learners are students. In the workplace, employees become learners when they participate in a training program or when novice managers engage in a structured mentoring program with senior managers. Homemakers become learners when they go to the library to take part in a parenting program. Community members become learners when they go to the local election center to be trained as poll workers.

We hardly need to mention the truism that learners differ on many dimensions, both in terms of physically observable conditions—such as age, gender, size, and appearance—and in terms of internal conditions—such as inherited traits and abilities, ethnic identity, socioeconomic background, prior knowledge of the subject matter, interests, and motivations. Many of these are discussed in Chapter 2 as factors that influence success in academic achievement. This virtually infinite variability is supported by recent neuroscience research, which has demonstrated that each individual's brain has a different pattern of interconnections among nodes and modules—a neural fingerprint, as it were (Bertolero and Bassett 2019, 29, 31). Each different pattern means differences in terms of attention, working memory, vocabulary, complex processing power, and so on.

Dealing with this variability is one of the greatest challenges of instructional planning and implementation, and experienced teachers have developed many techniques to cope. For example, to deal with variability in subject-matter mastery, students can be grouped into three clusters—struggling, average, and advanced—with some remediations offered to the struggling group and some enhancements added to the advanced group. Or learners can be arranged into two- or three-person collaborative teams for cooperative project activities, with teams periodically adjusted to provide support for those struggling and acceleration for those ready to move rapidly. In any event, learners will be learning in their own way at their own rate regardless of what the instructors are doing! This profound observation was captured in a cartoon showing two schoolboys walking to school, one—enrolled in an individualized instruction program—saying "I'm progressing at my own rate… Whose rate are you progressing at?"

Learners Produce Learning

Having constructed the complex mechanisms necessary for formal education, it is tempting for educators to imagine that they are somehow in full control of the learning process. They are not; learners are. You do not have to be a devotee of a particular educational philosophy to acknowledge that instructed learning is a voluntary activity. Learners attain new knowledge, skills, or attitudes only when they decide to engage in the activities designed to lead them there. Teachers can lay out the pathway and offer a hand of guidance, but learners have to do the walking. As a Chinese proverb says: *Shī fu lǐng jìn mén, xiū xíng zài gè rén*—Teachers open the door; you enter by yourself.

This is easiest to see in the case of cognitive skills. Mental constructions must be built by the learners themselves; meaning-making is at the heart of cognitive learning, according to contemporary theories of learning (Bruner 1998). Attitudes, interpersonal skills, and physical skills all have cognitive components; but even aside from that, they require engaged practice to develop. That is, attitudes and interpersonal or physical capabilities, too, are created by the learner. In any teaching–learning setting, students are the producers; their work products are their advancements in knowledge, skill, and attitudes. Teachers and other facilitators assist those doing the work, perhaps even serving as coproducers of some learned skills. Fellow students can also serve as coproducers; think of students in a study group who help each other figure out a geometry theorem.

It is tempting to think of instructors as "the workers" because they are the ones being paid to "get the job done" and the classroom is for them a workplace. No doubt, they are doing work—difficult, often exhausting work—but in terms of mastering the new knowledge or skill specified in the lesson objectives, only the learner's exertions can make learning happen.

Facilitator

Given that instruction entails purposive and controlled activities, who selects the objectives and drives the activities? Merrill does not include any concept equivalent to *teacher* or *instructor* in his glossary (2013, 461–467); most of his examples assume a mediated format of instruction. Frick's glossary (2019, 19) uses the term *teacher*, defined as "a person who intends to guide another person's learning." We agree with the definition but prefer the term *facilitator*. To use the word *teacher* for this function would falsely conjure up the image of an elementary or secondary school faculty member. *Instructor* is a more neutral term, but in British usage it is applied mainly to training or religious contexts. Further, the term in general has unwanted connotations, implying an authoritative, even somewhat coercive posture. Thus, we prefer the term *facilitator* to designate the person or device that supports and guides learners during an instructional event. It has gained considerable acceptance in the domain of corporate education; for example, it is promoted by Elaine Biech in *The Art and Science of Training* (2017) as "it implies that you are enabling learners; pulling it out of them rather than pushing learning toward them." In corporate education, the distinction between a trainer and a facilitator is a well-recognized one, with the differences revolving around authority. A trainer is seen as a subject-matter expert—with the higher standing that comes with superior knowledge—and one who takes the lead during instructional events. A facilitator may be a peer in terms of subject-matter expertise and may participate in give-and-take with learners rather than playing the dominant role.

To be a *facilitator* one does not have to be employed at an educational or training institution. We are using the term to refer to any person or device that supports and guides learners during an instructional event. College professors are facilitators when they create and implement lessons for their students. Kindergarten aides are facilitators when they play a role in a structured learning activity. Parents in the home are facilitators when helping their children with homework or even conducting homeschooling lessons. When an older student is tutoring a younger student, the tutor is playing the role of facilitator. As used here, *facilitator* is not an occupation, but the label for a role played in instructional events. As we shall see, mechanical or electronic devices can be programmed to guide learners through instructional activities. While that device is guiding the learner, it is playing the role of facilitator.

Conversely, people who are employed as teachers do not spend all their time playing the role of facilitator, as defined here. They also serve as curriculum planners, materials producers, test developers, evaluators, disciplinarians, caseworkers, event coordinators, friends, nurses, record keepers, and a dozen other functions. It is only when they are engaged in instructional activities that they play the role of facilitator, as defined here.

Facilitators Facilitate Learning

Dictionaries define "to facilitate" as "to make easy" or "ease a process." In our case, facilitators are easing the process of learning. According to contemporary learning theories, knowledge construction is primarily in the hands of learners; therefore, facilitators can encourage learners to invest effort in carrying out the mental, emotional, and psychomotor processes necessary for learning, but they cannot produce that learning. Facilitators can design lessons that are appealing and engaging and that provide suitable conditions to practice new skills. Facilitators and learners can be collaborators in a common enterprise. But only learners themselves can create meanings for themselves.

Merrill, in his comprehensive attempt to establish technical definitions for key terms in the field of instruction, prefers the term *promote learning* rather than *facilitate learning* to refer to what teachers and other instructors do (2013, 193). He feels that *promote* is a stronger term to describe the guidance and assistance offered by instructors; it connotes causality better than *facilitate*. We do not disagree; however, we prefer *facilitate* because it has a broader and softer connotation. Classroom teachers, using best practices in a well-focused lesson, do illustrate *promoting* learning, but peers quizzing each other in a study group illustrate something softer, hence *facilitating*. It also happens that *facilitate* is already widely accepted in the literature of education, especially of educational technology. For example, *facilitate learning* is the key phrase in the current definition of the field of educational technology (Januszewski and Molenda 2008). Thus, *facilitator* has a familiar and comfortable feel in educational discourse, while *promoter* would sound quite a sour note in the context of education.

It is important to point out that all the learning theories discussed at the beginning of this chapter are intended as *descriptions* of how the learning process takes place, not *prescriptions* of what should be done to induce efficient and effective learning. Learning theories do not necessarily lead directly to or even imply the use of any particular instructional strategies. As is discussed in greater depth in Chapter 12, no instructional prescriptions flow directly from any description of the learning process. Even given a "learner-centered" description of how humans learn, it is still true that any and all teaching–learning prescriptions, including teacher-centered presentations and demonstrations, can help learners carry out the "intentional process of constructing meaning from information and experience" (APA Task Force on Psychology in Education 1993).

Resources

Often overlooked in thinking about teaching and learning are *resources*, a third element of instruction, along with the *learner* and the *facilitator*. As Petroski (1998) points out, when Henry David Thoreau went into the Massachusetts woods to write *Walden*, his reflections upon simple living in natural surroundings, he took along some bare essentials. Thoreau lists all these necessities in painstaking detail, including needle and thread, matches, soap, telescope and microscope, blanket, and so on. What he failed to mention was the pencil he used to record all these thoughts. Some things are so familiar to us, so much a part of our everyday lives, that they become virtually invisible. Educationists focus so much on the nature of the learner and the contrivances of teachers that they tend to give little attention to the everyday materials and tools that are integrated into almost every instructional setting—the desks and chairs that make reading and writing convenient, the chalkboard or whiteboard that allows easy visualization of concepts, and so on.

Even textbooks are often overlooked by theoreticians. Textbooks are ubiquitous in formal education, from elementary school through university studies. In the corporate realm, training manuals and workbooks have long been a mainstay. The most recent survey indicates that about two-thirds of all training time is spent in face-to-face classrooms or some "blended" combination of classroom and online study (Training Magazine 2018). These modes of delivery are typically supported by print materials of some sort. Studies done at the elementary school level often find evidence that teachers rely on textbooks for selection of content and sequence of coverage (Sosniak and Stodolsky 1993). At the secondary school level, chapter-by-chapter readings are the core of most homework assignments. At the higher education level, examination questions seldom stray far from the contents of required textbooks. When you add up the time spent in the classroom interacting with materials plus the time spent outside the classroom on homework assignments (including reading the textbook), it is obvious that learners spend a sizable proportion of their instructional time using such resources (McCutcheon 1982). And yet, in all the volumes of advice on teaching methods, how much attention is given to textbooks?

Defining Resources

In Merrill's terms, the two major "instructional modes," the ways of "providing content to the learner" are telling and showing (Merrill 2013, 71). Telling is limited to verbal or digital information; showing is limited to analog representations, such as graphic materials. He does not go on to define the concept of *resources*, which we claim are the physical manifestations of telling and showing—the actual text, audio, or visual materials themselves. Frick, like Merrill, features "content" in his basic glossary, defining it as "signs of objects and objects selected by a teacher for student learning" (Frick 2019). By focusing on the visible manifestations of "content," Frick's definition is aligned with ours.

We use the term *resources* to refer to all the materials and devices that learners interact with during instructional events. This includes textbooks, slide shows, handouts, computer hardware and software, and the like. The resources used in instruction are discussed under two headings: (a) *instructional* resources—those that have information embedded in them; and (b) *real-world* resources—those that exist in nature and are occasionally borrowed for instructional use.

Instructional Resources

Some of the resources used in education and training are designed specifically to be used for instruction, for example, textbooks, work sheets, training videos, narrated slide presentations, computer-based games and simulations, alphabet blocks, recorded nursery songs, flash cards, podcast lectures and interviews, language learning CDs, Web tutorials, and whole courses online. These would be classified as *instructional resources*, as discussed in depth by Betrus (2008) as "resources by design." Current literature tends to focus on the use of newer, digital resources; but in terms of everyday practice, analog resources such as textbooks and training manuals, the overhead projector, chalkboards and whiteboards, and the videocassette recorder (VCR) are still used extensively in both corporate and academic settings. For example, photographic slides, in use since the 1850s, continue to be used for subjects where high definition images are critical, such as biology, veterinary medicine, optometry, and the visual arts. And kindergarten teachers still like to have phonograph players available—so easy to drop the needle on the right song. Thus, while current trends point toward an increased use of digital instructional resources, instructors continue to make ample use of analog instructional resources.

Real-World Resources

In addition to using *instructional* resources during instructional events, learners also interact with an infinite variety of *real-world* resources—things that are not created to be instructional but can be enlisted in the cause of education with some effort. Betrus refers to these as "resources by utilization" (2008, 213). For an everyday example, early childhood education makes use of blocks, pitchers, cups, and ladles. Elementary schools may keep pet animals in the classroom, such as guinea pigs, rabbits, rats, and fish. Students go on field trips to see and feel nature—at farms, zoos, lakes, and streams—or to experience adult workplaces, such as fire stations, hospitals, or factories, or to understand history by seeing and touching exhibits at museums and historic sites. Secondary school students may opt for vocational classes in which they use real-world tools in the kitchen, woodshop, auto-repair garage, or plumbing lab. They may also have assignments in academic classes that require them to read newspapers, watch television programs, or do Web searches. Postsecondary education can add even more exotic encounters with real-world resources with practicum work at archeological sites, in undersea exploration, at astronomical observatories, in musical and theatrical performances, and on the athletic field. When we say *real-world resources*, we are talking about all the people, places, and things that exist for their own purposes but can be pressed into the support of learning by creative instructors.

Mass education is impossible without resources, those designed as instructional and those that are borrowed temporarily as needed. The reach of teachers is extended and amplified by putting information into analog and digital recordings that can be accessed and used by learners anytime, anywhere. Learners can read or view these materials at their convenience and as frequently as they like, allowing repetition and practice far beyond the patience of a live instructor. The importance of this surrogate role played by resources will become dramatically obvious when we examine distance education, the most rapidly growing format of formal education.

The availability of both instructional and real-world resources makes it possible for autodidacts to create their own learning environments, using books, records and tapes, observation of masters, and Web resources to achieve the skills they feel impelled to pursue. An example is actor and musician Dudley Moore (1935–2002) who claimed to have learned jazz piano technique by listening to the vinyl records of jazz virtuoso Erroll Garner and transcribing what he heard, note by note.

Resources vs. Media

We have intentionally avoided using the term *media* up to this point in this chapter. In Chapter 1, we discussed how *media* as communication channels are routinely conflated with the messages transmitted through those channels. Here, we reiterate this distinction between the channel (*medium*) and the content that flows through that channel: speech, songs, images, text, sounds, music, gestures, dance, facial expressions, and body language. These packets of information are potential resources. However, they do not constitute *resources* unless and until they have been captured and stored in a manner that makes their subsequent retrieval convenient, i.e., when they have been transformed into printed or digital texts, printed or digital images, or audio/video recordings.

Communication Configuration

So far, we have discussed learner, facilitator, and resources as the three basic, observable elements of instruction. The term *element* is used in chemistry to designate substances that cannot be separated into simpler substances. But here *element* is used in a more general sense—the simplest component of a complex whole, that "complex whole" being an instructional event. There are other candidates for basic components, such as content, goals, and motivation, but since those things are not observable per se, they are not included in the present discussion, as important as they may be.

We want to add another critical component of an instructional event. It has not previously been recognized widely as a vital part of instruction, although Merrill comes close with his concept of *instructional mode*—which refers to what sorts of interactions facilitators and learners have among themselves (2013, 71). What we are referring to is the *communication configuration*. It is observable, but it is not a physical object; it is the communication pattern among learner, facilitator, and resources employed during an instructional event. This topic is pursued at greater length in Chapter 4, where we propose that these configurations can be organized into a typology, consisting of the following types: Presentation, Demonstration, Whole-Class Discussion, Small-Group Discussion, Tutorial, Repetition, Study, and Expression—each of which is discussed in the following Chapters 5–11.

Setting

Another element that is visibly part of any instructional event is the *setting* for the event. Frick uses the term *context* to refer to "the system environment of teacher and student that contains content" (Frick 2019). We intend much the same thing in our definition of *setting*: the physical surroundings in which the learner, facilitator, and resources interact. We intentionally avoid using the term *environment* in this discussion because it is nowadays often used in education discourse for something more esoteric than the physical surroundings of teaching–learning encounters.

Clearly, the spaces and furnishings that are available have an enormous effect on what sorts of resources and methods can be brought to bear. For example, such a simple thing as having chairs that can easily be moved into circles may determine whether discussion methods will be used. Classrooms without desks—often encountered in less-developed countries—limit learners' ability to read and write. Lecture halls without voice amplification constrain the number of listeners who can effectively receive the lectures. Heating and air conditioning or the lack thereof can make or break the convening of classes. These are mundane concerns, often outside the control of educators, but nevertheless constrain the instructional choices they make.

Nowadays, in the "first world" of industrialized nations, access to electrical services is taken for granted. However, in much of the rest of the world electricity is a scarce commodity. The term *energy poverty* came into popular use early in the twenty-first century, referring to the large numbers of people whose well-being is negatively affected by lack of access to power sources, especially electrical power. Energy poverty constrains education directly, by limiting access to audiovisual resources, especially the Web, in school, and making it difficult for students to read or do homework at home. Energy poverty affects education indirectly by reducing children's time for education when they are forced to spend hours foraging for firewood and water for their family, and by discouraging teachers from taking positions in non-electrified areas.

The issue of how the physical setting constrains the instructional enterprise is discussed under the heading of Frame Factors in Chapter 2.

Chapter Summary

Since this book primarily serves to introduce our notion of the basic elements of instruction, especially the new concept of communication configurations, the major purpose of this chapter is to put these concepts into the context of the conversation about the processes of learning and instruction.

Our brief overview of contemporary theories of learning highlights the support offered for various theories by research in neuroscience. These theories, although they seem to offer differing—even conflicting—explanations for how people learn, can better be viewed as different perspectives on the whole, broad scene of human learning. In that sense, each captures part of the truth. We conclude this section with a generic definition of learning as the acquisition of new—or the modification of existing—knowledge, skills, or attitudes resulting from the individual's interaction with the environment.

Some types of human learning occur naturally as the person matures, assuming they have normal sorts of interactions with other people and the natural environment along the way. Other types of learning require conscious effort to master, best accomplished with the guidance of a knowledgeable other person. This is the genesis of the process of instruction, which we define as a deliberate effort to provide learners with conditions suitable for achieving specified learning objectives. Further, to be considered successful, instruction should be humane, effective, and efficient.

In keeping with our goal of helping to build a basic working vocabulary of concepts in the domain of instruction, we begin by identifying the visible elements present within any instructional event: learner, facilitator, resources, setting, and the pattern of communication among them. The latter, communication configuration, is an overlooked element of the process, and we intend to illustrate the power of this concept in describing instructional situations—as is done in operational definitions in research projects—and in preparing an instructional plan—as is done in instructional design projects. This is the focus of the next chapter.

Works Cited

AECT Task Force on Definition and Terminology. 1977. *The Definition of Educational Technology*. Washington, DC: Association for Educational Communications and Technology (AECT).

APA Task Force on Psychology in Education. 1993. *Learner-Centered Psychological Principles: Guidelines for School Redesign and Reform*. Washington, DC: American Psychological Association and Mid-Continent Regional Educational Laboratory.

Bandura, Albert. 1977. *Social Learning Theory*. Englewood Cliffs, NJ: Prentice-Hall.

Bandura, Albert. 1986. *Social Foundations of Thought and Action: A Social Cognitive Theory*. Englewood Cliffs, NJ: Prentice-Hall.

Bertolero, Max, and Danielle S. Bassett. 2019. "How Matter Becomes Mind." *Scientific American* 321 (1): 26–33.

Betrus, Anthony Karl. 2008. "Resources." Chap. 8 in *Educational Technology: A Definition with Commentary*, edited by Alan Januszewski and Michael Molenda, 213–240. New York: Lawrence Erlbaum Associates.

Biech, Elaine. 2017. *The Art and Science of Training*. Alexandria, VA: ATD Press.

Bruner, Jerome S. 1998. *Acts of Meaning*. Cambridge, MA: Harvard University Press.
Bruner, Jerome S. 1966. *Toward a Theory of Instruction*. Cambridge, MA: The Belknap Press of Harvard University Press.
Bruner, Jerome S., Jacqueline J. Goodnow, and George A. Austin. 1956. *A Study of Thinking*. New York: John Wiley.
Cole, Michael W., Patryk Laurent, and Andrea Stocco. 2013. "Rapid Instructed Task Learning: A New Window into the Human Brain's Unique Capacity for Flexible Cognitive Control." *Cognitive, Affective, & Behavioral Neuroscience* 13 (1): 1–22.
Driscoll, Marcy P. 2004. *Psychology of Learning for Instruction*. 3rd ed. Boston, MA: Pearson Education.
Ellis, Rod. 1990. *Instructed Second Language Acquisition: Learning in the Classroom*. Oxford, UK: Basil Blackwell.
Etzel, Joset A., Michael W. Cole, Jeffrey M. Zacks, Kendrick N. Kay, and Todd S. Braver. 2016. "Reward Motivation Enhances Task Coding in Frontoparietal Cortex." *Cerebral Cortex* 26: 1647–1659. doi:10.1093/cercor/bhu327.
Frick, Theodore W. 2019. *Close Schools. Open Minds. Why We Need Educology for Improving Education Systems*. Accessed July 17, 2019. http://educology.indiana.edu/Frick/MRW%20chapters/educology.pdf.
Gagné, Robert M. 1965. *The Conditions of Learning*. New York: Hold, Rinehart and Winston.
Gagné, Robert M., and Robert Glaser. 1987. "Foundations in Learning Research." In *Instructional Technology Foundations*, edited by Robert M. Gagné, 49–83. Hillsdale, NJ: Lawrence Erlbaum Associates.
Gagné, Robert M., Leslie J. Briggs, and Walter W. Wager. 1992. *Principles of Instructional Design*. 4th ed. Fort Worth, TX: Harcourt Brace Jovanovich.
Geake, John G. 2009. *The Brain at School: Educational Neuroscience in the Classroom*. Maidenhead: Open University Press/McGraw-Hill.
Geary, David C. 2008. "An Evolutionarily Informed Education Science." *Educational Psychologist* 43 (4): 179–195.
Goldstein, Alvin G., and June E. Chance. 1970. "Visual Recognition Memory for Complex Configurations." *Perception and Psychophysics* 9: 237–241.
Greenspan, Stanley I., and Beryl Lieff Benderly. 1997. *The Growth of Mind: And the Endangered Origins of Intelligence*. Reading, MA: Addison-Wesley.
James, William. 1899. *Talks to Teachers on Psychology; and to Students on Some of Life's Ideals*. New York: Henry Holt and Company.
Januszewski, Alan, and Michael Molenda, eds. 2008. *Educational Technology: A Definition with Commentary*. New York: Lawrence Erlbaum Associates.
Kandel, Eric R. 2004. "The Molecular Biology of Memory Storage: A Dialog between Genes and Synapses." *Bioscience Reports* 24 (4/5): 477–517.
Kandel, Eric R. 2006. *In Search of Memory*. New York: W. W. Norton.
Kardas, Michael, and Ed O'Brien. 2018. "Easier Seen than Done: Merely Watching Others Perform Can Foster an Illusion of Skill Acquisition." *Psychological Science*, 29 (4): 521–536.
McCombs, Barbara L., and Donna Vakili. 2005. "A Learner-Centered Framework for E-Learning." *Teachers College Record* 107 (8): 1582–1600.
McCutcheon, Gail. 1982. "Textbook Use in a Central Ohio Classroom." *Annual Meeting of the American Educational Research Association*. New York City.
Merrill, M. David. 2013. *First Principles of Instruction*. San Francisco, CA: Pfeiffer.
Neisser, Ulric. 1967. *Cognitive Psychology*. Englewood Cliffs, NJ: Prentice-Hall.

Paas, Fred, and John Sweller. 2014. "Implications of Cognitive Load Theory for Multimedia Learning." In *The Cambridge Handbook of Multimedia Learning*, 2nd ed., edited by Richard E. Mayer, 27–42. New York: Cambridge University Press.

Paivio, Allan. 1971. *Imagery and Verbal Processes*. New York: Holt, Rinehart & Winston.

Petroski, Henry. 1998. *The Pencil: A History of Design and Circumstances*. New York: Alfred A. Knopf.

Phelps, Elizabeth A. 2006. "Emotion and Cognition: Insights from Studies of the Human Amygdala." *Annual Review of Psychology* 57: 27–53.

Reigeluth, Charles M., and Alison A. Carr-Chellman, eds. 2009a. *Instructional-Design Theories and Models: Building a Common Knowledge Base*. Vol. 3. New York: Routledge.

Reigeluth, Charles M., and Alison A. Carr-Chellman, eds. 2009b. "Situational Principles of Instruction." In *Instructional-Design Theories and Models: Building a Common Knowledge Base*, edited by Charles M. Reigeluth and Alison A. Carr-Chellman, 3:57–68. New York: Routledge.

Rizzolatti, Giacomo, and Corrado Sinigaglia. 2008. *Mirrors in the Brain: How Our Minds Share Actions, Emotions, and Experience*. Oxford, UK: Oxford University Press.

Skinner, B. F. 1953. *Science and Human Behavior*. New York: The Free Press.

Sosniak, Lauren A., and Susan S. Stodolsky. 1993. "Teachers and Textbooks: Materials Use in Four Fourth-Grade Classrooms." *Elementary School Journal* 93 (3): 249–275.

Stanley, Damian, Emma Ferneyhough, and Elizabeth A. Phelps. 2009. "Neural Perspectives on Emotion: Impact on Perception, Attention, and Memory." Chap. 42 in *Handbook of Neuroscience for the Behavioral Sciences*, edited by Gary G. Berntson and John T. Cacioppo, 2:829–838. Hoboken, NJ: John Wiley & Sons.

Training Magazine. 2018. "Industry Report." *Training*, November–December: 18–31.

Wellington, Arthur M. 1887. *The Economic Theory of the Location of Railways*. Revised and Enlarged Edition. New York: John Wiley and Sons.

Wile, David. 1996. "Why Doers Do." *Performance & Instruction* 35 (2): 30–35.

Communication Configurations and Methods

4

Adding to the Basic Elements

As introduced in Chapter 3, our list of basic elements begins with the most visible elements—a *learner* and a *facilitator* commonly using some sort of *resources* as they strive toward the goal of *instructed learning*. The term *element* is used in chemistry to designate substances that cannot be separated into simpler substances. But here *element* is used in a more general sense—the simplest component of a complex whole, that "complex whole" being an *instructional event* (discussed in Chapter 3). There are other candidates for basic components, such as goals and motivations, but since goals and motivation are not observable, they are not included in the present discussion, as important as they may be.

To the three most visible elements we add the *setting* in which they interact, as discussed in Chapter 3. The fifth basic element is not a physical object, but it is observable—the communication pattern among facilitator, learner, and resources during an instructional event. We refer to this communication pattern as a *communication configuration*—which we define as the pattern of the flow of information and control among learner, facilitator, and resources during an instructional event. This is the main topic of this chapter, in which we will argue that there is a finite set of configurations that have evolved for use in instruction and these can be arranged into a typology, a system for categorizing communication configurations. Having established that typology, in the latter half of this chapter we will explain how communication configurations can be viewed as components of teaching–learning patterns, which we will refer to as *methods*, a generalized pattern of activities that affords learners the opportunity to exercise the cognitive and/or motor and emotional processes necessary to achieve some instructed learning objective.

Evolution of Our Typology

Throughout human history, educators have devised many different arrangements for carrying out teaching–learning activities. These arrangements vary in size, from one facilitator and one learner to one facilitator and many learners. By definition, there can be no more than one facilitator at a time; a given audience can only listen to one person at a time and be directed by one person at a time, even if this role is rotated, as with "team teaching." The communication patterns may vary widely, from simple one-way transmission from one facilitator to a group of learners, to learners interacting amongst themselves, to individual learners interacting with resources, and so on.

Despite the myriad mathematical possibilities of combinations and permutations of these roles and communication patterns, a finite number of arrangements have evolved over the centuries. We propose that these arrangements can be organized into a typology, based on the physically observable elements of facilitator, learner, resources, and communication pattern.

This concept of a typology based on communication configuration has evolved over a period of four decades. It began with some prescient speculations by the eminent instructional theorist Robert Gagné and culminated many years later, after the boundaries of teaching and learning were stretched by the blossoming of Web-based distance education.

Gagné's Modes of Instruction

In the first edition of his groundbreaking book *Conditions of Learning*, Gagné referred to the different types of instructional arrangements as "modes" of instruction:

> Environments for learning consist of the various communication media arranged so as to perform their several functions by interaction with the student. The particular arrangements these media may have in relation to the student are usually called the modes of instruction
>
> *(Gagné 1965, 285).*

He outlined six different *modes* of instruction being commonly used (Gagné 1965, 285–294):

- tutoring: "interchange between a student and his tutor"
- lecture: "oral communication on the part of the teacher"
- recitation: "teacher 'heard' the students perform"
- discussion: "oral communication…between teacher and student…[and] interactions between students"

- laboratory: "a stimulus situation that brings the student into contact with actual objects and events"
- homework
  - self-instruction: "as [reading] a chapter in a textbook"
  - practice: "examples of previously learned principles"
  - projects: "organize a variety of activities for himself in such a way as to lead to the development of a product."

This construct of *modes* was repeated verbatim in the second edition of *Conditions of Learning* (Gagné 1977, 367–377), but it disappeared from all subsequent editions.

Molenda's First Adaptation of Gagné's Modes

It seemed that Gagné was onto an important idea here—that you could classify the various instructional arrangements according to the interaction pattern that characterized it. Although Gagné did not pursue this idea in later editions or in other works, Molenda sought to develop this notion further. He began by analyzing the communication flow within each category, using the basic ideas first proposed by Claude Shannon in his mathematical theory of communication (Shannon and Weaver 1963, 7). Information originates in a source, from which a message is sent by means of a transmitter through some communication channel, and then reaches a destination by means of a receiver. In the case of human communication, the receiver is the person's sensory apparatus and the destination is the brain. The original source can determine the success of transmission by receiving feedback from the destination, repeating the communication process in reverse.

Applying these insights to instructional encounters, it appears that there are three possible sources of information: the facilitator, the learner, and the resources employed, and each of those sources could also be a destination for a return message. Thus, not only can the facilitator provide feedback to the learner, so could resources, such as programmed instruction booklets or computer programs.

Therefore, focusing on the three major actors—facilitator, learner, and resources—and the communication patterns among them, Gagné's categories could be reinterpreted as follows (Molenda 1972):

- tutorial: two-way interchange between tutor (facilitator) and tutee (learner)
- lecture: one-way information flow from presenter (facilitator) to many receivers (learners)
- discussion: two-way information interchange among learners
- laboratory: learner acts on instructional or real-world materials (resources)
- independent study: learner acts on encoded, instructional materials (resources)
- practice: learner uses new skill repeatedly (may be guided by facilitator)

This seemed to be a useful classification system—simple and compact—that was reasonably successful in providing "buckets" into which one could place many of the instructional formats that one encounters in everyday teaching. The value of such a simplified typology is that the instructional designer would only have to choose one among a half-dozen options (e.g., discussion) rather than sifting through the dozens or hundreds of names or varying formats created for different discussion situations (e.g. buzz group, brainstorming, debriefing, workshopping, conversation groups for language learning, etc.). The assumption that accompanies this typology is that what is important is the communication pattern; it provides certain possibilities ("affordances" in the language of cognitive psychology) and imposes certain limits. Once you have chosen the mode of instruction, choosing the format boils down to logistical considerations. The particular manifestation of that mode—the format—may bring logistical advantages or disadvantages. For example, textbooks might be more readily available than Web pages for some audiences. However, it is the communication pattern that carries the pedagogical power and imposes some limitations. A given message, with its auditory and visual components, will have essentially the same learning effect whether it is delivered live, over broadcast television, or via DVD recording. Choices made for logistical considerations—time and money—can be crucial decisions, but they do not directly affect the pedagogy.

It also appears that certain modes lend themselves to different phases of the learning process. For example, an experiential activity might serve well at the beginning of a lesson to stimulate interest and provoke questions about a new topic. A lecture would be an efficient way to present new information to an audience whose curiosity is already aroused. A discussion can help learners digest new principles and apply them to their daily lives. Practice activities are often assigned as homework in order to develop confidence and speed in application. An experiential activity, such as a simulation game, might be used at the beginning of a lesson to arouse interest and provide a holistic framework for later discussion…or it might be used at the end of a lesson to provide a venue for applying new knowledge and skills to a realistic representation of real-world application.

Davies's "Methods"

A colleague of Molenda's at Indiana University, Ivor Davies, quite independently created a list of instructional arrangements, referring to them as "methods" (Davies 1981, 38–50). His list included: lecture, demonstration, discussion (with a number of subsidiary types—experiential small group, debate/seminar, case study, role playing, game), and independent study (including doing projects, working through programmed instruction, and viewing slide-tape presentations).

Davies's list, although not presented as a typology, overlapped significantly with Gagné's and Molenda's lists, and it also defined each "method" in terms of structural elements, as a typology would. It gave little attention to tutorial and experiential-learning arrangements, reflecting its grounding in the realm of corporate training rather than formal education. Consequently, it gave much more attention to group-experience arrangements such as small-group discussions, games, and role-plays as well as innovations of the time, such as programmed instruction and slide-tape presentations. All Davies's additions are reflected in later versions of the Molenda typology.

Berliner's "Activity Structures"

In the 1980s, David Berliner was studying the interactions between various treatments and various learner aptitudes. In the course of doing so, he found it necessary to find better operational definitions of the treatments he was manipulating.

> The titles of these treatments represent little more than descriptions of nominal categories with very unclear boundaries. If ATI research is to improve, better definition of treatment is necessary
>
> *(Berliner 1983, 2).*

Based on observations done in elementary school classrooms, Berliner identified eight types of "activity structures" that captured most of what transpired during instructional time in those classrooms, which he dubbed "a taxonomy of activity structures." (Although it does not actually meet the criteria for taxonomy, it could be considered a typology.) Berliner's categories:

- reading circle: in a small group, individuals read orally and discuss, under direction of teacher
- seatwork: working independently, students write responses as directed by materials
- two-way presentation: student and teacher communicate orally with each other
- one-way presentation: teacher communicates orally to group without response
- mediated presentation: students listen to or watch a presenter who is not available for conversation
- silent reading: individual students read without requirement of a response
- construction: student generates a product from materials
- games: activity employing rules or strategies that are gamelike (i.e., ludic).

A limitation is that Berliner's "taxonomy" pertains only to elementary education. In some cases, names of categories seem awkward, for example:

- "Two-way presentation" is misleading for describing an exchange between teacher and student. The term "presentation" connotes a one-way communication; if it is two-way it is a conversation, it is not just a series of presentations.

- "Mediated presentation" does not seem distinguishable from "one-way presentation." Both are essentially one-way flows of information. If the listener speaks up and the presenter responds, the activity shifts to another configuration.
- "Seatwork" and "silent reading" would seem to overlap a great deal, the only difference being that seatwork may require written responses.
- "Seatwork" and "construction" also appear to overlap, both requiring student creation of some sort of product that indicates what they have learned.

Stodolsky's "Instructional Formats"

Later, Susan Stodolsky (1988) conducted classroom research on the teaching of math and social studies at the elementary school level. She compared the amount of time students spent engaging in different "instructional formats" while studying math versus social studies. As operational definitions of different formats, Stodolsky identified 12 categories:
- seatwork: students working at their desks on assignments
  - diverse seatwork: students working at desks or other locations on a number of different tasks
  - individualized seatwork: students working at desks on individually assigned or chosen tasks
- recitation: short exchanges between teacher and students—calling on individuals to answer or read in turn
- discussion: similar to recitation but more exchanges among students
- lecture: teacher talks to students at some length
- demonstration: teacher shows how to do something
- test/quiz: students take oral or written test
- group work: students work on common tasks in small groups
- film audiovisual: students watch or listen to films or recordings
- contests/learning games: cognitive games or contests that may involve whole class
- student reports: individual students share information with whole class
- tutoring: teacher, other adult, or student tutors another student.

Her research demonstrated that elementary school teachers tend to apportion time somewhat differently in mathematics and social studies, using similar teaching–learning arrangements, but in different proportions. For example, seatwork occupied nearly half of all math learning time but less than 30 percent of social studies time, with much more social studies time spent in small-group work.

Her classification system, although presented merely as operational definitions for her research, actually could be seen as a typology. Like Gagné's and Molenda's, it focuses on the teacher–learner communication pattern as the main criterion for classification. It was intended to serve as a framework for quantifying the instructional activities in elementary school classrooms. Indeed, it served the purpose well, allowing Stodolsky to group different sorts of activities into a small number of categories. The proven utility of the classification system lends validity to the idea of basing a typology on teacher–learner communication patterns.

Further, Stodolsky acknowledged that any coding or classifying of classroom events needed to be able to break down the events into chunks according to the mode being employed at any moment because teachers often switched quickly from one mode to another: from lecture to demonstration, from demonstration to recitation, or from seatwork to tutoring. She referred to these chunks as "activity segments." This is the same concept as what we label as "instructional event." There is a semantic difference; Stodolsky's term implies that the activity is part of something larger—a segment. We make no assumption; each chunk simply exists—an event.

A limitation of Stodolsky's typology for present purposes is its rather narrow focus on elementary education. We are pursuing a typology that could encompass all manner of instructional arrangements: for nonformal as well as formal education, for all venues, and for all levels from the most basic to the most sophisticated. Some categories were too narrow; for example, expression was represented only by "student reports," and study was represented only by "seatwork." Stodolsky's "recitation" seems to describe the purpose of an instructional activity, not its physical configuration, which is basically a type of repeated practice or repetition. Otherwise, Stodolsky's typology overlapped significantly with Berliner's categories and Molenda's efforts to that point.

Molenda's Transitional Typologies

Over the years, Molenda's primitive 1972 typology evolved slowly until it was codified in print in the third edition of the textbook coauthored by Molenda, Robert Heinich, and James D. Russell (1989, 8–10). In that iteration, the typology was given the label of "methods," and the discussion of it was limited to two pages—consisting of brief definitions of each category. The eight categories in 1989 were:

- presentation
- demonstration
- drill-and-practice
- tutorial
- discovery
- gaming
- simulation
- problem-solving.

Beyond the brief descriptions, there was no discussion of the basis for the typology, and no further reference was made as to how these categories might be used in planning instruction. By the fifth edition of the textbook (Heinich et al. 1996,

9–12), Sharon E. Smaldino had been added to the author team, and the typology appeared with only minor amendment—adding the categories of discussion and cooperative learning groups, expanding the list to ten categories. The name of the typology remained "methods," referred to as "procedures of instruction that are selected to help learners achieve the objectives" (1996, 9). Beyond that, there was no further discussion of the basis for the typology or how it might be used.

Molenda dropped off the author team of that textbook after the fifth edition, but the concept of "methods" continued to appear in future editions, with little alteration. Indeed, the most recent edition, the twelfth, maintains the same categories as the fifth edition; the only significant change is that the typology is now called "learning strategies" (Smaldino, Lowther and Mims 2019, 66–74). Another change is that suggestions are given as to how "technology and media" may be incorporated into each category. However, as in the earlier editions, the list is not referred to as a typology, and there is no discussion of the basis for the categorization nor for the "learning strategies" name.

Meanwhile, after dropping off the textbook team, Molenda continued to modify the evolving typology in response to new perspectives prompted by advances in technology, particularly Web-based distance education, and in instructional theories, particularly the challenges posed by advocates of constructivism. In the late 1990s, Charles Reigeluth asked permission to put the Molenda typology into print in his book on instructional design theory (Reigeluth 1999, 23). The 1999 version of the Molenda typology included 11 categories:

- lecture/presentation
- demonstration/modeling
- tutorial
- drill-and-practice
- independent study
- discussion/seminar
- expression
- cooperative group
- games
- simulations
- discovery
- problem-solving/laboratory.

A Digital Age Typology

Throughout this period, Molenda was regularly presenting and discussing the typology in graduate classes on instructional design. Each semester's discussion raised questions that led to amendments to the typology. Then, in the early 2000s, he began teaching seminars on instructional design for distance education. When Molenda and his students began to study the pedagogical strategies of Web-based

116 Communication Configurations and Methods

distance courses, they found that the 1999 version of the typology did not provide very adequate "buckets" for holding the various activities that were most common in Web-based courses. This led to the realization that distance courses required numerous *learning* strategies but offered only a few different *teaching* strategies (mainly just presentation of new information). So, in order to portray both the learning and the teaching strategies being encountered by students, the typology needed to better reflect both teacher-controlled and learner-controlled arrangements. The major modification was to add the category of study, which encompassed the many activities that distant students did individually, such as reading texts and reflecting on their personal interpretation.

The expanded typology contained 13 categories. It is notable that these categories, although developed independently of Davies, Berliner, and Stodolsky, overlapped highly with each of their quasi-typologies, contributing to the validity of this approach of categorizing teaching–learning activities according to the visible interactions among facilitators, learners, and resources.

As a result of further discussions, especially when presenting at professional conferences, Molenda realized that his previous categories could be condensed by examining more strictly the communication patterns at the heart of each category. For example, "cooperative groups" actually interact in the form of a discussion. On the other hand, discussion really covered two somewhat different communication patterns; whole-class discussions revolve around the facilitator, while small-group discussions revolve around the learners themselves. Hence, discussion was subdivided under two different headings. Finally, after much consideration, "laboratory" was dropped from our list of configurations on the basis that, while it represented an important category of teaching–learning activity, it was not a specific, tangible arrangement of people and resources. Rather, it described an overall approach for "discovery" type learning that incorporated a number of different configurations. In our current iteration, *Problem-Based Learning* is the term employed in Chapter 9 to denote the strategic-level method encompassing "laboratory" or "discovery" type activities.

These amendments led to the current version presented in this book, with seven major categories, one of which was subdivided into two, hence a total of eight "buckets": Presentation, Demonstration, Whole-Class Discussion, Small-Group Discussion, Tutorial, Repetition, Study, and Expression.

The other refinement dealt with nomenclature. Gagné referred to his construct as *modes*. Berliner referred to *activity structures*. Stodolsky proposed a set of *instructional formats*. Earlier versions of the current typology had used the label *methods*—as Davies's typology also did, while Molenda's coauthors came to prefer the label *learning strategies*. Ultimately, the terms *methods*, *modes*, *strategies*, and *modalities* were rejected because all had prior meanings in the literature of education. *Instructional formats*, Stodolsky's term, was an attractive alternative because of its clarity and simplicity. However, in the field of educational technology the term *format* had a long history of referring to a particular manifestation of a class of media; for example, cassette and reel-to-reel tapes were two different *formats* of audio recordings.

The term *format* is better used to refer to the many manifestations of each broad configuration; for example, writing, speaking, painting, and dance are all formats for the Expression configuration, just as film, DVD, and Web video are different formats for the motion visual category of media. The decision was finally made to refer to this as a typology of *communication configurations*, using a label that had not been proposed previously, but which was a clear, straightforward description of the object of study.

Each of the eight categories may have many different-looking manifestations; for example, a private music lesson and the marching drills of an army squad would both be classified as a Repetition configuration. As different looking as they are, an observer should be able to walk into a room, attend to how the facilitator, learners, and resources are arranged, and describe what is going on using the labels specified here as communication configurations.

Next, we will examine each category of communication configuration and investigate the critical attributes of each.

Presentation

Probably the most commonly encountered configuration in formal education is the lecture or other type of oral presentation, such as a sermon, panel discussion, or symposium. The category of *Presentation* includes any one-way communication of information from a source to a number of receivers. Presentations may be given live and in-person, but they can also be transmitted to remote listeners through broadcast or computer technology. They may also be recorded as film, video, slide-tape, or computer-generated slideshow or slide deck. In this case, the source may not be a live person but rather some type of *resource*—a still or moving image, a graph or chart, a vocal or music recording, a narrated film or animation. Whatever the format, a presentation is defined as being a one-way flow of information from one source to multiple receivers.

> *Presentation*: A Facilitator (F), or some Instructional Resource (IR) playing the role of Facilitator, conveys information one-way to a number of Learners (L); the Facilitator or Instructional Resource controls the flow of communication (Figure 4.1).

The great advantage of presentations is their efficiency in communicating a message to many listeners or viewers simultaneously, especially if the audience is multiplied by means of sound amplification or broadcasting through communications media. Because presentations may be improvised or created at little cost, they can be both an efficient and an economical means of giving out information. Most instructional objectives, whether they are cognitive, affective, interpersonal, or psychomotor, require some amount of new information as part of the lesson, hence almost any lesson plan will include a Presentation at some point.

118 Communication Configurations and Methods

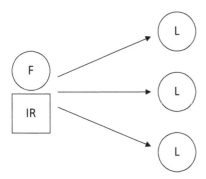

Figure 4.1 The Presentation Communication Configuration.

Presentations have the limitation of being only as useful as the thought and creativity that go into them. Nothing is more stultifying to an audience than a listless, monotonous, drone of a lecture. Even if well-crafted and artfully delivered, presentations can only fulfill one stage of the learning process—providing new information. Other configurations are needed to allow learners to process the new information and integrate it into their mental structure.

Demonstration

Instructors have long understood the power of demonstrations and visual examples as a way of making the abstract concrete, thus enabling learners to more easily fit new concepts or procedures into their mental schemata or behavioral repertoire. This tactic has been invoked as long as humans have been engaged in conscious instruction, in order to transmit what Geary (2008) refers to as biologically secondary knowledge. People of the Neolithic era surely taught flint flaking and basket weaving by having their children watch closely as they demonstrated their techniques. Today's equivalent are the ubiquitous Internet how-to videos used by millions for learning tasks large and small.

An instructional activity falls into the category of *Demonstration* if it entails showing an example of a concept or procedure. It could be a teacher holding up pictures of a horse and an otter as examples of mammals. Or it could be behavior modeling, such as a sales trainer conducting a role-playing exercise, himself playing the role of the salesman making a pitch. Facilitators can also model the thinking process, such as solving math problems: "The teacher modeling and thinking aloud while demonstrating how to solve a problem are examples of effective cognitive support" (Rosenshine 2012, 15).

> *Demonstration*: A Facilitator (F) or some Instructional Resource (IR) playing the role of Facilitator displays and explains an Example (Ex) of some process,

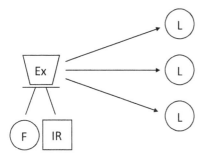

Figure 4.2 The Demonstration Communication Configuration. IR represents an Instructional Resource; EX represents an Example of the concept or behavior being demonstrated.

procedure, or other complex task to a number of Learners (L); the Facilitator controls the flow of communication (Figure 4.2).

Demonstrations play a crucial role in many types of learning by forging the link between abstraction and reality—such as the word "mammal" paired with pictures of familiar animals. For interpersonal skills and moral or spiritual goals nothing has more instructive clout than modeling the desired behavior.

On the other hand, demonstrations alone cannot be expected to carry the entire burden for skill acquisition. Repeated practice is a necessary follow-up: "Students need to spend additional time rephrasing, elaborating, and summarizing new material in order to store this material in their long-term memory" (Rosenshine 2012, 16). Further, for learners to gain ownership over the target knowledge, skill, or attitude they need to integrate it into their own repertoire, possibly through discussion, reflection, and self-expression.

Whole-Class Discussion

Learning by means of discussing the content with peers is a tactic that is supported by all theoretical perspectives. For behaviorists, discussion allows learners to practice using new knowledge under conditions of feedback from other learners. From a cognitivist perspective, discussion promotes active processing of the new knowledge, a necessary step for acquisition and long-term retention. For constructivists, learning is a process of constructing—individually and socially—meanings, meanings that are formed within a community of learners and hence require social negotiation with the group. The humanistic perspective seeks to develop self-actualized individuals through interaction with peers in a cooperative, supportive environment.

120 Communication Configurations and Methods

We distinguish between two different types of discussion based on two different patterns of communication—whole-class discussions and small-group discussions. In *Whole-Class Discussion*, the instructor remains in charge, leading the whole class in conversation, calling on one participant after another. The instructor as moderator controls the agenda and may encourage differing views to be voiced, cutting off conversation when a satisfactory end point is reached. By contrast, in *Small-Group Discussion* the participants are on an equal footing, deciding as a group how to proceed, sharing opinions as equals, and arriving at their own conclusions—all under the indirect supervision of the instructor.

> *Whole-Class Discussion*: A Facilitator (F) engages the whole class in a conversation in which Learners (L) take turns sharing information and opinions, with the Facilitator remaining at the center, setting the agenda and controlling the flow of communication (Figure 4.3).

One's ability to remember and *use* new knowledge depends on how deeply that knowledge is processed and talking about new concepts is an effective way to encourage the learner to think about the concept and to integrate it into one's repertoire. In most cases, discussion will be a break from the normal routine, giving participants a chance to shift attention, hear other voices, and perhaps ask questions or give opinions lurking in the backs of their minds. All learners, especially older ones, come to the classroom with their own life experiences and may welcome an opportunity to share those experiences with others.

Of course, some students will be uncomfortable with the shift into an activity that may be unfamiliar and may make them feel like they are being put "on the spot." Likewise, the instructor may also be apprehensive, as discussions are unpredictable and require instructors to surrender some control over the flow of information. To be effective, discussions of all types require preparation and thinking through contingencies beforehand.

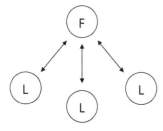

Figure 4.3 The Whole-Class Discussion Communication Configuration. The two-headed arrows indicate that communications flow to, from, and through the Facilitator.

Small-Group Discussion

To be a *Small-Group Discussion*, the facilitator must form the whole class into smaller groups and then step aside and allow the participants to take full control of the flow of information. The facilitator is responsible for logistics: when and where to meet, for how long, and with what rules of procedure. To have a fruitful discussion the participants need questions to answer, issues to discuss, or tasks to accomplish. With that logistical support they can enjoy the freedom to express their opinions and compare them with others' as they work toward accomplishing their goal.

> *Small-Group Discussion:* Two or more Learners (L) exchange information and opinions without the intermediation of a Facilitator; a Facilitator may set the agenda and control logistics, but Learners control the flow of communication within the group (Figure 4.4).

As mentioned above, all types of discussion have the benefit of encouraging learners to process new information, to integrate it into their own repertoire. In the case of distance education, Small-Group Discussion—conducted through chatrooms, e-mail, and discussion forums—is especially valuable because it may provide the only social learning venue for people who otherwise never meet. It not only helps distance learners feel part of a group, it also allows the "social negotiation" that constructivists view as vital to meaningful learning.

Even more than Whole-Class Discussions, Small-Group Discussions are prey to listlessness, argumentation, and wandering off-topic. They require extra preparation—possibly including some training and practice in how to perform effectively as a member of a task group—and supervision in order to stay on track and yield successful results.

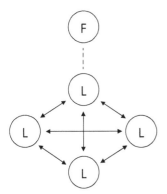

Figure 4.4 The Small-Group Discussion Communication Configuration. The two-headed arrows indicate that communications flow among the Learners; the Facilitator stands aside.

Tutorial

The *Tutorial* configuration, assuming an able tutor, is often considered the ideal teaching–learning configuration. It allows the maximum in individualization while requiring constant active participation by the tutee. In addition to formal student–teacher tutorials, other formats for this configuration include trade apprenticeships, on-the-job training next to a skilled practitioner, workplace mentoring, peer tutoring, and "writing buddies." The essence is a one-to-one rich interchange between a learner and another playing the role of facilitator.

> *Tutorial*: A person or device playing the role of Facilitator (F) interacts, intensively and substantively, one-to-one with a Learner (L) (or small group of Learners acting as one or taking turns); the Facilitator (tutor) and Learner (tutee) share control of two-way communication (Figure 4.5).

With just one learner to deal with, a tutor can remember and use past experience to cater to the tutee's needs, interests, strengths, and weaknesses. Suitably guided, the learner can remain actively engaged in processing new information: answering questions, raising new questions, finding connections with prior knowledge, and expressing their understandings in their own words, thus owning the knowledge.

The greatest drawback of the *Tutorial* configuration is its cost. In an era of mass education, only a small proportion of prospective learners could expect to receive actual tutoring from highly qualified tutors. Enlisting students to serve as tutors to other students—peer tutoring—has been developed as a reasonable substitute, replacing a costly professional tutor with an unpaid volunteer whose payoff is enhanced understanding of the subject matter for tutors themselves (Fisher and Frey 2019; Cohen, Kulik and Kulik 1982).

Repetition

One of the most powerful tactics for mastering new skills, whether cognitive, affective, interpersonal, or psychomotor, is to rehearse the new behavior repeatedly. The usual name for this activity is *practice,* but we choose the label *Repetition* for two reasons; first, to emphasize the importance of *repeated* rehearsal, and, second, to save the term *practice* to refer to the more generic notion of doing an activity or contemplating an idea, perhaps just once. In the more generic sense of *practice*, there is practice involved in many other configurations; for example: during Presentation, a

Figure 4.5 The Tutorial Communication Configuration.

learner may take notes, thus mentally practicing by restating the new ideas; during Discussion or Tutorial, a learner's responses may be rehearsals of their understanding of a new idea; during Expression, while writing an essay the learner is practicing when rethinking and restating his understanding of the new material.

In the *Repetition* configuration, we see the learner repeatedly performing all or part of the target skill. The need for repetitive drill is obvious in the case of psychomotor skills, such as in sports. But it is equally true for some types of cognitive skills, where overlearning is required for fluent performance—in reading, for example. In real life, most skilled performance requires a combination of cognitive, affective, interpersonal, and psychomotor abilities, practiced separately and together. As Rosenshine points out, "The best way to become an expert is through practice—thousands of hours of practice. The more the practice, the better the performance" (2012, 19).

We see Repetition in use when schoolchildren recite multiplication tables, and in the language lab, when learners practice the speech of a native speaker. Play rehearsal, musical instrument practice, and athletic training are all familiar venues for Repetition outside the classroom. Since repetitive drills are often perceived as boring, interest-arousing activities such as games are used to draw learners into repeated practice.

> *Repetition*: A Learner (L) performs repeatedly all or part of a specified Skill (S) in order to improve retention and proficiency (Figure 4.6).

Repetition can be done by the learner alone, but ideally with someone playing the role of facilitator (a role increasingly played by a computer program) to provide feedback on the performance. Alone, the learner is in control; with someone playing the role of facilitator, the teacher (or computer program) is typically in control.

Repetition is central to both behaviorist and cognitivist perspectives on learning theory. For behaviorists, when learners are repeating the desired behavior or attitude, they are increasing the likelihood of incorporating that skill into their repertoire, especially if the behavior is followed by reinforcers of some type. The cognitivist perspective recognizes that new information has to be processed in order

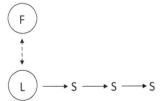

Figure 4.6 The Repetition Communication Configuration. The multiple Ss represents a mental or physical Skill that is repeated in order to be mastered.

to move from working memory to long-term memory, and the more episodes of processing under varying conditions, the surer the mastery.

On the other hand, repeated practice has some limitations. While repeated practice accounts for a fair amount of the variance in athletic performance, it accounts for a smaller amount of the variance in on-the-job performance that has a higher quotient of cognitive, affective, and interpersonal skills. In fields such as teaching or sales, innate ability plays a larger role. That is, in many professions—and even in athletics—people lacking the necessary intellectual or physical endowments can never achieve elite levels of performance, even with millions of repetitions.

Study

Both in formal and nonformal education, learners spend a large proportion of their learning time in independent study—reviewing notes, reading a textbook, browsing for new information on a topic, mentally rehearsing or attempting to memorize new material, or thinking about what is known and what remains to be learned. Information-processing research highlights the need to rephrase, elaborate, and summarize new information in order to commit it to long-term memory (Rosenshine 2012, 16). An appropriate configuration for these processes is *Study*, characterized by individual learners interacting with resources—instructional resources and their own inner resources. Examples of the latter include devising mnemonic aids and reflecting on personal experiences with the material being studied.

The *Study* configuration has risen in visibility in the age of distance education, when learners spend little to no time in traditional classroom activities, instead approaching cognitive skills largely through self-study and discussion with digital peers. The instructional resources they use may include e-textbooks, articles from online journals, podcasts, and Web videos.

> *Study*: A Learner (L) interacts with Instructional Resources (IR), or with Real-World Resources (RR), or with their own inner resources, without the direct supervision of a Facilitator (F), but often inspired or guided by someone playing the role of Facilitator. The Learner is in control of events, deciding exactly what to do and when to do it (Figure 4.7).

Going beyond rote learning to attain understanding of the new material and integration of it into one's own mental schema requires processing the information, such as summarizing the main ideas or drawing visual representations of those ideas, and such mental processes require individual effort. As indispensable as *Study* activities are for cognitive learning, they do not stand alone. Such learning becomes meaningful when it is complemented with discussion and testing in real-world contexts. Looking beyond the cognitive domain, affective growth requires social interaction; physical skills require practice with feedback; and interpersonal skills advance only in settings that allow communication with others.

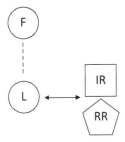

Figure 4.7 The Study Communication Configuration. The IR represents Instructional Resources and RR represents Real-World Resources; the two-headed arrow indicates that both may be controlled by the Learner and both can provide information to the Learner.

Expression

Many types of cognitive and aesthetic learning reach their height when learners take their new knowledge and skills and use them to express their thoughts, feelings, or artistic conceptions in tangible form—essays, research reports, drawings, graphs, paintings, photos, videos, prints, game designs, sculptures, dance routines, and the like.

Elementary forms of self-expression, such as oral conversations, are learned as biologically primary knowledge; they are not explicitly taught but rather evolve naturally in the home environment (Geary 2008). During formal education, people learn to communicate in a new and different form, developing biologically secondary communication skills through conscious instruction. Those receiving their oral or written communications do not necessarily share their background or experiences, so those communications have to be consciously crafted to bring the reader along.

In the *Expression* configuration, learners produce some tangible indication of what they have learned, in a form that may be verbal—such as an essay, book report, or speech—or nonverbal—such as a drawing, a graph, or a work of art—or a bodily movement—such as a dance or theatrical performance.

> *Expression*: A Learner (L) creates some type of tangible Product (P) in order to process some new knowledge, skill, or attitude; the experience may be structured and/or monitored by a Facilitator (F), but the Learner controls what is created and how it is created (Figure 4.8).

Technology has played a significant role in making *Expression* easier to accomplish and to share with others, allowing feedback to correct errors and sharpen thinking. The typewriter improved over handwriting; photocopy machines allowed easy sharing of print materials. By the late 1980s, computer-based word-processing software was inexpensive and usable enough to proliferate in educational institutions.

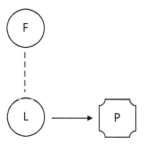

Figure 4.8 The Expression Communication Configuration. The P represents the tangible Product that is created by the Learner.

This made both the production of text and revision of text infinitely easier than it had been in the past. At the same time, audio and video recording technology were taking music, speech, and visual production out of the professional studio and into homes and classrooms. By the opening of the twenty-first century, the Web embraced all of these technologies, making multimedia presentations both easy to produce and easy to share around the world.

The Expression configuration, as valuable as it is for integration of knowledge and skills of all sorts, is not a configuration useful for receiving new knowledge. Other configurations—Presentation, Demonstration, and Study—are needed to provide the inputs to be processed through Expression.

Teaching vs. Learning Focus

Discussions of instructional events tend to focus on the activities of the facilitator or the teaching system (such as a computer program). Some configurations are teacher-centered: Presentation, Demonstration, and Tutorial. Others are more learner-centered: Discussion, Repetition, Study, and Expression. Historically, instructional theorists and practitioners alike have tended to give less attention to those activities that take place mostly outside the direct supervision of the facilitator. The situation has changed, thanks to the growing prominence of distance education, in which virtually everything takes place outside the direct supervision of the facilitator. The learner-centered half of the picture now has more light shining on it.

A Typical Lesson Employs a Variety of Configurations

It is important to point out that although communication configurations can be isolated in a "snapshot," they typically exist within a "movie," a constantly flowing and changing scene in which participants may move quickly from one configuration to another. As Rosenshine (2012, 19) points out, "research on cognitive processing supports the need for a teacher to assist students by providing for extensive reading of a variety of materials [i.e., Study], frequent review [i.e., Presentation], and discussion [i.e., Discussion] and application [i.e., Repetition] activities." Any given lesson may incorporate any or all of these configurations. The implementation of a variety of configurations within lesson development can be observed across all types of instructional levels and settings. We will give examples from three different realms—elementary education, higher education, and professional preparation.

Configurations in a Typical Lesson: Elementary School

An elementary school lesson might combine numerous configurations to maximize attention and motivation through brisk pacing and toggling between different sorts of activities. For example, a science lesson for second graders might cycle through many activities involving different configurations:

- The teacher begins by holding up a jar containing a tadpole (Demonstration) and asking children to guess what it is; individuals call out answers (Repetition in the form of recitation).
- She then states that the tadpole represents one stage in the life cycle of a frog and then announces the objectives of the lesson (Presentation).
- Using flash cards, the students then read new vocabulary terms in unison (Repetition).
- The teacher uses sketches on a whiteboard or a projected image to show all the stages in the life cycle of a tadpole (Demonstration).
- Pointing to images of each stage of life, students identify them in unison (Repetition).
- Students then work individually on worksheets to properly label the stages in the life cycle (Repetition in the form of recitation), which will serve as the assessment.
- Enrichment is a construction project: consulting a chapter in the textbook (Study) and using art supplies to create a frog life-cycle drawing (Expression).

Configurations in a Typical Lesson: Higher Education

In colleges and universities, professors often assume that their field of study has a "domain-specific" teaching methodology—a gut-level understanding of the best ways to impart the wisdom and know-how of their field to novices. No doubt, one will find vastly different sorts of activities going on in lecture halls, design studios, laboratories, and athletic fields. However, we contend that those activities can be described and classified into our common set of configuration categories.

For an example from higher education, we can look at an actual case study that was observed by one of the authors at a large university in the Midwestern United States. A mathematics professor on this campus, we will call him Prof. GV, had won numerous student-nominated awards for excellence in teaching. He had what could be called a cult following; his courses were always wait-listed, with hordes of students anxiously hoping to be admitted. We were eager to find out what methods he was using to attract this following. End-of-course evaluations revealed no technological secrets, only that he somehow was an amazing teacher who enticed students to love math.

A visit to his classroom revealed a well-equipped space, with smartboards, document cameras, and desktop computers for all. However, Prof. GV used none of these. Instead, he rolled out of the corner, out to the front of the room, a 1980s overhead projector. He began the lesson talking while showing a series of overhead transparencies (Presentation configuration); some contained diagrams and bulleted text to scaffold his lecture; others were blank, allowing him to work out solutions to problems by writing on the transparency with a marker (Demonstration configuration).

Students listened with rapt attention, occasionally interrupting the lecture with questions, which Prof. GV answered seriously and fully (Tutorial configuration). After the class, several students waited to talk further with Prof. GV (more Tutorial interactions). The students left with a set of problems to be worked out individually (Study configuration). They submitted their written solutions (Expression configuration) to Prof. GV, and he returned them with written comments and sometimes with oral remarks at the beginning of the next class (further Tutorials).

It was apparent that Prof. GV had refined his teaching techniques over the many years he had been teaching. His approach was based on carefully chosen and conscientiously executed methods that relied on communication configurations and technologies—speech, visual projection, printed and written materials—that had all the affordances he needed and were, in addition, inexpensive and reliable. Granted, he could have elicited student participation by using an electronic response device or by incorporating small-group discussion activities into the lecture. He could have expanded the size of his live audience and added a remote audience by using a microphone, document camera, and Web delivery system. But for the audience he was given and the objectives he was pursuing, he chose appropriate tools and used them effectively.

Configurations in a Typical Lesson: Professional Preparation

Professional preparation in fields such as law, medicine, and engineering is characterized by each field having a dominant paradigm for what constitutes proper training—what Shulman (2005) refers to as "signature pedagogies." Typically passed down from generation to generation, these pedagogical frameworks have survived the test of face validity—turning out practitioners who succeed professionally. Each field considers its methods to be "domain specific"; however we contend that each uses the same elements, the same building blocks, in constructing its pedagogy as every other group. For example, the legal profession famously employs the case method, using a "quasi-Socratic" questioning procedure during face-to-face classes. Yet, if we examine the concrete, operational procedures being used, we see elements common to other settings. For example, a law-school class using the case method might cycle through many activities involving different configurations:

- Before class, law students read the textbook (Study) and analyze the case being presented.
- Students then "brief the case," that is, they identify the facts, pinpoint the legal issues— "issue-spotting"—and state the ruling reached in the case. In doing this, they are "thinking like lawyers," and thus engaging in Repetition—practice of legal thinking.
- Pre-class preparation culminates in writing the brief (Expression configuration).
- In class, the main activity is a quasi-Socratic questioning of individual students—a form of Whole-Class Discussion. For the individuals being questioned, it is Repetition in the form of recitation—again, practicing "thinking like lawyers."
- During the discussion, individuals are taking notes (Expression), comparing the findings of the discussion with their own brief.
- After class, individuals review and summarize the conclusions reached in class, revising their briefs (Expression), often along with a study group (Small-Group Discussion).

What Communication Configurations Are Not

The concept of *communication configuration* is intended simply to give educators a common vocabulary for describing what they see and hear as they observe people engaged in instructed learning activities. Configurations are simply descriptions—snapshots—of how the participants are physically arranged and what patterns of communication are being used. The typology does not imply any sort of hierarchy. No configuration is better than another. Each has its strengths and limitations, which will be outlined in each of the subsequent chapters. Each has been the subject of voluminous research indicating the sorts of learning objectives for which it is well suited. It is not the purpose of this book to document that research extensively nor to argue for any particular approach to instruction. Each of the teaching–learning configurations can be employed in support of any number of different instructional approaches or instructional strategies.

Configurations Are Not Methods

The literature of pedagogy is rife with references to different "methods," and no two authors use the term with the same meaning. This issue is discussed at greater length at the end of this chapter, where an *instructional method* is defined as a generalized pattern of activities that affords learners the opportunity to exercise the cognitive and/or motor and emotional processes necessary to achieve some instructed learning objective.

A communication configuration, such as Presentation, does not comprise a method of instruction, nor a strategy, not even a tactic because it does not specify the learning activities that take place within the physical structure of the configuration. Each configuration can be employed within any larger strategy or method. For example, a lesson employing the so-called "discovery" method might well call for a prior reading assignment (Study) and a brief expository introduction (Presentation) before plunging participants into a simulation game that might include practice (Repetition) of desired decision processes. The game might be followed with a debriefing (Discussion) and a journal writing assignment (Expression), all wrapped up with the instructor's summary (Presentation). The overall approach of the lesson might be termed "discovery" or "experiential," but the lesson incorporates most or all of the different configurations.

Similarly, a lesson representing an expository approach might feature the lecture method, in which Presentation is the most visible configuration. But the lesson plan will very likely require learners to do textbook reading (Study), possibly a study group with other students (Discussion) and some sort of report or essay (Expression). The *method* could be called "lecture method," but the lesson employs multiple teaching–learning configurations.

For a final example, as discussed in Chapter 8, the Oxbridge system actually employs Study, Expression, and Demonstration in addition to tutorial activities. Again, one "method" but many communication configurations.

Next, in order to see how these configurations fit into the instructional toolkit, we will consider the various settings in which they may be used.

Different Configurations for Different Instructed Learning Settings

Affordances of Various Learning Settings and Configurations

Instruction can take place in a wide variety of settings; each can be said to offer certain communication *affordances* for instructed learning processes. We use the term *affordance* in the common, nontechnical sense of an opportunity offered by the setting to a learner (Rabinowitz and Shaw 2005). For example, a lecture hall offers the affordance of hearing verbal information, possibly supplemented with visual media.

Large-Group Setting: Presentation, Demonstration, and Whole-Class Discussion

One of the first settings that comes to mind when imagining instructional activities is the classroom. A common setting for the Presentation configuration, a classroom is a space artificially arranged to accommodate a large number of people, usually seated, in a way that they can comfortably see and hear a person speaking, and view any visual information—text, images, audiovisual shows, etc.—being presented by the latter. If the space and/or audience are so large that the person speaking is not clearly audible to all, a voice amplification system can be used—a microphone and one or more speakers; if the visual information being shown is not clearly visible to all—and if it is being shown via TV monitors or computer projection, this issue can be mitigated by setting up additional screens strategically positioned across the classroom space. This arrangement affords primarily the reception of spoken/verbal and visual information. The speaker could also pause to demonstrate a skill or facilitate the demonstration of various procedures or skills, for example, by bringing in people to role-play person-to-person interactions, common formats for the Demonstration configuration.

From time to time, the lecturer may pause and encourage audience members to ask questions or make comments. This interlude affords some few members of the audience to engage in interaction, sending as well as receiving verbal information; an extended dialogue of this sort would fit in the Tutorial configuration. However, if the lecturer wants to allow the audience to engage more actively with the ideas being presented or demonstrated, a Whole-Class Discussion can be launched, spontaneously or pre-planned. A Whole-Class Discussion does not require breaking the audience into smaller groups, so it can be conducted without finding other space or rearranging the furniture. The trade-off is that only a limited number of audience members get vocally involved, and the instructor controls the flow of conversation.

The lecture setup may be augmented by adding a whiteboard, which extends the affordances to written verbal information and symbols, such as flow charts, equations, and graphs. Whiteboards, even electronic ones, serve mainly for spontaneous instructor-generated material, highlighting key terms or roughly sketching visuals to illustrate relationships among concepts. More advanced hardware, such as overhead projection or tabletop video cameras allow large-screen projection of both spontaneously generated material and pre-prepared materials, such as outlines, drawings, graphs, and charts. All of these arrangements offer similar affordances: written verbal material and symbolic imagery, all augmenting spoken verbal information.

Various types of projectors can further enhance the sensory affordances of large-group instruction. Slides—whether based in film or computer media—may show photographic images, thus adding the affordance of pictorial information, as well as verbal and symbolic material. Motion images—from movie films to videos to computer animations—can add the affordance of moving pictures. If the still or motion images are accompanied by a soundtrack, one has a bimodal presentation, in which the verbal and visual channels can complement each other.

Of course, all these combinations of verbal and visual messages are only one-way presentations. If the presentation is live and face-to-face there is some opportunity to have limited two-way interaction; if it is prerecorded it is one-way only…until and unless there is a shift out of the large-group mode into individual seatwork or small-group discussion. Nevertheless, despite these limitations, the large-group presentation is an efficient way of disseminating new information.

Small-Group Setting: Tutorial and Small-Group Discussion

Recognizing the need for learners to process new information by thinking and talking about it, instructors can turn to the Small-Group Discussion or Tutorial configurations. These involve primarily verbal information exchange, although a tutor or discussant could demonstrate a skill or supplement their words with pictorial or symbolic images.

Dividing a large class into smaller clusters allows all members to participate in the conversation and many members to share in the control of the conversation. Learners can clarify their understanding of a topic by back-and-forth exchanges with fellow learners, people who are in a position to empathize with questions or confusions and help to resolve them. All learners, especially adults, value the opportunity to share their personal experiences and perspectives with others.

Collaborative learning requires the small-group setting. It may be implemented through Small-Group Discussion configuration or Tutorial configuration. These can be arranged in face-to-face meetings or in virtual meetings by means of online synchronous or asynchronous chatrooms or discussion forums. One-to-one discussions can be conducted face-to-face or online through e-mail, document sharing, discussion forums, or social media applications. Whatever the configuration, the benefit offered by collaborative learning is deeper learning due to the interactive, social, contextual, and student-owned processes activated by discussion.

Face-to-face tutorials, in which there is a rich exchange between tutor and tutee, lead both parties to respond to the material by talking about it. If tutor and tutee are peers, they are more likely to be empathetic about difficulties in grasping the point. Further, the tutor is likely to deepen their understanding of the subject matter through teaching it to someone else. If the tutor is in a superior position, he or she may provide a helpful model of how to think about the subject.

Tutorials delivered though digital devices allow the presentation of rich combinations of still and moving images, including lifelike simulations, in presenting new information or problems to learners. Learner responses, however, are limited to multiple-choice or verbal forms. Incidentally, note that most modules labeled as "Web tutorials" are nothing of the sort. They are usually recorded lectures or video demonstrations; there is nothing two-way about them.

Out-of-Classroom Realistic Setting or "Modified Reality" Setting: Repetition

Instructors may choose to send learners into real-world, natural settings for field studies, such as aquatic surveys, birdwatching, botanical or geological sample collecting, or archaeological digs. Here learners are in firsthand contact with real objects, people, and events. Internships and on-the-field athletic practices would be further examples. Somewhat more structured, but still authentic, settings include studio arts—practicing music, dance, painting, and sculpture. Settings such as these offer the affordances of three-dimensional, concrete experiences involving all the senses—not only seeing and hearing but also touching, tasting, and smelling.

Games and simulations represent a different sort of practice, a type that takes place in a simulated problem space, a "modified reality" setting. They allow learners to engage in interactions that are designed to look and feel similar to real-world settings, at least in some salient regards. They allow participants to explore a problem space, to understand the problem and try various possible solutions. Participants may work alone or as part of a team. Social simulations and team problem-solving activities mainly offer the affordance of verbal interaction. Multimedia games and simulations offer verbal, pictorial, and symbolic information and may add spoken verbal information, music, and natural sounds as complements.

Individual Study Setting: Study and Expression

The venue for instructed learning that is probably most often overlooked in discussions of instructional methods and strategies is that of individual private study. This sort of learning activity typically happens outside the classroom; hence, it often escapes the view of researchers, who tend to make observations of instruction by looking into classrooms.

In this setting the learner is engaged individually in interaction with various resources. Examples include homework, library research, textbook study, and worksheet exercises, all of which would be common formats for the Study configuration. The specific nature of the resources used determines what affordances are offered to the learner. Overall, being in private study gives the learner the time and space to contemplate, digest, and integrate new knowledge with prior knowledge.

Besides Study, the other configuration most closely associated with individual study is Expression; examples would include writing a term paper, keeping a journal, producing a podcast, or painting a picture. All are activities that require the learner to coalesce prior knowledge and lower-level skills with newly developing skills of creating something.

The most likely type of resource used in individual study for cognitive objectives is print material: books and worksheets. They support verbal learning, at least. Text materials often include visual complements, such as pictures and drawings (pictorial affordance) and charts and graphs (symbolic affordance).

If learners can be provided with analog and digital audiovisual media, such as slide-tape programs, PowerPoint presentations, and hypermedia programs they can experience simultaneous display of verbal and visual messages, affording the opportunity of bimodal learning: dual-coding of verbal and visual information. These tools would be especially helpful for mastering difficult concepts in chemistry, physics, biology, and other STEM fields.

Individual study can be enhanced further by augmenting the verbal information with motion media, in formats such as DVD analog recordings or digital media such as Web-based videos. These arrangements offer better opportunities to gain learner attention, hold it, and move from rote learning to deeper comprehension. Still, they are one-way communications, allowing little opportunity to test one's understanding or to move from inert knowledge to useful knowledge. Digital devices, whether desktop computers, laptops, pads, or smartphones, add another affordance lacking in textbooks and audiovisual recordings—true interaction with the material.

For expressive activities, learners are most likely to be turning to real-world resources rather than instructional resources—paint and brush, clay and potter's wheel, fabric and sewing machine, or possibly a dance partner. They afford learners the opportunity to touch, feel, and manipulate real objects, a necessary affordance for the mastery of higher-level psychomotor skills or combinations of psychomotor and cognitive skills.

Distance Education Setting

The evolution of distance education, from nineteenth-century correspondence study to twenty-first-century online learning, is told in Chapter 1. That discussion ends with a definition of distance education that we reiterate here:

> *Distance Education*: a program of some duration with specific learning goals, leading to formal recognition of achievement (such as course credit or professional certification), in which the learner is separated from the instructor and in which communication technologies facilitate dialogue between the remote student(s) and the instructor and possibly among the students themselves.

The fact that "the learner is separated from the instructor" in time and/or in space presents a particular challenge to this setting. Of course, distance students are also separated from other students and all the other resources and facilities that would ordinarily be found in a face-to-face educational institution. The easiest problem to overcome is access to resources for Study activities. Textbooks can be sent by mail. Other readings may be retrievable on the Web. Facilities for student Expression are also feasible to arrange. They are likely to own or easily acquire paper, pens, art supplies, and a computer to enable them to carry out Expression activities, either in terms of concrete products or online essays, discussion forum comments, or blogs.

Still there remains the challenge of compensating for the lack of a Facilitator. Centuries ago, nobody could have imagined that it would be possible to devise artificial means to replace many of the functions of the absent facilitator—presenting expert information, demonstrating new skills, observing practice exercises and giving appropriate feedback, arranging discussion with other learners, and grading learner performance. As it turns out, the information-presentation and demonstration functions have been relatively easy to replace, thanks to advances in printing and telecommunications media. Showing and telling could be recorded and transmitted to learners through broadcasting, audio and video recordings, or digital media transmitted over wired or wireless Web platforms.

It has been more challenging to provide for truly interactive Tutorial instruction, mental or physical practice that is observed by an instructor or mentor, who then provides appropriate feedback. Likewise, it has taken ingenuity and advances in software applications to arrange for effective Discussion activities among students. Finally, perhaps the most challenging task has been to find a way to facilitate hands-on Repetition activities with appropriate feedback for distance students—clinical labs, field experiences, social simulations, and the like.

Although much distance education—like much classroom instruction—remains fairly mundane and limited in its employment of the full panoply of teaching–learning methods, examples abound of cases in which ingenious means are used to implement innovative strategies in distance courses. Examples of each will be discussed in the respective chapters devoted to each configuration (Chapters 5 to 11).

Communication Configurations as the Building Blocks of *Methods*

Defining Methods

In Chapter 1, discussing the debate between Richard E. Clark and Robert Kozma, we pointed out that Clark contended that the active ingredient in media-comparison studies is not the medium but the *method*. At the time, Clark did not offer a clear definition of *method*, but in his original essay on the subject, "Reconsidering Research on Learning from Media" (Clark 1983, 449), he referred to a definition by Robert Glaser in Glaser's early attempt to outline the key elements of instructional design: "the conditions which can be implemented to foster the acquisition of competence" (Glaser 1976, 17), although Glaser did not give a name to this construct.

During the period of the so-called Clark–Kozma debate, the two primary participants never did agree on a definition of either *media* or *method*, which contributed to the rather long and inconclusive duration of the debate. However, Clark (1991) later paraphrased a definition proposed by Salomon (1979): "An *instructional method* is any way to shape information that activates, supplants, or compensates for the cognitive processes necessary for achievement or motivation." There are components of this definition that correspond with our own conception—and the generally held conception—of *method*, namely the activation of learning processes that lead to instructed learning. However, the wording "any way to shape information" is too broad and vague for our purposes.

More recently, Reigeluth and Carr-Chellman (2009) define *instructional method* as "anything that is done purposely to facilitate learning or human development" (21). Unfortunately, this definition suffers from being overly broad, as indicated by the same authors using the same definition for the larger concept of *instruction* (6). Other authors on this topic are even less helpful, using the term *method* very loosely without giving an explicit definition. We contend that a good definition begins with a concrete *genus*—the overarching category that encompasses everything falling under the *term*—and goes on to spell out limitations to exclude all things that are part of the genus but not of the term. For the *genus*, we reject overly broad and vague nouns, like "anything" or "any way." We are talking about a pattern of activities—visible actions of people. What sorts of activities? Those that afford learners the opportunity to exercise the faculties needed for successful learning. Therefore, we define *instructional method* as a generalized pattern of activities that affords learners the opportunity to exercise the cognitive and/or motor and emotional processes necessary to achieve some learning objective. We specify a "generalized" pattern of activities because we are not talking about individual instances but templates that can be applied to different subjects and different populations. We specify "cognitive and/or motor and emotional" processes to broaden our net to include all the domains of learning and to acknowledge that all learning has an emotional dimension. Like most of the definitions in this book, this is offered, not as a novel or stipulative definition, but rather as a precising definition. We intend to capture the generally held meaning of the term but in a way that is more precise than previous efforts.

Methods—Strategic and Tactical

Instructional methods can be applied at the strategic level—forming the framework for a lesson, even a whole curriculum, comprising a comprehensive, coherent educational program organized around specific principles from educational philosophy or psychology. Educators have designed whole elementary, secondary, college, and training curricula around a particular approach to pedagogy, that is, a method at the strategy level. Looking at individual lessons, strategic-level methods may provide the framework for the whole lesson, which might comprise a half-dozen or more instructional events, each with tactical-level methods applied. That lesson might, in turn, be part of a curriculum in which many different strategic-level methods and tactical-level methods are employed. Methods applied at the tactical level serve as components of a lesson plan. Any given lesson might include a number of different tactics to serve different components of the lesson—introducing new ideas, demonstrating how new skills are done, practicing the new skills, and so on.

Strategic-Level Methods

Strategic-level methods tend to follow one of two approaches—deductive or inductive. The deductive, or expository, approach is the one most people would incline toward as the default approach: Tell the learners the facts or principles you want them to learn; give them examples to illustrate The Point; then have them practice, working with the new knowledge or skill. In the inductive approach the learners are led to The Point through a process of discovery or construction of their own understanding of The Point. The process might include collecting data, analyzing and interpreting the findings, arriving at some generalizations about the phenomenon, and, finally, reaching a conclusion about the concept or principle being studied—the Point.

Strategic-Level Methods, Deductive

Deductive, or expository, methods focus on explicit presentation of content to learners through narration, explanation, and demonstration. They assume that information-processing is the core activity of learning, and that remembering new knowledge is a prerequisite to using it. Among the strategic-level methods that fit under the expository umbrella are:

- Self-Directed Learning (SDL)
- Direct Instruction (DI)
- Personalized System of Instruction (PSI)
- Individually Prescribed Instruction (IPI)
- Learning for Mastery (LFM)
- Peer Instruction
- Oxbridge system
- Programmed Tutoring
- computer-assisted intelligent tutoring.

Strategic-Level Methods, Inductive

Also known as inquiry learning, strategic-level methods of the "discovery" family focus on learning activities in which learners create, integrate, and generalize new knowledge by exploring a problem space. Learners are immersed in firsthand

138 Communication Configurations and Methods

experiences from which they are guided toward understanding of some specified concept, rule, or cognitive strategy—The Point. Among the strategic-level methods that fit under the inductive, or discovery, umbrella are:

- Montessori Method
- Problem-Based Learning (PBL)
- project-based learning
- case-based learning
- seminar
- Process-Oriented Guided Inquiry Learning (POGIL)
- cooperative learning.

Communication Configurations as Components of Methods

Methods, whether at the strategic level or the tactical level, must specify the teaching–learning arrangements under which learners may carry out the cognitive and/or motor processes necessary to achieve the specified objectives. Communication configurations comprise a convenient set of building blocks to construct these teaching–learning arrangements. Any given *method* can be viewed as some combination of communication configurations. This is easiest to see with tactical-level methods.

Tactical-Level Methods Based on Presentation

At the tactical level, methods that rely heavily on Presentation include:

- deductive or inductive concept teaching
- elaboration strategies—presenting analogies, paraphrasing, summarizing, comparing and contrasting.

Tactical-Level Methods Based on Demonstration

At the tactical level, among the methods that rely heavily on Demonstration are:

- Show and tell
- behavior modeling—live or recorded human performance is used to demonstrate a complex skill
- language laboratory—listening to the recorded voice of a native speaker.

Tactical-Level Methods Based on Whole-Class Discussion

At the tactical level, among the methods that rely heavily on Whole-Class Discussion are:

- interactive lecture—a lecture punctuated with pauses for audience participation
- Debriefing—whole-class discussion that follows use of a simulation or game.

Tactical-Level Methods Based on Small-Group Discussion

At the tactical level, among the methods that rely heavily on Small-Group Discussion are:

- buzz group—a brief, intense interchange among a few participants as a break-out session in a lecture setting
- collaborative learning—pairs or small groups interact, live or through synchronous discussion forums
- interteaching
- study groups—live or via video conferencing or Web conferencing.

Tactical-Level Methods Based on Tutorial

At the tactical level, among the methods that rely heavily on Tutorial are:

- coaching
- question and answer session
- cognitive apprenticeship—guided by a live mentor or computer-based simulation or tutorial.

Tactical-Level Methods Based on Repetition

At the tactical level, among the methods that rely heavily on Repetition, or repeated practice of the target skills, are:

- drill-and-practice
- guided practice—instructor teaches a small amount of new material, then supervises practice with feedback.

- recitation—learners study independently, then are called upon by the teacher to display what they have learned by reciting (or working a problem on the chalkboard) in front of the class.
- Instructional games—a structured, ludic activity in which participants follow prescribed rules that differ from those of real life as they strive to attain a challenging goal
- Instructional simulations—experiential activity involving learners in realistic problems in settings that are scaled-down versions of reality.
- Role-playing—learners play the roles of various types of people in order to practice interpersonal or communication skills under realistic conditions.

Tactical-Level Methods Based on Study

At the tactical level, among the methods that rely heavily on the Study configuration are:

- reading—reading assigned chapters in a textbook or class handouts
- listening—listening privately to an audio recording or podcast of spoken material
- watching—privately viewing an instructional video
- mnemonic devices—contrivances to aid memorization

Tactical-Level Methods Based on Expression

At the tactical level, among the methods that rely heavily on the Expression configuration are:

- note-taking
- book report
- research project or term paper
- Writing to Learn—involving the learner in doing a wide range of writing assignments in all areas of the curriculum
- Reflection—learners analyze their own internal cognitive processes and express them in speaking, writing or some other form, such as a drawing or cartoon.

Summary

Given the elements discussed in Chapter 3—facilitator, learner, setting, and resources—we can observe how these elements are arranged at different times, patterns that are distinguishable in terms of who is communicating with whom and in what direction the communication flows. Again, these things are visible and audible. We suggest that the multiplicity of instructional arrangements can be categorized into eight different "buckets," which we call communication configurations: Presentation, Demonstration, Whole-Class Discussion, Small-Group Discussion, Tutorial, Repetition, Study, and Expression.

This chapter asserts the claim that any time an instructional event is taking place, an observer could identify the basic elements that are present and could classify the activities as conforming to one of the communication configurations described above. Configurations can change from moment to moment throughout a lesson, and a group can be subdivided into smaller groups or individuals engaged in different configurations at the same time. Both face-to-face and distance education arrangements utilize the same set of configurations, although in different formats and in very different proportions. Most lesson objectives require putting learners through a succession of configurations as they move toward the learning goal, for example, starting with Presentation and Demonstration, moving into Discussion, then providing opportunities for Repetition—possibly in an interactive, experiential setting such as a simulation or game, followed by individual Study, possibly culminating in Expression, as with a project report or tangible product.

The chapter concludes with the concept of instructional methods, providing a definition, examples and an extensive list of commonly used methods, both at the strategic level and the tactical level. Methods can be viewed as consisting of some combination of communication configurations and hence can be classified according to which configuration is prominent in each method.

The following seven chapters deal with each of the communication configurations in turn. Each is examined in terms of its definition, its origins, its formats, its strengths and limitations, its best practices, and its possible incorporation into various methods.

Works Cited

Berliner, David C. 1983. "Developing Conceptions of Classroom Environments: Some Light on the T in Classroom Studies of ATI." *Educational Psychologist* 18 (1): 1–13.

Clark, Richard E. 1983. "Reconsidering Research on Learning from Media." *Review of Educational Research* 53 (4): 445–459.

Clark, Richard E. 1991. "When Researchers Swim Upstream: Reflections on an Unpopular Argument About Learning from Media." *Educational Technology* 31 (2): 34–40.

Cohen, Peter A., James A. Kulik, and Chen-Lin C. Kulik. 1982. "Educational Outcomes of Tutoring: A Meta-Analysis of Findings." *American Educational Research Journal* 19 (2): 237–248.

Davies, Ivor K. 1981. *Instructional Technique*. New York: McGraw-Hill.

Fisher, Douglas, and Nancy Frey. 2019. "Peer Tutoring: 'To Teach is to Learn Twice.'" *Journal of Adolescent & Adult Literacy* 62 (5): 583–586.

Gagné, Robert M. 1965. *The Conditions of Learning*. New York: Holt, Rinehart and Winston.

Gagné, Robert M. 1977. *The Conditions of Learning*. 2nd ed. New York: Holt, Rinehart and Winston.

Geary, David C. 2008. "An Evolutionarily Informed Education Science." *Educational Psychologist* 43 (4): 179–195.

Glaser, Robert. 1976. "Components of a Psychology of Instruction: Toward a Science of Design." *Review of Educational Research* 46 (1): 1–24.

Heinich, Robert, Michael Molenda, and James D. Russell. 1989. *Instructional Media and the New Technologies of Instruction*. 3rd ed. New York: Macmillan.

Heinich, Robert, Michael Molenda, James D. Russell, and Sharon E. Smaldino. 1996. *Instructional Media and Technologies for Learning*. 5th ed. Englewood Cliffs, NJ: Prentice-Hall.

Molenda, Michael. 1972. Instructional Design Basics, unpublished class lecture notes. Bloomington, IN.

Rabinowitz, Mitchell, and Emily J. Shaw. 2005. "Psychology, Instructional Design, and the Use of Technology: Behavioral, Cognitive, and Affordances Perspectives." *Educational Technology* 45 (3): 49–54.

Reigeluth, Charles M., ed. 1999. *Instructional-Design Theories and Models: A New Paradigm of Instructional Theory*. Vol. 2. Mahwah, NJ: Lawrence Erlbaum Associates.

Reigeluth, Charles M., and Alison A. Carr-Chellman. 2009. "Understanding Instructional Theory." In *Instructional-Design Theories and Models: Building a Common Knowledge Base*, edited by Charles M. Reigeluth and Alison A. Carr-Chellman, 3:3–26. New York: Taylor & Francis.

Rosenshine, Barak. 2012. "Principles of Instruction: Research-Based Strategies that All Teachers Should Know." *American Educator* 36 (1): 12–19, 39.

Salomon, Gavriel. 1979. *The Interaction of Media, Cognition, and Learning*. Mahwah, NJ: Lawrence Erlbaum.

Shannon, Claude E., and Warren Weaver. 1963. *The Mathematical Theory of Communication*. Urbana, IL: University of Illinois Press.

Shulman, Lee. 2005. "Signature Pedagogies in the Professions." *Daedalus* 134 (3): 52–59.

Smaldino, Sharon E., Deborah L. Lowther, and Clif Mims. 2019. *Instructional Technology and Media for Learning*. 12th ed. New York: Pearson Education.

Stodolsky, Susan S. 1988. *The Subject Matters: Classroom Activities in Math and Social Studies*. Chicago, IL: University of Chicago Press.

Presentation   5

We begin our survey of communication configurations with those that are most frequently employed in large-group classroom settings—Presentation, Demonstration, and Whole-Class and Small-Group Discussion. The first two, Presentation and Demonstration, are the most "teacher-centered" (as opposed to "learner-centered"), depending entirely on the instructor's selection of content, gathering of sources and materials, and choice of time and place of delivery.

Presentation Defined

Fitting into the category of Presentation are the many and varied ways facilitators transmit information to multiple learners simultaneously.

> *Presentation*: A Facilitator (F), or some Instructional Resource (IR) playing the role of Facilitator, conveys information one-way to a number of Learners (L); the Facilitator or Instructional Resource controls the flow of communication (Figure 5.1).

Facilitators are using the Presentation configuration when they are speaking or showing visual or verbal information, such as with an image projector or electronic slide show. The learning of verbal information can also profit from examples, verbal or audiovisual. Merrill (2002) emphasizes the value of *portrayal*—a visual or tangible example—as a complement to the presentation of new information: "Instruction is far more effective when it also includes the portrayal level in that the information is demonstrated via specific situations or cases" (48).

As we discuss below, the Presentation configuration can accommodate a wide variety of one-way communications. In addition, instructors can switch

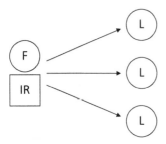

Figure 5.1 The Presentation Communication Configuration.

back and forth to other configurations during the course of a lecture. When instructors pause to pose a question and receive a response from an individual, they are switching to Tutorial mode. When they pause to allow discussion among the learners, they are switching to Discussion mode. Learners are in the Presentation mode as long as the pattern of one-talking-to-many is maintained. By definition then, individuals reading printed materials or watching videos are not participating in Presentation configuration, they are engaging in Study (see Chapter 10).

Formats Associated with Presentation Configuration

The most obvious format for employing the Presentation configuration is a lecture or any sort of oral presentation, the "most common method for training adults worldwide," according to Ruth Colvin Clark, highly regarded corporate consultant and research synthesizer (R. C. Clark 2015, 231). However, many other formats are encountered, both in live, face-to-face instruction and in online education settings. Other formats may involve a group of people, as in a panel discussion. Although the panelists might interact among themselves, it is still a Presentation from the standpoint of the audience—one source reaching many receivers. Some formats may involve no people at all, just still or moving images—with or without sound. If a speaker writes some text or draws some graphic images on a chalkboard or whiteboard, those displays would also be examples of the Presentation configuration.

Showing a video recording or slide set would take place in a Presentation configuration. In the definition above, this would be an example of "some Resource playing the role of Facilitator." In distance education settings, users who are viewing a slide set or video in a synchronous broadcast or videoconference are participating in a Presentation. If they are looking at the same material in a self-paced manner, stopping, starting, and reviewing as desired, they are in the Study configuration.

Examples of Formats for the Presentation Configuration

Verbal Monologue

A verbal monologue may be experienced live face-to-face or live via some broadcasting vehicle, such as radio, television, or Web videoconference. For example:

- lecture or speech, by instructor, student, or outside resource person
- tour guide's spiel
- museum docent's commentary
- sermons or moral lessons at church service.

Verbal-Audiovisual Monologue

A verbal-audiovisual monologue is like a verbal monologue, with the addition of audio and/or visual information sources, which may be presented live or in a recorded form. Many presenters include graphs, charts, photos, and video clips in their presentation in order to provide a concrete representation of certain facts or concepts in their lecture. Merrill (20022013) refers to such representations as *portrayals*. Like the verbal monologue, it can be experienced face-to-face or via some broadcast or Web vehicle. Examples:

- "chalk talk"—instructor talks and draws diagrams on chalkboard/whiteboard
- speaker uses overhead image projection
- lecture recital—musician talks about music, illustrating points by playing music
- PowerPoint presentation—speaker plus electronic slide set
- showing worked examples in mathematics on a chalkboard
- travelogue—speaker accompanies travel talk with film or video recording
- paintings made to inspire religious devotion or advocate a political viewpoint.

Recorded Audiovisual Showing

As indicated in the definition of Presentation above, learners can receive instructional messages from Resources directly, in a group setting or individually. When used individually, in the Study configuration, such resources usually consist of recordings combining auditory and visual messages. Such recorded material has traditionally been the "backbone" of distance-education courses, especially of contemporary MOOCs. When audiovisual recordings are received in a group setting, learners are in the Presentation configuration. A notable feature of recordings is that they preclude the possibility of asking questions or holding discussions of the material. Some examples:

- live lectures recorded for later playback
- instructional films and videos designed to support conceptual learning objectives
- movies made to promote a cause or drive home a social message
- animated simulations of concepts that are otherwise abstract
- Sesame Street animated video segments, combining song, dance, mime, and lyrics to convey a specific conceptual point (e.g., "C is for Cookie")
- recordings of music to support music appreciation
- audio (e.g., historical voices or song lyrics) or video clips (e.g., news stories or documentary reportage) inserted into lectures.

Group Performance

A group performance entails two or more people interacting among themselves for a didactic or persuasive purpose in front of an audience, live or at a distant reception site. It may be recorded in the form of a documentary or dramatic film. For example:

- panel discussion, debate, or symposium
- dramatic role-play or skit (not a Demonstration of a skill but a drama to make a didactic or propaganda point)
- didactic stage play, such as the "morality plays" of the Middle Ages, twentieth-century Chinese "revolutionary operas," or Sesame Street live-action skits between film segments
- choral performance of songs meant to be informational or persuasive
- filmed drama with propaganda purpose, such as *The Battleship Potemkin*.

Early distance education courses tended to rely on "canned" lectures as the backbone of the course, in the form of audio or video recordings or narrated slide presentations, as did the MOOCs of the 2010s. Traditional, university-based online courses nowadays are more likely to use electronic textbooks, instructor-prepared notes, or digital slide presentations as the backbone. When they are used by individual learners at home on an "on-demand" basis, they would be Resources being used in the Study configuration (discussed in depth in Chapter 10). That is, the material is under the control of the learner; users may stop, start, or repeat as desired. The heavy reliance on the Study configuration is one of the hallmarks of distance education versus face-to-face (F2F) education.

Indeed, it is increasingly difficult to categorize courses or programs of study as either "distance" or "F2F." First, conventional F2F courses have always included some use of Resources other than the instructor and various forms of out-of-class study. Second, nowadays many F2F courses/programs require students to do some of their study online, referred to as *blended learning*. Third, many F2F courses these days use learning management systems (LMS) to house instructional materials and facilitate course grading, further blurring the boundaries between mediated and F2F instruction. Finally, courses that are primarily online experiences, including some MOOCs, provide F2F opportunities for students, setting up "meet-ups" at central locations for F2F discussion or group project work.

As discussed in Chapter 1, it is tempting to get caught up in the enthusiasm over the latest new "trending" media format or program type (such as MOOCs), but the fact is that any format—analog or digital—is fully capable of doing the job of information presentation. Delivery systems certainly differ in terms of their logistical advantages: One may be cheaper for a specific setting; another may reach more people simultaneously; another may have lower production costs; and another simply may be more convenient. For example, in a distance education course, it might be desirable to bring the voice of a guest expert into the class. It would usually be more cost-efficient to make a recording of that person, to be played back in future renditions of the course than to ask the person to come back and perform live again and again. The choice boils down to time, cost, and context factors, not inherent superiority. These formats differ in many ways, but they share in common the capacity to carry one-way transmissions of information to numbers of learners simultaneously.

Note again that, in our terms, it is not the speech, slide set, YouTube video, or broadcast program that constitutes the Presentation configuration. Rather, these are *resources* that could be used in a variety of settings, in a variety of communication configurations. We are using the term *Presentation* to refer to the arrangement among facilitator, learner, and resources—the physical arrangement of one information source sending messages out to an audience of multiple people.

The Presentation Configuration Seldom Stands Alone

We are not suggesting that the use of the Presentation configuration—or any other configuration—would or should constitute the whole of any lesson. As described in Chapter 4, each instructional event would be a "snapshot" taken from the "movie" of the live, flowing lesson and each instructional event might employ a different configuration. That is, any well-designed lesson will carry the learner through a series of experiences suitable for each stage of the instructed learning process. Robert Gagné (1985), for example, proposed that a comprehensive lesson entails several stages (which he calls *events of instruction*):

- gaining attention
- informing learner of the objective and activating motivation
- stimulating recall of prior knowledge
- presenting the stimulus material
- providing learning guidance
- eliciting performance
- providing feedback and assessing performance

- and enhancing retention and transfer (304).

The second-grade science lesson described in Chapter 4 featured a rapid sequence of activities in different configurations: Demonstration (to gain attention, inform about objectives, and motivate), Repetition (to elicit performance), Presentation (to present new stimulus material), Repetition (to elicit performance), Demonstration (to provide learning guidance), Repetition (more performance with feedback), Study (enhancing retention), and Expression (for assessment and enhancing transfer).

Evolution of Presentation

It is difficult to know for certain what instructional methods were used in early societies, especially before the development of written language. The earliest glimpses we have of organized education outside the home derive from Egypt and Sumer, where the earliest forms of writing evolved. Men who knew how to write and read taught literacy skills mainly by reciting texts and having students copy them. By the time of the Classical period of Greece, the 400s BC, itinerant scholars who called themselves Sophists used lectures and the "Sophistic dialogue," a form of group discussion (Saettler 1990, 24–26). In Rome during the Republic period, dictation of text by the teacher and choral recitation by students was certainly prominent, as was private reading followed by individual recitation before the teacher (Robinson 1965, 111). Another of the early documented uses of lectures for educational purposes is the Yeshiva, established at least by the third century AD. This Jewish institution, established to encourage the study of traditional religious texts, uses the *chavrusa*—a one-to-one student interchange—as the primary means of study. However, the yeshiva system also relies on a daily *shiur*—an in-depth lecture given by a rabbi well-versed in the Torah; and students also attend a weekly *shiur* summing up the week's study of a given topic (*Encyclopedia Judaica*, 2nd ed., s.v. "yeshiva").

The contemporary concept of the lecture stems from the practices in the medieval university, where books (and professors) were in short supply. To accommodate large numbers of students, the instructor would read from an original source (*lecture* means "reading") while the students copied the material for later private reading (Saettler 1990). Over time, as books became more readily available, the lecture evolved into the instructor's commentaries on the text.

The lecture method was adapted to schooling for children by the great Czech pedagogical innovator, Johan Amos Comenius (1592–1670). As he spells out in *Didactica Magna* (The Great Didactic Art), the classroom itself was arranged so that the teacher was clearly visible and audible, and the master teacher introduced new material through oral presentation (Comenius and Keatinge 1967). Learners were divided into groups of ten (*decuria*), each of which was overseen by an aide, who followed the methods modeled by the master teacher. This leveraging of the master teacher made schooling accessible to larger numbers and at an affordable cost, one of Comenius's great utopian aims.

In the eighteenth and nineteenth centuries, as the psychological bases of pedagogy were being established, no theoretician was advocating for the lecture as the ideal format for learning—quite the opposite. Nevertheless, by the end of this period the lecture was firmly ensconced as the principal experience of the school day, at all levels beyond elementary school, in all parts of the Western world. How did this happen? The answer is not clear or singular. At the older European universities, the lecture was well established as a core activity going back centuries, as already described. By modern times, the student experience at most European universities consisted of little more than attending lectures and taking end-of-year examinations (except in Germany, where research and laboratory work held sway, and Great Britain, where tutorial and seminar predominated). The colleges that sprang up in colonial America, originally boxed into the English classical curriculum, were revolutionized in the late 1700s by a wave of academics inspired by the Scottish Enlightenment at the universities of Glasgow and Edinburgh. They came to America as missionaries for the liberal, humanistic, and democratic spirit that was making Scotland a leader in science and industry (Herman 2001). New colleges sprang up faster than expert professors were being produced. They opened their doors to all qualified students, creating a torrent of demand that necessitated a larger ratio of students to faculty than the English tutorial system, pushing educational method toward group lectures rather than tutorial. This trend gained steam after the American Civil War when federal land grants helped plant large universities in each of the growing number of Western states.

The Cognitive Science and Neuroscience of Auditory and Visual Learning

Educationists at least as far back as Comenius in the seventeenth century discussed the advantages of employing visual images in the task of promoting understanding of verbal texts. Later generations of educators, inspired by Comenius, joined him in challenging the hegemony of the Word in education, or, as they called it, *verbalism*—parroting words empty of substance. They advocated supplementing verbal instruction with auditory and visual stimuli, although the scientific basis for this was still sketchy.

Comenius's illustrated textbook, *Orbis Sensualium Pictus* (The Visible World in Pictures), published in 1658, featured full-page copperplate prints that showed several related images within a realistic context, such as fishermen using different devices to catch fish (Comenius 1967). These illustrations were placed on pages facing printed texts discussing "fishing," allowing the learner to read the text and easily refer back-and-forth to the pictures as needed. As discussed in Chapter 1, some would call this *multimedia learning*, although we prefer *bimodal* or *multimodal*. Regardless of how this concept is labeled, the neurological processes behind it are anything but simple. To appreciate the complexities of creating the content that is delivered in the Presentation configuration, it is helpful to understand a bit about the cognitive science and neuroscience underlying the processes of learning from auditory messages and visual messages, and later, both combined. We explore these underlying factors in this chapter, Presentation, but the processes of learning by hearing and seeing are common to all of the communication configurations, so there is no need to repeat this story in later chapters.

Sensory Processes

It was not until the twentieth century that researchers understood the mechanisms that allowed people to perceive, process, and understand information presented through any symbol system, much less multiple ones at once. To begin with, neuropsychologists define *sensory modalities* as the several categories of impressions triggered by external stimuli—roughly speaking, the five senses: seeing, hearing, smell, taste, and touch (includes temperature, pain, and pressure). Each of these sensory modalities consists of a complex chain of electrical and chemical signals that flow through the sensory systems and into the brain (Ivry 2009). Of course, humans experience perceptions through many sensory modalities at the same time, whether we are consciously aware of all those signals or not. This constant "multimodal perception" means that many regions of the brain have to work together to organize these overlapping signals. Thus, when we sit in a classroom and contemplate a bar graph projected on a screen, we form a memory of that concept that includes not only the look of the graph and the meaning of the accompanying words but also the smell of the room, the sound of the speaker's voice, the feel of the chair, and even the temperature of the room, especially if it is notably hot or cold. The goal of the instructor is to ensure that the informational content is more salient than the other sensory perceptions and, therefore, that it is stored in a way that it will easily be retrieved when needed.

Of all the sensory modalities, seeing and hearing are the ones that carry most of the information-transmission burden in the instructional process. We are so used to seeing and hearing simultaneously that we must consciously step back to examine the properties of each separately.

Auditory Learning

The spoken word is the basis of virtually all instruction. Until the invention of writing, there was no other way of conveying information from one person to the next, one generation to the next. The ear has long been the portal of human learning. The printing press eventually allowed the storage and retrieval of visual information—words and pictures—in a form readable by the eye; later, digital storage and retrieval made those words and pictures transmissible without moving books from one place to another, making them quickly and cheaply available to many people dispersed in many places. Nevertheless, even in an age of abundant visual media, auditory transmission of speech, music, and other sounds retains a prominent place in the instructional tool kit.

For a brief overview of the neuroscience behind auditory learning, we will confine ourselves to the processing of human language. Sound waves produced by speech travel from the outer ear to the middle ear to the inner ear, where they are transduced into electrical signals. Those signals are primarily processed in the auditory cortex (part of the temporal lobe, near the center of the brain). From there, information appears to follow two different pathways for further processing. The ventral stream ultimately connects to the middle temporal gyrus, responsible for sound recognition and extraction of meaning from sentences. The dorsal stream leads to the inferior frontal gyrus, responsible for verbal working memory and speech production. Recent fMRI observations have tended to support this model, although the degree of specialization of the "two streams" is downplayed in favor of a more holistic "give-and-take" view (Kraus and White-Schwoch 2015).

Language Comprehension

As language originates as an auditory phenomenon, it is not surprising to find that the area controlling language comprehension is adjacent to the auditory cortex, where the parietal lobe meets the temporal lobe, known as *Wernicke's area*, since its discovery by Carl Wernicke in 1874. More recently, fMRI observations have shown that language comprehension occurs more broadly in the temporal lobe (Poeppel, Idsardi and van Wassenhove 2008). Indeed, as we discuss below, it involves many parts of the brain.

Language Production

Language production is usually localized in the left cerebral hemisphere. Because this function is closely linked to movement of the mouth and tongue, it is not surprising to find that it is located next to the mouth-control area, the precentral gyrus, traditionally referred to as *Broca's area* after Pierre Paul Broca, who identified it in 1861. More recent fMRI observations have shown that other nearby areas are also involved, hence the new term, *Broca's region*. This region is also involved in interpreting hand gestures, including sign language. Further, recent fMRI observations have also indicated that the areas around Broca's region are involved in working memory, for nonlinguistic as well as linguistic tasks (D'Esposito et al. 1999).

Audio in Learning Domains Other Than Language

Indeed, vast domains of human learning *require* auditory transmission: musical performance, foreign language acquisition, driver education, flight training, sports training, medical diagnoses of organ function—such as listening to the heart and lungs, and any other learning situation in which sound discrimination is paramount or in which the learner cannot be reading while learning. This includes the whole realm of cognitive learning for children and adults who have not mastered the skills of reading.

While some learning tasks demand audio resources with specific qualities, such as musical compositions, foreign language utterances, or engine noises, information delivered through human speech fulfills the need in many other cases. Even though speech is ephemeral, we use it because of its unmatched expressive power. The human voice can create a mood, appeal to emotions, amuse, sadden, and persuade like no other medium (Winn 1993, 117). Thus, audio resources can play a number of roles in instruction: Speech can convey verbal information and create an emotional link to that information; music can be presented as a performance or it can be used as an adjunct, directing listeners' attention toward specific points; real sounds can serve as examples for discrimination practice while artificial sound effects can, like music, punctuate the narration, directing attention to key points.

Using Audio Resources

As ubiquitous as audio resources are, nevertheless there is little guidance that educators can glean from research in deciding how to best shape auditory messages (Calandra, Barron and Thompson-Sellers 2008, 589). For example, one of the most popular guides to instructional design (Morrison et al. 2013) devotes six pages to text layout guidelines and six to pictures and graphics, but none to audio resources. Barron (2004) provides a comprehensive compilation of research on the use of the spoken word in instruction but offers few design guidelines that are not highly conditioned. This becomes more understandable when we consider how complex is the neurological process of auditory learning, as described above. According to Kraus and White-Schwoch (2015, 643), "the auditory system should be thought of as a distributed, but integrated, circuit." They describe the auditory learning process as one that engages cognitive, sensorimotor, and reward systems functioning together to interact with other neural modules—as discussed in Chapter 3—to constantly remodel the state of the mind, which is the more physically accurate way to think of learning.

Visual Learning

The Cognitive Science View

The early basic research on visual perception was done outside the field of education. One relevant strand of visual learning research began in Germany with Gestalt psychology, precursor to cognitive psychology, pioneered by Max Wertheimer (1944) and elaborated by Kurt Koffka and Wolfgang Köhler. They were attempting to describe how humans perceived stimuli and used cognitive processes to understand and solve problems. Another strand of cognitive research, focusing on the formation of mental models, was begun by Kenneth Craik (1943) in England, and elaborated by Johnson-Laird (1983). Meanwhile, Canadian Allan Paivio was doing studies of how words and pictures are processed, developing what became known as dual-coding theory (1971). Generalizations gathered from these sorts of basic research were compiled by American audiovisual researchers, Malcolm "Mac" Fleming and Howard Levie (1978) in the form of message design principles, later updated to include a growing body of literature (Fleming and Levie 1993).

The Neuroscience View

More recently, with the advent of computer-mediated imaging devices, cognitive science findings are able to be tested by neuroscience methods—observing the electrical patterns in the brains of living subjects. We must preface our overview of insights from cognitive neuroscience by reminding ourselves that learning through the sensory modality of *seeing* includes reading—the decoding of verbal texts—as well as the interpretation of realistic and graphic images. Perception of any visual images—images or printed words—begins with light passing through the cornea and lens onto the retina, where the image is transduced into electrical pulses, which pass along the optic nerve to the visual cortex, the largest system in the human brain, located in the occipital lobe of the primary cerebral cortex, the most posterior region of the brain. Making sense of the incoming stimuli requires several steps—recognition, categorization, and encoding. The processed information from the visual cortex is subsequently sent to other regions of the brain to be analyzed and utilized. As described above in regard to auditory processing, there appear to be two main pathways that visual messages follow. According to Goodale and Milner (1992), the ventral, or perceptual, stream computes a detailed map of the world from visual input, which can then be used for cognitive operations (which may help explain why we say "I see" when we comprehend something). The dorsal, or action, stream transforms incoming visual information to the requisite head-centered coordinate system for skilled motor functioning. This specialization allows the brain to recognize objects and patterns quickly without a significant conscious effort, leaving other cortical regions free to perform other computations such as those responsible for executive functioning and decision making. In other words, you can duck away from the rock thrown at your head while trying to understand what is happening.

New visual information needs to be stored in memory in a way that it can be retrieved when needed. This process is aided, according to schema theory, by preexisting *schemata*—mental structures or frameworks (Rumelhart 1980). The new information is easy to store and retrieve if it fits into the learner's existing mental framework. Thus, people can organize new perceptions into schemata quickly and automatically without conscious thought as long as they fit. Unfortunately, since schemata have a tendency to resist change, even in the face of contradictory information, one of the difficult tasks of educators is to help learners break out of the mental boxes that may be preventing them from understanding new concepts.

In any event, as we will discuss below under dual-coding theory, verbal decoding and image interpretation entail different neural processing systems. We revisit this important point in our concluding thoughts in Chapter 12.

Reading

The comprehension of written text involves a number of brain regions, the temporal lobe—for phonological awareness and discriminating sounds—and the frontal lobe, especially Broca's region, as discussed above regarding language comprehension. Since reading comprehension requires speech comprehension, all the auditory processes discussed above—such as Wernicke's area—are pertinent. Indeed, recent neuroscience research finds that reading involves activity in four lobes—temporal, frontal, parietal, and occipital—across both brain hemispheres. In addition, reading depends on pathways in the white matter—nerve tissues surrounded by a white myelin sheath—found below the surface of the brain. Especially important are the white-matter pathways that connect the language centers with the visual information centers (Yeatman et al. 2012). These pathways strengthen as children grow older and practice the subskills associated with reading (e.g., decode single words, expand vocabulary, and understand sentences).

Writing

Although writing clearly is part of the Expression configuration (Chapter 11), we explore its neurological bases in order to round out our overview of the cognitive science and neuroscience underlying different learning tasks. Given that writing is dependent on (spoken) language comprehension, language production, and fine motor skills, it is not surprising that it entails cooperation from several regions of the brain, especially the left temporal lobe (Wernicke's area for receptive speech) and the left frontal lobe (Broca's region for expressive speech) and another area, known as *Exner's writing area*, named for Sigmund Exner who identified this area in 1881, which is located adjacent to Broca's region. Exner's area translates auditory images transferred from the language areas into the motor impulses that enable writing (Joseph, n.d.). It appears that there are at least two stages involved in writing: (1) a linguistic stage for translating auditory and visual information into symbols for letters and numbers; and (2) a motor-expressive stage for activating the hand and finger movements of writing. Coordination requires extensive interconnections between Broca's region and Exner's area (Joseph, n.d.).

Visuals in Other Learning Domains

So far, we have dwelt on the reading of verbal material as a principal use of the eye—the sensory modality of vision. Of course, myriad other types of visual imagery play an enormous role in every domain of learning—cognitive, affective, interpersonal, and psychomotor skills. One of the clearest rationales for the role of visuals in the cognitive domain was offered by General Semantics, a field conceived by Korzybski (1933) and interpreted by Hayakawa (1941). One of its primary principles was expressed in the epigram, "the map is not the territory," pointing out words are mere symbols for the things we want to talk about. The General Semanticists emphasized that the more abstract your representation, the greater latitude you leave for misinterpretation. The only sure way to communicate accurately is to show the thing you are referring to, or at least a visual representation of it. Regardless of any special merits of visuals, they can complement verbal presentations by providing listeners with *concrete referents*—images of things—that words alone cannot convey. For someone who has never seen an ostrich, a picture quickly accomplishes what a thousand words struggle vainly to do.

Regarding the affective domain, there is an unspoken affective objective in every instructor's mind—that students should appreciate and value the subject matter. This is a prompt to make the instructional conditions, especially the resources that are used, as appealing as possible. This includes incorporating graphics to illustrate abstract relationships, photographs to illustrate people and places, and videos to portray ideas realistically. In the 1920s when motion pictures were an experimental notion in education, numerous large-scale studies were conducted to discover what films did well and not so well. One major finding, which today seems self-evident, is that films are most useful when they depict events that require motion in order to be understood, such as historical events or dynamic physical processes (F. N. Freeman 1924, 77–78). Further, it was found that films made the biggest impact when they used the format of a drama. Similarly, a photograph can pack a powerful punch if it contains dramatic content. Compare one photograph of the horrors of a Nazi death camp with a thick volume of written description. Humans do not separate their emotional responses from their intellectual responses; they blend together. Successful visual representations, like successful speeches, have high impact when they hitch their informational message to a compelling story.

Interpersonal skills rely on real-life practice to master; but along the way, behavior models shown in video clips are an effective way to portray desired behaviors. Psychomotor skills range from handwriting to on-the-job tool use to team sports. These types of skills, perhaps more than others, depend on diagrams, photos, and action videos for learners to observe and emulate the target skills.

Combining Auditory and Visual Messages

A theory that has proven to be quite robust posits that humans use two distinct types of codes—pictorial and verbal—for representing information in the brain (Paivio 1971). This *dual-coding theory* proposes that visual and verbal information are processed differently (analog codes for images; symbolic codes for words and numbers) and along different pathways in the brain, creating separate representations for information (Sternberg and Sternberg 2002, 281). Experiments using positron emission tomography (PET) have supported Paivio's theory. However, they have found that both visual and verbal stimuli activate *both* of the separate pathways, to some extent, suggesting that the executive control function of the brain selects a combination of pathways depending on the nature of the mental task (Mazoyer et al. 2002).

"Multimedia" (or Multimodal) Learning

Coding a message two or more different ways increases the chance of remembering that item compared to coding it only one way. This simple idea is at the heart of so-called "multimedia learning," discussed as a problematic construct in Chapter 1. As we pointed out in Chapter 1, those researching this topic define multimedia learning as simply "learning from words (e.g., spoken or printed text) and pictures (e.g., illustrations, photos, maps, graphs, animation, or video)" (Mayer 2014, ix). As Mayer goes on to say, these conditions are met when a lecturer draws a diagram on a chalkboard during a lecture or when a student reads a textbook with illustrations (Mayer 2014, 2–3). We would prefer to term this condition as bimodal learning (two sensory modalities).

The concept of using words plus images to synergistic effect might seem quite straightforward, but matters actually become quite complicated when auditory signals are combined with visual signals in different forms, as when learners are viewing a slide show with a narration (the sensory modality of hearing—linguistic) and slides that include both text and images (the sensory modality of seeing—linguistic and pictorial). This now becomes a multimodal condition.

Each word or image is considered an external representation of an idea (which the designer hopes will become an internal representation within the learner). As Schnotz puts it, "These representations can take different forms, such as spoken text, written text, maps, drawings, graphs, and sound" (2014, 75). Each representation, auditory or visual, can, in Schnotz's terms, serve as a description or a depiction. Merrill makes the same point but uses the terms telling and showing (Merrill 2013, 71). Descriptions frequently take the form of words, spoken or written. Depictions may take the form of pictures, graphics, or models—representations that have some resemblance to the thing pictured (Schnotz 2014, 76).

Each type of representation is itself quite complicated neurologically. Cognitive science research suggests that when we are reading or listening to verbal information (descriptions) the brain actually is processing several levels of representation—from comprehending the sounds of the words, to determining the conceptual meaning of the words, to blending the elements into a verbal proposition—a sort of logical equation of the ideas in the text (Schnotz 2014, 77). Likewise, when looking at a picture (depiction) the brain is again processing several levels of representation—from simply perceiving the image to forming a visual mental model of the thing depicted. To analyze the instructional issues involved in different bimodal and multimodal combinations we need to scrutinize each problem separately.

Spoken Words vs. Written Words

Mentally interpreting messages that simultaneously present auditory linguistic information (description) and visual linguistic information (description) raises the problem of split attention (Mayer and Moreno 1998). That is, listeners must choose between paying attention to the visible words on the screen or the audible words, possibly missing important information from both as the speaker quickly goes on to the next slide. To reduce the possible confusion, this condition should be avoided, or at least the two messages should be highly consistent with each other (Fleming and Levie 1993); for example, just putting a few key words on the screen while speaking a whole sentence that includes those key words.

Spoken Words vs. Images

The problem of split attention arises again if a speaker is talking about one thing (description, auditory) while showing a projected image (depiction, visual) of something different. The listener has to choose to attend to one signal or the other, perhaps trying to make sense of the visual image, meanwhile ignoring the oral narration. Imagine a lecture about Union army uniforms in the American Civil War while showing a portrait of a Confederate army general (a slide left over from an earlier talking point).

Written Words vs. Images

Consider the case of a lecturer projecting a slide showing a graph along with written text explaining the graph (assume the lecturer stays silent to allow reading the slide). Viewers again have to decide how to split their attention between the visual description and the visual depiction. They will probably scan back and forth, hoping to grasp the point before the slide changes. What is happening neurologically is that all the information must enter working memory through the visual pathways, forcing the visual processing system to switch between verbal visual feature analysis and graphemic input analysis (Schnotz 2014, 89). The recommended solution to this problem is that visual presentations should be accompanied with vocal narration rather than printed text. Mayer (2014, 134) dubs this the modality principle. However, even this generalization is limited to live presentations. When learners are in the self-study mode and have time to view and read at their own pace, and to review the material as needed, printed text is superior to audio narration.

Words plus Images

Words and images work together supportively if the words and pictures are semantically related to each other and if they are presented close to each other—spatially in a textbook or temporally in a lecture. Schnotz refers to these as the coherence condition and the contiguity condition (Schnotz 2014, 89). The coherence principle was stated succinctly earlier by Winn (1993, 118): "When narration accompanies a message in another modality, the relationship between the two messages must be strong and apparent."

Other design principles for the Presentation configuration can be found in Fleming and Levie (1993) and Mayer (2014). Perhaps the wisest advice is given by Winn:

> Even if it were possible to develop an exhaustive list of principles to guide the message designer directly in a reliable and consistent manner, one might question whether this might not ultimately be self-defeating. Design well done is a dynamic and creative process, not a mechanically applied technique. All the principles in the world cannot guarantee that what is designed will be effective, attractive, motivating, or even acceptable.
>
> *(1993, 119)*

In the end, we can conclude that there is no inherent instructional benefit in appealing to any particular sensory modality or employing any particular combination of media. The success of any instructional intervention depends on providing the learners whatever instructional conditions—including linguistic and pictorial representations—they need to master the task.

Strengths and Limitations of Presentation

Strengths

The Presentation configuration is virtually ubiquitous in live classroom instruction because instructional objectives, whether cognitive, affective, interpersonal, or psychomotor, almost always entail imparting some new information. Transmitting the information is the first step of a process that must also include opportunities to practice new skills with feedback and may include other activities to improve retention and transfer. The information that is transmitted may be verbal, visual, auditory, or some combination. All of these types of information can be conveyed efficiently to large groups in the Presentation configuration. So, efficiency is the first strength of Presentation, but there are many others, detailed here.

Efficiency

First and foremost, presentations are time- and cost-efficient vehicles for simply conveying information. One sender can reach a large number of receivers with information at one time, especially if the message is amplified acoustically or through communications media. And, as the saying goes, "Talk is cheap." An oral message can be improvised with little preparation and transmitted at little cost. Little wonder that it is the most common mode of instruction. In many areas of the world, printed material may be scarce and expensive, or literacy limited, so a lecture may be the only practical way of informing listeners of vital information. In poor rural areas, radio broadcasts, for example, about crop diseases, have proven to be life-saving channels of information. Even in wealthier settings, the Presentation configuration can reach more students at lower cost than any other. In fact, in corporate training, the Presentation configuration is so pervasive that it has become necessary for instructional designers to remind trainers that "Telling Ain't Training" (Stolovitch and Keeps 2002). But if the objective is simply the comprehension and retention of some information, a Presentation activity that is well structured and well executed can be effective (R. C. Clark 2015, 231–233) as well as efficient.

Novel and Critical Information

In the classroom, printed material, used in the Study mode, may be superior in terms of straightforward information conveyance because it allows students to progress at their preferred rate, to review, and to skip known material. But sometimes the lecturer has knowledge that is not readily available in print, such as unpublished research, personal experiences, or informal anecdotes. Further, lectures allow the instructor to point out conflicting viewpoints, highlight critical features, or adapt the material to the needs of a specific audience. Instructors' questions and comments can stimulate students' interest in the issues.

The Narrative as a Way of Constructing and Remembering Meanings

One of the most innate and universal of human traits is storytelling. When ancient texts are found, they usually contain stories, such as the Epic of Gilgamesh. The teachings of ancient sages are often encapsulated in parables, stories meant to exemplify moral lessons, such as Jesus's parable of the Prodigal Son. Parables are found not only in Christian literature but also in Jewish, Zen Buddhist, Native American, and well, nearly all world literature, oral or written. It appears that humans are wired to remember—and be emotionally moved by—information woven into story form. As Jerome Bruner observed in 1991 ("The Narrative Construction of Reality"), "It was perhaps a decade ago that psychologists became alive to the possibility of narrative as a form not only of representing but of constituting reality" (5). We now understand that narratives put abstract ideas into a context, helping learners integrate the new knowledge into their schemata; this aids retention and ability to transfer this knowledge to similar contexts. This accounts for the success of cases studies as a pedagogical technique in business education. How often do former students report that they don't remember all that much of a professor's lectures, but they remember the "war stories" he told—in essence, parables with a lesson embedded in them? More recently, narrative structures have become ubiquitous in the virtual environment, as in serious games and simulations. Embedding material in a narrative story line, then, can be a powerful way of using the Presentation configuration.

Persuasion

When the goal is persuasion, winning the listener over to a different opinion, human speech can be a powerful instrument, especially when experienced face-to-face. Think of sales pitches or political addresses. In 1860, a young lawyer from Illinois carefully prepared a speech recounting—as in a legal brief—the evidence that the Founding Fathers would not have approved of the expansion of the institution of slavery into the new Western states. When Abraham Lincoln gave this famous address at Cooper Union in New York City, newspapers reported that, at the conclusion, men shouted wildly and threw their hats in the air. One interviewee proclaimed:

> When I came out of the hall, my face glowing with excitement and my frame all a-quiver, a friend with his eyes aglow, asked me what I thought of Abe Lincoln, the rail-splitter. I said: 'He's the greatest man since St. Paul.'
>
> *(A. A. Freeman 1960, 86)*

Thus, Presentation retains a prominent role in formal and informal education because, as Fleming and Levie put it in their synthesis of research on message design:

> Human speech is the most powerful and expressive medium the designer has available....It is the easiest way for the message designer to create mood, to appeal to emotions, to lighten or make more serious the 'tone' of a message, to amuse, to sadden, to persuade, to coax, to chide, or to cajole.
>
> *(1993, 117)*

Social Presence

A frequently overlooked aspect of lecturing is the mere presence of an authority figure in front of the room. That "social presence" can be a critical factor in establishing the overall environment for learning. Just think about the change in atmosphere within a classroom when the instructor enters the room and proceeds to the center of the stage. One of the challenges of distance education is to overcome the absence or diminution of the social presence of a live instructor. This is discussed further in Chapter 10.

Role Modeling

There is a tacit dimension to instruction as well as an explicit dimension. Learners are absorbing more than just the content of a lecture. Lectures also expose students to ways of thinking and feeling about a subject. Whether conscious of it or not, lecturers serve as role models for how to think about issues in the field (behavior modeling is discussed at length in Chapter 6). A lecturer who exhibits passion for the subject matter can have an impact far beyond the mere presentation of information. Research indicates that teacher enthusiasm is a major factor in sparking student interest in the subject matter (Csikszentmihalyi and McCormack 1986).

Limitations

You're Leading; Is Anyone Following?

Presentations are, by definition, primarily one-way. Lecturers have difficulty determining if their message is being comprehended. Body language, including sleeping bodies (!), provides some feedback; eye contact helps; pausing for questions or comments helps; but basically, the train keeps moving whether the listener is "on board" or not. It is well established that the minds of listeners can comprehend at a faster rate than most speakers speak, so the potential for daydreaming is high to begin with. At best, a lecture is aimed at the middle range of learner comprehension ability. Invariably, the quicker minds yearn to speed up while the slower ones pray for a slowdown.

Source Credibility

Aristotle was the first scholar to comment on the importance of credibility on audience perceptions of speaker effectiveness. His observations were confirmed by the ground-breaking research of Hovland, Janis, and Kelley (1953) and pursued by many subsequent researchers. We now understand that much of what people believe and remember from a presentation depends on their summary appraisal of the speaker, what is known as *terminal credibility*. If, for example, the audience perceived that the speaker was less than competent, lost composure, or acted in an unsociable way, terminal credibility would be low. On the other hand, teachers who are perceived as "caring" have been found to leave students with positive feelings about the course and positive estimation of their learning growth (Teven and McCroskey 1997).

Objectives Beyond Information

Most educational objectives—even those that just pertain to the cognitive domain—aim to go beyond the mere rote learning of verbal information. Most courses of study demand applied skills, evaluative abilities, or even creative abilities. These require practice that cannot be conducted in the Presentation mode. Beyond that are the domains of interpersonal skills, affective proficiency, and psychomotor dexterity, most of which are also beyond the range of Presentations. Years ago, a university administrator in Kuwait confided in one of the authors:

> We usually hire our academic employees from Egypt, but I've given up finding a photography instructor from there. We bring them here and they can't take a picture or develop film. They say, "All I know is from lectures. I can *tell* you how to take a picture or develop film, but I can't actually do it."

The Default Mode

Like any configuration, Presentation can be badly used. Who hasn't sat in a classroom praying for the end of a long, tedious lecture? Even wise words, if delivered in a monotone, can stupefy. Poorly organized thoughts are unlikely to inspire coherent understanding of the subject matter. Perhaps the greatest limitation of presentations is that they tempt instructors to fall back on the easy expedient of simply talking about the subject rather than using alternative methods to engage learners and to allow them to think critically, to evaluate, or to practice new skills.

Best Practices for Using the Presentation Configuration

Advice for the Facilitator

Encourage Engagement

Presentations can be employed effectively or poorly. They can be exciting and engaging or dull and deadly. As with any configuration, the trick is to engage learners, to get them thinking actively, not just passively receiving information. Any type of presentation is more likely to arouse listener engagement if it incorporates features such as these, suggested by McKeachie (1999):

1. Start with a question. Stimulate curiosity by beginning with an unsettled issue (e.g., "Does a child's intelligence come from genetic endowment or from their life experiences?"). Or cite a case that is in the news (e.g., "Did the mayoral candidate use statistics properly when she defended the crime rate?"). Periodically inject other questions. If listeners answer the questions mentally, they are processing the content; this is the essence of *engagement* (R. C. Clark 2015, 65).
2. Regain attention. Even under the best of circumstances, it is difficult for listeners to maintain attention to oral presentations longer than about ten minutes. Presenters can regain attention by changing the format (e.g., switching from chalkboard to a projected image or handing off to a different speaker). If you are turning to another subject, change the slide or turn off the projection. Break off the presentation to summarize main points or pause for questions. This gives listeners a chance to catch up, digest, and clear up confusions.
3. Close the sale. Give an emphatic conclusion—summarize main points, point out remaining controversies, or ask for and answer remaining questions.

Avoid Cognitive Overload

Presenters must be aware of the capacity of their audience to absorb the ideas they are presenting, known as *cognitive load*. It is true that the mind can follow verbal presentations faster than most speakers can speak, but this is only true if the information is largely familiar material. If the information is largely new to the listeners, it cannot be unleashed in a torrent. Listeners need time to connect the new to the old, to fit it into their cognitive structure. As discussed in Chapter 3,

Paas and Sweller (2014) distinguish among three types of cognitive load: *intrinsic*, the inherent complexity of the material being studied; *extraneous*, information that is distracting; and *germane*, information that is relevant to the learning task. Thus, presenters want to avoid the extraneous and focus on the germane.

The first step for speakers is to ration their words and visuals—both the total number and the amount of new information in each sentence or image. A pie chart can help illustrate the revenue streams of a business, but ten pie charts in a row or even a couple of very complex ones can overwhelm the viewer's interest in even trying to continue processing. Successful presenters also resist *cognitive competition*—deluging participants with multiple signals at one time: If a slide has text in it, let viewers read it rather than talking while they are trying to read. As discussed earlier, showing a picture of something and talking about something else forces the listener to "toggle" back-and-forth mentally, possibly missing both points, the picture and the talk (R. C. Clark 2015, 113). Well-designed presentations incorporate "signposts," clear indications of what to focus attention on, to ensure that listeners use their limited capacity for the most important points. One way to signpost is to provide an outline to follow—possibly a verbal outline or a diagram that shows the relationships of the parts of the main topic.

Contextualize

Information is more likely to be retained and transferred if it is presented in context: How does this new information relate to what we already know? How can these procedures be used on the job? So, follow a lean explanation with an application exercise (R. C. Clark 2015, 158). This principle goes back to schema theory, discussed earlier in this chapter. Learners can process new information more efficiently if it fits into preexisting categories. Many lecturers start by reminding listeners of previous topics covered, showing how the current material fits with that. Another way to create a context is to illustrate major points with stories. In the case of training within an organization, stories that are based within the organization help learners visualize the application of new concepts in a familiar setting, connecting to their existing cognitive structure.

Personalize

Research in neuroscience indicates that humans invest more mental effort in social interactions than in impersonal activities. Thus, they "are unconsciously compelled to process information more deeply when the lesson embeds social cues" (R. C. Clark 2015, 128). This means speaking with a relaxed, friendly persona—using "I" and "you," paying attention when interacting with learners, and using polite phrases when giving suggestions to learners. As mentioned above with regard to source credibility, when learners perceive that their teachers care about them they tend to find them more credible, the course more valuable, and to learn more themselves (Teven and McCroskey 1997).

Make the Abstract Concrete

As discussed at length above, it can be most helpful to show a picture or draw a diagram, or at least provide vivid verbal examples. New concepts are learned by contrasting examples with non-examples.

Employ Mnemonic Devices

Students often come up with their own mnemonic devices for helping them remember multifaceted ideas. Recent research indicates that mnemonic devices function much like the schemata, discussed in Chapter 3, to help make information "stickier." They are a natural way for the mind to manage information storage (Belleza 1987). Instructors can help by using mnemonic devices in their presentations, such as an acronym to stand for a phrase, such as "The Five Ws and One H of a good newspaper story." Or they can put their key points into rhyming phrases. "Chunking" large lists into smaller portions helps reduce cognitive overload and aids retention; for example, "the eight varieties of grass seed can be grouped into four that are good for shade and four that are good for sun."

Use Audiovisual Showmanship

The recasting of an oral presentation into an audiovisual format, such as a slide show or video, does not per se amplify its instructional value. It is more likely to make an impact if the mediated presentation incorporates proven psychological principles, like those discussed above. When it comes to using a media presentation in front of an audience, no one is expected to have the flair of a circus ringmaster, but presenters are expected to avoid gaffes like:

- Not having the presentation ready to show. Check twice to be sure the projector is set up properly and your program is ready for showing. Nothing sucks credibility out of a room like "How do you turn this thing on?"
- Failing to take care of the lighting: "Does anyone know where the light switch is?" Have an assistant standing by to operate the light switch or curtains.
- Parking yourself out of the spotlight. When a projector is shining on a screen, eyes follow the light. If you want attention back on yourself, turn off the projector and turn up the room lights. Be conscious of where the audience

attention is. If a stranger wanders into the room, stop talking until people turn their attention back to the speaker.

Advice for the Learner

Before the presentation, get into the right conceptual frame; consciously think about what you already know about the topic. If it is a course with a series of lectures, review notes from the previous lecture.

During the presentation, stay engaged: Maintain eye contact with the speaker, ask questions, and volunteer answers to questions. Taking notes during a lecture serves two purposes: creating the notes helps to process the material, which helps later recall (Gagné and Driscoll 1988); and having the notes allows later review, which further fosters retention. Focus on understanding the material, taking enough notes to remind you of the main ideas. It helps to have some shorthand abbreviations and symbols to reduce the amount of time writing. Leave space in your notes to allow for editing or adding material later. Highlight points that the speaker emphasizes or repeats; use indenting to list supporting points.

After the presentation, review notes within 24 hours; if you wait longer, you will not be refreshing your memory but learning all over again. Edit and highlight now while you still remember the points emphasized by the speaker. Compare and discuss notes with another conscientious student. As a practical matter, it would be preferable to use a loose-leaf notebook to make it easier to amplify and rearrange your notes as you gain insights through further reading and reflection.

Methods Featuring the Presentation Configuration

Most presentations can be and should be paired with other configurations to create robust lessons. New knowledge, if retained at all, may remain inert. To become an active part of the learner's repertoire, the received information needs to be used in some way. Many different methods—discussed in Chapter 4—have been devised to combine various configurations into potent learning experiences. Let us examine some well-established methods to see in detail how Presentation plays a key role in them.

Strategic-Level

Lecture Method (Presentation + Supplements)

Viewed as a strategic-level method, the lecture method provides a template for a whole lesson, a whole course of study, or even a whole curriculum. Adoption of the lecture method does not mean exclusive use of Presentation for all parts of all lessons; rather, it means that units are organized around the Presentation portion and the other portions are viewed as supplements, to be conducted before or after a presentation. Such supplements often take the form of Discussions and Repetition activities. For example, college courses are often described as lecture courses, or lecture-discussion, or lecture-lab. Supplementary activities can also be interspersed *within* a presentation—described below as an "interactive lecture."

Knowledge Lesson (Presentation + Discussion + Study + Expression)

This is one of the most widely used strategic-level methods for cognitive objectives; Davies (1981, 50) refers to it as the framework for a *knowledge lesson*. The lesson begins with a short lecture, providing listeners with some basic facts, concepts, or principles. This is followed by one or more Discussion formats, occupying the larger part of the meeting time, to allow learners to process the material. The lesson concludes with a task assignment meant to consolidate the new knowledge into the learner's repertoire, usually in a form that would require some Study followed by Expression—a written or oral report.

Tactical-Level

Interactive Lecture (Presentation + Discussion and/or Tutorial)

A lecture or audiovisual presentation can become interactive by pausing to have a question-and-answer period; each interaction with a participant serves as a mini-Tutorial. Facilitators can interrupt a lecture and ask listeners to break into buzz groups (see Chapter 6); give them a challenging question to consider, a reporting task, and a short period of discussion time. Many more ideas are found in Thiagarajan (2012).

Deductive Concept Teaching (Presentation/ Demonstration + Repetition during Presentation)

Used when the objective is to teach a new concept, the instructor presents the concept, explains it, and gives some examples and non-examples to illustrate the critical attributes of the concept. For concrete concepts, where the critical attributes are visible, Demonstration may be used to show rather than just tell what the concept is all about. Participants can then practice using the new concept (Repetition) during the presentation, using techniques such as those discussed above: raise a hand, share with a neighbor, response card, electronic response system, or responsive handout.

Inductive Concept Teaching (Repetition + Presentation)

An inductive—or "discovery"—approach to concept teaching requires learners to figure out how a new concept works. It turns the teaching procedure upside down. Instead of beginning by presenting and explaining the new concept, the instructor begins by showing many examples of the concept in use, challenging learners to detect the critical attributes, the features that distinguish this concept from other concepts, then concluding by restating and clarifying (Presentation) the learners' discoveries (Collins and Stevens 1983).

Seatwork (Presentation + In-Class Repetition)

Following Presentation or Demonstration to introduce a new concept, principle, or procedure, after Presentation the learners work individually in-class using responsive handouts to practice using the new material.

Homework (Presentation + At-Home Repetition)

Following Presentation or Demonstration to introduce a new concept, principle, or procedure, learners work individually at home using responsive handouts or other homework assignments to practice using the new material.

Note-Taking (Presentation + Expression)

See "Advice for the Learner" above regarding note-taking. Taking notes while listening to a lecture is an effective method of processing new material—what is most important, what is most relevant to your objective, and what the text means, translated into your own words.

Brainstorming (Presentation + Whole-Class Discussion)

Brainstorming can be used with an unfamiliar audience *before* the presentation to get a sense of their preconceptions or misconceptions, *during* a presentation to flesh out an idea with examples contributed by the audience, or *after* a presentation to generate "take-aways." Begin with an open-ended question (e.g., "What are some *positive* aspects of being a serf in the Middle Ages?"); have participants call out responses without self-censorship or judgment of others' responses; record all responses on a whiteboard. Then repeat the process, posing another question, perhaps another side of an issue (e.g., "What are some *negative* aspects of being a serf in the Middle Ages?"). Lead a discussion to cluster similar responses; then discuss conclusions that may be drawn. Detailed instructions for conducting brainstorming sessions are found in Chapter 7 under "Whole-Class Discussion."

Chapter Summary

Our exploration of the eight communication configurations outlined in Chapter 4 begins at the "teacher-centered" end of the spectrum with the Presentation configuration, which is defined as the arrangement in which some person (or some resource playing the role of facilitator), conveys information one-way to a number of learners; the facilitator or resource controls the flow of communication. In addition to the familiar lecture, the Presentation configuration can accommodate a number of formats that can be grouped into the categories of verbal monologue (e.g., an oral lecture) , verbal-audiovisual monologue (e.g., a travel talk accompanied by a film), group performance (e.g., a dramatic role-play), and audiovisual showing (e.g., a Sesame Street animated video clip).

The Presentation configuration has a long track record in education, originally serving the purpose of conveying the content of a book to a group of students, later transitioning to commentary on the text. It has maintained a prominent place in corporate training as well as higher education, as it remains an inexpensive and convenient vehicle for passing along new and critical information.

The strengths, limitations, and best practices for using the Presentation configuration are best understood against a background of the cognitive science and neuroscience behind auditory and visual learning. The sensory modalities of hearing and seeing each entail complex neurological processes. Auditory stimuli are processed in the auditory cortex, near the center of the brain; visual stimuli are processed in the visual cortex, at the very back of the brain. Both types of stimuli (speech and printed text primarily) are then routed through two separate pathways to other parts of the brain for further processing and storage; since speech and text both involve language comprehension, they are interconnected, linking neural activities distributed widely throughout the brain.

The complexity of the underlying cognitive processes makes "multimodal" learning a complicated matter. Creating multimodal learning experiences requires careful organization of spoken words vs. written words, spoken words vs. images, written words vs. images, and words and images combined. The Presentation configuration excels as an efficient way of communicating, when novel or critical information must be understood. It can also carry dramatic power, making its messages more memorable and persuasive. The very physical presence of a speaker changes the climate of a classroom, and the speaker can serve as a role model for thinking about a subject. The limitations of the Presentation configuration center on the fact that it can fulfill only one step in the larger process of mastering new knowledge and skills. Further, it depends on ability of the presenter to gain attention and credibility.

Best practices for employing Presentation largely revolve around helping listeners incorporate the new information into their mental frameworks, or schemata—by contextualizing the material, providing concrete examples, and suggesting mnemonic devices…all while avoiding cognitive overload and avoiding gaffes in using audiovisual media. Listeners can help themselves by thoughtful note-taking and later review of those notes.

Presentations seldom stand alone to reach the objectives of a lesson. There are number of templates, which we call "methods" in Chapter 4, for combining Presentation with other configurations. At the strategic level are the so-called "lecture method" itself and lectures interspersed with interactive episodes ("interactive lectures"). The knowledge lesson includes a package of follow-up activities to make a complete learning experience out of the lecture. Some methods are devised for the tactical level, to be used as part of a lesson, such as inductive and deductive concept-teaching methods and brainstorming. The intent of all of these methods is to stimulate the sort of mental processing that listening alone may not accomplish.

Works Cited

Barron, Ann E. 2004. "Auditory Instruction." Chap. 35 in *Handbook of Research on Educational Communications and Technology*, 2nd ed., edited by David H. Jonassen, 949–978. Mahwah, NJ: Lawrence Erlbaum Associates.

Belleza, Francis S. 1987. "Mnemonic Devices and Memory Schemas." In *Imagery and Related Mnemonic Processes*, edited by Mark A. Daniel and Michael Pressley, 34–55. New York: Springer-Verlag.

Bruner, Jerome. 1991. "The Narrative Construction of Reality." *Critical Inquiry* 18 (Autumn): 1–21.

Calandra, Brendan, Ann E. Barron, and Ingrid Thompson-Sellers. 2008. "Audio Use in E-Learning: What, Why, When, and How?" *International Journal on E-Learning* 7 (4): 589–601.

Clark, Ruth Colvin. 2015. *Evidence-Based Training Methods: A Guide for Training Professionals*. 2nd ed. Alexandria, VA: ATD Press.

Collins, Allan, and Albert A. Stevens. 1983. "A Cognitive Theory of Inquiry Teaching." In *Instructional-Design Theories and Models: An Overview of Their Current Status*, edited by Charles M. Reigeluth, 247–278. Hillsdale, NJ: Lawrence Erlbaum Associates.

Comenius, Johann Amos. 1967. *Orbis Sensualium Pictus: Facsimile of the 3rd London Edition 1672 with an Introduction by James Bowen*. Sydney, Australia: Sydney University Press.

Comenius, John Amos, and Maurice W. Keatinge. 1967. *The Great Didactic of John Amos Comenius*. New York: Russell & Russell.

Craik, Kenneth. 1943. *The Nature of Explanation*. Cambridge, UK: Cambridge University Press.
Csikszentmihalyi, Mihaly, and Jane McCormack. 1986. "The Influence of Teachers." *Phi Delta Kappan* 67 (6): 415–419.
Davies, Ivor K. 1981. *Instructional Technique*. New York: McGraw-Hill.
D'Esposito, Mark, Bradley R. Postle, Dana Ballard, and Jessica Lease. 1999. "Maintenance Versus Manipulation of Information Held in Working Memory: An Event-Related fMRI Study." *Brain and Cognition* 41 (1): 66–86. doi:10.1006/brcg.1999.1096.
Fleming, Malcolm, and W. Howard Levie. 1978. *Instructional Message Design: Principles from the Behavioral Sciences*. Englewood Cliffs, NJ: Educational Technology Publications.
Fleming, Malcolm, and W. Howard Levie, eds. 1993. *Instructional Message Design: Principles from the Behavioral Sciences*. 2nd ed. Englewood Cliffs, NJ: Educational Technology Publications.
Freeman, Andrew A. 1960. *Abraham Lincoln Goes to New York*. New York: Coward-McCann.
Freeman, Frank N. 1924. *Visual Education*. Chicago, IL: University of Chicago Press.
Gagné, Robert M. 1985. *The Conditions of Learning*. 4th ed. New York: Holt, Rinehart, and Winston.
Gagné, Robert M., and Marcy P. Driscoll. 1988. *Essentials of Learning for Instruction*. 2nd ed. Englewood Cliffs, NJ: Prentice-Hall.
Goodale, Melvyn A., and A. David Milner. 1992. "Separate Visual Pathways for Perception and Action." *Trends in Neurosciences* 15 (1): 20–25. doi:10.1016/0166-2236(92)90344-8.
Hayakawa, Samuel I. 1941. *Language in Action: A Guide to Accurate Thinking, Reading, and Writing*. New York: Harcourt, Brace.
Herman, Arthur. 2001. *How the Scots Invented the Modern World*. New York: Crown Publishers.
Hovland, Carl I., Irving L. Janis, and Harold H. Kelley. 1953. *Communication and Persuasion: Psychological Studies of Opinion Change*. New Haven, CT: Yale University Press.
Ivry, Richard. 2009. *Cognitive Neuroscience: The Biology of the Mind*. New York: W. W. Norton.
Johnson-Laird, Philip N. 1983. *Mental Models: Towards a Cognitive Science of Language, Inference, and Consciousness*. Cambridge, MA: Harvard University Press.
Joseph, Rhawn Gabriel. n.d. *Agraphia: Disorders of Writing*. Accessed January 25, 2020. http://brainmind.com/Agraphia.html.
Korzybski, Alfred. 1933. *Science and Sanity: An Introduction to non-Aristotelian Systems and General Semantics*. New York: The International Non-Aristotelian Library Publishing Co.
Kraus, Nina, and Travis White-Schwoch. 2015. "Unraveling the Biology of Auditory Learning: A Cognitive-Sensorimotor-Reward Framework." *Trends in Cognitive Sciences* 19 (11): 642–654.
Mayer, Richard E., ed. 2014. *The Cambridge Handbook of Multimedia Learning*. 2nd ed. New York: Cambridge University Press.
Mayer, Richard E., and Roxana Moreno. 1998. "A Split-Attention Effect in Multimedia Learning: Evidence for Dual Processing Systems in Working Memory." *Journal of Educational Psychology* 90 (2): 312–320.
Mazoyer, Bernard, Nathalie Tzourio-Mazoyer, Angelique Mazard, Michel Denis, and Emmanuel Mellet. 2002. "Neural Bases of Image and Language Interactions." *International Journal of Psychology* 37 (4): 204–208.
McKeachie, Wilbert J. 1999. *Teaching Tips*. 10th ed. Boston, MA: Houghton Mifflin Company.
Merrill, M. David. 2002. "First Principles of Instruction." *Educational Technology Research and Development* 50 (3): 43–59.
Merrill, M. David. 2013. *First Principles of Instruction*. San Francisco, CA: Pfeiffer.

Morrison, Gary R., Steven M. Ross, Howard K. Kalman, and Jerrold E. Kemp. 2013. *Designing Effective Instruction*. 7th ed. New York: John Wiley & Sons.
Paas, Fred, and John Sweller. 2014. "Implications of Cognitive Load Theory for Multimedia Learning." In *The Cambridge Handbook of Multimedia Learning*, 2nd ed., edited by Richard E. Mayer, 27–42. New York: Cambridge University Press.
Paivio, Allan. 1971. *Imagery and Verbal Processes*. New York: Holt, Rinehart & Winston.
Poeppel, David, William J. Idsardi, and Virginie van Wassenhove. 2008. "Speech Perception at the Interface of Neurobiology and Linguistics." *Philosophical Transactions of the Royal Society of London* 363 (1493): 1071–1086. doi:10.1098/rstb.2007.2160.
Robinson, Cyril E. 1965. *Apollo History of Rome*. New York: Thomas Y. Crowell Co.
Rumelhart, David E. 1980. "Schemata: The Building Blocks of Cognition." Chap. 2 in *Theoretical Issues in Reading Comprehension*, edited by Rand J. Spiro, Bertram C. Bruce and William F. Brewer, 33–58. Hillsdale, NJ: Lawrence Erlbaum Associates.
Saettler, Paul. 1990. *The Evolution of American Educational Technology*. Englewood, CO: Libraries Unlimited.
Schnotz, Wolfgang. 2014. "Integrated Model of Text and Picture Comprehension." In *The Cambridge Handbook of Multimedia Learning*, 2nd ed., edited by Richard E. Mayer, 72–103. New York: Cambridge University Press.
Sternberg, Robert J., and Karin Sternberg. 2002. *Cognitive Psychology*. 6th ed. Belmont, CA: Wadsworth.
Stolovitch, Harold D., and Erica J. Keeps. 2002. *Telling Ain't Training*. Alexandria, VA: American Society for Training & Development.
Teven, Jason J., and James C. McCroskey. 1997. "The Relationship of Perceived Teacher Caring with Student Learning and Teacher Evaluation." *Communication Education* 46 (1): 1–9.
Thiagarajan, Sivasailam. 2012. *Thiagi's Interactive Lectures*. Alexandria, VA: ASTD Press.
Wertheimer, Max. 1944. "Gestalt Theory [English translation of 'Über Gestalttheorie' 1924/5]." *Social Research* 11: 78–99.
Winn, William. 1993. "Perception Principles." Chap. 2 in *Instructional Message Design*, 2nd ed., edited by Malcolm Fleming and W. Howard Levie, 55–127. Englewood Cliffs, NJ: Educational Technology Publications.
Yeatman, Jason D., Robert F. Dougherty, Michal Ben-Shachar, and Brian A. Wandell. 2012. "Development of White Matter and Reading Skills." *Proceedings of the National Academy of Sciences* 109 (44): E3045–E3053. doi:10.1073/pnas.1206792109.

Demonstration   6

Demonstration is the second of the communication configurations that are most "teacher-centered," in the sense that, like Presentation, Demonstration depends entirely on the instructor's selection of content, gathering of sources and materials, and choice of time and place of delivery. It requires a separate category because it represents a different message type and serves a different function than Presentation.

Just as people learn complex behaviors better when shown a behavioral model, they also learn complex mental skills by observing someone thinking through a problem. Elementary school teachers demonstrate, by talking aloud, how to think through a math problem. Instructors may also share transcripts or recordings of students who model the desired thought process. Another way of viewing the role of Demonstration is to see it as the crucial bridge between theory and application. It is one thing to comprehend a rule or principle on an abstract level; it is another to be able to put it into practice. Living examples and role models *show* how to make the transition.

Demonstration Defined

By dictionary definition, *demonstration* can have the "philosophical" meaning of "making evident by reasoning" (Oxford English Dictionary, 2nd ed. 1989); thus, one could end an argument by claiming that your point has been *demonstrated*. But we are using *demonstration* in a more concrete sense: "the exhibition and explanation of specimens and practical operations, as a method of instruction in a science or art" (Oxford English Dictionary, 2nd ed. 1989). This configuration is similar to Presentation, differing in that the source is not a speaker but a real object, a mechanical model, a computer simulation, or one or more live humans, showing how some procedure or complex task is done. The focus is on the thing being

Demonstration

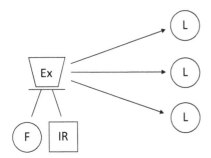

Figure 6.1 The Demonstration Communication Configuration. IR represents an Instructional Resource; EX represents an Example of the process, procedure, or task being demonstrated.

shown. A speaker will probably comment on the procedure, or the demonstrator may do so. Our definition:

> *Demonstration*: A Facilitator (F) or some Instructional Resource (IR) playing the role of Facilitator displays and explains an Example (Ex) of some process, procedure, or other complex task to a number of Learners (L); the Facilitator controls the flow of communication (Figure 6.1).

Instructors are using the Demonstration configuration when they pause a Presentation and show a video clip of someone performing a skill being discussed. The Demonstration configuration can be the primary one for lessons based on observing expert performance, coupled with practice of the desired skill, as the *sensei* in a *dojo* or the yoga instructor in her studio.

Formats associated with Demonstration

Science Experiment

Instructors of physics and chemistry frequently use dramatic experiments performed in front of the class—such as the explosion of sodium dropping into a vessel of water—as a way to capture attention, arouse curiosity, and stoke interest in a new topic. However, more mundane experimental demonstrations are also common; they are used to convert an abstract principle into a sensory experience—calling upon neural pathways other than that of language comprehension.

Live Experiment

- physics teacher demonstrates "torque" with a meter stick hanging from a ring stand and a set of weights attached to the meter stick
- science instructor demonstrates the visible light spectrum by shining a lightbulb through a diffraction grating, gradually turning up the light intensity
- the "Cartesian diver": suspend a small floating object—such as an eyedropper or soy sauce packet—in a large plastic bottle, tighten cap, squeeze on sides of bottle to make the object descend.

For purposes of distance education or blended learning classes, dynamic experiments such as those described above may be recorded for subsequent asynchronous delivery in a different place at a different time. In such a situation, these recordings would be considered Resources, which would most likely be used by individual learners in the Study configuration that we describe in Chapter 10, with individuals being able to pause, stop, start, and replay the recordings as needed. In contrast, if a group or class of learners were to view a live telecast of a dynamic experiment synchronously that would assuredly represent the Demonstration configuration.

Physical Model

Models, three-dimensional representations of real things, are among the oldest of technological innovations in education. Their use goes back to colonial times in America, when globes, orreries (movable models of the solar system), and pulleys and levers in a frame were often found at colleges, alongside physics laboratory equipment. By the 1830s, an oversize abacus—or numeral frame, a globe, and geometrical solids were standard items in schools (C. Anderson 1962). These devices, again, offer an alternative to linguistic representation, operating in the brain as metaphors rather than just verbal symbols.

Static Model

- an oversize model of a clock, to show hours and minutes
- cutaway model of a house with underground utilities for architectural study
- cutaway mock-up of a jet engine
- 3D anatomical model of human body, with circulatory system and organs exposed.

Dynamic Model

- oversize human DNA strand with manipulable nucleotides
- working model of a windmill
- dynamic model showing blood circulation through heart and lungs
- dynamic model showing planetary movements and/or eclipses—a modern orrery.

Animated Portrayal of a Process or Procedure

Defined as a sequence of graphics that change over time, thus resulting in apparent motion, animation has been found effective in illustrating the complex procedures and the structural and functional relationships among objects and events (Park and Gittelman 1992). To show a complex process that may not be visible in real life (e.g., because it is so small or it happens over such a large area or because it happens so quickly or so slowly), a video animation may offer an ideal alternative.

- slow-motion video of process of mitosis, cells reproducing
- 2D motion graphics illustrating the formation of kidney stones
- 2D motion graphics visualization to raise awareness of overpopulation
- 3D motion graphics visualization of the dynamic forces of the water cycle
- 2D or 3D motion graphics visualization of various types of jet propulsion systems.

When such recordings are shown in a live, large-group setting, learners would be in the Demonstration configuration. If the recordings are viewed individually, as in online learning, they would be Resources, being used in the Study configuration.

Behavior Modeling

For learning procedures or more complex behaviors, an effective strategy is to show a person performing the target skills (Yelon 1996, 165–184). Athletic training makes constant use of Demonstration to show the correct way to make different plays, such as shooting free throws in basketball or serving a volleyball. Behavior modeling can be shown in many formats. As described in Chapter 8, the tutorial method used at Oxford and Cambridge entails weekly encounters with a tutor, during which the student typically presents orally the substance of the paper she has been working on. In many cases, one or more other students are also present. For those other students, the oral presentation and defense are a Demonstration; the student presenter is modeling a behavior that they wish to master as well.

Live Role Play

- salesperson encounter with customer
- employer–employee conflict scenario
- historical reenactors, as on Civil War battlefield
- theatrical plays that have a propaganda purpose or moral lesson to impart.

Recorded Role Play

- salesperson encounter with customer scenario, captured on video
- employer–employee conflict scenario, captured on video
- Staged dramatization, possibly scripted, of teacher–student interactions, for teacher education classes
- television situation comedies that show positive or negative examples of family relationships.

When such recordings are shown in a live, large-group setting, learners would be in the Demonstration configuration. If the recordings are viewed individually, as in online learning, they would be Resources, being used in the Study configuration.

Live Motor-Skills Demonstration

- in-person teachers or experts who model the process of solving a problem
- baseball coach demonstrates grip for throwing curveball
- shadowing an executive in a corporate setting
- "sitting next to Nelly": the part of on-the-job training in which an experienced worker shows a neophyte how to perform a function.

In addition, more advanced students often serve as behavioral models for younger or less advanced students. By their comportment, they show others how to succeed as students. In dealing with specific subject-matter skills, students can also serve as useful demonstrators. If they exhibit mastery of a target skill, it encourages other students to believe that they can do it too.

- softball coach asks skilled player to demonstrate how she slides into a base.

Recorded Motor-Skills Demonstration

- basketball coach shows slow-motion video of proper free-throw technique
- how-to-do-it educational television broadcasts—e.g., painting techniques, cooking demonstrations, or yoga exercises
- YouTube "how to" videos, such as do-it-yourself projects.

When such recordings are shown in a live, large-group setting, learners would be in the Demonstration configuration. If the recordings are viewed individually, as in online learning, they would be Resources, being used in the Study configuration.

These formats differ in many ways, but they share in common the concrete portrayal of natural or social processes, procedural tasks, complex skills, or attitudes.

Evolution of Demonstration

Early Forms of Cultural Learning

If we could revisit human life in prehistoric times, we would undoubtedly find a lot of learning by demonstration. Debate has raged for over a century about the origins of vocal language, generally tracing its development roughly to the time of the emergence of *Homo sapiens*. Whether or not Stone Age people could learn through spoken communication, we can be quite certain that they were learning via demonstration. Pottery making, basket weaving, flint flaking, spear hunting, and all the other survival skills of early humans were learned by observing expert performers. Children watched adults in their community and absorbed the skills they observed. Jerome Bruner reported on observations done in the 1960s among people living the hunter-gatherer lifestyle:

> Most of what we would call instruction is through showing. And there is no practice or drill as such, save in the form of play modeled directly on adult models—play hunting, play bossing, play exchanging, play baby tending, play house making.
>
> *(1966, 151).*

Conscious Use of Behavioral Models

In *De Re Militari*, a book still read by military trainers, Vegetius (writing around AD 400) describes how Romans trained their legions for marching, physical fitness, and weapons handling. Exact methods are not explained, but we can deduce that weapons training would have resembled today's behavior modeling—demonstrations by masters followed by repeated practice.

Classical Greek theater evolved originally as means of promulgating moral lessons; this tradition continues in modern plays and films, sometimes consciously, sometimes unconsciously. Medieval art was almost exclusively devoted to portraying religious themes. Sculptures on the outsides of cathedrals and paintings inside them vividly depicted the consequences of sin and the rewards of virtue. The intention was explicitly educational, to show "right behavior" and urge compliance. Medieval tomb sculptures showed the magnificence of the nobles buried within and the grief suffered by those left behind, incorporating the donor into the history of the community.

We do not know precisely how medieval guilds conducted training of new members; this was part of the "trade secrets" that guilds were established to protect. However, given that most guilds involved manual crafts, it is a safe bet that most training took the form of behavior modeling—observation of masters and practice under their experienced eye.

Modern Behavior Modeling

The use of a human demonstrator to illustrate how to carry out some physically observable skill is referred to as behavior modeling. It can be employed as the first step in the process of teaching complex skills, usually involving attitudes and mental decisions as well as the physical actions. Culinary students stand beside experienced chefs as they chop and stir. A lab instructor demonstrates to chemistry lab students how to use a rubber pipet bulb to pipet solutions from one container to another. Medical students observe a physician informing a patient of his diagnosis and treatment options, with special attention to communicating compassionate concern to the patient. The martial arts *sensei* stands in the midst of a small group of students and performs every technique over and over, slowly at first, so that they can see every step in the action.

Teacher as a Behavioral Model: From Aristotle to Cognitive Apprenticeship

Going back to the Classical era in Europe, seekers for knowledge have looked for sages to whom they could attach themselves as acolytes. Famously, Socrates (470–399 BC) was the teacher of Plato (*c.* 427–*c.* 347 BC), who became the teacher of Aristotle (384–322 BC), who became the teacher of Alexander the Great. We know Socrates, Plato, and Aristotle as "philosophers," but their occupation was teacher, teaching those things that were most important for an affluent young man to master, especially rhetoric, oratory, and reasoning—all aimed toward attaining *areté*, meaning "excellence" or "moral virtue." Meanwhile in ancient India, noble families traditionally sent their young men off to *gurukuls*—wholistic learning environments located within the homes or compounds of revered *gurus*—where they would spend several years striving to acquire the latter's wisdom and insights via a culturally specific model of apprenticeship.

In the eighteenth century, the ancient Greek ideals mentioned above were emulated by Scottish universities. Lecturers such as Francis Hutcheson (1694–1746) at the University of Glasgow and his successors, as leaders of the Scottish Enlightenment, proposed daring new theories about the place of humans in the universe, carrying their followers into the realms of science and mathematics in addition to philosophy in order to inform a modern concept of *areté*. One of those leaders, John Witherspoon (1723–1794), ventured to the colony of New Jersey in 1768 to become president of Princeton, bringing the humanistic ideals of the Scottish Enlightenment to the New World. He taught moral philosophy, divinity, rhetoric, history, and French; and he preached at the college chapel on Sundays—an archetype of the educator as charismatic role model (Herman 2001).

Although modern academic institutions have reduced their claims to moral leadership, teachers and professors still serve as role models, at least for how to think and behave within their profession. Thus, one of the major justifications for live classroom meetings is that they expose students to exemplars worthy of emulation. Even if all the informational content is forgotten, students may come away more motivated to pursue the subject and steeped in the ways of thinking about problems in their field. This recognition of the tacit dimension of schooling goes under the banner of *cognitive apprenticeship*, discussed further below.

Cognitive Science and Neuroscience Behind Demonstration

Imitation and Mirror Neurons

As discussed in Chapter 3, Albert Bandura (1977) proposed that people frequently acquired new skills, even quite complex procedures, by merely observing another person (or a video recording of another person) performing the target behavior…or even just being told how to do it. Bandura's "social learning theory" gave a theoretical structure to Bruner's earlier observations of imitative learning, discussed above. About 30 years after Bandura's experiments, neuroscience researchers independently discovered *mirror neurons*. These neurons fire both when an organism acts and when that organism observes the same action being performed by another (Rizzolatti and Sinigaglia 2008), constituting a form of learning without prompting, practice, or reinforcement. However, some major caveats are in order; first, the learner—whether a primate or a human—must consider the behavior model to be worthy of imitation; and, second, the learner must possess the prerequisite skills for the new learning task. Someone with a good working knowledge of the French language might gain oral interpretation skills by listening to a skilled actor read a poem, while a novice would profit little from the example. Experiments have shown that novices who watch a skilled juggler juggle bowling pins may go away with a good deal of confidence in their ability to replicate this skill, but without prerequisite experience with unbalanced objects like bowling pins, they invariably fail.

Cognitive Apprenticeship

Today this theoretical structure is represented by *cognitive apprenticeship*, the thrust of which is to bring the tacit dimension of behavior modeling processes "into the open, where students can observe, enact, and practice them with help from the teacher" (Collins, Brown and Newman 1987). Through modeling and coaching, instructors can support the three stages of skill acquisition: the cognitive stage (declarative understanding of the skill), the associative stage (correcting misconceptions and errors in understanding and strengthening correct connections), and the autonomous stage (skill executed with conscious thought) (J. R. Anderson 2000).

Acquiring New Knowledge

Sometimes the instructional objective entails, not whole new behavioral repertoires, but cognitive comprehension. As discussed in Chapter 5, for the brain to form internal representations of the things and ideas being taught, it needs to receive external representations of those things and ideas. According to Schnotz, "these representations can take different forms, such as spoken text, written text, maps, drawings, graphs, and sound" (2014, 75). As varied as these forms can be, they fall into two basic categories—*description* and *depiction*. Pictures, graphics, or models would be *depictions*—representations that have some resemblance to the thing pictured (Schnotz 2014, 76). Cognitive science research suggests that when we are looking at a visual representation, such as a working model or a human actor (*depictions*), the neural processing system follows pathways different from language comprehension, thus providing a representation in the brain that could be complementary to the linguistic representations of the narrative that accompanies the demonstration—two different ways of storing the new information.

Why Demonstration? Strengths and Limitations

Strengths

Demonstrations provide a critical link in the learning process—connecting abstract ideas to specific, concrete instances. Humans are much better equipped to learn by example than by exhortation. Many complex skills can hardly be taught by any other method. Nobody ever gained proficiency in surgery or martial arts from a book or a lecture. Consequently, Demonstration has been used ever since humans became human, so both givers and receivers of Demonstration are well accustomed to using this method.

The "Show" of "Show and Tell"

Humans generally struggle to fit new abstract information into their mental schemata or into their behavioral repertoire. They do much better when shown an example of a concept or a concrete portrayal of a procedure. This is actually a crucial step in the learning process; new ideas are unlikely to be remembered, much less applied, unless the learner has translated the teacher's abstract pronouncement into his own words or pictures. A baseball coach could talk all day about how to throw a curveball; but until he demonstrates the grip, the windup, and the delivery, the greenhorn pitcher is not going to progress.

Limitations

Demonstrations are, by definition, primarily one-way and teacher-controlled. They do not accommodate individual differences unless adapted and repeated to conform to the needs of individuals. Demonstrations are converted into usable skills only if followed by Repetition.

Some forms of Demonstration, such as behavior modeling, can be quite labor-intensive, hence expensive. The cost barrier can be reduced by using off-the-shelf video portrayals of the desired performance.

Like any configuration, Demonstrations can be badly used. Because they are so commonplace, it is easy for instructors to be haphazard about conducting a demonstration. Learning does not naturally follow just because some sort of offhand example has been shown. As with any other configuration, careful preparation and thoughtful procedures yield the best results, as discussed below.

Best Practices for Using Demonstrations

As with other modes of instruction, learners need to be put in the right mental set and given experiences that hold their attention and draw them into active engagement.

Behavior Modeling

Demonstrating human performance, which can involve rather complex objectives, including concepts, principles, physical skills, and attitudes, requires a five-step process:

1. Inform learners exactly what they will be expected to be able to *do* after the demonstration.

2. Direct learners' attention to the *critical features or steps* of the behavior, picture, video, or dramatization they are about to see.
3. Direct learners to *remember* each step in the process to be shown.
4. *Call out* each step in the process as it is shown.
5. Give learners *practice* in carrying out the target skill (Yelon 1996).

Procedure and Process Learning

One of the first principles of Merrill's approach to instructional design is that "learning is promoted when learners observe a demonstration of the knowledge and skill to be learned" (Merrill 2013, 23). To Merrill, it is critical that the demonstration be consistent with the learning task. For a procedure ("how to"), therefore, the steps should be illustrated as well as the consequences associated with each step. For a process ("what happens"), the demonstration should portray the conditions required for the process to work (e.g., ingredients for a chemical reaction) and the results of the process (e.g., liquid changes color). Further, Merrill contends that the learning of procedures and processes is enhanced when the instructor explicitly calls attention to the critical aspects of the process or procedure (23).

Metacognition

To help learners develop the metacognitive skill of self-monitoring, the instructor or a subject-matter expert can model the process—perform a task and reflect aloud so students can observe how it's done.

Methods Featuring the Demonstration Configuration

Strategic-Level

Skills Practice (Demonstration + Repetition)

A demonstration would have a limited chance of making a permanent impact on the learner's repertoire without being followed by some opportunity for Repetition. A tutorial mode with one-to-one coaching would be ideal. Next best would be a computer-based program that was able to receive users' responses and give appropriate feedback. This could range from a simple multiple-choice verbal test program to a highly responsive, remote-controlled videogame device, like the Wii system, for practicing physical skills. At the lower end of the scale would be a demonstration with independent practice without expert feedback, such as watching a video on proper golf swing and then hitting a bucket of balls.

184 Demonstration

As described above, for many types of practical skills, the instructional cycle may start with behavior modeling—the instructor demonstrating the correct technique—and then proceed to supervised Repetition. This is the essence of the "skills practice" method.

Behavior Modeling and Executive Coaching (Demonstration + Tutorial)

Productive performance in the workplace requires a myriad of interpersonal skills, many of which are tacit. Part of the "art" of job interviewing is to detect whether candidates have the intangible personal qualities to succeed in a given organization. Some interpersonal skills are considered critical and teachable and, in fact, corporations probably spend more effort teaching interpersonal skills than any other kind. Two well-established corporate training methods depend on a combination of Demonstration and Tutorial.

Behavior Modeling

Sales training is a classic venue for behavior modeling. The learner is shown video modules of "right" and "wrong" ways to sell to a certain class of customer, then given the opportunity to role-play with a tutor, usually an experienced salesperson. The tutor gives feedback and further practice ensues until the required level of mastery is attained.

Executive Coaching

Organizations that are large enough to have a sizable cohort of upper management often invest in programs that link up-and-coming managers with experienced executives. Typically, the junior member will spend time shadowing the senior member, observing the executive at work; this is the Demonstration component. Learners then go back to their current duties and attempt to put their observations into practice. They remain in contact with their "tutors" through regular meetings and/or e-mail; this is the Tutorial component. This allows a two-way conversation about progress in the specified "growth" areas.

Tactical-Level

Show and Tell (Presentation + Demonstration)

A demonstration would rarely stand alone. It would almost always be given in some sort of context, most commonly being embedded in or introduced by a

Presentation of some sort. For example, there is a long tradition in chemistry education of using dramatic demonstrations of chemical reactions to attract student interest and provoke thinking about the underlying processes.

Chapter Summary

The Demonstration configuration has a special role as a vehicle for bridging the gap between theory and application. Comprehending a fact, principle, or procedure can be achieved by just hearing a well-organized verbal presentation, but being able to put that fact, principle, or procedure into practice requires living examples and role models.

In the Demonstration configuration, a facilitator (or a substitute in the form of a resource person or mediated presentation) displays and explains an instance—an example—of some process, procedure, or other complex task to some learner(s). Many different formats may serve as vehicles for demonstrations: science experiments, physical models (e.g., cutaway mock-ups, working models, graphic animations), and behavioral models (including role-plays and motor-skill demonstrations). Consciously or not, the teacher herself is constantly modeling how to feel about and how to think about the subject being taught. As different as these formats are, they share the concrete portrayal of natural or social processes, procedural tasks, complex skills, or attitudes.

The cognitive science behind the Demonstration configuration begins with the neural processing of auditory and visual representations, as discussed in Chapter 5; this would apply to learners' responses to experiments, models, and animated simulations. However, the learning of complex human psychomotor skills may be better viewed through the lens of Bandura's social learning theory, which appears to have its basis in the extraordinary phenomenon of "mirror neurons," a distinctive neural process that enables primates and humans to imitate the actions of others merely by watching them perform. This applies not only to explicit, observable behaviors but also to the tacit dimension. We can learn to think like and feel like our role models, which is more-or-less what is referred to as cognitive apprenticeship.

Guidelines for getting the most impact from various types of demonstration are provided by Yelon and Merrill, using somewhat different terms, but following quite congruent steps: informing learners of the objective, directing attention to critical features of the performance, asking learners to remember what they are about to see, explicitly pointing out key steps—and consequences—as they occur, and giving learners the opportunity to practice following the demonstration.

Over time, educators have devised several methods or templates for combining Demonstration with other configurations to carry out the steps recommended by Yelon and Merrill. These include "skills practice" (Demonstration followed by Repetition), "behavior modeling" and "coaching" (Demonstration accompanied by Tutorial), and "show and tell" (Demonstration accompanying Presentation).

Works Cited

Anderson, Charnel. 1962. *Technology in American Education 1650–1900.* Volume 1 of series: New Media for Instruction, Office of Education, Bulletin 1962, No. 19, U.S. Department of Health, Education, and Welfare, Washington, DC: U.S. Government Printing Office, 53 pages.

Anderson, John R. 2000. *Cognitive Psychology and Its Implications.* New York: Worth Publishers.

Bandura, Albert. 1977. *Social Learning Theory.* Englewood Cliffs, NJ: Prentice-Hall.

Bruner, Jerome S. 1966. *Toward a Theory of Instruction.* Cambridge, MA: The Belknap Press of Harvard University Press.

Collins, Allan, John Seely Brown, and Susan E. Newman. 1987. *Cognitive Apprenticeship: Teaching the Craft of Reading, Writing and Mathematics.* Technical Report No. 403, Center for the Study of Reading, University of Illinois. Cambridge, MA: Bolt Beranek and Newman, 27 pages.

Herman, Arthur. 2001. *How the Scots Invented the Modern World.* New York: Crown Publishers.

Merrill, M. David. 2013. *First Principles of Instruction.* San Francisco, CA: Pfeiffer.

Park, Ok-choon, and Stuart S. Gittelman. 1992. "Selective Use of Animation and Feedback in Computer-Based Instruction." *Educational Technology Research and Development* 40 (4): 27–38.

Rizzolatti, Giacomo, and Corrado Sinigaglia. 2008. *Mirrors in the Brain: How Our Minds Share Actions, Emotions, and Experience.* Oxford, UK: Oxford University Press.

Schnotz, Wolfgang. 2014. "Integrated Model of Text and Picture Comprehension." In *The Cambridge Handbook of Multimedia Learning,* 2nd ed., edited by Richard E. Mayer, 72–103. New York: Cambridge University Press.

Yelon, Stephen L. 1996. *Powerful Principles of Instruction.* White Plains, NY: Longman Publishers USA.

Discussion 7

The Discussion configuration differs from Presentation and Demonstration in that the locus of control may be partially shared with or even largely shifted onto the learners. The root meaning of *discuss* is to shake apart, suggesting the analysis of a topic by dissecting it and examining it. To educators, it refers to the analysis that is done by learners' sharing their thoughts and feelings about a topic.

Discussion Defined

Discussion involves the exchange of ideas and feelings among learners. It may be employed before a Presentation to arouse interest in the topic. It is more commonly used after a Presentation to allow learners to digest the new information, to internalize it, by talking about it in their own words. Discussion can also reveal misconceptions that need to be addressed.

This configuration includes two variants that differ in terms of control of the process. Whole-Class Discussion retains the traditional classroom setup with the instructor in charge; all conversation flows through the latter, who guides the conversation.

> *Whole-Class Discussion*: A Facilitator (F) engages the whole class in a conversation in which Learners (L) take turns sharing information and opinions, with the Facilitator remaining at the center, setting the agenda and controlling the flow of communication (Figure 7.1).

Small-Group Discussion breaks the class into subgroups and the members of the small groups control their own flow of communication. Once the activity is launched, learners decide what happens next.

188 Discussion

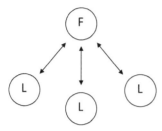

Figure 7.1 The Whole-Class Discussion Communication Configuration. The two-headed arrows indicate that communications flow to, from, and through the Facilitator.

Small-Group Discussion: Two or more Learners (L) exchange information and opinions without the intermediation of a Facilitator (F); a Facilitator may set the agenda and control logistics, but Learners control the flow of communication within the group (Figure 7.2).

Note that learner control of the conversation is a critical attribute of Small-Group Discussion. Oftentimes, instructors say "let's pause for some discussion," but what ensues is a series of question-and-answer exchanges between the instructor and different students individually. If such an interchange actually proceeds into an in-depth substantive exchange aimed at altering or supporting the learner's growing understanding, it could be viewed as an instance of Tutorial, the topic of Chapter 8.

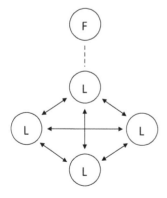

Figure 7.2 The Small-Group Discussion Communication Configuration. The two-headed arrows indicate that communications flow among the Learners; the Facilitator stands aside.

Distinguishing Whole-Class Discussion from Recitation

Another type of teacher–student interaction, commonly referred to as *recitation*, could be conflated with Discussion. In *recitation*, the teacher calls upon a student to answer a question; the teacher gives feedback to the student's reply and either continues with further questions or goes to another student for another question-and-answer sequence. There is no "collaborative construction of knowledge," just checking for comprehension (Wilkinson 2009). Although the term is rarely encountered in pedagogical parlance today, *recitation* was a prominent feature of American education from the colonial grammar school to the early twentieth-century college classroom, as illustrated by this description in a 1917 nursing education journal (Suhrie 1917):

> [Recitation is] that type of class-room exercise in which the instructor, in conference with the collective body of students to whom a given assignment has been made in either textbook, library, or laboratory work, attempts to ascertain the extent to which they have solved the problems proposed, fixed the habits desired, or memorized the principles involved in the assignment. At its worst it has little educational value. At its best it aims to assist the student in properly estimating his own progress and to reveal to him the imperfections of his method of work
>
> *(611–612).*

Clearly, the intent is assessing progress, not developing new insights into the material. To qualify as Discussion, learners must "have considerable agency in the construction of knowledge, understanding, or interpretation" (Wilkinson 2009, 330).

By contrast, in the Whole-Class Discussion configuration, while the facilitator remains in charge as moderator, all audience members are invited to volunteer to respond. Listeners who respond to the leader's prompts are addressing the whole group; all are expected to pay attention and all are invited to respond to her remarks. The audience responses may become a conversation, possibly branching off into unanticipated directions.

Distinguishing Instructed Learning from Natural Learning

For something to fit our definition of Discussion, it has to be formally set up with explicit instructional intent. While arguably the larger part of human learning occurs informally via lived experiences, let us remember that the communication configurations presented in this book do not deal with such natural learning. Some commonly experienced "discussion" formats, such as adult book clubs, probably would not fit our definition of Discussion because they are informal and not explicitly instructional in intent. Book club discussions of fiction works usually aim to enhance readers' experience with the book being read, not necessarily to learn anything specific beyond that, even though informal learning can and does occur in the process. In the case of nonfiction books, the purpose may also be entertainment or appreciation of the work itself, with any learning occurring mostly as a side effect. Only if there is an intention to gain new knowledge or understanding of the history or geography being described or of the scientific principles underlying the book, or the like, would the discussion be labeled instructional. In that case, the guidelines for small-group discussion would be relevant.

Formats Associated with Discussion

One of the obstacles to classifying the various types of discussions is that in the educational research literature there is a disturbing lack of clarity about what is counted as an instance of "discussion." As Dudley-Marling points out in his review of literature, "Most serious of all, with the exception of a few studies, researchers have been virtually silent on what they mean by 'discussion'" (Dudley-Marling 2013, 5). This deficiency in operational definitions was one of the factors impelling us to compose the typology outlined in this book and to devote special attention to specifying the formats for each communication configuration. In reality, discussions vary widely in scope—they may be as brief as a few minutes or as long as a several-hour seminar—and in structure; they may be tightly controlled or freewheeling. To make some sense of the many different arrangements for discussion, we will treat them in three categories: whole-class, small-group, and dyad.

Whole-Class

As defined above, whole-class formats treat the whole audience, large or small, as one intact group, and the facilitator serves a moderator. Examples:

- seminar, particularly an open-ended one in which students guide the direction
- Paideia seminar, a whole-class, structured method for analyzing a text
- break in lecture for whole-class interaction, such as brainstorming
- debriefing that follows a whole-class use of a simulation or game.

Small-Group

As defined above, in the small-group formats, learners are divided into sets of three to perhaps ten or twelve participants, each set holding its own conversation, controlled by the participants. Examples:

- buzz group—a brief, intense interchange among a few participants as a breakout session in a lecture setting
- T-group—sensitivity training exercise for attitude and behavior change
- panel discussion (a Discussion for the panelists, a Presentation for listeners)
- debate (a Discussion for the debaters, a Presentation for listeners)
- collaborative learning, teams of two to perhaps six, work together live or through synchronous chats or forums or asynchronous threaded discussion forums
- study groups, live or via video conferencing or Web conferencing
- "small groups" for Bible study in religious congregations
- "workshopping" a play in a rehearsal setting or a short story in a writing seminar
- interactive cultural conversations with foreign students via video Web conferencing.

Dyad

In proposing dyads—two-person groups—as a vehicle for Discussion, we are aware of the fine line that separates such usages from tutoring, which is explored in the next chapter. The key is that in the Discussion mode neither participant is playing the role of "knowledgeable other." Each of the two are searchers, trying to come to new understandings through mutual exchange.

After the "cognitive revolution" of the 1960s, a number of innovations emerged, aimed at helping students spend more of their academic time in one-to-one peer conversations. Thus, attention shifted to the *dyad* arrangement, led by Marcel Goldschmid's development of the "learning cell" (Goldschmid 1971) at the Swiss Federal Institute of Technology. Students are randomly assigned to dyads, and they take turns asking and answering questions about assigned readings, with the instructor visiting dyads to give feedback. This is akin to the *chavrusa* discussion format in the *yeshiva* system, mentioned earlier in this chapter. Other examples of discussion dyads:

- "interteaching"—like the "learning cell," students assigned to pairs to discuss a structured list of questions over an extended period
- Peer Instruction—students pair up with a neighbor to discuss a challenging question in the middle of a lecture (discussed below as a Method)
- conversation partners in live or online language learning.

Mediated Discussion Formats

Distance Education

In the days before computers, one of the major shortcomings of correspondence study and other forms of distance education was the difficulty of arranging any sort of peer-to-peer discussion. As soon as computers became networked—around the 1990s—educators began to explore ways to utilize them for conversations between and among learners. At first it was simple e-mail, allowing individuals to converse with other individuals, share files, and thus collaborate on some sort of written assignment. A little later, conferencing software allowed more than two participants to share in the same (keyboard) conversation. By the end of the 1990s, there were dozens of applications that allowed synchronous and asynchronous interaction via keyboard—from brainstorming to chatting to preparing collaborative reports. Also emerging around this time was discussion around a video presentation; as remote students watched a video together, they could make on-screen annotations through their keyboards, thus stimulating back-and-forth conversations about each other's annotations.

By the 2010s, many different synchronous tools and platforms for collaboration were available, later to include voice communication, such as Blackboard Collaborate, Google Hangouts, Skype, and Adobe Connect. Eventually, virtually all the platforms used for computer-based distance education have come to incorporate tools such as these. Such synchronous tools have the limitation of requiring all participants to be signed in at the same time, which can pose challenges for distance education programs that enroll students across multiple time zones.

In cases where users are not all available to interact at the same time, meaningful interaction can still be arranged through asynchronous tools such as e-mail, discussion forums, document-sharing, and wikis, which can allow sound and images in addition to text, and which allow dispersed learners to collaborate on joint projects.

In short, what had originally been a shortcoming of distance education—having to communicate electronically—has become an advantage. Now, online tools allow a range of apparently infinitely scalable possibilities for interaction and collaboration that surpass those of the everyday face-to-face classroom. This is particularly true in terms of bringing together diverse groups of learners. Online tools enable communication amongst learners of different ages, cultures, nations, and socioeconomic backgrounds—in ways that can be much more challenging to achieve face-to-face, given the geographical, socioeconomic, cultural, and communicative distances between different groups of learners.

Blended Learning

Indeed, the possibilities for synchronous and asynchronous communication have grown so enormously that they have encouraged educators to seek ways to bring mediated activities that were traditionally the province of distance education into the F2F classroom. This phenomenon is known as *blended learning*, a combination of F2F and computer-mediated experiences (Graham 2006). Schools, universities, corporations, and military services around the world design programs of study such that learners can enjoy the benefits of both F2F and distance formats. For example, a corporate training course might be based in a live classroom for a combination of

Presentation and Whole-Class Discussion; then participants might download some practice exercises to a smartphone, which they can work on while commuting via public transit. They could share their answers with their virtual study group via text messages or an asynchronous discussion forum, and the group could collaborate by means of a wiki or shared document to prepare a group report.

The blended learning phenomenon spread widely in the 2010s. Some educators who were unfamiliar with its distance education roots and who thought they discovered something new dubbed it "the flipped classroom." By this they meant that the work normally done in the classroom—listening to a lecture—could now be done by viewing a recorded version at home, freeing class time for Discussion or Repetition, doing the sort of processing of the information traditionally done through study groups or homework assignments outside of class. Thus, the allocation of class time is "flipped" compared to traditional practice.

These formats—whole-class, small-group, dyadic, or distance—differ in terms of how many students are involved, what role the Facilitator plays, and how structured their interactions are. They share the critical attribute of engaging learners in active conversation about a topic. They are all intended to take learners out of the passive listening mode and into a more active, dynamic process.

The Evolution of Discussion

Early Historical Traditions

Uses of student-to-student discussion for educational purposes in the distant past are not well documented. During the early eras of formal education, expertise was presumed to be the province of the teacher and any written texts that were available. One of the few documented applications of Discussion in formal education is the Yeshiva, the Jewish institution that focuses on the study of traditional religious texts, which can be traced back at least to the third century AD. In a yeshiva, the primary means of study was (and remains) the *chavrusa*, a student-to-student discussion of the text under consideration. The *chavrusa* sessions were interspersed with daily and weekly *shiurim*—lectures by knowledgeable experts; but the *chavrusa* was primary. Unlike a tutorial relationship, the *chavrusa* requires each student to analyze the text and develop a coherent construction of the meaning, which he explains to his partner. The partner analyzes that construction, questions any weak points, and presents his own reasoning. They continue the give-and-take until they arrive at a consensual meaning.

At the University of Oxford, the use of the tutors is documented back to the fifteenth century, but the "tutorial system" as we know it today was instituted late in the nineteenth century. In that system, students meet regularly with an academic supervisor—a *don*—and a small group of fellow students, who—in addition to one-to-one tutoring—are led through a discussion among those students of assigned readings and essays (Markham 1967).

Democratic Perspective

In America, through the late nineteenth century and into twentieth century, the resources available for education—qualified teachers, adequate facilities, books, and libraries—gradually improved. It then became possible to implement the more flexible and more democratic methods of instruction being proposed by philosophers of education such as John Dewey (1916). This school of thought views individuals as inseparable from their society. Hence, education is a social activity, which, in a democratic society, should be conducted along democratic lines. Ideally, students work with others on meaningful problems, sharing responsibility and sharing their perspectives through Discussion. More recent advocates, such as Brookfield and Preskill (2005), posit that discussion is the very process that makes democracy possible: "discussion helps students learn the processes and habits of democratic discourse" (30).

Shift to Student-Centered Psychology

World War I saw American psychologists gaining experience in applying their methods to practical problems, such as selection and training of troops. The post–World War I period brought the first empirical research on teaching methods, including discussion (McKeachie 1990, 189). Interest in "student-centered" methods surged in the years after World War II, impelled by new psychological perspectives, such as Carl Rogers's "client-centered therapy" and the group-dynamics movement inspired by Kurt Lewin's work (McKeachie 1990, 191). Application of these ideas in college teaching led to a major research project on methods, including discussion, at the University of Michigan in the 1940s. The results generally showed "no significant difference" for different treatments, presaging a plethora of later studies reaching the same conclusion for other innovations (Guetzkow, Kelly and McKeachie 1954). To their credit, the authors acknowledged that the experimental treatment occupied only a small part of the overall course experience in their University of Michigan study, a factor not often reported as a limitation in similar studies. They also commented on a limiting factor emphasized by Dudley-Marling (2013) in his literature review—that the outcome measures were seldom if ever sensitive to the measurement of the sorts of conceptual change that Discussion advocates claim to be the outcome of well-executed discussion: "deep, engaged learning."

In the 1960s, the influx of "baby boom" students created pressures on American universities to accommodate larger cadres of students, giving them incentive to experiment with instructional methods that could maintain quality without increasing faculty size. Independent study and student-centered discussion methods flourished. Meanwhile, in elementary and secondary education and adult education, similar forces, including the "cognitive revolution" and burgeoning post–World War II enrollments, created conditions for experimenting with student-centered methods.

Cognitive Science and Neuroscience Behind Discussion

To begin with, when learners discuss among themselves, they are engaging in speech, so the neural pathways described in Chapter 5 under "Language Comprehension" and "Language Production" apply here as well. More important, there are relevant findings from neuroscience specifically about how the brain reacts during person-to-person communications. In Chapter 8, we will consider the neural processes involved in relationships between therapist and client or mentor and mentee. When trust is established, "attunement" between the parties helps to alleviate the subconscious fear that may be aroused when the learner is abandoning a previous position and developing a more critical posture. This has been well established in research on therapist–client relationships (S. Johnson 2006).

However, more recent neuroscience research in the Basque Country, using electroencephalography (EEG), reveals that when two people are conversing, even if they are strangers, their brains work to synchronize neural oscillations, creating a connection that allows each to work toward the common goal of clear communication (Pérez, Carreiras and Duñabeitia 2017). This sort of synchronizing is referred to as "neural entrainment," a process in which electrical activity in ensembles of cortical neurons adjust to synchronize with the periodic vibrations of an external source, in this case, oral narratives spoken by another person. Thus, the sorts of conversations that occur during discussion can promote an atmosphere of trust that enhances mutual receptivity to each other's ideas. Of course, this neuroscientific insight is especially relevant to the Tutorial configuration, so this finding is discussed in Chapter 8 as well.

Strengths and Limitations: Why Discussion?

Humans have long understood that the creation of usable knowledge requires more than the transmission of information from expert to novice. Receivers need opportunities to clarify and refine their understanding through back-and-forth exchanges with others, not just experts but especially with fellow learners. Fellow learners can empathize with each other, understand each other's struggles, and offer solutions suited to the level of the novice. All learners, but especially adult learners, appreciate the opportunity to share their personal experiences with others. Aside from what may or may not be happening inside the head of the learner, we can *see* when learners are talking amongst themselves; we can see people leaning forward to listen or make a point; we can feel the energy level rising. The switch from passive listening to active discussion is palpable. You do not have to be committed to any particular theory of learning to value active engagement over passivity.

Strengths

Practice

The ability to remember, and certainly to *use*, new information depends on how deeply the learner processes that information. Through Discussion learners can strengthen and deepen their grasp of the material by going through the process of thinking about it and talking about it—comparing and contrasting it with prior knowledge, explaining it to someone else, summarizing it, and so on. In Chapter 9, we examine the role of Repetition in learning; Discussion is one convenient way of engaging learners in *practice* in the cognitive domain. If we want them to be able to integrate new knowledge into their repertoire and to be able to apply that knowledge, why not give them a chance to practice those skills? Further, in Discussion learners are practicing under circumstances in which they receive corrective feedback as they proceed, an ideal condition for Repetition, as discussed in Chapter 9.

Fitting into Existing Schemata

All learners come to the classroom with a store of life experience. Discussion allows them to bring those experiences into play, thus honoring the value of those experiences, while advancing the educational goal of building on existing cognitive structures or schemata. Learners are more likely to retain and use knowledge that they perceive as relevant to their own lives. When learners hear other members of their own cohort verbalize their ideas, giving examples from their own lives, they come to understand that other people have different perspectives, worthy of respect. They come away with a richer conceptualization than if they only heard from a textbook or lecturer.

Limitations

Avoiding Participation

First, no instructional activity is useful if students do not take part in it, as lectures are of no value if the audience members are not listening. Likewise, discussion periods can be passive experiences. Rocca's review of the literature on discussion in postsecondary classrooms (2010) reveals that relatively few students participate, even when offered the opportunity. Such dodging of accountability is easier in a whole-class discussion in a large class than in a more intimate setting, such as a seminar or small-group discussion. It can be overcome, but with the expenditure of extra effort in training and motivating the class members.

Sociocultural Barriers among Discussants

Diversity in a learning community is a two-sided coin. It offers great opportunities, but it can also erect barriers if issues are not addressed. Discussion is unique among the various communication configurations in how it can broaden horizons and deepen understanding by taking advantage of the diversity—of race, ethnicity, language, class, gender, sexual orientation, ability, etc.—that is inherent within any group of human beings (Brookfield and Preskill 2005). The authors go so far as to say that "without a willingness to confront and exploit differences, very little of real value or meaning can emerge" (124). At the same time, these differences can represent differences in perceived power relationships that can inhibit free and candid exchange of ideas if left unaddressed. As one example of potential barriers, consider gender's complex role: (a) men tend to talk more often and they tend to assume the role of small-group reporter; (b) women are much more likely to preface their contribution with a self-deprecatory remark and to express feelings associated with pain and suffering; (c) men are more likely to express feelings of anger and to make sarcastic comments (Roulis 2005).

In addition to gender, socioeconomic status and race are at least as important in determining who gets to speak, for how long, and whose voice is taken seriously (Roulis 2005). When discussants differ as to native language—or even accent—their peers may make stereotyping judgments about them, diminishing the value of their contributions or making them self-conscious about even speaking at all. All these are potential limitations to productive discussion, but they are not insuperable barriers. In the "Best Practices" section below, we will mention some steps that can ameliorate these difficulties.

Primarily for Cognitive Objectives

Second, the Discussion configuration—even when students do participate—provides practice primarily in the cognitive domain. It is all about speech comprehension and retention of verbal concepts and principles. If the Discussion format requires some conscious attention to the feelings of other participants, learners may be developing some skills in the interpersonal domain, although that is usually considered a concomitant skill, not a target skill. Also, it is quite likely that participants in a discussion will develop greater interest in or even fondness for the subject matter, adding an affective facet to the cognitive knowledge. But, again, this would usually be an implicit or concomitant type of learning, not one of the target skills.

Trade-off between Time Expended and Increased Retention

Third, discussion requires more time to "cover" material than straightforward Presentation and Demonstration. Outside observers and administrators might question the expenditure of time in a way that may not appear to be directly headed to the goal of "covering" all the content of a course. The instructor may have to justify use of this strategy; in contrast, lectures are traditionally perceived as a "gold standard" in Method A vs. Method B comparison studies and are thus seldom questioned.

Facilitator Skill Set

Fourth, arranging a productive discussion requires extra effort if one is working in a lecture-based environment. It requires skills that are not necessarily picked up along the way by many people who play the role of Facilitator. In the case of whole-class discussion, the instructor remains in charge but plays a different role. A discussion leader is more of a moderator or host, occasionally a devil's advocate, occasionally a referee, but not a didact or preacher. This role change can pose a psychological hurdle. Anyone would be hesitant to leave their comfort zone and embark on a venture whose outcome is uncertain. The discussion leader accepts responsibility for keeping students engaged, motivated, and contributing. The role is easier for someone who is outgoing and enthusiastic by nature.

Not only are most instructors at home with the lecture method, so are most learners. It might require a period of trial-and-error learning for both the instructor and her students before they feel confident about investing effort in learning via Discussion. Some suggestions are given below under "Facilitating Task Groups and Cooperative Learning Groups."

Best Practices in Conducting Discussions

Discussion episodes typically are aimed primarily at cognitive objectives. But even when cognitive objectives are primary, there are usually implicit, concomitant goals of an interpersonal and affective nature. Instructors hope that students will develop a disposition toward respectful communication and, ultimately, toward democratic behavior (Brookfield and Preskill 2005); these are interpersonal objectives. Instructors also hope that students will come to have greater enthusiasm about the topic after discussion; this is an affective objective. Needless to say, these goals are not met by chance. Careful preparation enhances the likelihood of success, as is true of any teaching–learning activity.

For groups of diverse backgrounds, that advance preparation could include steps to help reduce the potential barriers to easy communication. When it comes to *socioeconomic* and *cultural* divides, Brookfield and Preskill (2005) recommend (a) getting participants to talk about themselves as members of cultural groups or social classes; (b) giving participants space and time to point out that their perspective is not being taken seriously; (c) providing an outlet for expressing anger or sorrow;

(d) monitoring the discussion for signs of insensitivity; and (e) introducing frequent perception checks, which involves describing what one thinks a particular participant is feeling and requesting that they confirm or correct this description.

Detailing ways in which classroom expectations and rituals can be altered to help learners find new ways of talking about and across *gender*, Roulis (2005) recommends: (a) relational talk—beginning discussion-based courses with personal disclosure; (b) establishing ground rules granting learners license to stumble in conversation without feeling stigmatized; and (c) rapport talk—introducing periods of women-only discussion, alternated with periods of men-only discussion. She also suggests more complex strategies such as: (a) beginning discussions with standpoint statements—having learners write down a few demographic descriptors that fit them; (b) having learners generate personal preference lists—the things they most enjoy doing in their lives; (c) using texts drawn from popular culture to alert learners to ways in which they perpetuate or subvert stereotypes about how men and women talk; and (d) having learners evaluate how a discussion went.

Whole-Class Discussion

Preparation: Arrange Common Experience

If the aim is to have some conversation that delves into a deeper layer of understanding, some advance preparation is required. First, ideally, a discussion should be based on some common experience. It puts all participants on a level playing field, even those who are new to subject, and even those who have not done the assigned readings. This common experience could be a video clip, a staged role-play, autobiographical testimony, or even a field experience. After the presentation, a leading question can initiate discussion, such as "Why do you think _____ did what you just witnessed?"

Preparation: Provocative Questions

In any event, the discussion leader should come in with prepared questions, beginning with broad, provocative questions to prompt initial response. The instructor could, for example, adopt a controversial position and invite disagreement (making it clear that this is an artificial posture). It is helpful to inform listeners that they should take half-a-minute to think about their response before opening the floor to discussion. Once the dialogue is flowing, narrower questions can be posed, if necessary, to focus attention on the target concepts. With written questions in hand, the leader will feel more confident about maintaining control and steering the dialogue in the desired direction.

Start with Ground Rules

Announcing some ground rules for discussion helps participants feel more comfortable about speaking up. Examples of ground rules are found below under "Small-Group Discussion." Suggestions for conducting brainstorming sessions are outlined below.

While under Way

A quotidian detail, but an important one, is to record key words of students' responses on a chalkboard or whiteboard, or a graphics tablet in the case of distance education. This serves two purposes: first, it validates the voice of the student, seeing their words on the screen; second, it serves as a record of the discussion, providing a handy means to summarize at the end.

It might be necessary to interrupt the discussion to comment on the process. Pointing out positive and negative behavior helps the group learn how to dialogue productively. This does not mean breaking into a lecture. Allow the process to play out. If conversation lags, revisit earlier comments. Challenge them or point out gaps in responses so far. On the other hand, if too many want to get into the conversation at once, consider breaking temporarily into small groups (see below), each dealing with one part of the topic. The process does not have to flow neatly; some chaos can be stimulating.

If nonparticipation is an issue, the instructor can ask everyone to write down an answer to the instructor's question. After a pause to write, nonparticipants can be invited to tell what they wrote.

Discussions at a Distance

Whole-class discussion in a distance education setting may be constrained or facilitated by the software available to students. Most course management systems include applications that allow various, flexible forms of communication between and among students. Live, synchronous chatrooms can operate much like a face-to-face class as long as participants follow some guidelines for how to jump into the conversation. Asynchronous discussion forums can provide a structured format for dialogue, with the advantage of allowing users the time to process others' comments and compose coherent responses. One advantage of these online tools is that they may allow wider participation. Students who are shy or apprehensive may remain passive in the classroom, but may jump into the fray in the online environment when they have time to form and even check their responses before typing them.

Brainstorming

The purpose of *brainstorming* is to generate creative thinking about a problem. Brainstorming is often used to introduce a new topic or new problem. The activity encourages a flurry of ideas, regardless of their practicality. It should be fast-paced and freewheeling. Brainstorming discussions have some additional ground rules:

- Initial "storming" phase
  - Appoint a recorder to record all ideas.
  - Don't self-censor; the initial goal is to gather lots of ideas, however wild. "Quantity over quality."
  - No evaluation of other people's ideas.
  - Build on other people's ideas; nobody has ownership.
- "Sifting" phase
  - Discard only the most impractical ideas.
  - Discuss ways to combine ideas.
  - Reach tentative conclusions by general consensus.
- Final "decision" phase
  - Keep original goal in mind.
  - If bogged down, talk about why.
  - Group ideas into categories.
  - Establish and apply evaluative criteria.
  - Reach final decision or decide on what needs further study.

Small-Group Discussion

Preparation

Like any instructional activity, small-group discussions are more productive if the instructor or trainer plans the logistics ahead of time. For example:

- Pre-assign groups and designate where they will meet.
- Print out or prominently display the assigned group tasks.
- Provide needed materials—whiteboard, markers, name tags, etc.

Start with Ground Rules

Instructors can keep the energy level high by announcing very short time limits on each phase of discussion. Counting down the minutes remaining helps instill a sense of urgency. Time is always precious, so let participants know you are looking for efficiency. Of course, if the topic is a sensitive one requiring emotional processing, groups should be given the time necessary to let everyone speak and respond. In fact, in such cases, the ground rules (see below) may specify that the session is not over until each member has spoken.

When learners are broken into small groups, even for brief, occasional episodes, it is recommended to institute some ground rules in order to keep the conversation focused and productive:

- Listen actively and attentively to others.
- Do not interrupt others.
- Speak up if you have an idea that has not been represented.
- Speak from your own experience: "I think . . .," not "Most people would say . . ."
- Disagree politely; critique ideas, not people; sarcasm tears down trust.
- Stay on task.
- Speak only loudly enough to be heard in your group.

Assign Roles

If small groups are going to be used as a regular feature of a class or training session, it is worthwhile to assign members to specific roles, and then rotate these roles so that everyone has a chance at every role. Some roles that are particularly useful:

- coordinator (one per group): convenes the group; keeps the discussion focused; pushes for closure
- recorder (one per group): takes notes of group deliberations; presents the group's findings
- explorer (any number): adopts an "outsider" mentality; seeks out divergent opinions beyond the required readings; finds outside sources of data or opinion
- evaluator (one per group): leaves the group and sits with another group to appraise the quality of their interactions and conclusions; completes a checklist to be given to the group. It is especially educative for participants to serve as evaluators of the functionality of their group or other groups. By evaluating others, they develop sensitivity to the behaviors that make groups successful.

Cooperative/Collaborative Learning Group

If an instructor is planning to use group-based learning as a major feature of a course of learning, the management of group dynamics becomes a necessity. A popular framework for thinking about group processes is the Forming-Storming-Norming-Performing model proposed by Bruce Tuckman (1965). When a group is first formed, it goes through a phase of orientation—meeting each other, finding out about what tasks lie ahead, and beginning to think outside their own individual interests. At the "storming" phase, some individuals might clash over issues of dominance or shirking or simply over how best to proceed. If the group survives the turbulence, they enter the "norming" phase in which they accept each other's faults, recognize each other's strengths, form a group identity, and get on with the mission, thus entering the "performing" phase.

Assisting Group Dynamics

Understanding that groups need some time and practice in order to become functional is an important first step—"forewarned is forearmed." Instructors need not become experts in group dynamics to be helpful to groups as they move through the phases of growth. During the "norming" stage they can, first, take care in forming groups: distributing domineering types across groups rather than clustering them together and distributing mature, facilitative types across groups. The instructor and other more mature members of each group can serve as role models for tolerance and patience as groups become oriented. If some groups experience turbulence during the "storming" phase, the leader can meet with them, serving as a resource to answer their questions and to suggest ways to face up to their conflicts and resolve them. Being a model for mutual trust and patience can be helpful. As groups move into "norming" and "performing," it would be helpful to get feedback from the group members about how they perceive their progress. A simple checklist with space for open-ended comments can help identify unmet needs. Be ready to spend time with each team to be a resource and simply to communicate your interest in their success.

Incentives for Cooperation

A primary requirement of true cooperative learning is that members of the group actually share responsibility and have a stake in each other's mastery of the objective. This sharing mentality can be encouraged by thoughtful management of incentives. For example, for a manual skill objective, an industrial trainer assigned trainees to groups of four to practice the operation of several items of equipment. They were given written directions and told to help each other master the machine operations. They were advised that they would be tested by having *one* member selected at random to demonstrate operation of each machine; that person represented the group, pass or fail.

A Template for Cooperative Learning

In formal education, a well-established format for cooperative learning is *Student Teams-Achievement Divisions (STAD)*, a protocol developed by Robert Slavin and associates at Johns Hopkins University in the 1990s (Slavin 1995). In STAD, students are placed in four-person teams, all of which are equally mixed in terms of ability, ethnicity, and gender. Following whole-class activities, teams work together using worksheets and other resources in order to help each other improve proficiency. Students are tested individually, but teams are given points based on total performance of all team members. This scoring system is designed to encourage interdependence and achievement motivation.

Methods Featuring the Discussion Configuration

Whole-Class Discussion

Interactive Lecture (Presentation + Whole-Class Discussion)

Discussion activities are often used in conjunction with the Presentation configuration, either to wrap up a topic or to interrupt a lecture episode with some active work with the material. When using a more inductive approach, Discussion can be used before a Presentation as a way of arousing curiosity about the topic and highlighting the issues that need to be covered. Communication is one-way in Presentation configuration, but interspersing Discussion episodes lends interaction to the overall experience.

Vicarious Interaction

A popular variation of the *interactive lecture* is known as the *Fishbowl method*. It tends to be used as a complement to a lecture class. One small group of approximately four students is chosen by the instructor to engage in a discussion—at the front of the room or in the center with others forming a circle around them. As they discuss the questions proffered by the instructor, the other students listen and take notes; they may participate by handing notes to discussants. Since the majority of the class is not physically involved in the discussion, for them it is a Demonstration—of the mechanics of small-group discussion (a useful way to train novices on using discussion methods) and of the ways of handling the ideas being considered.

The *Fishbowl method* can be adapted to distance education. Sutton (2001) proposes the term *vicarious interaction* to describe the process of observing other students engaged in discussion, such as lurking on a discussion forum or reading argumentative blogs or wiki comments. She suggests that learners can derive some—but not all—of the benefits of discussion vicariously.

Debriefing (Experiential Activity + Whole-Class Discussion)

Originally referring to the post-action, intelligence-gathering interviews with military operatives, the meaning of *debriefing* has expanded to include group discussions following some animating, perhaps dramatic, real or lifelike experience (Pearson and Smith 1985). The initial experiential, hands-on activity may range from children going on a field trip to a farm to adults playing a social simulation game. All participants gather after the event and talk about their experiences and the meaning of those experiences in terms of the original learning objectives; the discussion is usually moderated by someone with expertise in the subject matter being studied. See also "Methods" in Chapter 9 for a discussion of debriefing in the simulation and game context.

Seminar (Study + Whole-Class Discussion)

Best suited to smaller class sizes, students convene to discuss readings or laboratory projects recently completed. The convener/moderator is usually someone more experienced than the learners and may interject expert opinions as well as guiding discussion among learners, who do most of the talking. The broad *seminar* model has been adapted many times to fine-tune the process for specific learning domains or educational settings; we will mention two variations: the Harkness Discussion and the Paideia Seminar.

The Harkness Discussion

The Harkness Discussion is named for the philanthropist who funded its development at Phillips Exeter Academy; it is best suited to smaller class sizes. Students do assigned readings and prepare questions to ask their classmates. Seated in an oval, facing each other, one of the students begins by asking a question, asking for volunteers to respond, and serving as temporary discussion leader. Other students then take turns asking questions and responding. The teacher stays in the background, while the students act as a team to guide the discussion (Smith and Foley 2009).

The Paideia Seminar

The Paideia Seminar is named for a curriculum plan proposed by philosopher Mortimer Adler (1982). In this curriculum, one of the three main instructional methods is a type of seminar in which discussion is based on the reading of primary materials, not textbooks. Teachers lead the discussion with challenging questions;

student respond freely. The Paideia seminar is more dependent on expert teacher guidance than other formats of Discussion.

Brainstorming (Presentation + Whole-Class Discussion)

Brainstorming is described earlier in this chapter under "Best Practices for Whole-Class Discussion." As mentioned earlier, the purpose of brainstorming is to generate creative thinking about a problem, often used to pique interest in a new topic, prior to a presentation, or to conclude a unit of study with a problem to be solved.

Small-Group Discussion

Buzz Group (Presentation + Small-Group Discussion)

We are using the term *buzz group* to refer generically to small, short-duration "breakout" groups (three to five persons) that are formed on-the-spot in an impromptu fashion as part of a larger lecture session. They typically invite audience members to render some opinion or share some personal experience relevant to the topic of study (Brookfield and Preskill 2005). After a short discussion period, the moderator gathers a sampling of responses from different groups.

Study Group (Study + Small-Group Discussion)

Discussions are also useful for processing material that has just been read, as when students form a *study group* to support their reading of a textbook or to work out their responses to an assigned homework task. This type of discussion group is typically self-organized and self-managed and may convene regularly over the period of a semester. As with other Discussion activities, much of the learning comes from, first, coming to the meetings prepared—having done the readings, having prepared questions to ask, etc.; second, being required to formulate one's own thoughts on the subject at hand, and third, listening to the perspectives of others.

Online Study Group

Currently, much of the interest in this method is focused on its use in distance education—the *online study group*. During the pre-Internet era of distance education various configurations developed to allow remote students to view video presentations synchronously, with the ability to stop and start the video and pause for discussion as desired . . . referred to as *collaborative video viewing*. With the advent of MOOCs, the challenge of providing student interaction is magnified many-fold, since hundreds or thousands of individuals may be taking a given course. Various versions of collaborative video viewing, adapted for different platforms, have gained support from students, and may become the method of choice for promoting learner-to-learner social and conceptual interaction during MOOC participation (Li et al. 2014).

Cooperative/Collaborative Learning Groups (Study + Small-Group Discussion + Expression)

Small groups can be established for longer lasting periods of collaborative work toward an assigned goal, thus combining Discussion with Expression, the development of a prescribed product or solution to a problem. Cooperative learning is associated with formal education, especially at the K–12 level (Johnson and Johnson 1999). The burgeoning of online tools for collaboration in the 1990s coincided with a philosophical shift, advocated by some educators, toward a sociocultural view of learning. This view recognizes that whenever people learn in a group setting they are affected by the social connections and cultural values of the group; learning always has a social context. The concept of cooperative learning is to involve students in group activities that encourage them to become—and to see themselves as—members of a community, tapping into the collective intelligence of a community of learners, with the understanding that the whole is more than the sum of its parts:

> Cooperative learning provides an environment in which students can reflect upon their newly acquired knowledge, process what they are learning by talking with and actively listening to their peers, and develop a common understanding about various topics.
>
> *(Dean et al. 2012, 37)*

There is not a canonical version of cooperative learning, but the shared attributes of all versions include (a) positive interdependence among group members, and (b) individual accountability (Dean et al. 2012).

Many variations have been devised to offer novel procedures for packaging collaborative learning. For example, in *Gallery Walk* small groups gather around posters placed around the classroom by the teacher, each proposing provocative ideas or questions (Vogt and Echevarria 2008).

Online Collaborative Learning

Collaborative learning has been logically advanced and apparently rendered infinitely scalable in recent decades, initially via online asynchronous discussion forums (e.g., "electronic cafés") and synchronous forums (e.g., chatrooms), and subsequently via specialized collaborative platforms and vast mediated social networks on the Web. For example, the *Gallery Walk* method described above can be adapted to Web courses or MOOCs by arranging for groups to create a Web page as the output of their deliberations.

Self-Organized Learning Environments (Repetition + Small-Group Discussion)

Many experiential activities employ Discussion as part of the instructional event. For example, most experienced instructional game or simulation users believe that the debriefing after the game or simulation is when learning is crystalized and internalized. Debriefing is usually set up as a whole-class discussion, structured by leading questions that will guide players toward understanding the lessons hidden in the game play.

A famous example of the successful combination of hands-on Repetition with Discussion, known as the "Hole in the Wall Project," occurred in Delhi, India, in 1999. British educational technologist Sugata Mitra—along with coinvestigators from an Indian for-profit training company called National Institute of Information Technology (NIIT) where he served as chief scientist at the time—set up a computer in an alcove in a slum neighborhood and observed as children came to tinker with the computer. Without any guidance at all, the children gradually figured out how to accomplish tasks with the computer. They took turns exploring functions, explaining what they discovered to others and letting them try it. As they developed a vocabulary to describe various procedures, they held informal discussions to decide on shortcuts or how to explore other functions. The experiment was repeated in other sites with comparable results. From it grew a pedagogical theory, self-organized learning environments (SOLE), for learning technology skills by exploration and discussion (Mitra and Crawley 2014).

Dyads

The two examples we offer as methods for using the Dyad format are both based on the notion that a good way to master a subject is to teach it to another. In both Peer Instruction and interteaching, students involved in formal classes take turns playing the role of facilitator, massaging their own understanding of a topic by explaining it to another.

Peer Instruction (Presentation + Dyad Discussion + Expression)

Peer Instruction (PI) is a highly structured method developed by Eric Mazur to engage students during a class session by requiring them to explain key concepts to peers. After a short presentation, listeners are given a challenging conceptual question; they have a few minutes of quiet reflection to formulate an answer and write it down. Students then discuss their answers with peers sitting near them, trying to convince them to accept their answer. After a short discussion period, the instructor collects the answers, explains the preferred answer, and moves on to the next topic (Crouch and Mazur 2001). This method has been adapted to the elementary school level as the *Think-Pair-Share method*.

Interteaching or Learning Cell (Study + Dyad Discussion + Expression)

Interteaching was developed by Boyce and Hineline (2002) as a means of applying behavioral learning theory to classroom instruction. Meeting in a traditional classroom setting, rotating pairs of students—"where 'total involvement' is maintained by natural contingencies of social interaction" (Boyce and Hineline 2002, 219)—take turns asking and answering problem-oriented questions prepared by the instructor, based on assigned readings. At the end of the 30-minute session they complete a report form, indicating issues that require further explanation. These reports aid the instructor in preparing lectures. A similar procedure, the *learning cell*, was developed by Marcel Goldschmid (1971), as described earlier in this chapter.

Chapter Summary

Discussion involves the exchange of ideas and feelings among learners. It is the first of the several communication configurations sequentially described in this book that attempts to move the locus of control over the learning experience away from the facilitator and at least partway towards the learner.

Whole-Class Discussion retains the normal classroom setup with the instructor in charge; all conversations flow through the facilitator, who guides the conversation. Typical formats for whole-class discussions include the seminar, brainstorming, and debriefing after immersive learning experiences. In contrast, Small-Group Discussion breaks the class into subgroups and the members of the small groups control their own flow of communication. Typical formats for small-group discussions include buzz groups, collaborative learning teams, study groups, and online chatrooms and discussion forums. The smallest possible group is the dyad; typical formats for two-person discussions include "interteaching," peer instruction, and foreign language conversation partners.

While its use for educational purposes in the distant past is not well documented, it has always been part of the instructional landscape and has become more and more prominent as the constructivist perspective on learning has gained dominance. Discussion is widely employed today across K–12/higher education and corporate training contexts, and across F2F, blended, and distance education settings. Within online learning, including MOOCs, contemporary technological tools/platforms have rendered various Discussion arrangements increasingly accessible to learners and almost infinitely scalable.

Neuroscience research suggests Discussion may help provoke a sort of neural synchronization that helps establish a receptive atmosphere that cannot be matched via other communication configurations. Like any other configuration, Discussion has its advantages and drawbacks from a pedagogical standpoint, and needs to be conceptualized and implemented with appropriate, strategic intention in order for it to help meet pedagogical goals. Discussion—if deployed effectively—can allow for vastly expanded interaction between learners and maximization of a learning community's collective intelligence.

Works Cited

Adler, Mortimer J. 1982. *The Paideia Proposal: An Educational Manifesto*. New York: Simon & Schuster.

Boyce, Thomas E., and Philip N. Hineline. 2002. "Interteaching: A Strategy for Enhancing the User-Friendliness of Behavioral Arrangements in the College Classroom." *The Behavior Analyst* 25: 215–226.

Brookfield, Stephen D., and Stephen Preskill. 2005. *Discussion as a Way of Teaching: Tools and Techniques for Democratic Classrooms*. 2nd ed. San Francisco, CA: Jossey-Bass.

Crouch, Catherine H., and Eric Mazur. 2001. "Peer Instruction: Ten Years of Experience and Results." *American Journal of Physics* 69 (9): 970–977.

Dean, Ceri B., Elizabeth Ross Hubbell, Howard Pitler, and Bj Stone. 2012. *Classroom Instruction That Works*. 2nd ed. Alexandria, VA: ASCD.

Dewey, John. 1916. *Democracy and Education: An Introduction to the Philosophy of Education*. New York: Macmillan.

Dudley-Marling, Curt. 2013. "Discussion in Postsecondary Classrooms: A Review of the Literature." *SAGE Open* 3 (4): 1–13.

Goldschmid, Marcel. 1971. "The Learning Cell: An Instructional Innovation." *Learning and Development* 2: 1–6.

Graham, Charles R. 2006. "Blended Learning Systems: Definition, Current Trends, and Future Direction." In *The Handbook of Blended Learning: Global Perspectives, Local Designs*, edited by Curtis J. Bonk and Charles R. Graham, 3–21. San Francisco, CA: Pfeiffer.

Guetzkow, Harold, E. Lowell Kelly, and Wilbert J. McKeachie. 1954. "An Experimental Comparison of Recitation, Discussion, and Tutorial Methods in College Teaching." *Journal of Educational Psychology* 45 (4): 193–207.

Johnson, David W., and Roger T. Johnson. 1999. *Learning Together and Alone: Cooperative, Competitive, and Individualistic Learning*. 5th ed. Boston, MA: Allyn and Bacon.

Johnson, Sandra. 2006. "The Neuroscience of the Mentor–Learner Relationship." *New Directions for Adult and Continuing Education* 110: 63–69.

Li, Nan, Verma Himanshu, Afroditi Skevi, Guillaume Zufferey, Jan Blom, and Pierre Dillenbourg. 2014. "Watching MOOCs Together; Investigating Co-located MOOC Study Groups." *Distance Education* 35 (2): 217–233. doi:10.1080/01587919.2014.917708.

Markham, Felix. 1967. *Oxford*. London: Weidenfeld & Nicolson.

McKeachie, Wilbert J. 1990. "Research on College Teaching: The Historical Background." *Journal of Educational Psychology* 82 (2): 189–200.

Mitra, Sugata, and Emma Crawley. 2014. "Effectiveness of Self-Organised Learning by Children: Gateshead Experiments." *Journal of Education and Human Development* 3 (3): 79–88. doi:10.15640/jehd.v3n3a6.

Pearson, Margot, and David Smith. 1985. "Debriefing in Experience-Based Learning." Chap. 4 in *Reflection: Turning Experience into Learning*, edited by David Boud, Rosemary Keough, and David Walker, 69–84. New York: Routledge Falmer.

Pérez, Alejandro, Manuel Carreiras, and Jon Andoni Duñabeitia. 2017. "Brain-to-Brain Entrainment: EEG Interbrain Synchronization While Speaking and Listening." *Scientific Reports* 7 (4190): 1–12. doi:10.1038/s41598-017-04464-4.

Rocca, Kelly A. 2010. "Student Participation in the College Classroom: An Extended Multidisciplinary Literature Review." *Communication Education* 59 (2): 185–213. doi:10.1080/03634520903505936.

Roulis, Eleni. 2005. "Discussing Across Gender Differences." Chap. 8 in *Discussion as a Way of Teaching: Tools and Techniques for Democratic Classrooms*, 2nd ed., edited by Stephen D. Brookfield and Stephen Preskill, 148–167. San Francisco, CA: Jossey-Bass.

Slavin, Robert E. 1995. *Cooperative Learning*. 2nd ed. Boston, MA: Allyn & Bacon.

Smith, Lawrence A., and Margaret Foley. 2009. "Partners in a Human Enterprise: Harkness Teaching in the History Classroom." *The History Teacher* 42 (4): 477–496.

Suhrie, Ambrose L. 1917. "The Aim and Method of Recitation." *The American Journal of Nursing* 17 (7): 611–615.

Sutton, Leah A. 2001. "The Principle of Vicarious Interaction in Computer-Mediated Communications." *International Journal of Educational Telecommunications* 7 (3): 223–242.

Tuckman, Bruce W. 1965. "Developmental Sequence in Small Groups." *Psychological Bulletin* 63 (6): 384–399.

Vogt, MaryEllen, and Jana Echevarria. 2008. *99 Ideas and Activities for Teaching English Learners with the SIOP Model*. Boston, MA: Allyn & Bacon.

Wilkinson, Ian A. G. 2009. "Discussion Methods." In *Psychology of Classroom Learning: An Encyclopedia*, edited by Eric M. Anderman and Lynley H. Anderman, 330–336. Detroit, MI: Macmillan Reference.

Tutorial 8

The Tutorial configuration, like the Discussion configuration, represents a step in the direction away from the "teacher-centered" instruction of the Presentation configuration. The tutor/facilitator still maintains considerable control over events, setting the agenda and giving minute-by-minute guidance, but so does the learner, whose responses dictate what happens next. A Tutorial configuration can exist and persist only as long as the tutee/learner continues to play an active role, responding to the tutor's prompts, receiving feedback, and agreeing on what to do next. Similar to the dyad format of Discussion, tutorial arrangements usually involve two persons, but in the case of Tutorial, one of them plays the role of "knowledgeable other"—more like a facilitator than a fellow learner.

Tutorial Defined

First, a caveat: The term *tutorial* is used very loosely in general pedagogical discourse. At many universities, so-called tutorials are merely small classes conducted in seminar fashion. On the Web, a so-called *tutorial* is typically a straightforward informational narrative and a so-called *video tutorial* is usually just a step-by-step how-to demonstration. In the educational technology literature, *tutorial* tends to describe any self-contained, self-paced instructional module that presents instruction, provides practice, gives feedback, and tests for comprehension, all without the need for human intervention. Here, the term is used in a more literal sense, referring to a one-to-one interchange in which the learner is constantly making responses and receiving intensive, substantive, and nuanced feedback from a tutor. Our definition, below, therefore, is a *precising* definition—taking the lexical, or dictionary, definition and adding critical attributes in order to make the meaning precise enough for scholarly discourse.

Figure 8.1 The Tutorial Communication Configuration.

In our definition, as with the other configurations, the term *facilitator* is used to label the person (or device) that takes the lead in the dyad, the one who plays the role of the more knowledgeable person. The facilitator in a tutorial relationship could be an actual professional educator, a paraprofessional, a parent, a sibling, a student of about the same age (peer tutoring), or an older student (cross-age). The Tutorial configuration is being employed whenever a "knowledgeable other" is engaging an individual in intensive, substantive discussion of a topic of study. Our definition:

> *Tutorial:* A person or device playing the role of Facilitator (F) interacts, intensively and substantively, one-to-one with a Learner (L) (or small group of Learners acting as one or taking turns); the Facilitator (tutor) and Learner (tutee) share control of two-way communication (Figure 8.1).

Instructors are using the Tutorial configuration not only when they consciously set up dyads for specified sorts of interaction but also if they interrupt a lecture to engage a listener in a substantive dialogue in response to a question. At that moment, they have switched from Presentation configuration to Tutorial configuration. Likewise, if a class is divided into groups for Small-Group Discussion activities, when the instructor joins a group, listens, then engages one person with substantive reaction or advice, that becomes a Tutorial interaction.

Formats Associated with Tutorial

Facilitator–Learner (F2F)

The most obvious format for a Tutorial is the classic case of an experienced teacher sitting next to a learner, engaged in a back-and-forth dialogue; as the aphorism goes, "Mark Hopkins (president of Williams College from 1836 to 1872) on one end of a log and a student on the other." Live, F2F tutoring has the attributes that other formats seek to emulate: a source that has subject-matter expertise and instructional expertise, located in the same place, where body language and nuances of speech can inform the understanding of each other, and where back-and-forth repartee can range unfettered. For example:

- apprenticeship in trades and crafts
- the part of on-the-job training in which an experienced worker shows and tells the trainee how the job is done; in British parlance, "sitting next to Nelly"

- mentoring among professionals in the workplace
- live conversational practice with a native speaker for language learning
- athletic coaching [Note: This topic will be treated more thoroughly in Chapter 9 because in sports and athletics, with motor skills being the dominant issue, repetitious practice is the central focus of instructional strategy, with tutoring being mainly an adjunct to Repetition. It will also be included in the discussion of "methods" at the end of this chapter, where "coaching" will be classified as a method that combines Tutorial with Repetition.]

Facilitator–Learner (Mediated)

During the twenty-first century, more and more instructors are finding themselves having to navigate how to teach in settings other than traditional F2F classrooms. In this process, they are often finding that some of the issues raised by blended and online learning are in fact opportunities in disguise. One of the major challenges of teaching in the online mode is figuring out how to compensate for the loss of social presence in the classroom, especially the presence of a facilitator. A significant part of the day-to-day motivation of learners in the live classroom is having an appointment with someone who may be an inspiration and is at least an unwitting role model. How can that traditional, reassuring F2F presence be replaced?

Ironically, it turns out that contemporary blended/online learning actually makes it *more likely* that learners will have frequent, quality one-to-one communication with the person playing the role of facilitator. E-mail and synchronous chat sessions (which often allow side conversations) actually allow more opportunities for personal contact than is usually found in the typical face-to-face large-group classroom. Instructors often feel obliged to make an extra effort to connect with learners they cannot physically see, a feeling less likely to occur in a traditional classroom. They may assign weekly journals to be sent via e-mail, opening the door to dialogue that helps build a mentoring relationship. Indeed, once the door is opened and the instructor welcomes learners' questions and concerns, the latter's expectations for speedy and voluminous communication may actually become problematic in terms of the instructor's time management. Overall, well-designed distance courses offer substantial opportunity for the Tutorial configuration. For example:

- e-mail exchanges between facilitator and learners: feedback on project work or journals, or other conversations provoked by questions raised by one of the correspondents
- facilitator participation in synchronous chat sessions with learners.

Learner–Learner

Students have always helped other students as long as there has been organized education. Older children helping younger children was a major feature of the nineteenth-century one-room schoolhouse. However, since the 1960s there has been an effort to surround peer tutoring and near-peer tutoring with more structure and to study its dynamics. In elementary schools, peer tutoring is used mainly in math and reading education. Several varieties of student-to-student tutoring have been validated (Robinson, Schofield and Steers-Wentzell 2005) and have gained widespread adoption, particularly in elementary education:

- same-age peer tutoring—one particular model pairs academically strong high school students with peers who are at risk for failure; the tutors may be compensated or given academic credit. An example in higher education is peer editing, or "writing buddies," who comment on each other's drafts before submission
- cross-age peer tutoring—older students, typically at a higher grade level, are paired with younger students (e.g., middle school with elementary school); most commonly, they offer compensatory help in reading or mathematics skills.
- reciprocal peer tutoring—pairs of students take turns acting tutor and tutee. One well-developed model, "Classwide Peer Tutoring" (CWPT) incorporates a contest format in which each student is paired with another and assigned to a team (with high, average, and low ability students balanced on each team). Student pairs practice academic tasks, with each student serving as tutor and tutee while acquiring points for their team (Greenwood 1997).
- programmed tutoring (PT)—pairs the learner with a tutor who has been trained to follow a structured pattern: When the tutee struggles to complete a step, the tutor gives hints ("brightening"), taking the learner back to something he already knows, then helps him to move forward again (Ellson et al. 1965). During the early 1980s, PT was validated in comparison studies (Cohen, Kulik and Kulik 1982) and was recognized by the US Department of Education as one of the half-dozen most successful innovations of its time.

Learner–Learner (Mediated)

Enormous educational, technological, and cultural shifts starting a few years prior to the turn of the millennium—namely, the proliferation of blended and online learning, the advent of ever-more-portable computing from "ultraportable" laptops to tablets to ever-more-powerful handheld devices, and the success of social media networking, in becoming arguably the most potent sociocultural force in current times, have rendered mediated communication between and amongst learners ubiquitous; cue the Internet meme showing a group of kids sitting together on a park bench texting each other instead of talking. In this new reality, learners do not appear to be worrying too much about "loss of social presence" issues as they wholeheartedly embrace mediated communication in seemingly every aspect of their lives—so why should learning-related communication be any different? As explained earlier, in today's world Web-based distance education actually makes it *more likely* that learners will have frequent, quality one-to-one communication with teachers, and this equally applies to peer-to-peer communication as well—offering substantial opportunities for mediated peer tutoring. For example:

- Dozens of creative ideas for stimulating structured interactions among online learners are found in Bonk and Khoo (2014); for example—Scholar/Scientist/Innovator Role Play, Interactive Learner Questioning and Discussion, and Video Annotations (asynchronous talk while watching videos).

Print–Learner: Programmed Instruction

Programmed instruction (PI) was originally devised by B. F. Skinner (1904–1990) in the 1950s as an alternative to the passive large-group lecture method. The meticulously organized printed software at first was incorporated into what came to be called a "teaching machine," a box with a window through which the user could read a scroll that contained chunks of information followed by a question; there was a slot in the window, allowing the user to write a response on the scroll and then advance it to see the correct answer. This format was based on the behaviorist principle that learners should practice desired behaviors as opposed to sitting and listening, and that each occurrence of a desired behavior should be followed by a reinforcer of some sort, in this case "knowledge of correct response." Before long, other investigators—including Skinner himself—were disposing of the machine and transforming the scroll into printed pages in a book, arranged so that the reader would encounter the question on one page, write or select a response, then turn the page to see the correct answer (Molenda 2008b). Some specific examples are:

- "teaching machine"—printed software enclosed in a device that controls page-turning
- "linear" PI books and booklets
- "branching" PI books and booklets—originally developed by Norman Crowder and widely emulated, branching programs present informational frames followed by multiple choice questions; depending on the user's selected answer they might be directed to remedial material or to more advanced material (Crowder 1962). As discussed below, the branching PI format was later adapted to delivery via computer-assisted instruction.

Computer–Learner: Intelligent Tutoring

Research and development have gone on since the 1960s, with each generation producing a combination of hardware and software that provides more robust learning experiences: more stimulating audiovisual material, more varied types of input—not just pushing buttons but speaking, drawing, or manipulating control devices, and more powerful ability to judge learner responses and provide feedback adapted to the learner's needs. The goal is *intelligent tutoring*, tutoring guided by artificial intelligence, that meets the "gold standard," represented by Bloom's meta-analysis of the effectiveness of human tutors (Bloom 1984). For example:

- AutoTutor, a pedagogical agent that holds a conversation with learners in natural language and simulates the dialogue moves of human tutors as well as ideal pedagogical strategies (Graesser 2016)
- TutorIT, a patented authoring and delivery system for computer-based lessons, mainly in mathematics (Scandura 2015)
- ZOSMAT, a software package that can be used by individual learners or by teachers as an aid to instructor-to-student tutoring; it tracks personal information, learning status with respect to the learning objectives, and performance on tests (Keleş 2009).

Wide-scale adoption of intelligent tutoring systems is impeded by the difficulty and expense of creating software that offers a semantically connected conceptualization of the content to be taught, a way of knowing what the learner does and does not understand—and provides appropriate feedback, and a delivery method that adapts to individual performance.

Evolution of Tutorial

Ancient Roots

Like Demonstration, tutorial activities undoubtedly go back into the mists of prehistoric times. Just as Stone Age children learned by watching their parents as they hunted, gathered, and made pottery and other tools, surely they must also have interjected questions about what they saw. At any rate, they would have been able to do this after communicative speech had evolved. And the parents surely gave them small tasks to do and gave them corrective feedback on their work. Such interchanges were precursors to the Tutorial configuration.

It was not until the Classical era in Athens, around 420 BC, that formal education beyond the elementary level became commonplace, and then only for young men from affluent families who could afford to pay fees. Sons of nobility received tutorial education at home; others with the means attended classes with "sophists," who used lectures and group discussion techniques.

Roman children of wealthy families also received their early education in their homes from private tutors. After the conquest of the Greek colonies in southern Italy in the third century BC, it became fashionable to import enslaved Greek scholars as tutors to wealthy families. Later, during the Empire period, formal schooling outside the home evolved into a system parallel to the modern one of elementary, secondary, and higher education. The highest level, *rhetor*, training for oratory and public life, seems to have been done through private tutors.

Medieval to Modern

In medieval Europe, heir to Roman traditions, monastic and cathedral schools sprang up to teach reading and writing in Latin. Students seeking higher education eventually formed guilds, later known as universities, in Bologna, Paris, Oxford, Salamanca, and other towns. Instructional methods revolved around the book—reading, copying, and memorizing classic texts (Saettler 1990). Meanwhile, young men learning a trade spent seven years as apprentices in medieval guilds. Methods of teaching the craft were regarded as trade secrets, but we can assume that Demonstration and Tutorial were the most common configurations.

In England, during the medieval period and beyond, church authorities conducted "grammar schools," devoted mainly to learning Latin as a first step toward religious careers. Aristocratic families tended to disdain the harsh conditions of these schools and hired tutors to educate their sons at home until ready for the university. Tutors, usually local clergymen or recent university graduates, taught reading, writing, mathematics, and basic Latin and Greek, in addition to the social graces.

The "tutorial method" eventually became the favored approach at two leading universities; Oxford and Cambridge became famous for their placement of tutorial instruction at the heart of their curriculum, beginning in the mid-nineteenth century. The system has been constantly modified since then, but the essentials remain. A student is assigned a tutor or "don" in their major area of study; the tutor gives the student a weekly assignment for a written paper; and student meets with the tutor and perhaps another student or two for a critique and discussion of the paper.

Contemporary Developments

During the twentieth century, schools and colleges tended to adopt the whole-class lecture and recitation style of instruction formulated by Comenius in the seventeenth century, as described in Chapter 5. Tutoring was seen as a supplementary method, helping students catch up with or get ahead of their classes. But by the latter part of the twentieth century, the whole-class method was perceived to have reached a plateau in terms of qualitative improvement. The search for more efficient and effective alternative approaches led to renewed interest in bringing the best of the tutorial system back in a way that was sustainable for mass education, as Eugene Oxhandler put it "bringing the 'dons' up to date" (1963).

Computer-Assisted Instruction—Local, then Distributed on the Web

As clever as the mechanical teaching machines of the 1960s came to be, they could not offer the responsiveness to individual needs, both intellectual and social, that human tutors could. Attention shifted to the burgeoning field of computer technology for a better solution. An early effort at computer-assisted instruction, the PLATO project, began at the University of Illinois in 1961, aiming to produce cost-efficient instruction using networked inexpensive terminals and a simplified programming language for instruction, TUTOR. Early programs were basically drill-and-practice with some degree of branching, but a wide variety of subject matter was developed at the college level. Over time, terminals at outlying universities were connected to the central mainframe in a timesharing system, growing to hundreds of sites and thousands of hours of material available across the college curriculum. As software development continued, more varied sorts of instructional strategies became possible, including discovery-oriented methods (Molenda 2008a). The PLATO system pioneered online forums and message boards, e-mail, chat rooms, instant messaging, remote screen sharing, and multiplayer games, leading to the emergence of what was perhaps the world's first online community (Woolley 1994).

The advent of the Internet in the 1990s, especially with the World Wide Web becoming the most popular Internet protocol around 1993, made it possible for these functionalities to be made available to learners—in or out of educational institutions—everywhere. With programs residing on the Web, they could be tapped from anywhere in the world that could access the Internet. That did not mean that truly tutorial instruction was now available to all, but it provided a venue in which various types of person-to-person interchanges were now easy and affordable.

Cognitive Science and Neuroscience Behind Tutorial

To begin with, when tutors and tutees talk among themselves, they are engaging in speech, so the neural pathways described in Chapter 5 under "Language Comprehension" and "Language Production" pertain here as well. More important, there are relevant findings from neuroscience specifically about how the brain reacts during person-to-person communications.

There has been a good deal of neuroscience research on the neural processes involved in relationships between therapist and client or mentor and mentee. When trust is established, we can observe a flood of biochemical reactions (dopamine, serotonin, and norepinephrine), enhancing the growth and connectivity of neural networks associated with learning, helping to move the receiver's thinking activities into the brain regions where reflection and abstract thinking take place (Johnson 2006, 64).

In Chapter 3 we discussed the special role that fear plays in the learning process—avoidance of situations that would threaten the security of our beliefs, which is what is happening when we are developing greater cognitive flexibility, going from certainty to critical analysis. When the mentor and learner are "attuned" to each other, that bond

> creates the holding environment that assists the learner in moving his or her emotions from the limbic area to the higher regions of the brain (orbito-frontal cortex), where "the voice of reason" is found and the learner can self-modulate those fears.
>
> (Johnson 2006, 66)

Through these mechanisms, reflective and critical thought can be fostered through a trusting relationship between the tutor and tutee, mentor and mentee. Further, as discussed in Chapter 7, studies of brain functions when two people are conversing show that a synchronization of neural oscillations takes place. This physical harmonization facilitates communication with each other (Pérez, Carreiras and Duñabeitia 2017). Thus, the sorts of conversations that occur during tutorial activities can promote an atmosphere of trust that enhances mutual receptivity to each other's ideas.

Strengths and Limitations: Why Tutorial?

Strengths

Record of Success

Tutorial methods have been embraced by stakeholders as long as there has been formal education. For those able to afford it, it has always been the preferred choice. Parents and educators have tweaked and tinkered with the details, but nowhere have they abandoned it in favor of some other configuration. The Tutorial configuration, assuming an able tutor, offers the best of all instructional conditions: There is a high proportion of "time on task"; learners must be engaged with the material, processing it mentally to make it their own; learners receive immediate and personalized corrective feedback and ample opportunity to practice until mastery is achieved.

The programmed instruction movement of the 1950s and 1960s lent credence to the notion that individual learners could benefit from carefully structured self-instructional programs. The limitation in early designs was the inability of paper or mechanical products to respond to anything more than multiple-choice selections by learners. Ellson's programmed tutoring (PT) proved to be a reliable and effective design for keeping the careful structure of the program while adding the flexibility of human judgment in responding to learner performance (Ellson et al. 1965). Thanks to efforts like this, a number of structured tutoring programs were developed, and by 1982 a meta-analysis of these programs (Cohen, Kulik and Kulik 1982) concluded that "tutored students outperformed control students on examinations, and they also developed positive attitudes toward the subject matter covered in the tutorial programs" (237). Another meta-analysis, by Benjamin Bloom (1984), lent authority to the growing interest in developing structured programs to channel human tutors' efforts more effectively. Walberg's massive meta-analysis of all different sorts of treatments (Walberg 1984), discussed at length in Chapter 2, ranked *tutorial instruction* as the number one treatment in terms of learning outcomes, with an exceptional effect size of 2.0. Around the same time, Ellson (1986) conducted an exhaustive critical analysis of the literature on educational innovations, seeking experimental treatments that were more than twice as productive as the control treatment. Among the 125 studies that met this criterion, about 70 percent represented some type of programmed instruction, structured tutoring, or programmed teaching (a category including Engelmann's Direct Instruction)—all of which could be put under the umbrella of the Tutorial configuration. Thus, by the 1990s, structured tutoring was considered the "gold standard" for effective instruction.

Individual Differences

With just one learner to deal with, a skilled tutor can store information about the learner's past accomplishments, needs, and interests and can call upon that stored information to decide what path to follow at the moment, thus making the Tutorial more adaptable to individual differences than any other configuration. Meanwhile, the learner is constantly active, in various ways practicing the target skills. Skills are demonstrated and practiced, not just verbalized. This satisfies the behavioral theorist, who sees lots of practice of desired behaviors with many opportunities for reinforcement. It also satisfies the cognitive theorist, who sees a teacher providing scaffolding for a learner who is creating his own understandings as he talks about the material.

Can be Implemented by Peer Volunteers

In the case of *peer tutoring* or *cross-age tutoring*, students benefit from hearing the subject matter from someone around their own age and status. Peer tutors are able to empathize more easily with tutees because they have experienced similar struggles not so long ago. For the tutee, it is less risky to betray weakness to a fellow student than to a judgmental teacher. The institution benefits from shifting the cost of tutoring onto volunteers, volunteers who also profit in terms of improving their own achievement. As a side benefit, the *tutors* in the 65 studies covered in the meta-analysis discussed above (Cohen, Kulik and Kulik 1982), who were generally student peers or near-peers, "gained a better understanding of and developed more positive attitudes toward the subject matter" (237).

Limitations

Expensive Because Labor-Intensive

In the Tutorial configuration, someone playing the role of tutor elicits some sort of performance from the learner—solving an arithmetic problem, analyzing a poem, welding a seam, or whatever, and then provides confirmation or corrective feedback about that performance. The value to the learner is commensurate with the skill of the tutor in evaluating his response and selecting the most appropriate feedback. Such an arrangement, one-to-one guidance, is highly labor-intensive and therefore expensive. To address the cost issue, inventive educationists have turned to specially formatted print materials, computers, and even peer learners (whose labor is usually contributed gratis) as tutors. The challenge is to arrange the printed material, program the computer, or train the student tutor sufficiently to provide continuing motivation and quality feedback to the tutee.

Requires Restructuring of Traditional Classroom

Back in the first quarter of the twentieth century, Maria Montessori brought her revolutionary plan for early childhood education to the United States, to great public acclaim. In the decades that followed, educational innovators such as Frederic Burk, Carleton W. Washburne, Helen Parkhurst, and Henry Clinton Morrison had developed school restructuring plans based on programs of individualized instruction. In the 1960s, large-scale school implementation projects were conducted on the implementation of programmed instruction. During the 1970s and 1980s, the US Department of Education funded a major national effort to disseminate demonstrably effective educational innovations in American schools. All of these efforts scored local successes in test cases, but none reached massive adoption within the public education system. The basic underlying fact is that all of these systemic innovations require fundamental restructuring of school organization and classroom routines. Administrators then, as now, were resistant to a leap into the unknown (Saettler 1990, 297–302). As Larry Cuban (1986) observed, regarding teachers and technological innovations,

> Within this school and classroom organizational framework, the culture of teaching, itself shaped in part by structural arrangements, further funnels both newcomers and veterans into teaching regularities, where certain "wisdom" is crafted and reinforced as essential to classroom survival.
>
> *(64–65)*

Best Practices for Using Tutorials

Advice for the Facilitator

Before Tutoring

Before considering the techniques of tutoring itself, instructors must first be willing to shift roles from "sage on the stage" to "guide on the side." Here we are referring particularly to secondary and postsecondary education, and to corporate training as well. Prior to the nineteenth century, tutors at English universities were primarily charged with shaping young men into compliant practitioners of orthodox religion, good manners, and proper dress. After rational humanism chipped away at the authority of the Church, the didactic aspect of the tutorial relationship came to supersede the pastoral one. In short, the academic tutor's role nowadays is not to tell tutees *what* to think but to teach them *how* to think. The goal, especially in the traditional academic disciplines, is to encourage *deep learning* as opposed to surface learning. That is, actively creating one's own interpretation of knowledge, integrated into one's own cognitive structure instead of passively receiving and reproducing knowledge passed along by others. To accomplish this goal, the academic tutor poses questions and problems that stimulate the learner to work through the available resources to prepare and defend a solution.

More often, instructors are working in an institutional setting in which large-group instruction is the norm. Tutoring individual students one-at-a-time is not an option. In such cases, instructors can turn to the next best expedient, peer or cross-age tutoring. Here, fellow students at the same level or at a more advanced level temporarily play the role of tutor to other students. To make this arrangement work the overall instructor must, first, plan how to assign students to teams and to provide the time and space to meet. Second, they need to screen candidates and make sure they have the necessary knowledge of the subject and the temperament to act as tutor. Third, instructors must train tutors and give them the tools they need to do a good job—tools such as job aids or scripts outlining the steps in the tutoring process, checklists, record sheets to keep track of their efforts and the learners' progress, and the like. While the tutoring is taking place, they need to supervise and be ready to intervene as needed, and periodically assess how well the sessions are proceeding.

While Tutoring

Over time, the requirements of good tutoring have become quite well understood. The tutor, whether a peer or an experienced teacher, first must be able to see the challenges of the lesson from the tutee's perspective, starting from where the learner is. If their help is not relevant, it will have no effect. The help that is given must be understandable to the tutee. This is why peer tutoring often succeeds—being able to empathize because the tutor is not that far removed from tutee's own world. Explanations need to be spelled out in a clear and logical order. As discussed above, in structured tutoring, the tutor is trained to begin with hints or prompts that are minimal, gradually increasing them as needed, even taking a step back to previously mastered material and building from there.

Of course, nothing happens until the tutee practices the new knowledge or skill, at which point the tutor must be ready to confirm or correct. Better than a book or a machine, a living tutor should be able to judge when a bit of social reinforcement is merited—a smile, a nod, a word of encouragement.

In the business or organizational setting, mentoring or coaching typically emphasizes using questioning techniques to build up the learner's thought processes, as in academic tutoring. The goal is personal insight and lasting change—deep learning—not just the accumulation of new knowledge at a superficial level. As with any type of tutoring, this requires empathizing with the learner's situation, helping them formulate personal goals, and giving appropriate feedback about their performance.

Advice for the Learner

As with any instructional activity, the learner's disposition is crucial to success. As a tutee, the learner must buy into the objectives, be willing to accept constructive feedback, and willingly do the practice or study prescribed by the tutor. A truism among educators is that learning is highly dependent on amount of invested mental effort (AIME): The more effort you put into your study, the more you get out of it. This conclusion is based on a wide body of research in cognitive science, education, and social psychology.

Methods Featuring the Tutorial Configuration

Strategic Level

The Oxbridge System (Study + Tutorial + Expression + Demonstration)

The classical Oxford-Cambridge methodology combines face time with a tutor with an extended period of Study—reading textbooks, pursuing other sources in the library, perhaps consulting online Resources—followed by the preparation of a written paper (Expression), which is presented to the tutor in oral or written form. Converting secondhand knowledge into one's own interpretation, stated in one's own words, is one of the most efficacious ways of attaining mastery of higher-level cognitive skills. In practice, the Oxbridge system usually also involves other students in the tutee's oral presentation; for those students, the tutee's performance serves as a Demonstration, behavior modeling.

Programmed Tutoring (PT) (Study + Tutorial)

Designed as a stand-alone method for individualized instruction, PT pairs the learner with a tutor who has been trained to follow a structured pattern: When the tutee struggles to complete a step, the tutor gives hints ("brightening"), taking the learner back to something he already knows, then helps him to move forward again. Tutorial sessions are usually preceded by the learner engaging in some sort of Study activity, such as reading a textbook or handout.

Class-Wide Peer Tutoring (CWPT) (Study + Tutorial)

CWPT implements a form of reciprocal peer tutoring within whole classes of students. Meant to largely replace lectures in elementary education and to accommodate diverse populations, CWPT incorporates a contest format in which each student is paired with another and assigned to a team (with high, average, and low ability students balanced on each team). Student pairs work on tasks specific to the subject matter, with each student serving as tutor and tutee while acquiring points for their team.

Athletic coaching (Repetition + Tutorial)

As mentioned earlier in this chapter, developing high-level sports and athletic skills requires a great amount of Repetition, repetitive practice of whole-skills or part-skills. Such practice would usually be accompanied by some means of observing and giving feedback on the performance, whether by a live coach or a video recording for self-evaluation. However, in some cases the guidance given by a coach can rise to the level of Tutorial—intensive and substantive back-and-forth discussion of tactics and strategies. Cognitive coaching, as with an employee mentoring program is discussed under "Methods" in Chapter 6.

Employee Mentoring (Repetition + Study + Tutorial)

New employees, interns, and mid-career employees develop on-the-job through mentoring programs in which they are paired, one-to-one or one-to-several with more seasoned employees. The content of mentoring programs tends to revolve around career exploration, corporate culture, and "soft skills" development. The mentoring program typically requires Study of business practices through print and mobile devices plus regular meetings with the mentor, when the learner may be assigned a real-world task (Repetition configuration) such as chairing a meeting or organizing a conference, that is considered a "stretch" assignment.

Computer-Assisted Intelligent Tutoring (Study + Practice + Tutorial)

Traditional twentieth-century computer-assisted instruction (CAI) was largely limited to presenting information, offering questions or practice exercises, and giving prerecorded feedback to individual learners. *Intelligent tutoring* aims to employ artificial intelligence (AI) to track individual progress and to judge learner responses and provide feedback adapted to the learner's needs. Such devices are intended to potentially stand alone, offering tutorial instruction in places and at times when human tutoring is not feasible.

Tactical Level

Question & Answer (Presentation + Tutorial)

In a large-group lecture setting, there is often an opportunity for the facilitator and individual learners to engage in a question-and-answer interlude. When the lecturer pauses the presentation to accept questions, the configuration switches from Presentation to

Whole-Class Discussion. If that interchange evolves into a deeper, longer exchange with a particular learner, it could meet the definition of a Tutorial session.

Chapter Summary

Like the Discussion configuration, Tutorial represents another step away from "teacher-centered" instruction, since the learner shares control with the tutor. In Tutorial a human or a device, such as a computer, can play the role of facilitator/tutor, who interacts intensively and substantively with the learner or perhaps a small group; tutor and tutee share control.

Although the stereotyped image of a tutorial involves an expert working one-on-one with a novice (such as a skilled tradesman and an apprentice or a business executive mentoring a novice), in practice, many other formats are possible. Because such tutoring is labor-intensive, and expertise is scarce and expensive, alternative formats have been developed and tested to replace the expert-tutor with more abundant and affordable sources. In schools, it is quite common now to have whole classes organized to implement peer or near-peer tutoring, or even class-wide peer tutoring, in which all students are paired with those of differing abilities and they rotate the roles of tutor and tutee. Printed materials, in the form of linear or branching programmed texts, can also be structured to offer at least a quasi-tutorial experience. A longtime goal of computer advocates is to develop a robust and flexible device for *intelligent tutoring*; some substantial products are available, such as AutoTutor and TutorIT, but that dream is still short of being fulfilled. Nevertheless, what had long been the favored educational method for social and economic elites has been adapted successfully to mass education by twentieth-century innovators who devised structured-tutoring innovations that have become the "gold standard" against which other innovations are measured.

In the twenty-first century, the Tutorial configuration has escaped the bonds of elite one-to-one tutelage and has been translated into forms that can be applied to large populations of ordinary learners. Programmed Tutoring and Classwide Peer Tutoring provide frameworks for allowing elementary and secondary education students to play the role of tutor. Computer-based intelligent tutoring systems give individualized feedback without the intervention of a human tutor. In corporate training and education, mentoring programs allow seasoned employees to act as guides to newer employees as they grow through "stretch" assignments performed in the real workplace.

Works Cited

Bloom, Benjamin. 1984. "The 2 Sigma Problem: The Search for Methods of Group Instruction as effective as One-to-One Tutoring." *Educational Researcher* 13 (6): 4–16.

Bonk, Curtis J., and Elaine Khoo. 2014. *Adding Some TEC-VARIETY: 100+ Activities for Motivating and Retaining Learners Online*. Bloomington, IN: Open World Books. Accessed February 10, 2020. http://tec-variety.com.

Cohen, Peter A., James A. Kulik, and Chen-Lin C. Kulik. 1982. "Educational Outcomes of Tutoring: A Meta-Analysis of Findings." *American Educational Research Journal* 19 (2): 237–248.

Crowder, Norman A. 1962. "Intrinsic and Extrinsic Programming." In *Programmed Learning and Computer-Based Instruction*, edited by J. E. Coulson, 55–66. New York: Wiley & Sons.

Cuban, Larry. 1986. *Teachers and Machines: The Classroom Use of Technology Since 1920*. New York: Teachers College Press.

Ellson, Douglas G. 1986. *Improving the Productivity of Teaching: 125 Exhibits*. Bloomington, IN: Phi Delta Kappa.

Ellson, Douglas G., Larry Barber, T. L. Engle, and Leonard Kampwerth. 1965. "Programed Tutoring: A Teaching Aid and a Research Tool." *Reading Research Quarterly* 1 (1): 77–127.

Graesser, Arthur C. 2016. "Conversations with AutoTutor Help Students Learn." *International Journal of Artificial Intelligence in Education* 26: 124–132. doi:10.1007/s40593-015-0086-4.

Greenwood, Charles. 1997. "Classwide Peer Tutoring." *Behavior and Social Issues* 7 (1): 53–57.

Johnson, Sandra. 2006. "The Neuroscience of the Mentor–Learner Relationship." *New Directions for Adult and Continuing Education* 110: 63–69.

Keleş, Aytürk. 2009. "ZOSMAT: Web-Based Intelligent Tutoring System for Teaching–Learning Process." *Expert Systems with Applications* 36 (2): 1229–1239.

Molenda, Michael. 2008a. "Historical Foundations." Chap. 1 in *Handbook of Research on Educational Communications and Technology*, edited by J. Michael Spector, M. David Merrill, Jeroen van Merriënboer, and Marcy P. Driscoll, 3–28. New York: Lawrence Erlbaum Associates.

Molenda, Michael. 2008b. "The Programmed Instruction Era: When Effectiveness Mattered." *TechTrends* 52: 52–58.

Oxhandler, Eugene K. 1963. "Bringing the 'Dons' Up to Date." *Audiovisual Instruction* 8: 566–569.

Pérez, Alejandro, Manuel Carreiras, and Jon Andoni Duñabeitia. 2017. "Brain-to-Brain Entrainment: EEG Interbrain Synchronization While Speaking and Listening." *Scientific Reports* 7 (4190): 1–12. doi:10.1038/s41598-017-04464-4.

Robinson, Debbie R., Janet Ward Schofield, and Katrina L. Steers-Wentzell. 2005. "Peer and Cross-Age Tutoring in Math: Outcomes and Their Design Implications." *Educational Psychology Review* 17: 327–362.

Saettler, Paul. 1990. *The Evolution of American Educational Technology*. Englewood, CO: Libraries Unlimited.

Scandura, Joseph M. 2015. "AuthorIT & TutorIT: An Intelligent Tutor Authoring and Delivery System You Can Use." *Technology, Instruction, Cognition and Learning* 10: 173–202.

Walberg, Herbert J. 1984. "Improving the Productivity of America's Schools." *Educational Leadership* 41 (8): 19–27.

Woolley, David R. 1994. *PLATO: The Emergence of Online Community*. Accessed February 12, 2020. http://just.thinkofit.com/plato-the-emergence-of-online-community/.

Repetition 9

Repetition is the configuration in which a learner is repeatedly practicing a new mental or physical skill. One could say that practice is the "active ingredient" of virtually all types of learning activities. In discussions and tutorial sessions, if learners are processing new information coming from tutors or fellow discussants, working with the material in order to understand it better, they are practicing cognitive skills. In games, simulations, and expressive activities, if learners are making decisions, trying to see what works, perhaps creating work products, and in other ways, *doing* the skills they are trying to master, they are practicing. Even relatively passive activities such as listening to a lecture, watching a demonstration, or reading a book result in learning gains only to the extent that the learner mentally manipulates the material—comparing and contrasting the information against prior knowledge and personal experiences, thinking about possible applications, committing certain information to memory, and so on. When educationists talk about "engagement," they are talking about practice. Hence, practice is a feature of virtually every configuration. What places an instructional event into the Repetition configuration is that it features *repeated* instances of practice without the accompaniment of other features, such as the presentation or the demonstration of new information.

Repetition differs from other configurations in that it can take place without the physical presence of a facilitator. Learners can and do carry out repetitive practice on their own, whether it is the mental practice of memorizing a list of vocabulary words or the physical practice of swinging a golf club. However, a coach or some other type of facilitator is usually in the background, setting the learning goal, prescribing the repetition routine, or holding the learner accountable for doing the practice. That coach, if physically present, can also offer corrective feedback on the practice efforts.

Repetition Defined

Instructors are using the Repetition configuration when they give learners the opportunity to try out a new skill multiple times, for example, directing the rehearsal of a scene from a play or overseeing a group of rangers who are orienteering in an unfamiliar forest. Sports coaches spend a large portion of their time organizing and critiquing individual performance during drills. For some athletic venues, fellow players may take turns playing the role of Facilitator; for example, weightlifters who take turn "spotting" each other or football players who lead drills of others who play the same position.

> *Repetition*: A Learner (L) performs repeatedly all or part of a specified Skill (S) in order to improve retention and proficiency (Figure 9.1).

Repetition can be done by the learner (L) alone, but ideally with someone playing the role of Facilitator (a role increasingly played by a computer program) to provide feedback on the performance. Alone, the learner is in control; with someone—a human or a computer program—playing the role of Facilitator, that someone is typically in control.

Formats Associated with Repetition

A clear example of Repetition in action is military "basic training." Recruits undergo an array of drills on skills such as marching, hand-to-hand combat, rifle maintenance, and marksmanship. Through repetition with corrective feedback, the recruits learn to perform these functions with accuracy and automaticity.

Repetition is also a vital component of mastery of cognitive skills as well as of physical skills. When given new information, concepts, or principles to master, students need to devote time to rephrasing, summarizing, and elaborating the new material—what is referred to in information-processing theory as "encoding through elaborative rehearsal" (Sternberg and Williams 2010). Practice can also

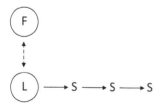

Figure 9.1 The Repetition Communication Configuration. The multiple Ss represent a mental or physical Skill that is repeated in order to be mastered.

refine skills that are primarily attitudinal—such as respect for ecological values, or interpersonal—such as diplomacy or leadership.

Formats for Repetition can be grouped into the categories of solo practice, group practice, and supervised practice, according to the extent of corrective feedback received from others. In solo practice, the only feedback is one's own appraisal of how successful the attempted action had been. Group practice allows for critique by others in the group. Supervised practice features feedback from a "knowledgeable other," such as a coach.

For each category, the type of practice could be overt physical practice or covert mental practice.

Formats for Solo Practice

Formats for solo practice include, for example:

- memorization drills, such as reciting multiplication tables
- a violinist practicing alone at home
- learning foreign language vocabulary by drilling with flash cards
- refining pronunciation of a foreign language in a language lab
- reading and rereading a poem to commit it to memory
- doing homework math problems
- playing word puzzles or games via smartphone app to build vocabulary
- practicing therapy skills, such as cardiopulmonary resuscitation (CPR), on manikins or other simulated patients
- working in a real-world setting as an intern or volunteer
- clinical practice in medicine and nursing
- clinical practice in education, teacher training
- using a programmed device that gives practice and feedback on target skills
- taking practice tests
- playing an instructional video game
- using a physical simulator, such as a flight simulator
- refining tennis strokes by playing against a tennis ball machine
- doing practice putts on a putting green before beginning a golf match
- developing soccer skills by juggling a ball between left and right feet.

Formats for Group Practice

Formats for group practice include, for example:

- actors rehearsing a scene informally, without a director
- a chamber music ensemble rehearsing informally, without a conductor

- develop team skills in baseball with drills, such as relays to home plate, pitcher fielding bunts, etc.
- develop team skills in soccer, such as passing drills
- choral response to questions during a presentation
- whole-class memorization drill by chanting together, "group recitation"
- participation in an instructional social simulation exercise.

Formats for Supervised Practice

Supervised practice refers to Repetition situations in which learners are monitored and given corrective feedback as they practice. Instructional events involving Repetition with supervision could be classified as Tutorial if the monitoring is done one-to-one and there is a richness to the quantity and quality of communication between tutor and tutee. Formats for supervised practice would include, for example:

- participating in an orchestra rehearsal with a conductor
- rehearsing a play under the supervision of the director
- church choir practice
- team-building exercises
- lecture recitation—question-and-answer quizzing of students during lecture
- textbook recitation—teacher quizzes students in class about their comprehension of assigned readings from a textbook
- participation in a multiplayer instructional game or simulation game, with the feedback in the form of other players' responses or a scoring system.

"Modified Reality" Formats

Some formats for the Repetition configuration—those involving game or simulation features—ought to be discussed at greater length, due to their popularity and their special potential for impact on instructed learning. What all these formats have in common is that they incorporate repeated practice into a framework of what could be called *modified reality*. That is, games, simulations, and simulation games all immerse learners into settings in which reality has been modified in some purposeful way—simplified, in the case of simulations, and completely invented, in the case of games.

First, some definitions are needed. The terms simulation, game, and simulation game are often used interchangeably. Since these terms actually have different meanings and different applications, they will be discussed separately. A *simulation* is an abstraction or simplification of some real-life situation or process. The thing being simplified can be as uncomplicated as a manikin that represents a human body for purposes of CPR training. Or it could be as complex as a computerized flight simulator that offers a highly realistic rendition of flying an airplane. A more comprehensive definition of *computer-based instructional simulation* is: "algorithmic, dynamic, often simplified models of real-world or hypothetical phenomena that contain features that not only allow but promote the exploration of ideas, manipulation of parameters, observation of events, and testing of questions" (Girault et al. 2016).

A *game* is defined as a ludic (playful) activity in which participants follow prescribed rules that differ from those of real life as they strive to attain a challenging goal—the outcome of which is uncertain. "Striving to attain a challenging goal" does not necessarily have to involve competition with other players. The competition may be against some standard (such as "par" in golf), against their own previous score, or against the designer of the game, as in video games that have multiple levels of difficulty. Communication games, for example, represent a type of game activity in which participants agree to suspend the normal rules of interpersonal communication in order to pursue such goals as self-awareness, empathy, and sensitivity (Heinich et al. 1996, 326). Instructional games may be simple adaptations of traditional games such as tic-tac-toe, rummy, concentration, and bingo, or they may be designed from scratch by instructors or by commercial developers. As long as they do not involve modified reality—imaginative role-playing or fantasy scenarios—they would be classified as Repetition activities, vehicles for repetitious practice of skills such as reading and mathematics.

A *simulation game* combines the attributes of a simulation (role-playing, a model of reality) with the attributes of a game (striving toward a goal, specific rules). Like a simulation, it may be relatively high or low in its modeling of reality. Like a game, it may or may not entail competition (Heinich et al. 1996, 332).

Physical Simulators

Many types of psychomotor skills require practice under conditions of high feedback, giving the learner the feel of the action. The repeated practice required to attain such competencies, such as driving a car or piloting an airplane, could entail high costs and high risks. Hence, simulators are often used as scaled-down versions of the living reality. Indeed, nowadays flight crews on most airlines receive most of their training in flight simulators, saving a fortune on fuel, not to mention the reduction of risk to life and limb. Simulators are also used for more mundane skills, such as mock-ups used for training in chiseling and welding. Such devices, if they do not incorporate imaginative role-playing or intricate problem-solving, can simply be formats for Repetition. They can be valuable substitutes for practice routines that would otherwise be expensive or risky. For science education, biological and chemical processes can be studied through simulations that allow users to experiment without the cost of specimens or the risk of unleashing harmful chemical reactions. *Biologica* allows students to experiment with genetics. *Dance of the Planets* is an animation of the solar system, allowing real-time exploration of the planets without leaving the astronomy classroom.

Simulation Exercises

Elementary students participate in simulations when they set up a pretend grocery store and practice being the customer, the shopkeeper, the checkout clerk, the stocker, and so on. An acting company might arrange a rough approximation of a stage set to walk through their parts at an early stage of rehearsal.

In corporate training, fast-food restaurant management trainees might practice supervising a crew in a mock-up of a typical restaurant kitchen. The training facility for a major plastics manufacturer contains a lab set up with trays of chemicals and equipment needed to simulate the actual plastics manufacturing practice; trainees learn how to control the temperature, flow rate, and mixing speed of the chemicals in a safe, scaled-down version of the real thing. International banking companies train traders for cross-cultural negotiations by arranging realistic simulations of meetings with foreign counterparts.

Simulations of human interactions typically put participants into roles within a scenario, interacting with other participants who are playing other roles—a scaled-down version of a real-life encounter between people with different motivations and interests. Social simulations can vary greatly in the extent to which they fully reflect the realities of the situation they are intended to model. A simulation that incorporates too many details of a complex situation might be too complicated for novices. On the other hand, if the model is oversimplified, it may fail to communicate its intended point. A well-designed simulation provides a faithful model of those elements that are most salient to the immediate objective, and, ideally, the designer informs the instructor and participants about elements that have been simplified or eliminated completely. For business settings, the simulation might take the form of an "in-basket" exercise, in which learners cope with problems presented in the form of messages coming into an executive's in-basket. They are not interacting with other players. Learners must prioritize issues and make decisions while working under deadline pressures, as they would in a real business.

Case Studies

When lawyers were trained simply by apprenticing themselves to an attorney, they learned legal principles and strategies by being involved in the cases handled by that attorney. It was a matter of learning primarily through behavior modeling. At the same time, apprentices were learning that judges dealt with the cases before them by referring to previous cases and the precedents set by previous decisions. Thus, legal education has always involved "thinking like a lawyer," meaning dissecting the various courts' reasoning on previous cases and applying those rationales to the current matter.

Formal legal education in the United States eventually took root in universities. As academic programs were formed, they faced the issue of creating a curriculum for educating lawyers, and quite early on, the case method was adopted as a core pedagogical method. The Harvard Law School curriculum was based around the case method by 1870. Others followed their lead quite rapidly, and soon it was the norm.

A case used in law school typically reports the ruling of an appellate court. It might be just a few pages long or more than 100 pages long, including the facts of the case and the rulings of the court. From this, the student must prepare a "brief," a summary of the case, touching upon the facts, the issues, and the legal reasoning applied. By repeated practice on many cases, the student develops generalized habits of analysis necessary for functioning as a lawyer.

As discussed in Chapter 4 and Chapter 8, law school instructors often use a quasi-Socratic dialogue to parse a chosen student's analysis of the case. The vigorous questioning of the student is meant to serve as a virtual field experience for the class; the other students are also immersed in the case and imagine themselves in the place of the examinee and mentally formulate their own responses. Instructors can reinforce the group involvement by spontaneously calling on other students to step in at any time.

The case method spread to business schools after World War I and to public administration in the 1940s, although with adaptations of the law school method, relying more on group discussion of various solutions to problems, since there is not "one correct answer" or authoritative historical precedents when analyzing complex business or governmental problems.

The education of physicians has long included study of specific cases, here meaning the written documentation regarding the symptoms and treatment of patients. However, it was not until the 1980s that McMaster University Faculty of Health Sciences adopted the case method as part of their adoption of problem-based learning as their core pedagogy. Since then, this approach has been embraced by many other programs for training health professionals (Servant-Miklos 2019).

Cases are developed differently and used differently in law, business, public administration, and medicine, but all involve immersing learners in a realistic situation that has been scaled down but that retains salient features of real-life problems in that field. The total process may involve individual study, small-group discussion, and the reporting of conclusions at the end; but all entail immersion in a problem space and interacting with Resources (such as, in the case of medicine, the results of diagnostic tests) and other learners to reach a resolution.

In business school, for example, the immersion is done through a detailed verbal description of the case: a specific business, the context in which that business operates (e.g., regulations that constrain its operations), the characters involved, and the events that led to the difficult decisions those characters must now make. Students are then assigned to teams and possibly assigned to specific roles, such as representing major antagonists in the case. Participants then may seek outside sources of information, hear presentations by experts in various areas, and engage in ongoing discussions within the team before concluding with their recommended solution to the problem, usually a written report (Barnes et al. 1994).

Role-Plays

A *role-play* is an activity in which two or some small number of individuals act out a brief encounter, playing assigned roles and pursuing specified goals within a defined setting. Role-plays are especially valuable for pursuing interpersonal skill development, particularly how to handle delicate problems—terminating an employee, denying service to a customer, explaining the store's return policy, or even physically intervening with an out-of-control patient in a hospital. In academic settings, role-plays can help participants empathize with the perspectives of other people; for example, playing the school cafeteria manager discussing menus with a parent or playing an artist explaining his work to a skeptical critic.

Sometimes a role-play is employed as a demonstration in front of a class. The scene being played out gives raw material for the class to discuss afterward: Who did what and why? In this case, the activity would be classified as a Demonstration for the class members and as a Repetition for the actual participants in the action. If a role-play exercise is being organized to involve the whole class at one time, the class would be broken into small groups of three or four people. There may be a dozen or more similar scenes being played out simultaneously. In such a case, the instructor may add an additional member to each team to act as an observer, a surrogate for the instructor (Davis and Davis 1998, 330–342).

Games

Play has long been appreciated as a beneficial element of child development, but it was not taken seriously as an educational tool until recent times, with some exceptions. One notable exception was the Czech philosopher and educator Comenius (1592–1670), who opposed the punitive character of schools of his time, proposing instead to introduce children "to knowledge of the prime things that are in the world, by sport and merry pastime" (Comenius and Keatinge 1967). Most other educators adhered to the conventional wisdom that study was serious and that lessons were more likely to be retained if accompanied by strokes of a switch; hence, the old song lyric "Reading and 'riting and 'rithmetic; taught to the tune of the hick'ry stick."

By the late nineteenth century, the kindergarten movement and, by the early twentieth century, the Montessori movement had demonstrated the superiority of a more nurturing, playful environment. Elementary schools, too, lost their austere tone and took on a developmental approach. Play began to receive serious scholarly attention in the mid-twentieth century, spurred by the groundbreaking work of Johan Huizinga in *Homo Ludens* (Huizinga 1955). He popularized the concept of the "ludic," referring to an activity that has an element of fun and is not aimed at accomplishing anything productive.

Games, although they do suspend some of the rules of reality, do not necessarily entail learners' immersion into an imaginary scenario, as simulations and simulation games do. Hence, games are more likely to be the vehicle for straightforward repetitive practice of desired skills, as opposed to being the vehicles for discovery learning, as simulation games tend to be. A simple example would be the child's card game Authors, which provides practice in pairing American authors with their books in a card game similar to Go Fish. Through repetitive play of the cards, users gradually associate authors with their works, but players are never immersed in an imaginary scenario.

Instructional Games

Educators began to take interest in games as a format for increasing the quality and quantity of Repetition in the 1960s. The distinction between play and reality makes games feel more like entertainment than labor. Striving to attain a goal makes them motivational. A game designed to be instructional will be structured such that most of the players' time is spent practicing skills specified in the objectives, and the scoring system will be set up to reward decisions and behaviors consistent with the objectives. Thus, if the game is well designed and implemented, the participants will be motivated to increase their *amount of invested mental effort* (AIME), will practice a lot of desired behaviors, and will persist in performing what might otherwise be a tedious drill-and-practice routine.

Simple games are used at even the earliest educational levels. For example, a traditional childhood game such as *Mother, May I* is used in Montessori schools and kindergartens to teach politeness and attention to rules. *Big Fish, Little Fish* is a traditional card game through which children can learn some basic science principles of predator fish and their prey.

In the United States, interest in innovative formats such as games blossomed in the period following the Elementary and Secondary Education Act (ESEA) of 1965. Title III of ESEA offered grants for research and development of innovative instructional materials. Those that proved effective were widely disseminated through the National Diffusion Network. For example, many different games were developed for subskills of reading, such as card-based games in which players try to combine cards to form words, or *Road Race*, a board game in which players move around a track based on the number of words they have made. For math skills, Mathematics Pentathlon provided a package of 20 games for different math concepts, linked to actual tournament competitions within schools and between schools. Begun in 1979, the games and organizational structure were still widely used into the 2020s (see www.mathpentath.org/). By being placed in a competitive framework, hours of repeated practice of math skills can feel like an exciting adventure rather than a tedious drill.

In addition to games designed from scratch, educators have often adapted familiar games such as tic-tac-toe, rummy, Concentration, and bingo to instructional uses; for example, substituting alphabet cards for number cards and following the rules of rummy to form words. Either such parlor games or newly designed games may have frameworks that allow them to be adapted to different subject matters; these are referred to as *frame games* (Stolovitch and Thiagarajan 1980). The common feature of all of the types of games discussed here is that they are a novel departure from regular classroom activities, and hence attractive. Learners tend to persist in spending more "time on task" when engaged in a fun activity.

Computer-Based Instructional Games

Independently of the scholarly and educational interest in games, recreational video games became a popular fascination in the 1980s. Originally appearing as large, stand-alone stations in amusement arcades, the format gradually morphed into video game consoles connected to television sets in the home—such as the PlayStation, Xbox, and Nintendo Wii. Later still, games were miniaturized to fit into laptop computers, tablets, and smartphones. By 2013, computer-based leisure games were ubiquitous in society, and a majority of Americans reported playing one or more games. Educators could not ignore students' fascination with, even addiction to, game-playing. At first, teachers merely used game-playing as a reward for completing an instructional task. But eventually educators ventured out to find computer games that actually focused on skills transferable beyond the game itself.

In general, computer games suffer some limitations in the academic setting. Those that students find attractive tend to be designed as recreational games and do not offer good matches with curricular goals. When teachers use game-design software to create their own games that do fit the academic curriculum, the products tend to lack the visual appeal and other entertaining features that draw students to recreational games.

However, there are off-the-shelf products that manage to hold student interest while offering legitimate practice of target skills. One of the earliest computer games specifically designed for mathematics education was *Darts*, developed in the early 1970s by the PLATO project at University of Illinois. Using an early, primitive graphic interface, users won points by aiming "darts" at "water balloons" that represented estimates of different fractions. In the 1990s, a project at University of British Columbia developed *Super Tangrams*, in which users practiced transformational geometry by solving a series of visual puzzles. A Web-based product of the early 2000s, *ASTRA EAGLE*, involved a series of games for solving simple equations, mapping x and y coordinates, and other such skills, in which users moved to more advanced levels when they correctly answered all the questions at the current level. Similar games are available for drill-and-practice in reading and language arts in the elementary school curriculum.

Even physical education has discovered ways to incorporate computer-based games. Twenty-first century developments in user interfaces allowed physical movements to be detected by the computer, allowing users to practice physical skills with the computer. The Wii remote controller, introduced in 2006, was a handheld pointing device that detected movement in three dimensions, thus allowing users to compete with the computer in games such as tennis. Later, a "balance board" input device allowed users to do exercises, introducing a new genre of computer games, "exergames." The dozens of exergames that are commercially available offer a multitude of options for activities that can fit into school and college physical education curricula, as well as private use for self-training.

In addition to examples such as these of straightforward practice activities, there are a host of educational games that also have simulation features, creating more of an authentic problem-solving environment—discussed below.

Gamification

As educators and trainers observed the growing incidence of game-playing among their students and trainees, they began to seek ways to harness the motivational power of game-playing in their instructional programs. *Gamification* is the label applied to the process of adding game-like elements to traditional education and training courses. For example, a major accounting firm wanted to increase the rate of use and of completion of its online leadership-development modules. They instituted two changes to the program: first, awarding "badges" for completion of modules, and second, displaying a "leaderboard" in the online course, indicating the individual trainee's standing compared to other comparable trainees.

Similar interventions have been applied in academic courses, usually to combat student procrastination and to motivate higher rates and higher quality of practice. A typical intervention is to break the course assignments into smaller steps, with evaluation and feedback after each step completed. These assignments might be described as "missions" or "quests" and the whole set of assignments postured under a *Star Wars* type story line with the most successful players proclaimed with heroic labels. The purpose of gamification is, as it is with the use of individual games, to promote a higher voluntary rate of practice among learners. It is found primarily in online courses or blended courses where the Repetition component is done in online modules.

The secret to the success of many instructional innovations, such as gamification, is that it forces a careful scrutiny of exactly what objectives need to be attained by the learners, how individuals can be provided with enough individual practice opportunities to meet those objectives, how learners can get quick and helpful feedback from that practice, and how completion of objectives will be measured. Going through a systematic analysis of this sort is itself an innovation, one that can yield benefits.

Simulation Games

Because they combine the characteristics of both simulations and games, instructional simulation games have advantages in common with both formats. One of the major rationales for using the simulation-game format is that it provides conditions for holistic learning. That is, through the modeling of reality and through the players' interactions as they strive to succeed, learners encounter a whole and dynamic view of the process being studied. Conventional instruction tends to segment reality into separate packages (e.g., biology, mathematics, psychology), but that is not how the real world is organized. Through simulation games, learners can see the whole process—with its dynamic interrelationships—in action.

Computer-Based Instructional Simulation Games

Since the 1970s, the home entertainment industry was offering sophisticated simulation games that were fun to play but also had relevance to social studies. One of the earliest and most popular was *Oregon Trail*, which allowed students to play the role of a settler planning a journey westward to Oregon and then suffering all the challenges of crossing the plains, deserts, and mountains with insufficient resources. An updated version was still in use in 2017. In the mid-1980s came *Pirates!*, in which players could participate in complex models of trade and conflict in the Caribbean in the seventeenth century. In the 1990s came *Civilization* and *SimCity*, in which players could build virtual cities and civilizations step by step, with real historical and demographic data programmed into the game's algorithms. Because of perceived educational value, this genre of products began to be called "edutainment." One of the most successful was *Where in the World is Carmen San Diego?*, in which players attempt to arrest criminals by gathering data about their whereabouts, in effect, learning to use a world almanac.

During this period, some commercial developers aimed to create video games aimed directly at the school market, such as *Math Blaster*, which made arithmetic drill-and-practice more fun (Squire 2003). Ultimately, these efforts failed to make an impact on teaching practices in schools, like the "multimedia" products promoted by publishers in the audiovisual era of the 1960s, for reasons having partly to do with the economics of education and power relationships in schools.

The edutainment genre has not yet made major inroads into formal education or corporate training, but some designers who earned their spurs in that genre eventually became involved in university research and development projects, leading to the "serious games" movement. Current "serious game" projects entail immersion in complex environments, for example, serving as a university president trying to successfully pursue the mission of their institution. "Serious game" products have not yet emerged that have found widespread adoption in academic disciplines as such. In corporate training, a number of simulation-games have been devised for particular companies, but other than the sorts of business games discussed earlier, they have not yet gained widespread adoption.

The new frontier is in the use of hand-held devices and smartphones to access technical simulations. Technicians now go into the field with devices that enable them to quickly trouble-shoot problems in electromechanical systems. Sales people receive updated customer information, short instructional modules, and podcasts while out making calls. The next step is to enable them to practice in realistic simulations or simulation games.

Repetition in Distance Education

Perhaps the most intractable hurdle for distance education has been to find ways to enable learners to have sufficient opportunities for Repetition when the facilitator and learner are separated by time and/or space. Solutions for knowledge-type objectives are fairly straightforward, but as the learning tasks move into the psychomotor domain, solutions are more challenging. If the task being taught requires special equipment or facilities to practice, how can these be provided at myriad distance locations? And if the learner's performance needs to be judged and corrected individually by someone with special expertise, how can this be done, even with a two-way synchronous media connection?

Cognitive Objectives

For many academic subjects and many cognitive objectives, the appropriate practice is primarily mental practice, requiring no special equipment or facilities. Nowadays, with the major delivery system for distance education being the Internet, through e-mail exchanges, discussion forums, and chat rooms, students can share their thinking with peers and get feedback from them. They can work in pairs or small groups to prepare authentic products, such as a stock purchase recommendation, a weather forecast, a newspaper article, a cash-flow statement, a patient diagnosis, a statistical analysis of retail data, a critique of a poem, or the like.

A novel approach to the challenge of repetitive practice at a distance was tried in the 1970s in Nicaragua via broadcast radio. Mathematics lessons spoken over the radio incorporated embedded questions followed by a pause and then confirmation of the correct answer. To the students in classrooms around the country, it felt like the radio teacher was listening to their choral responses and congratulating them on their correct answers (Suppes, Searle and Friend 1980). The "pseudo-interactive" radio project, sponsored by the U.S. Agency for International Development, was so successful that it was expanded to other subjects and other countries.

Interpersonal Objectives

For attitudinal or interpersonal skills, face-to-face practice with other people is often required. Role-plays or scenarios enacted over audio or video conferencing can substitute in part for the required practice, but only in part.

Psychomotor Objectives

For psychomotor skills, such as equipment operation, tool use, sports performance, and the like, there is no substitute for hands-on, realistic, repeated practice. A prominent example of these sorts of objectives is clinical practice, a core portion of professional training in medicine, dentistry, nursing, and other health professions. Technological solutions have been developed to address pieces of this problem; for example, high-fidelity computerized human patient simulator manikins have been widely adopted in medical education (Harder 2010). Even more advanced simulators are in use that provide high-resolution 3D images of dental procedures and can track the user's movements, correcting them before major mistakes are made (Yu et al. 2017). Virtual reality (VR) applications have also been applied to the procedures of examining and treating patients. However, these 3D and VR systems have largely been limited to on-site laboratory installations and are expensive in terms of development costs and staffing costs, given that they require a high teacher-to-student ratio (Dutile, Wright and Beauchesne 2011). Thus, for example, a nurse practitioner could practice diagnosing the illness of patient who is a thousand miles away, having access to two-way video and an array of lab tests, but he could not realistically practice administering an intravenous infusion in a video conference. The solution is to shift many types of Repetition to off-line venues. In professions in which precise performance is a life-and-death matter, such as nursing, dentistry, and medicine, online courses shift clinical practice to designated locations where learners can gather with certified professionals to conduct hands-on practice with expert feedback.

The potential scope of this problem was dramatized in 2020 during the Coronavirus (COVID-19) pandemic, when higher education institutions in the United States and around the world ceased F2F classes to retard spread of the contagion. Instructors were suddenly faced with the task of shifting overnight to online teaching. For most, technology was readily available to conduct activities in the Presentation, Demonstration, Discussion, Tutorial, Study, and Expression configurations, but Repetition—a vital component of many fields of study—posed a real challenge, and not just in health sciences and other laboratory-based fields. The piano teacher could offer a Demonstration of proper technique via some videoconferencing tool, but how could students practice without pianos in their homes or wherever they were sequestered? With schools closed, how could Teacher Education students gain practice in teaching? What had been rhetorical questions suddenly became very real.

Evolution of Repetition

Memorization by Copying and Reciting Texts

As a pedagogical tool, Repetition has served as a primary means to mastery of the basic skills of literacy and numeracy since ancient times, as documented by Aspinwall (1913) in his prodigious survey of the history of education. Basic education was widespread in ancient Egypt from the Old Kingdom to the Late New Kingdom, and it was characterized by rote memorization and copying of classical texts (2). In imperial China, from around the twentieth century BC until the twentieth century AD, education was dominated by the examination system, which led to "exact imitation" of classical texts, "study aloud in concert," and "rapid repetition" (6)—and similar methods were also common in basic education in India during that period (8).

Repetitive Drills for Physical Skills

In Europe, during the later stages of the Roman Empire, Vegetius (*fl.* 4th or 5th century AD) describes Roman military training in *De Re Militari*, a book still consulted by military trainers. Marching, physical fitness, and weapons handling skills were accomplished by constant drilling under the watchful eyes of officers who had themselves undergone the same training in their youth.

Later, during the early Christian period, monastic schools offered instruction to those aspiring to religious careers but also accommodating others seeking basic education; here, as in earlier times, the routine featured memorization of texts, taking dictation to copy books, and individual recitation (Aspinwall 1913, 49).

Recitation Mode

As discussed in Chapter 8, from the medieval period onward in England, children attended "grammar schools," where students copied Latin texts and spent hours chanting Latin declensions and conjugations, a form of group Repetition. Later, as the focus shifted from Latin to reading in one's own native language, chanting faded as a major activity because students were no longer learning declensions and conjugations of a foreign language by rote. Instead, practice was largely covert. Typically, teachers dictated a text, students copied it, memorized it (covert practice), then demonstrated their mastery by reciting the text back to the teacher (overt practice). On the American frontier—New York and Pennsylvania—in the early 1800s, many schools followed the Lancaster monitorial system from Great Britain, in which older students were trained to teach younger ones, allowing one qualified teacher to oversee a whole school (emulating the classroom model developed in the 1600s by Comenius, as discussed in Chapter 5). They followed the recitation model for reading and writing, as described above. For arithmetic, students copied the teacher's solution to a problem on a slate, erased the slate, and attempted new sample problems (Saettler 1990). By the twentieth century, this method evolved somewhat, with mimeographed sheets replacing slates. The recitation format of the nineteenth century continues down to the present time in slightly modified form, as teachers intersperse questioning of students during their lectures ("lecture recitation") or begin lessons by quizzing students on their assigned textbook readings ("textbook recitation").

Cognitive Science and Neuroscience behind Repetition

More Repetition, More Myelin

Many different sorts of skills, in different domains—cognitive, affective, motor, interpersonal, are all attained and maintained through repetitive practice. Each involves a complex combination of brain modules. However, there is a common physiological process underlying all these processes. Activities such as composing a poem, throwing a basketball, or driving a car trigger a pattern of electrical signals through the neurons. With practice, the axons that connect the neurons come to be coated with myelin, thus speeding up the signals following that path. The more signals, the more myelin. The more myelin, the faster and stronger the nerve impulses. These hyped-up pathways make our behavioral patterns more fluent, more automatized (Shen 2013). One study, for example, found a direct correlation between the amount of piano practice done during childhood and adolescence and white matter (myelin) density in regions of the brain related to finger motor skills and visual and auditory processing (Bengtsson et al. 2005).

Motor Skill Learning

While it is generally accepted that motor skills become automatized with sufficient practice, recent cognitive and neuroscience research sketches a more complicated picture, in which even automatized skills may come under conscious control. Willingham (1998) proposed a neuropsychological theory of motor skill learning that offers an explanation of how conscious and unconscious processes may interact to improve performance. His control-based learning theory (COBALT) proposes that "different cognitive components of motor control are subserved by anatomically distinct parts of the brain" (558–559) and that each of these four components utilize different forms of representation. The third process plans the sequence of movements; the fourth process, based in the spinal cord, locates the body in relation to the movements. Importantly, Willingham proposes a "dual-mode principle" to explain—in an original way—how motor skills can be performed under conscious control as well as under automatic control. COBALT also accounts for the benefits that have been demonstrated for mental practice of motor skills, and thus provides a theoretical basis for the role of coaching in improving physical performance.

Incidentally, the dual-mode principle also helps understand the phenomenon of "choking under pressure," which can be explained as the player using the conscious mode when the unconscious mode would result in greater accuracy (Willingham 1998, 576). The conscious mode might work well for a novice, but once the skill has been overlearned, the unconscious pathway guides performance more effectively (578).

There is an apparent paradox in that motor skill learning requires proprioceptive feedback, yet clearly such skills can be learned through mental practice or observation alone (Bandura's social learning theory, discussed in Chapter 3). Willingham's "dual-mode principle" resolves this paradox by proposing that the unconscious mode of learning requires proprioceptive feedback but the *conscious* mode does not (Willingham 1998, 575).

More recent research has supported Willingham's COBALT theory. Krakauer and Mazzoni (2011) conclude that:

> These results are interesting because they go against the idea that as tasks become well practiced and automatic, they break free of explicit control. The possibility that explicit cognitive processes can always enhance overlearned skills suggests an interesting difference between skill learning and adaptation.
> *(641)*

Neuroimaging studies have allowed new insights into neuroplasticity—the functional reorganization of the architecture of gray and white matter—that occurs during the acquisition, consolidation, and retention of motor skills (Dayan and Cohen 2011). In general, though, they support and explain previously discovered principles of motor skill learning, rather than overturning them. For example: "Motor skills are typically learned slowly over multiple training sessions until performance reaches near asymptotic levels" (443); and "reward during practice improves long-term retention of a sequential motor skill" (450).

Issues in Repetition

Whole-Task or Part-Task?

When doing Repetition, should the learner perform the whole task each time, or is it more efficacious to do part of the task? The answer is clearest in the psychomotor domain. Here, simply repeating whole performances in a routine way does not necessarily lead to greater expertise. For complex skills, it is often useful to focus on one subskill at a time. Or another way of looking at the problem is to begin with tasks that are initially outside one's current repertoire but can be mastered with a few hours of practice focused on critical aspects, and by gradually refining performance through repetitions after feedback. In athletics, maintenance of high-level skills requires constant repetitive drills on component skills, such as practicing free throws in basketball.

For complex learning tasks that may involve a combination of concepts, procedures, and even physical skills, whole-task practice is recommended. Begin with performance of the simplest version of the whole task that is still fairly representative of the ultimate task; then practice a more complex version of the task, and so on, until the desired level of complexity is reached. This is the essence of Reigeluth's "elaboration theory" (Reigeluth et al. 1980) and Merrill's "pebble-in-the-pond" design prescription (Merrill 2002). Cognitive load theory proposes adding "scaffolds" to whole-task practice—performance supports that are embedded in the instructional system to give hints and coaching to the learner (van Merriënboer, Kirschner and Kester 2003).

Overt or Covert Practice?

Mental imagery or mental rehearsal are terms used to refer to covert mental practice without any physical movement. In sports, the usual term is "visualization," imagining a future situation and thinking about the steps needed to be successful. Musicians also use this technique to mentally rehearse a performance while resting, traveling, or otherwise prevented from physically rehearsing. Research indicates that covert practice can have a moderate, positive impact on performance (Driskell, Cooper and Moran 1994). It depends, though, on the type of task, the elapsed time between visualizing and performing, and the duration of the covert practice. Not surprisingly, covert practice is better suited to cognitive tasks rather than physical ones, or the cognitive components of actions that entail a combination of mental and physical exertion (Driskell, Cooper and Moran 1994, 485).

Overt practice, in general, yields more positive gains than covert, especially for objectives that entail psychomotor learning. From a practical standpoint, the only way an instructor can be certain that anyone is practicing anything is to be able to see and hear the activity.

Massed Practice or Spaced Practice?

In the military comedy film *Stripes*, John Winger's platoon fails to properly go through basic training and are about to fail graduation. But the night before the graduation ceremony, John motivates his mates to spend the night in intensive practice drills. The next morning, they wow the generals with an impressive display of precision drills. Unfortunately, such an instructional strategy works only in fiction. Research indicates that spaced practice is superior, both for greater retention and to reduce fatigue and error along the way; this applies both to motor skills (Sage 1984) and cognitive skills (National Academies of Sciences 2018, 99). "Cramming" the night before an exam might allow the learner to scrape by, but long-term retention will be minimal (Rohrer and Taylor 2006).

How Many Repetitions?

In the classroom, on the sports field, and in the workplace, large amounts of repetition are often necessary in order to reach the goal of "overlearning," practicing newly acquired skills beyond mere initial mastery to the point of automaticity. An example is a well-known American baseball player of the 1950s, George "Shotgun" Shuba. His nickname came from his unique ability to consistently hit the ball hard on a line. His secret was that he practiced daily at home with a rope tied to the ceiling. He tied knots to represent the strike zone and swung a bat at that area at least 600 times a day.

The point of overlearning is to make the new skill fluent and automatic so that performance does not require use of working memory, which is always in limited supply (R. C. Clark 2015, 209). For example, when the student of Greek has mastered the Greek alphabet to the extent that they can read a sentence without thinking about the individual letters, they can move on to higher level tasks such as translation. You cannot speak a foreign language if you have to stop and mentally run through six possible verb endings for the present tense before forming a verb; those verb endings must become automatized through repetition before you can have a conversation.

There is no firm rule for determining how many repetitions are required to reach either initial mastery or automaticity. There was a brief fashion several years ago for a "10,000 hour" rule—proposing that someone with reasonable native ability needed that amount of practice to reach "elite" performance standards—promulgated by Gladwell (2008), who was interpreting the work of Ericsson (Ericsson, Krampe and Tesch-Romer 1993). First, this assumes that the performer starts out with all the necessary mental and physical abilities to become elite. If they do not, they will never excel, no matter how much they practice, as Gladwell later conceded. Second, individuals with similar genetic endowments may reach mastery with very different amounts of repetitions. Hambrick and his colleagues (2018) propose a comprehensive, multifactorial model of expertise that gives recognition to the contributions of both genetic endowment and practice. Ericsson's (1993) original concept of "deliberate practice" has come to be interpreted more broadly—even by Ericsson himself (2020)—as simply analyzing the learner's skill gaps and focusing on those gaps in practice sessions, usually with the assistance of a knowledgeable coach (R. C. Clark 2015).

How Much Guidance?

A rigorous definition of inductive or discovery learning would stipulate that learners are not given the target concepts or principles but must find them independently, given certain resources. If learners are left to struggle with little or no guidance, the hard-earned learning—whatever it might end up being—would probably be well remembered, but would it be worth the trade-off in terms of effectiveness (remembering the right things) and efficiency (the cost of the pursuit)? The fact that humans "figure things out" without much assistance in their daily living is not an argument to do the same thing in educational and training settings. The whole point of instruction, as discussed in Chapter 3, is to accomplish vital learning tasks more effectively and more efficiently than everyday "muddling through."

In reality, educators debate not about giving guidance but how much guidance to give. In comparison studies, minimal guidance does not fare well in terms of effectiveness or efficiency. The consensus is that certain types of guidance are invaluable, especially worked examples, ample feedback, and "scaffolding" of various sorts—templates, modeling a task, advice, or coaching (Clark, Kirschner and Sweller 2012). See the description of the Process-Oriented Guided Inquiry Learning (POGIL) method later in this chapter for examples of learner guidance. Discovery learning does not have to be "sink or swim."

Strengths and Limitations: Why Repetition?

Many different theories of instruction place a high value on repetition, but for different reasons. An early rationale for repetition came from stimulus-response theory; as Guthrie (1942) stated it:

> In learning any skill, what must be acquired is not an association or any series of associations, but many thousands of associations that will connect specific movements with specific situations. One lesson or trial is all that is necessary to learn to depress the brake pedal on a car. Learning to drive a car, however, requires a varied experience which will cause the pedal to be depressed in many situations and left severely alone in many others.
>
> *(36)*

Operant conditioning theory proposes that learners must exhibit some observable response in order to be provided with a reinforcer that will strengthen that behavior. In this view, a learning cycle consists of repeated responses followed by reinforcers delivered according to a schedule of reinforcement. The more repetitions with reinforcement, the more durable the response (Skinner 1953).

Cognitive information processing (CIP) theory posits that learners store new knowledge in long-term memory with the benefit of repetitive practice that is varied in time, place, and conditions (Atkinson and Shiffrin 1968). Constructivist learning theory emphasizes learners' construction of their own unique conceptual structures; hence, it advocates activity in complex, realistic, and relevant environments. To develop a robust conceptualization of complex material, it is necessary for learners to "crisscross" the landscape of the new material multiple times, viewing the material from multiple perspectives. In this sense, constructivist theory supports experiences that are repeated numerous times under varying conditions (Driscoll 2005, 105).

Looking beyond the cognitive domain, attitude formation can also be facilitated through structured repeated practice; the key is evoking a response that represents a step toward the target attitude. The original attitude can be changed by a series of small steps, gaining a new equilibrium at each step (Kamradt and Kamradt 1999).

The domain in which Repetition is most clearly the dominant configuration is psychomotor learning, ubiquitous in athletics, musical performance, military training, and the workplace. Mastery of new physical skills requires repetitive cycles of practice-and-feedback under varying conditions (Romiszowski 1999).

Regardless of theoretical orientation, it is clear that appropriate practice, repeated under varying conditions, is the linchpin of many different instructional programs. According to the National Research Council's authoritative review of research on learning:

> One of the simplest rules is that practice increases learning; in the brain, there is a similar relationship between the amount of experience in a complex environment and the amount of structural change
>
> *(National Research Council 2000, 125).*

There are three major commonsense justifications for giving prominence to Repetition. First, information that is received and comprehended but not used is quickly forgotten; some type of practice with the material helps integrate the new knowledge into the learner's cognitive structure (*schema* theory). Second, repeated practice helps connect the intangible, abstract concepts with physical movements and the emotions that are associated with those actions; activities—especially those that have some emotional overlay—are more readily remembered and those memories will carry the abstractions with them. Third, visible practice gives the instructor some indication of student progress. An observer can see and hear what learners are doing and can compare those behaviors with the educational objectives.

Strengths

Getting down to basics, there is probably no instructional activity with greater payoff than actually repeatedly *performing* the skill or using the knowledge or emitting the emotional response that is the goal of the lesson. By repeating the target behavior, the learner is increasingly the likelihood that it will be performed again in the future, especially if it is accompanied by some sort of reinforcer or corrective feedback.

Limitations

Some advocates have overpromised regarding the value of Repetition in achieving expertise, such as the "10,000-hour" claim discussed earlier. The fact is that people with exceptional innate talent can achieve and maintain elite-level skill with less practice, while those without the necessary physical or mental gifts can never achieve elite levels of performance with a million repetitions.

The value of repetition also varies with the nature of the task being learned. For sports and athletics, practice accounts for about one-fifth of the variance in performance. In vocations requiring a combination of cognitive, motor, and interpersonal skills—such as teaching, sales, or piloting airplanes—practice seems to play a smaller role (Hambrick et al. 2018). Innate ability matters a great deal.

Regardless of its theoretical merits, practice sometimes gets short shrift in formal education because it requires conditions other than the teacher-led, lecture-dominant traditional classroom. As just one dramatic example, observe the profusion of facilities and personnel that must be assembled by an American university to enable its football team to garner the practice necessary to compete interscholastically.

Best Practices for Using Repetition

Advice for the Facilitator

Repetition Itself

Repetition may be conducted in an intimate tutorial setting, as in a piano lesson; in a classroom setting, such as a high school physics class; or in a field setting, such as sales team members in a car dealership. In any case, the challenge is to make sure that each individual engages in the specified practice. Even in a one-to-one situation, it is possible for the mentor to dominate the practice session by talking about and demonstrating the new material, rather than letting the learner practice. The learner should be doing the work at least half the time (Yelon 1996, 190).

A lecture-type class can be modified to allow individual practice by interspersing whole-class or small-group discussions (see Chapter 7) or question-and-answer with response cards or other techniques (as discussed at length in Chapter 5 under Interactive Lecture).

Instructors who are overseeing practice in field settings are sometimes hesitant to set learners loose, fearful that they might hurt themselves, damage property, or "get lost," figuratively or literally. But it does not have to be an all-or-nothing choice.

In many cases it is possible to allow them to get involved a bit at a time—that is, a part-task rather than whole-task approach. For example, for a middle-school ecology outing, students could put seine nets in place in a stream and then collect the nets to examine them for aquatic insects. The instructor or science adviser could do the identification of insects, with students entering the data into a spreadsheet. After further experiences, students could do the identification themselves, as well as analyzing the statistical data collected—moving from part-task involvement to whole-task.

In any of these settings, one way of ensuring that learners get the *quantity* of practice they need—and the *quality* of practice they need—is to provide them with a checklist of the critical features of the target skill. A checklist will allow them to evaluate and document their own performance or the performance of a peer more systematically. Completed checklists can provide a record of practice both for the learner and the instructor (Yelon 1996, 275–276).

Appropriately Realistic Practice

The conditions of practice ought to match the conditions of the ultimate educational goal. Who would you rather have giving you an intravenous injection? (A) Someone who had read a Red Cross booklet on injections? (B) Someone who had watched a video demonstration of injections? (C) Someone who had injected fluid into an orange? Or (D) someone who had successfully infused several live humans with a syringe? A, B, and C could well be *necessary* steps in the learning the injection process, but only D is *sufficient* in including the real-world conditions relevant to this task. Part-task practice has a vital role to play, but at some point, each individual learner must have the opportunity to practice the whole task under realistic conditions. A simple way to judge the appropriateness of practice activities is to compare those activities to the intended final test. For example, if the objective is for learners to apply a physics principle to a problem, both the test and the practice activities need to require learners to apply that principle to previously unseen cases (Yelon 1996, 197).

If it is important to be able to perform the target skill automatically, students must be urged to practice outside of class repeatedly. Just as string players need to practice a new piece of music over and over in order to "stuff the notes into their fingers," so must actors repeat their lines or speakers rehearse their speeches until they can be performed without thinking about each word or each gesture.

Keep the Practice Interesting

To maintain learner interest, vary the practice exercises—some easy, some challenging (Keller 2010). A bit of humor also helps. Practice items can include characters who have humorous names or who are involved in humorous situations. Keep the sessions short and distribute them over time, both for the sake of interest and for the sake of long-term retention. Of course, as discussed above, putting the practice items into a game format can increase learners' motivation to start the task and persist through many repetitions.

Provide Appropriate Feedback

As important as ensuring appropriate practice is providing feedback on learner performance. The term "feedback" is borrowed from cybernetics, where it refers to the furnishing of data concerning the operation of a machine back to the machine itself, so that subsequent operations can be altered or corrected. The term is used in pedagogy with very much the same meaning—furnishing information to correct future behavior (Hattie and Timperley 2007).

Feedback may come from the learner's personal experience, e.g., experiencing the "feel" of a solid hit with a golf club; or it may be provided by a technological device, e.g., a video game that adds points for every successful math problem solved correctly; or it may come from another human—interpersonal feedback, e.g. a football coach adjusting the stance of a lineman or a medical clinic trainer using signals ("event markers") to indicate correct performance, discussed below.

The first, feedback from one's own personal experience, is the easiest to acquire but the least useful. It is difficult to objectively observe one's own performance while performing; and, likely as not, the performer is not sure of what the optimal execution looks like anyway.

The second, device-controlled feedback, can be more objective and more accurate than personal perceptions. An audio or video recording can be played back to compare the learner's motions to desired motions. An instructional computer program can provide continuous monitoring and objective correction. However, there are few types of performance that a computer program can actually observe—keystrokes, yes; multiple-choice selections, yes; numerical solutions to math problems, yes; images on a graphics tablet or touchscreen, yes; but athletic performance, artistic products, body language, persuasive arguments, interpersonal relationships…not so much.

The third type, interpersonal feedback, is most likely to be able to make fine discriminations between appropriate and inappropriate responses. People, especially those with special expertise, are better able to judge behavioral responses and give appropriate feedback than learners themselves or computer software. In addition, there is the intangible value of the human touch. Fellow students, instructors, or expert judges can craft their feedback in a way that is most helpful to the learner. In the context of instructional games and simulations, providing explanatory feedback, rather than just correct/incorrect or a number of points—a form of scaffolding—has proven to enhance learning (Mayer and Johnson 2010). In the distance education context, feedback may be offered in the form of text—such as e-mails or discussion forum comments, in the form of audio commentary—such as podcasts, or in visual form—such as screen shots of model answers to questions or "screencasts," short movies made showing some portion of a desktop that the instructor can narrate.

A fourth type, *event-marking*—better known as "clicker training"—begun as a dolphin training technique, has found a niche market in teaching psychomotor skills in fields such as clinical practice in medicine or dentistry. The basic notion, borrowed from operant conditioning, is to provide a signal—a click, a flicker of flashlight, a spoken "good"—every time the learner completes a step in a complex procedure successfully. The *event*, successful performance, is *marked* by an audible or visible signal (Konkel 2016). Martin Levy, an orthopedic surgeon, learned to use a clicker in training dogs. He later adapted the technique to training surgeons on basic psychomotor skills, such as knot-tying. He found that the clicker was more effective than verbal praise or criticism because it removed the emotional element, focusing attention solely on the learner's physical actions (Vedantam et al. 2018). This is congruent with the conclusions of Hattie and Timperley's meta-analysis (2007): that feedback is more effective when it reinforces correct responses (84), when it provides information on correct rather than incorrect responses, and when it builds on changes from previous trials (85).

Case Study Method

As with the Discussion configuration, many instructors find it difficult to abandon the security of the lecture format, in which content, timing, and sequence are under the control of the Facilitator. The case method—any heuristic approach—democratizes the classroom, with Facilitator and Learner sharing control and sharing responsibility for content, timing, and sequence.

Management of a learner-centered activity requires a plan as much as or more than a teacher-centered activity. When using the case method, the instructor must come in with a class plan. This plan will deal with time management—how much time is allocated for each step in the process—and content management—how to make sure that the salient points are addressed (Barbazette 2004).

It is always beneficial to begin with some framing of the activity: What are we doing and why are we doing it? What do we expect to gain from this case study? Students will have more confidence in the venture if they are convinced that the instructor has prepared all the logistics: Who will be doing what, when, and where?

Whether operating as a whole-class discussion or a small-group discussion, each discussion group must have an outline of the questions to be addressed. For case study, the questions fall into several categories:

- Facts of the case: Who are the actors? What is the setting? What are the issues at stake?

- Analysis of events: What happened? Why?
- Evaluation: So what? Why are these issues important?
- Decision: What is the best course of action?
- Speculation: What if the circumstances were different?

To bring closure to the session, the instructor will want to summarize what came out in the discussion and what lessons were learned. Here it is important not to end with a pre-planned lecture, which would signal that the students' efforts were inconsequential. The summary should contain the words and thoughts expressed by the students, condensed for easier digestion.

Role Plays, Simulations, and Simulation Games

Introducing the Activity

"Modified reality" activities provide the group with a rich hoard of experiences with the subject matter. There will be a lot to talk about. Participants may be willing to venture some hypotheses about "what works" in this problem space. But those experiences and ideas are unlikely to be integrated into the learner's repertoire without some advance framing and some after-action follow-up.

Any heuristic activity needs to be preceded by some framing: What is the objective of the activity? Sometimes a simulation game has a hidden agenda, for example, *Star Power*, reveals social class fault lines, but it is preferable for the participants to discover this themselves rather being told in advance. What is the time limit? What are the ground rules?

Of course, more complex simulation games will have their own instructions. These should be dealt with as quickly as possible to avoid dampening the enthusiasm of participants to dive in and begin playing. Players may be given printed instructions, which can be consulted later as needed. Roles must be assigned; groups must be formed; then participants head to their assigned areas.

Conducting the Activity

Experienced game directors like to keep the action brisk in order to keep energy levels high. Role-plays are usually best limited to five minutes or less; otherwise there may be too much material to remember and analyze in the debriefing. As mentioned earlier, if a class is broken into multiple play groups it is recommended to assign one team member in each group to act as an observer. If observers are given a checklist of what to look for, and a place to record comments, the debriefing can get off to a quick start, focusing on the salient points.

Concluding the Activity: Debriefing

Heuristic activities, which can be experientially rich, emotionally intense, and cognitively complex, require some unpacking in order to bring learners around to the original learning objectives. A whole-class discussion, structured as a debriefing, provides a robust framework for cycling through the needed phases of consolidating learning. The 4D process provides an outline for successful debriefings:

1. Decompression. As the activity ends, participants may be feeling exhilaration, frustration, anxiety, pride in success, or inadequacy in failure. Letting participants talk about these feelings helps them to return to an emotional equilibrium. For games, there will be some sort of scorekeeping, so winners can talk about their successful strategies, and losers can bemoan the obstacles they faced. Would people in the real-world situation have similar feelings? Were there aspects of the game that felt "unfair?" If there was a "hidden agenda" in the scenario, this would be the time to reveal it.
2. Description. The next objective is to have participants describe what they experienced during the activity. Who did what to whom? What was the meaning of these experiences? What principles could one deduce from the positive and negative outcomes of different strategies?
3. Drawing comparisons. To encourage transfer from the game to real life, participants can compare and contrast the game outcomes with what they would expect to happen in real life. What elements were missing from the simulation? Would the things that happened in the simulation happen in real life?
4. Deriving lessons. The final phase is to verbalize clearly what was learned from the simulation-game experience. What lessons can we take away? How might (doctors, managers, public officials) approach this type of problem more effectively? For corporate trainees: Can these ideas be used in our workplace? For students: What new understandings have we gained? (Heinich et al. 1996, 336)

Advice for Learners

Some configurations—Study, Discussion, Expression, and Repetition—by their very nature, place responsibility for learning squarely on the shoulders of the Learner. To prosper in these configurations, learners must come prepared, especially for the case method, in which they must study the case and prepare a brief before class. They must be willing to contribute to the discussion, including taking chances in venturing opinions. They must also respect the contributions of others (see the ground rules for Discussion in Chapter 8). As with instructors, not all students are equally suited dispositionally to be good discussants. For some, it will be a stretch. But passivity is not an option if learning is the goal.

In the case of athletic skills, it is assumed that learners will find the time and place to do repetitions without the presence of the coach. However, mindless repetition of drills can be a trap. When we repeat a habitual behavior over and over, we may assume that we are getting better, but we are more likely just reinforcing current habits, not improving our skill. And the habits might be bad habits.

As mentioned earlier in this chapter, the process of systematically organizing practice to focus on specific subskills is called deliberate practice. Its purpose is to improve performance in a conscious manner. Take, for example, soccer player A, who wants to improve her goal-scoring ability. For her daily practice, she might set up a dozen balls and practice kicking them into the goal, then repeat. Meanwhile, player B enlists the help of an assistant to play goalie and retrieve balls; she then practices hitting specific corners of the goal to avoid the blocks of the goalie…and takes twice as many attempts in the time available because she has a retriever helping her. Which player is more likely to improve?

Another way to make deliberate practice more effective is to measure the results. Player B could set up a video camera to record her shots, enabling her to count the misses and judge whether they were long, short, right, or left of the target. If there is a pattern to the misses, she can catch it and correct it. Better yet, player B can go one step further to make her practice more productive—get a coach. Elite players of solo sports like skiing, tennis, and golf rely on coaches to help set improvement goals and track progress toward those goals.

Methods Featuring the Repetition Configuration

Strategic Level

Direct Instruction (Presentation/Demonstration + Repetition)

Direct Instruction (DI) is a specific procedure developed by Siegfried Engelmann in the 1960s to accelerate the learning curve of young children, especially those who are educationally and economically disadvantaged. The teacher begins by presenting or demonstrating a small chunk of new material and asking for an overt response from the small group. All students in the group respond vocally to the teacher's cues in unison after a signal from the teacher. The teacher listens to the responses and gives appropriate feedback. Direct Instruction has been evaluated in hundreds of comparison studies over the years and consistently ranks among the most effective innovations for teaching reading and math skills at the elementary level (Engelmann and Carnine 1991).

Skills Lesson (Presentation + Demonstration + Repetition)

This is a common pattern for a lesson emphasizing the mastery of specific skills. It begins with a Presentation explaining the target skill (15 percent of the time), followed by a Demonstration (25 percent of the time) of the skill by the instructor or a master performer. It concludes by spending the greater part of the lesson in practice (60 percent of the time) guided by the instructor or a skills coach (Davies 1981, 50).

Process-Oriented Guided Inquiry Learning (POGIL) (Presentation + Simulation + Discussion)

POGIL is widely used in secondary and higher education classes in STEM subjects. A POGIL lesson begins with introductory teacher talk (Presentation), then students divide into groups of three with assigned roles—manager, computer operator, and recorder. The groups typically use interactive computer simulations, one computer per group, to explore the topic for the day. Their exploration is guided by a specific set of questions provided by the instructor. Typically, the first few questions build on students' prior knowledge; later questions are designed to promote the recognition of patterns in the simulation data, leading toward some concept development. The instructor circulates, giving tutorial help where needed. The teams talk about and agree upon their answers to the questions (Small-Group Discussion). The answers are shared as part of general discussion with the whole class (Whole-Class Discussion). The instructor ends by summing up the main concepts learned (Presentation) (Vanags, Pammer and Brinker 2013).

Case Study Method (Study + Discussion + Repetition in "Modified Reality" + Expression)

Whole courses—even some curricula—in law schools, business schools, and medical schools are designed around the case method. Learners study realistic case descriptions, discuss them in teams, and formulate solutions to the problems raised, as explained at length earlier in this chapter.

Instructional Game (Repetition within a Ludic Context)

As described above in this chapter, a game—a ludic activity in which participants follow prescribed rules that differ from those of real life as they strive to attain a challenging goal—can become the frame for repeated practice of desired behaviors, developing both cognitive and other types of skills. The key is to assure that players spend most of their time practicing the target skills, not extraneous activities, such as throwing dice or spinning spinners.

Instructional Simulation (Repetition within a "Modified Reality" Context)

As described above in this chapter, a simulation exercise—such as a case study, a role-play, or some other social simulation—allows learners to rehearse cognitive, affective, interpersonal, or psychomotor skills in a realistic context, but one that is scaled-down to simplify reality and to reduce physical or emotional risks.

Instructional Simulation Game (Repetition within both Game and Simulation Conditions)

As described above in this chapter, instructional simulation games combine the features of simulations and games to provide a holistic and realistic context to rehearse cognitive, affective, interpersonal, or psychomotor skills.

Problem-Based Learning (PBL) (Repetition within "Modified Reality" Conditions + Study + Discussion)

PBL is a powerful arrangement for inductive, or "discovery," learning. In the more common—deductive—approach, the lesson begins by telling learners the facts, principles, or procedures they are to learn—The Point, followed by guided practice of those skills. An inductive approach, sometimes characterized as a "constructivist learning environment," turns this process upside-down. It begins by immersing the learners in a problem—often in the form of a game or simulation or case study—and letting them grapple with the problem (Repetition configuration), giving minimal guidance while they explore and develop their own interpretation of the problem. At the end, a debriefing (Discussion configuration) is held to allow learners to voice their understandings and be led toward The Point.

Thus, in PBL learners are immersed in a problem space in which they are free to explore real-world resources and instructional resources (hence, the Study configuration will often be included), possibly in collaboration with other learners (Discussion), making decisions and practicing skills that lead to attainment of some instructed learning goal. A facilitator usually structures the situation and may monitor the experience, but learners are in control of the exploratory process.

PBL became established as a specific method for inductive learning in medical education in the 1980s (Barrow and Tamblyn 1980). The aim was to have medical students "thinking like doctors" right from the beginning of their training.

Tactical Level

Drill-and-Practice (Repetition in a Contrived Setting)

Both cognitive and psychomotor skills can be acquired by systematic repetition of desired behaviors. For physical skills "by repeating the essential movements in successive practice trials, the learner discovers the kinesthetic cues that signal the difference between error and error-free performance" (Gagné and Medsker 1996). Drill-and-practice promotes the acquisition of cognitive knowledge or skill through repeated rehearsal of specific knowledge, concept, or procedural problems. The subskills built through drill-and-practice may become the building blocks for more meaningful learning.

Recitation (Repetition in Group Setting)

Learners study independently, then are called upon by the instructor to display what they have learned by reciting (or working a problem on the chalkboard) in front of the class.

Guided Cognitive Practice (Repetition + Tutorial)

Combining tutorial help with Repetition goes beyond the routine feedback that a coach gives during practice exercises. When dealing with cognitive objectives, it is helpful to go beyond just confirming or correcting the learner's attempts to display a skill. After teaching a small amount of new material, checking student comprehension and discussing misunderstandings can go a long way toward preventing misunderstandings. If tutorial assistance from the instructor is not feasible, students can be paired up and asked to check each other's work. Ideally, for cognitive skills, they would talk about how they reached their answer. Unless the covert mental practice is made overt, it is difficult to evaluate or correct.

Physical Coaching (Repetition + Tutorial)

In the case of learning psychomotor skills, such as trade apprenticeships or athletic training, "guided practice" is referred to as coaching, in which much of the learner's time and effort are devoted mainly to repetitive practice of the new skills to be mastered. For physical skills, there is no substitute for repetitions, and the corrective advice of a skilled coach can ensure that those repetitions are correct, not ingraining bad habits. Cognitive coaching is also discussed under "Methods" in Chapter 6, and athletic coaching is discussed under "Methods" in Chapter 8.

Memorization (Study + Repetition)

As discussed in Chapter 10, when learners are in the Study mode, they may spend a large proportion of their time in some sort of repetitive practice; for example, consciously trying to memorize a list of foreign vocabulary words by repeating them aloud or covertly.

Debriefing (Repetition in Simulation or Game + Discussion)

It is universally recognized among researchers in simulation-gaming that much of the benefit derived from simulations and games results from the post-activity discussion, or debriefing. As Wouters et al. (2013) point out, "serious games are more effective when they are supplemented with other instructional methods…[game players] gain intuitive knowledge, but they are not prompted to verbalize the new knowledge and so do not anchor it more profoundly in their knowledge base" (260). Debriefing prompts participants to verbalize their insights, thus storing them as explicit declarative knowledge.

Chapter Summary

Repetition is the configuration in which a learner is repeatedly practicing a new mental or physical skill, with or without the benefit of a coach. One could say that practice is the "active ingredient" of virtually all types of learning activities. Formats for Repetition can be grouped into the categories of solo practice, group practice, and supervised practice, according to the extent of corrective feedback received from others. Examples of solo practice include reciting multiplication tables, musicians practicing alone, doing math homework problems, and working in a real-world setting as an intern. Examples of group practice include actors rehearsing a scene, a soccer team's passing drills, participation in a role-play exercise, or choral response during a presentation. Examples of supervised practice include orchestra rehearsal led by a conductor, church choir practice, or in-class textbook recitation.

Another class of formats is of special interest—the "modified reality" formats, various forms of simulations and games. Simulations, such as case studies, role-plays, and physical simulators, allow safe practice in scaled-down settings. Games add a ludic element and manipulation of the normal laws of nature and society; not scaled-down rules, but *different* rules apply. Games designed for specifically instructional purposes aim to offer focused, repeated practice of desired behaviors in a more motivating setting than ordinary practice. Both instructional games and instructional simulation games have been adapted to computer delivery, making them available on-demand. The popularity of computer-based entertainment games has led to a trend to add game-like elements—such as badges and leaderboard—to college courses and corporate training programs.

Distance education delivery offers particular challenges to offering Repetition activities remotely. Participants can practice cognitive skills through e-mail exchanges, discussion forum comments, and team project work conducted via document sharing, text chats, and video conferencing. Some interpersonal skill practice can be attained through audio and video conferencing. For motor skills, such as clinical practice in medicine, off-line laboratory settings are the norm, although considerable progress has been made in virtual-reality and 3D technology, allowing some limited sorts of practice for those who can afford it.

Repetition has a long pedigree as a means of teaching literacy and numeracy from the time of ancient civilizations, evolving into recitation routines in the Middle Ages. A broader range of more flexible formats have evolved in modern times, particularly in the form of F2F and computer-based simulations and games. Our understanding of the underlying physiology of motor skill learning has advanced along with advances in neurological imaging technology. Motor skills are interrelated with cognitive skills, each involving distinct parts of the brain simultaneously. Willingham's "dual-mode" theory offers an understanding of how even automatized skills can be brought under conscious control, helping to understand how coaching can serve the practice of psychomotor skills.

Research on Repetition has revolved around several key issues. Concerning whole- versus part-task practice, focusing on subskills is often justified, but generally, whole-task practice, as in Reigeluth's elaboration theory, is preferable in order to help the learner a maintain a holistic perspective of a complex learning task. Distributed practice provides greater long-term retention than massed practice, and overt practice is superior to covert practice, but there is no general rule for how much practice is required for mastery. On the other hand, the evidence is quite clear that instruction proceeds more effectively when learners receive ongoing guidance, or scaffolding, rather than being thrust into "authentic" problems with minimal guidance.

Repetition, as an instructional strategy, is recommended by virtually all schools of learning theory, but for different reasons. However, it is possible to oversell the value of Repetition, as with the purported "10,000 hours of practice to attain elite level skill." Innate ability has considerable weight in the process of attaining high levels of achievement in any domain, from cognitive to motor skills.

Best practices include ensuring that the practice is realistic vis-à-vis the ultimate application goal, that it is attractive in order to attain persistence, and that it receives appropriate feedback—usually meaning immediate and focused not only on the "how" but the "why." Case studies, games, and simulations all have protocols for their use, from introduction through debriefing. Indeed, in many cases, the debriefing yields the most important and most lasting learning outcomes of the activity.

Repetition plays a key role in many different instructional methods. At the strategic level, Direct Instruction, the skills lesson, and POGIL represent powerful combinations of Repetition with other configurations. At the tactical level, drill-and-practice, recitation, guided cognitive practice, coaching, interactive lectures, memorization, games, simulations, and debriefing each combine Repetition with other configurations to yield powerful instructional methods.

Works Cited

Aspinwall, William B. 1913. *Outlines of the History of Education*. New York: Macmillan.
Atkinson, Richard C., and Richard M. Shiffrin. 1968. "Human Memory: A Proposed System and Its Control Processes." In *The Psychology of Learning and Motivation*, edited by Kenneth W. Spence and Janet Taylor Spence, 2:89–195. New York: Academic Press.
Barbazette, Jean. 2004. *Instant Case Studies: How to Design, Adapt, and Use Case Studies in Teaching*. San Francisco, CA: Pfeiffer.
Barnes, Louis B., Roland Christensen, Abby J. Hansen, and C. Roland Christensen. 1994. *Teaching and the Case Method: Text, Cases, and Readings*. 3rd ed. Boston, MA: Harvard Business School Press.
Bengtsson, Sara L., Zoltan Nagy, Stefan Skare, Lea Forsman, Hans Forssberg, and Fredrick Ullen. 2005. "Extensive Piano Practicing Has Regionally Specific Effects on White Matter Development." *Nature Neuroscience* 8 (9): 1148–1150. doi:10.1038/nn1516.
Clark, Richard E., Paul A. Kirschner, and John Sweller. 2012. "Putting Students on the Path to Learning: The Case for Fully Guided Instruction." *American Educator* 36: 6–11.
Clark, Ruth Colvin. 2015. *Evidence-Based Training Methods: A Guide for Training Professionals*. 2nd ed. Alexandria, VA: ATD Press.
Comenius, Johann Amos. 1967. *Orbis Sensualium Pictus: Facsimile of the 3rd London Edition 1672 with an Introduction by James Bowen*. Sydney, NSW: Sydney University Press.
Comenius, John Amos, and Maurice W. Keatinge. 1967. *The Great Didactic of John Amos Comenius*. New York: Russell & Russell.
Davies, Ivor K. 1981. *Instructional Technique*. New York: McGraw-Hill.
Davis, James R., and Adelaide B. Davis. 1998. *Effective Training Strategies: A Comprehensive Guide to Maximizing Learning in Organizations*. San Francisco, CA: Berrett-Koehler Publishers.
Dayan, Eran, and Leonardo G. Cohen. 2011. "Neuroplasticity Subserving Motor Skill Learning." *Neuron* 72: 443–453.
Dean, Ceri B., Elizabeth Ross Hubbell, Howard Pitler, and Bj Stone. 2012. *Classroom Instruction that Works*. 2nd ed. Alexandria, VA: ASCD.

Driscoll, Marcy P. 2000. *Psychology of Learning for Instruction*. 2nd ed. Boston, MA: Allyn and Bacon.

——. 2005. *Psychology of Learning for Instruction*. 3rd ed. Boston, MA: Pearson Allyn and Bacon.

Driskell, James E., Carolyn Cooper, and Aidan Moran. 1994. "Does Mental Practice Enhance Performance?" *Journal of Applied Psychology* 79: 481–492.

Dutile, Colleen, Nancy Wright, and Michelle Beauchesne. 2011. "Virtual Clinical Education: Going the Full Distance in Nursing Education." *Newborn & Infant Nursing Reviews* 11 (1): 43–48.

Engelmann, Siegfried, and Douglas Carnine. 1991. *Theory of Instruction: Principles and Applications*. Revised edition. Eugene, OR: NIFDI Press.

Ericsson, K. Anders. 2020. "Towards a Science of the Acquisition of Expert Performance in Sports: Clarifying the Differences Between Deliberate Practice and Other Types of Practice." *Journal of Sports Sciences* 38 (2): 159–176. doi:10.1080/02640414.2019.168861.

Ericsson, K. Anders, Ralf Th. Krampe, and Clemens Tesch-Romer. 1993. "The Role of Deliberate Practice in the Acquisition of Expert Performance." *Psychological Review* 100: 363–406.

Gagné, Robert M., and Karen L. Medsker. 1996. *The Conditions of Learning: Training Applications*. Fort Worth, TX: Harcourt Brace.

Girault, Isabelle, Melanie Peffer, Augusto Chiocarriello, Maggie Renken, and Kathrin Otrel-Cass. 2016. "Computer Simulations on a Multidimensional Continuum: A Definition and Examples." In *Simulations as Scaffolds in Science Education. SpringerBriefs in Educational Communications and Technology*, by Maggie Renken, Melanie Peffer, Kathrin Otrel-Cass, Isabelle Girault and Augusto Chiocarriello, 5–14. Cham: Springer. Accessed March 11, 2020. doi:10.1007/978-3-319-24615-4_2.

Gladwell, Malcolm. 2008. *Outliers*. New York: Little, Brown.

Guthrie, Edwin R. 1942. *Conditioning: A Theory of Learning in Terms of Stimulus, Response, and Association*. Vol. 2, *The Psychology of Learning*, Chap. 1 in *The Forty-First Yearbook of the National Society for the Study of Education*, edited by Nelson B. Henry, 17–60. Chicago, IL: University of Chicago Press. doi:https://doi-org.proxyiub.uits.iu.edu/10.1037/11335-001.

Hambrick, David Z., Alexander P. Burgoyne, Brooke N. Macnamara, and Fredrik Ullen. 2018. "Toward a Multifactorial Model of Expertise: Beyond Born versus Made." *Annals of the New York Academy of Sciences* 1423 (1): 284–295. doi:10.1111/nyas.13586.

Harder, B. Nicole. 2010. "Use of Simulation in Teaching and Learning in Health Sciences: A Systematic Review." *Journal of Nursing Education* 49 (1): 23–28. Accessed February 10, 2020. doi:10.3928/01484834-20090828-08.

Hattie, John, and Helen Timperley. 2007. "The Power of Feedback." *Review of Educational Research* 77 (1): 81–112.

Heinich, Robert, Michael Molenda, James D. Russell, and Sharon E. Smaldino. 1996. *Instructional Media and Technologies for Learning*. 5th ed. Englewood Cliffs, NJ: Prentice-Hall.

Huizinga, Johan. 1955. *Homo Ludens: A Study of the Play-Element in Culture*. Boston, MA: Beacon Press.

Kamradt, Thomas F., and Elizabeth J. Kamradt. 1999. "Structured Design for Attitudinal Instruction." In *Instructional-Design Theories and Models*, vol. 2, *A New Paradigm of Instructional Theory*, edited by Charles M. Reigeluth, 563–590. Mahwah, NJ: Lawrence Erlbaum Associates.

Keller, John M. 2010. *Motivational Design for Learning and Performance: The ARCS Model Approach*. New York: Springer Science + Business Media.

Konkel, Lindsey. 2016. "Positive Reinforcement Helps Surgeons Learn." *Scientific American*, March 9. Accessed February 20, 2020. https://www.scientificamerican.com/article/positive-reinforcement-helps-surgeons-learn/.

Krakauer, John W., and Pietro Mazzoni. 2011. "Human Sensorimotor Learning: Adaptation, Skill, and Beyond." *Current Opinion in Neurobiology* 21: 636–644.

Mayer, Richard E., ed. 2014. *The Cambridge Handbook of Multimedia Learning*. 2nd ed. New York: Cambridge University Press.

Mayer, Richard E., and Cheryl L. Johnson. 2010. "Adding Instructional Features that Promote Learning in a Game-Like Environment." *Journal of Educational Computing Research* 42 (3): 241–265.

Merrill, M. David. 2002. "A Pebble in the Pond Model for Instructional Design." *Performance Improvement* 41 (7): 41–46. doi:10.1002/pfi.4140410709.

National Academies of Sciences, Engineering, and Medicine. 2018. *How People Learn II: Learners, Contexts, and Cultures*. Washington, DC: The National Academies Press.

National Research Council. 2000. *How People Learn: Brain, Mind, Experience, and School*. Expanded Edition. Washington, DC: The National Academies Press. doi:10.17226/9853.

Reigeluth, Charles M., M. David Merrill, Brent G. Wilson, and Reginald T. Spiller. 1980. "The Elaboration Theory of Instruction: A Model for Sequencing and Synthesizing Instruction." *Instructional Science* 9: 195–219.

Rohrer, Doug, and Kelli Taylor. 2006. "The Effects of Overlearning and Distributed Practice on the Retention of Mathematics Knowledge." *Applied Cognitive Psychology* 20: 1209–1224. Accessed December 4, 2017. https://search-ebscohost-com.proxyiub.uits.iu.edu/login.aspx?direct=true&db=eric&AN=ED505642&site=eds-live&scope=site.

Romiszowski, A. J. 1999. "The Development of Physical Skills: Instruction in the Psychomotor Domain." In *Instructional-Design Theories and Models*, vol. 2, *A New Paradigm of Instructional Theory*, edited by Charles M. Reigeluth, 457–481. Mahwah, NJ: Lawrence Erlbaum Associates.

Saettler, Paul. 1990. *The Evolution of American Educational Technology*. Englewood, CO: Libraries Unlimited.

Sage, George H. 1984. *Motor Learning and Control: A Neuropsychological Approach*. Dubuque, IA: William C. Brown.

Servant-Miklos, Virginie F. C. 2019. "The Harvard Connection: How the Case Method Spawned Problem-Based Learning at McMaster University." *Health Professions Education* 5 (3): 163–171. Accessed March 12, 2020. doi:10.1016/j.hpe.2018.07.004.

Shen, Jason. 2013. "Why Practice Actually Makes Perfect: How to Rewire Your Brain for Better Performance." *Buffer*. Accessed February 4, 2020. https://buffer.com/resources/why-practice-actually-makes-perfect-how-to-rewire-your-brain-for-better-performance.

Skinner, B. F. 1953. *Science and Human Behavior*. New York: The Free Press.

Squire, Kurt. 2003. "Video Games in Education." *International Journal of Intelligent Simulations and Gaming* 2 (1): 1–16.

Sternberg, Robert J., and Wendy M. Williams. 2010. *Educational Psychology*. 2nd ed. Upper Saddle River, NJ: Pearson Education.

Stolovitch, Harold D., and Sivasailam Thiagarajan. 1980. *Frame Games*. Englewood Cliffs, NJ: Educational Technology Publications.

Suppes, Patrick, Barbara Searle, and Jamesine Friend. 1980. *Radio Mathematics in Nicaragua*. Stanford, CA: Institute for Mathematical Studies in the Social Sciences, Stanford University.

van Merriënboer, Jeroen J. G., Paul A. Kirschner, and Liesbeth Kester. 2003. "Taking the Load Off a Learner's Mind: Instructional Design for Complex Learning." *Educational Psychologist* 38 (1): 5–13.

Vanags, Thea, Kristen Pammer, and Jay Brinker. 2013. "Process-Oriented Guided-Inquiry Learning Improves Long-Term Retention." *Advances in Physiology Education* 37: 233–241. Accessed February 3, 2020. doi:10.1152/advan.00104.2012.

Vedantam, Shankar, Jennifer Schmidt, Thomas Lu, and Tara Boyle. 2018. *When Things Click: The Power of Judgment-Free Learning.* Performed by Shankar Vedantam. June 4. Accessed March 11, 2020. https://www.npr.org/2020/02/03/802422904/when-things-click-the-power-of-judgment-free-learning.

Von Bergen, C.W., Barlow Soper, and Gary T. Rosenthal. 1997. "Selected Alternative Training Techniques in HRD." *Human Resource Development Quarterly* 8 (4): 281–294.

Weibell, Christian J. 2011. *Principles of Learning: 7 Principles to Guide Personalized, Student-Centered Learning in the Technology-Enhanced, Blended Learning Environment.* July 4. Accessed December 11, 2018. https://principlesoflearning.wordpress.com/dissertation/chapter-4-results/themes-identified/repetition/.

Willingham, Daniel B. 1998. "A Neuropsychological Theory of Motor Skill Learning." *Psychological Review* 105 (3): 558–584.

Wouters, Pieter, Christof van Nimwegen, Herre van Oostendorf, and Erik D. van der Spek. 2013. "A Meta-Analysis of the Cognitive and Motivational Effects of Serious Games." *Journal of Educational Psychology* 105 (2): 249–265.

Yelon, Stephen L. 1996. *Powerful Principles of Instruction.* New York: Longman.

Yu, Hao, Chang Yuan Zhang, Si Hui Zhang, Hui Cheng, and Jiang Chen. 2017. "Virtual Simulation Teaching Centre in Dental Education: A Report from Fujian Medical University, China." *The Chinese Journal of Dental Research* 20 (3): 173–177. doi:10.3290/j.cjdr.a38773.

Study 10

The Study configuration differs from most other configurations in that it focuses on the solitary learner, who exercises control of the time, place, and sequence of the activity. This makes it clearly the most learner-centered of all the communication configurations detailed in this book, and the polar philosophical opposite of Presentation, which is purely instructor-centered. Reading a textbook, browsing through a library collection, taking notes, pondering the larger meaning of a text, examining specimens or artworks in a museum, observing plants, animals, and other natural phenomena—all are components of Study, in which learners interact with various instructional resources, real-world resources, and their own inner mental resources. This is where a great deal of academic learning takes place, yet it is little discussed in pedagogical theories.

Study Defined

Of all the configurations, Study is the one most broadly defined and most capacious of varied forms and purposes. It encompasses all the cases in which Learners, by themselves, interact with Instructional Resources, Real-World Resources, or with their own inner resources. Since our typology is based on observable states, what observable state do all these types of investigation have in common? What we see is an individual working alone, perhaps reading a book, a map, or a chart—perhaps looking at a screen display, perhaps examining some specimens, possibly taking notes all the while. Typically, there is no instructor present nor other learners. The learner is usually acting under the indirect influence of an instructor or mentor, most likely pursuing an assignment aimed at a learning goal.

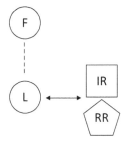

Figure 10.1 The Study Communication Configuration. The IR represents Instructional Resources and RR represents Real-World Resources; the two-headed arrow indicates that both may be controlled by the Learner and both can provide information to the Learner.

Study: A Learner (L) interacts with Instructional Resources (IR), or with Real-World Resources (RR), or with their own inner resources, without the direct supervision of a Facilitator (F), but often inspired or guided by someone playing the role of Facilitator. The Learner is in control of events, deciding exactly what to do and when to do it (Figure 10.1).

Formats Associated with Study

Using Instructional Resources

When learners are interacting one-on-one with materials prepared for specific instructional purposes, they are doing Study with Instructional Resources. The most obvious example is reading a chapter from a textbook as a homework assignment. Other formats for Study with Instructional Resources include:

- reading handouts prepared by the instructor
- listening privately to an audio recording or podcast of spoken material
- listening privately to an audio recording of a musical performance
- viewing a narrated PowerPoint presentation
- watching privately an instructional video, such as a Web "tutorial"
- reading a blog.

Using Real-World Resources

In addition to using instructional resources during Study, learners may also interact with a variety of real-world resources—things that are not created to be instructional but can be enlisted in the cause of education with some effort. Betrus refers to these as "resources by utilization" (Betrus 2008, 213). For an everyday example, early childhood education makes use of blocks, pitchers, cups, and ladles. Elementary schools may keep pet animals in the classroom. Students may also be directed to observe natural phenomena—at farms, zoos, lakes, and streams—or to see and touch specimens at museums. Formats for Real-World Resources might include:

- examining living biological specimens, such as flowers or frogs in a lab setting, botanical garden, or zoo
- examining preserved biological specimens in a natural history museum
- observing natural phenomena, such as clouds or waves outdoors
- analyzing a set of buildings in terms of their architectural styles
- comparing human artifacts at an anthropological or historical museum.

Using One's Own Inner Resources

When learners are working individually, thinking about the subject matter, and planning how to approach challenging material, they are using their own inner resources to develop learning strategies. An example would be using mnemonic strategies when reading a textbook chapter: preview the chapter, pay attention to headings, highlight salient points, and review. Other examples for Study with Inner Resources include:

- consciously planning a study schedule for a difficult subject
- during class, staying engaged by asking and answering questions
- taking lecture notes purposefully
- reviewing lecture notes after class, highlighting salient points
- after reading a section of text, closing the book and trying to restate the main points
- if not comprehending, checking other sources—maybe Googling for assistance
- devising or using mnemonic devices to memorize lists of information
- reflecting after a lecture or after completing a project.

The Use of Study in Distance Education

The very earliest versions of correspondence study were firmly based on the use of the Study configuration. Students were sent printed lessons via postal mail that required careful reading of the material and possibly a search for other sources in a library. The lesson typically concluded with a written assignment of some sort, which was mailed back to the person playing the role of Teacher, who evaluated the work, gave feedback to the learner, and possibly engaged in further tutorial conversation by mail.

When this model was first converted to Internet delivery, audio and video recordings were not easy or cheap to transmit, so text-based materials—typically the instructor's lecture notes—along with static visuals formed the backbone of the course. Thus, learners spent much of their learning time in the Study configuration, reading and digesting the aforementioned materials.

With the advance of technology, especially the World Wide Web, it has become more common to replace the written texts with audio or video presentations by the instructor or some subject-matter expert. Still, online learners—sitting alone at home or in the workplace—spend much of their time in Study. They can supplement the course presentations with books or journals from libraries, with virtual visits to museums and art galleries, or with the myriad other information sources available through the Web. All of these activities fall into the category of Study.

The Evolution of Study

Forming a Thoughtful Person

Study is deeply rooted in pedagogical traditions around the world. Within the Western cultural context, classical Greek and Roman philosophers postulated that the goal of education was to form "character"—habits of thought that led to "right behavior," not just the accumulation of knowledge and skills. Philosophers sought to inculcate habits of thoughtful response to challenges rather than just emotional reflexes. The surest way to accomplish this end was to pair the learner with an exemplary role model: Alexander the Great learned from Aristotle, who had learned from Plato, who had learned from Socrates. Quintilian (c. AD 35–c. 100) extended this learning model down to the earliest years of life. In his multivolume work on rhetoric, he digressed to comment on childhood education. He advised parents to take care in selecting nurses and pedagogues for their children, since right habits and interests must be cultivated while the mind is pliable and imitative of those in close association (Bloomer 2011).

But what about all those poor souls who were not fortunate enough to have an exemplary tutor? By the time of the Middle Ages in Europe, written manuscripts that captured the ideas of the leading thinkers were available to be read and copied at monasteries all across that continent. It was not the same as having Aristotle at your side, but it was an affordable alternative. Private study became one of the major preoccupations of clerics in monasteries and, later, of students in schools attached to monasteries and cathedrals (Saettler 1990). Recent research in cognitive neuroscience reveals that reading—a function that is not native to the human brain as oral language is—demands highly complex activities in the brain, involving four different lobes and all five layers of the brain (Wolf 2018, 20). Further, deep reading inculcates analytical and generative competencies that no other human activity can rival (Wolf 2018, 35–68). Thus, it may be that the process of reading itself constitutes the gateway to "forming a thoughtful person."

Printing Brings Study to the Masses

With the invention of the printing press in the mid-fifteenth century, reading burst out of the confines of the monastery into European society at large. It became possible for scholars to possess their own books and study them at leisure. The Dutch humanist scholar Desiderius Erasmus (1466–1536) wrote hugely popular texts, among the earliest "best sellers" of the printing press, devoted to self-improvement through independent study. Much of his writing dealt with religious issues, and his constant theme was that behavior based on inner conviction was what mattered, not outward displays of piety, a theme he elaborated in his most popular work *Enchiridion Militis Christiani* or *Handbook of a Christian Knight* (Erasmus 1905).

Later in the sixteenth century, Montaigne (1533–1592) devoted a number of his famous *Essais* to educational methods. He championed active learning through travel and social interaction, combined with reflection, deriving lessons for oneself from those firsthand life experiences, as opposed to passive ingestion of the ideas of others (Montaigne 2006). Contemporary educators epitomize this idea in a simple formula: Experience + Reflection = Growth.

Psychologizing about Study

William James's famous treatise, *Talks to Teachers on Psychology* (1899), has little to say about Study explicitly. It is broadly about human behaviors and how they are learned; so, like many who theorize about education, James focused on events taking place under the direct supervision of the teacher—student behaviors in the classroom. Still, only about 30 years later, A.C. Mace (1932) produced a whole volume of advice on how to effectively manage independent study, based on findings of the rapidly growing discipline of psychology. He was able to offer research-based recommendations on learning from lectures and readings, how to write papers, and how to prepare for exams. Mace's advice was sound enough to stand the test of time, being reprinted regularly until his death in 1971.

Study for Self-Education

For many, independent study is not a choice but a necessity. Able thinkers, young and old, have found ways to educate themselves even when deprived of access to teachers and schools. In the middle of the twentieth century an autodidact,

Eric Hoffer, burst upon the literary scene with the publication of *The True Believer* (Hoffer 1951), an original and groundbreaking inquiry into the mentality of totalitarianism. With little education beyond the rudiments of reading and writing, Hoffer spent his life as a migrant worker, prospector, and longshoreman. But he occupied his leisure time with books (especially Montaigne's *Essais*), pursuing his own quest to understand why humans behave as they do. He eventually published a dozen books—beginning after age 50—and had a literary prize named after him.

Besides being central to nonformal self-education, Study is also a backbone of formal education. Textbooks have long been and still are among the most ubiquitous of all pedagogical tools. The whole premise of the textbook is that students can gain knowledge by the private reading of text. Whether in face-to-face or distance settings, there is a strong tendency for instructors to shape lectures, homework, and tests around a textbook. Given the centrality of textbooks to most curricula, it is curious that few teachers actually teach their students how to study from textbooks, and that few teacher training programs give focused attention to teaching with textbooks.

Technology for Study

In corporate training, Malcolm Knowles initiated a trend with the publication of *Self-Directed Learning* (Knowles 1975). He advocated the efficiency of replacing training classes with self-instructional material that could be used at the time and place most convenient for trainees, perhaps even on their *own* time rather than the company's time. The self-directed learning (SDL) literature also emphasized the value of learners' taking responsibility for their own learning, meanwhile developing the discipline and study skills that would serve them well in life, in terms that would have made Erasmus and Montaigne proud. During the 1990s, when this concept was at its greatest popularity, SDL flourished under many different labels, including autodidactic learning, autonomous learning, adult learning projects, and self-education.

For training designers, the easy expedient for implementing SDL was simply to take the existing training lectures and convert them to print manuals distributed at will to those who lacked the specified knowledge. The more enterprising attempted to capture learners' attention and motivation by packaging self-instructional lessons in the form of slide-cassette programs or video clips that could be controlled by individual users in learning carrels. In the ideal case, these instructional units were structured to require learner response with some form of feedback, moving from the Study configuration to the Repetition configuration. Later, as computers became commonplace in the corporate setting, the audiovisual units tended to be converted for delivery through freestanding computers or through monitors connected to a local network.

The claimed advantage of these advanced technology formats was the ability to individualize—to enable learners to select their own content and proceed through a program at their own pace. The invention of hypertext and later hypermedia allowed learners to proceed not only at their own pace but along their own individual path by following links embedded in the text that allowed the reader to jump from one page to another. After the creation of the World Wide Web and the development of Web browsers, most hypermedia programs came to be delivered through the Web rather than through stand-alone computers or local networks.

The waning of the SDL trend can probably be attributed to the forces of human nature. Experience has demonstrated that would-be learners need more than access to materials in order to master swaths of knowledge. They need the motivation to get started and to persist, and they need guidance in judging where their knowledge/skill gaps are and how best to fill them. If access to texts and audiovisual materials were sufficient, universities would need only libraries, no classrooms or labs or dorms.

The Cognitive Revolution

Since the era of Comenius, educationists have tended to put the spotlight on teacher-controlled processes of teaching and learning. The lecture-based classroom is the stereotype that springs to mind when imagining "school" or "college." It is paradoxical that just at the time when resources for self-education were exploding, thanks to the World Wide Web, schools were more focused than ever on evaluating *teachers'* performance and making students more subservient than ever to a strict regime of drilling and testing.

At least on the front of research-and-theory, the spotlight began to shift back to the inner life of learners as the so-called "cognitive revolution" picked up steam in the 1980s and 1990s. The concept of *metacognition*—thinking about one's own thought processes—afforded new visibility to processes used by learners during Study. Research was showing that successful learners reflect on their thinking, set goals, monitor their progress, and respond appropriately if they find themselves falling short of their own expectations. Called "cognitive strategies" today, they are reminiscent of the "habits of mind" spoken of by the sages of the Classical era. In fact, although *metacognition* may be a relatively new label, the idea of examining one's conscious thought processes has been a topic of lively concern since the dawn of psychology as a discipline. As early as 1912, Professor Edward B. Titchener, founder of the largest program in Psychology at the time, presented a rationale and detailed methodology for understanding *introspection*, a concept close to what we know as metacognition (Titchener 1912).

As the cognitive revolution reached into the 1990s, reform-minded educationists under the banner of Constructivism championed learners' construction of their own meanings as they attempt to make sense of their experiences. Their perspective put self-awareness of cognitive processes—thinking about thinking—at the heart of the learning process. So, by the turn of the twenty-first century, the private mental world of the learner was back in the spotlight, and with it renewed interest in the ways and means of using Study profitably.

Cognitive Science and Neuroscience behind Study

Of all the sensory modalities, seeing and hearing are the ones that carry most of the information-transmission burden in Study. The underlying physiological processes of seeing and hearing are already explained in Chapter 5, so will not be repeated here. However, we would call attention to the section headed ""Multimedia" (or Multimodal) Learning." Instructional resources created for Study purposes—books, handouts, podcasts, slide sets, and the like—are subject to the same design guidelines discussed in terms of Presentations in Chapter 5. That is, the problem of split attention arises when learners encounter narrated slides sets containing verbal displays with voice narrations; if they are not completely complementary, the learner must choose to tune out one or the other; similarly, for graphic images and voice narration (Mayer and Moreno 1998). The same problem arises with graphic images accompanied by verbal text. All information has to enter working memory through the visual pathways, forcing the visual processing system to switch between nonverbal visual feature analysis and graphemic input analysis (Schnotz 2014, 89). Thus, visual presentations should be accompanied with vocal narration rather than printed text.

Words *plus* images work together supportively if the words and pictures are semantically related to each other *and* if they are presented close to each other—spatially in a textbook or temporally in a slide set. Schnotz refers to these as the *coherence* condition and the *contiguity* condition (Schnotz 2014, 89). The coherence principle was stated succinctly by Winn (1993, 118): "When narration accompanies a message in another modality, the relationship between the two messages must be strong and apparent."

Strengths and Limitations: Why Study?

Strengths

Study is the one configuration that can stand alone as a method of self-education. It is possible to educate yourself—at least in terms of declarative knowledge—without attending lectures, receiving tutorials, participating in discussion groups, working in laboratories, or writing reports. Reading, viewing pictures and videos, and reflecting can take you a long way, especially with the rich resources readily available on the Web. Indeed, autodidacts have proven that learners can accomplish great things even without *any* instructional activities other than Study. Of course, they profited from the noninstructional but nevertheless educative processes of interacting with the world and other people in everyday life.

Study combined with other teaching–learning experiences can, of course, take you even further than just Study alone. That is, you can not only deepen and broaden your understanding of declarative knowledge but also develop procedural skills, attitudes, values, and physical skills by applying Study techniques in combination with teaching–learning activities focused on interpersonal, affective, and psychomotor practice.

People can become expert learners if they are able and willing to apply an array of conscious learning strategies to their work. Information becomes usable knowledge when it has been digested and made part of one's own repertoire. Individuals can succeed as learners if they apply effective Study strategies—regardless of how poor the lectures, discussions, tutorials, or laboratory activities to which they are exposed.

Limitations

Study carried out in isolation can be stunted and warped without the learner's being aware of it. Ideas must be tested in social interaction to challenge the individual's egocentric thinking. The more advanced cognitive capabilities develop through social interaction. Self-education solely through reading other people's ideas would be limited not only in the scope of the content but also in terms of what domains of learning could be mastered. Applied skills, especially psychomotor skills, require real-world practice with feedback. Interpersonal skills require interaction with others. Affective abilities, too, grow through experiences with one's social milieu.

Best Practices for Using Study

Study Itself

Advice for the Facilitator

In recent centuries, really since the era of Comenius, interest in classroom-based methods has far outpaced interest in the techniques of private study. This focus has been driven by societal needs to expand educational opportunity, meaning more schools, more classrooms, and more teachers to be managed. Political forces inevitably demand measures of accountability for all the money spent—measures such as counting the credentials of teachers and counting the number of minutes students spend in the classroom in the presence of a licensed teacher (the infamous "Carnegie unit"). So, it is not surprising that the amount of research devoted to classroom teaching methods vastly overshadows that on study skills.

Teaching Self-Regulation Process Skills

However, that gap may be shrinking due to the growth of cognitive science research. Inquiry into the inner workings of the mind have yielded helpful guidance for what are termed "executive control processes" or "self-regulated learning." When students are facing unfamiliar challenges—such as group projects, case study methods, service learning, or field work—they may waste time and effort on trial-and-error attempts to cope with these expectations. Instead, this is an opportunity to help students develop their own self-regulation processes. Instructors can provide specific guidance in how to handle the new expectations, perhaps providing checklists for steps in the process—and inviting students to share ideas on what worked for them (Weinstein 2006).

Advice for the Learner

One of the major goals of Study is simply to remember more of what we hear in lectures and what we read in books. That is, we want to be able to retain salient information in long-term memory and to retrieve it when needed. Long-term memory is a capability that seems to rely on relatively permanent changes in neural connections spread throughout the brain. Specifically, we are talking about declarative memory—conscious recall of facts and understandings—when we are dealing with Study. The other major classification of memory, procedural memory, deals with knowing how to *do* things and it depends much more heavily on other configurations, especially Repetition.

Most strategies for making Study more productive can be described as metacognitive strategies; that is, they are based on thinking about one's own thinking. Metacognitive strategies are the processes of planning, monitoring, and assessing one's own learning (McGuire and Angelo 2016). Some of the strategies that have proven to be most helpful are: (1) organizing your thoughts before beginning a project; for example, preparing an outline before writing a paper; (2) setting up consequences for performance; for example, complete the outline before going for a coffee break; (3) self-verbalization; for example, in a study group, talk about steps of solving a problem; and (4) self-evaluation; for example, checking your work with a critical eye before handing it in. With practice, these strategies can become habits, thus bolstering one's study skills.

Strategies for Reading Textbooks

Whether they are students in school or college or trainees in businesses or other organizations, learners tend to spend a large proportion of their time-on-task reading textbooks or training manuals. Regardless of educational level or the subject matter, there are some general strategies that pertain to getting the most out of time spent with texts. There are different formulations for these strategies, but they boil down to following a sequence of tactical steps:

a) begin by establishing the purpose for reading this work—what you want to get out of it
b) survey the book or chapter—see it in context and get a sense of the territory covered by skimming the whole book or chapter, paying attention to main headings
c) read the text thoughtfully, highlighting key ideas (wait until reaching the end of a section before deciding what to highlight) and jotting down questions
d) review, perhaps by constructing an outline of the main ideas and supporting points; reread difficult portions and test your understanding by restating in your own words; if possible, discuss the material with another reader or just recite the main points aloud privately as this helps the transition from short-term to long-term memory.

Using Mnemonic Devices

Considering how much of academic success is based on remembering things—facts, principles, procedures, and the like—it is notable how little attention is given to mnemonics in programs of teacher education or the training of trainers. Nevertheless, there has been considerable educational research on the topic of mnemonic devices and related aspects of storing and retrieving remembered information. A leading researcher, Francis S. Belleza, proposes that there is a great deal of overlap between our knowledge of mental schemata and our knowledge of so-called mnemonic devices, which are often thought of as complicated and somewhat unnatural. He suggests that "mnemonic devices are simpler than memory schemas but seem complicated because the learner is very much aware of their operation" (Belleza 1987: 34).

In any event, there are numerous procedures recommended for memorizing different sorts of educational material. They can be condensed into several general steps:

- Focus attention on the material—take notes, highlight, underline.
- Create a personal connection with the material:
  - Greek and Roman orators remembered each part of a speech by visualizing walking from one room in their house to another, seeing familiar objects, which they would associate with key words.
  - Create an acronym from the first letter of each word in a list; e.g., POSDCORB stands for the main responsibilities of a public administrator—Planning, Organizing, Staffing, Directing, Coordinating, Reporting, and Budgeting.

- Arrange key words into a visual pattern or draw a visual symbol for key ideas; create your own emoji.
- Arrange key words or phrases into a rhythmic pattern, e.g., "the product of the means equals the product of the extremes"; say it out loud; chant it like a nursery rhyme; or sing it like a commercial jingle.
- The more sensory connections you make, the more memorable it will be.
- Practice the memorized material until you are confident; repetition is the key to remembering.

Methods Featuring the Study Configuration

Strategic Level

Self-Directed Learning (SDL) (Study + Expression)

As discussed earlier in this chapter, SDL is a curricular arrangement in which individual learners, in the Study configuration, work separately with specified resources, such as training manuals, textbooks, workbooks, slide sets, or programmed devices, to pursue target objectives. Learners may have wide leeway in deciding whether and when to study. Assessment typically involves the Expression configuration—a post-test, essay, project, or product—to demonstrate mastery of the target skill.

Oxbridge System (Study + Expression + Tutorial + Demonstration)

See Chapter 8 for a description of the Oxbridge system of reinforcing Study with weekly Tutorial sessions; these sessions usually involve other students, for whom the tutee's oral presentation serves as behavior modeling (Demonstration).

Learning for Mastery (LFM) and Personalized System of Instruction (PSI) (Repetition + Study)

Although LFM has been applied to group-paced instruction, it is better suited to an independent study setting, as is PSI. In both methods, material is organized around clearly stated objectives, and instruction is divided into small units. Individual learners work through the units, getting individual corrective feedback and other sorts of learning guidance; they can advance to the next unit only upon successful completion of the current one.

Tactical Level

Research Projects (Study + Expression)

Undoubtedly, the most valuable way of amplifying the impact of Study is to follow reading and reflection with Expression. Constructing a document written in your own words is one of the most productive paths to converting the verbal information that has been ingested into a meaningful component of your long-term memory. As the adage goes, "How can I know what I think until I see what I say?" That is why teachers are so fond of assigning reports, essays, and term papers. They encourage the learner to construct a coherent argument, which can be examined by the teacher, providing the basis for constructive feedback. Teachers also know well that there is no better way to master a topic than to teach it to someone else. As discussed in Chapter 8, the Oxbridge system requires students to do assigned reading and then prepare an essay crystalizing their thinking on the topic. They then present that essay either in oral or written form for critique by their tutor and sometimes by other students. This sort of intellectual conversation is the backbone of formal education.

Note-Taking (Study + Expression)

As with taking notes while listening to lectures (see "Advice to the Learner" in Chapter 5), taking notes while doing assigned readings or library research is an effective method of processing new material—what is most important, what is most relevant to your objective, and what the text means, translated into your own words.

Study Group (Study + Expression + Discussion)

See Chapter 7, Advice for the Learner, regarding organizing for small-group work.

Chapter Summary

Study—an individual Learner interacting with Instructional Resources, Real-World Resources, or with inner resources alone, without the direct supervision of a Facilitator—is underappreciated as a configuration for learning, considering how much formal education depends on individual learners working outside the classroom, reading textbooks and other resources, and sifting through the material to retain key points.

Formats for Study include such activities such as reading textbooks, listening to podcasts, and viewing narrated slide shows and videos. Or the learner might be taking notes at a lecture, reviewing previous notes, or planning a mnemonic device to remember main ideas. In distance education, learners are still assigned readings, but they can also summon up Web resources, such as how-to videos and podcasts.

Historically, private Study was a rare privilege until the printing press made books more widely available. Early popular authors, such as Erasmus and Montaigne, helped create a bank of scholarly thought that made self-education possible, but it was not until the twentieth century that psychologists began to tackle issues related to learning from books. In the corporate realm, by the 1970s, when both printed and audiovisual resources were widely and inexpensively available for individual use, there was a trend toward shifting from classroom presentations to individual, self-paced study. Then, as now with computers and the Web, access to resources was not the barrier to independent study—a motivational framework was.

Nowadays, the cognitive underpinnings of Study—such as metacognition—are better understood, and better guidance can be offered to independent learners. Learners can take advantage of such metacognitive strategies as preparing outlines, arranging contingencies for meeting performance goals, self-verbalization, self-evaluation, and preparing mnemonic devices.

Like Repetition, Study is connected with most other configurations. Most instructional methods include a step during which learners read, watch, or listen to instructional resources privately. The Oxbridge System and Learning for Mastery rely heavily on independent study, as do student projects and case-based learning. Bringing that research and study to fruition then requires some sort of written or constructed work as a culminating activity, which leads to the topic of the next chapter: the Expression configuration.

Works Cited

Belleza, Francis S. 1987. "Mnemonic Devices and Memory Schemas." Chap. 2 in *Imagery and Related Mnemonic Processes*, edited by Mark A. McDaniel and Michael Pressley, 34–55. New York: Springer. Accessed December 1, 2017. doi:10.1007/978-1-4612-4676-3_2.

Betrus, Anthony Karl. 2008. "Resources." Chap. 8 in *Educational Technology: A Definition with Commentary*, edited by Alan Januszewski and Michael Molenda, 213–240. New York: Lawrence Erlbaum Associates.

Bloomer, W. Martin. 2011. "Quintilian on the Child as a Learning Subject." *The Classical World* 105 (1): 109–137. Accessed 8 11, 2019. https://www.jstor.org/stable/41303490.

Erasmus, Desiderius. 1905. *A Book Called in Latin Enchiridion Militis Christiani and in English The Manual of the Christian Knight....* London: Methuen and Co.

Hoffer, Eric. 1951. *The True Believer*. New York: Harper & Brothers.

James, William. 1899. *Talks to Teachers on Psychology; and to Students on Some of Life's Ideals*. New York: Henry Holt and Company.

Knowles, Malcolm S. 1975. *Self-Directed Learning: A Guide for Learners and Teachers*. New York: Cambridge, The Adult Education Co.

Mace, Cecil Alec. 1932. *The Psychology of Study*. London: Methuen.

Mayer, Richard E., and Roxana Moreno. 1998. "A Split-Attention Effect in Multimedia Learning: Evidence for Dual Processing Systems in Working Memory." *Journal of Educational Psychology* 90 (2): 312–320.

McGuire, Saundra Yancy, and Thomas Angelo. 2016. *Teach Students How to Learn: Strategies You Can Incorporate into Any Course to Improve Student Metacognition, Study Skills, and Motivation.* Sterling, VA: Stylus Publishing.

Montaigne, Michel de. 2006. *Book 1, Chapter 25: On the Education of Children.* Edited by Charles Cotton and William Carew Hazlitt. Project Gutenberg. September 17. Accessed December 4, 2017. https://www.gutenberg.org/files/3600/3600-h/3600-h.htm#link2HCH0025.

Saettler, Paul. 1990. *The Evolution of American Educational Technology.* Englewood, CO: Libraries Unlimited.

Schnotz, Wolfgang. 2014. "Integrated Model of Text and Picture Comprehension." In *The Cambridge Handbook of Multimedia Learning,* 2nd ed., edited by Richard E. Mayer, 72–103. New York: Cambridge University Press.

Titchener, Edward B. 1912. "The Schema of Introspection." *American Journal of Psychology* 23: 485–508.

Weinstein, Claire Ellen. 2006. "Teaching Students How to Become More Strategic and Self-Regulated Learners." Chap. 23 in *Teaching Tips: Strategies, Research, and Theory for College and University Teachers,* edited by Wilbert McKeachie and Marilla Svinicki, 300–317. Boston, MA: Houghton-Mifflin.

Winn, William. 1993. "Perception Principles." Chap. 2 in *Instructional Message Design,* edited by Malcolm Fleming and W. Howard Levie, 55–127. Englewood Cliffs, NJ: Educational Technology Publications.

Wolf, Maryanne. 2018. *Reader, Come Home.* New York: HarperCollins.

Expression

11

The Expression configuration—along with Study—differs from the other communication configurations in that it centers almost entirely and exclusively on the learner, who typically exercises nearly complete control over the time, place, and sequence of the activity. Expression encompasses all instances where learners express their thoughts and feelings through writing, speaking, construction, and artistic creations. The role of the facilitator in this configuration chiefly focuses on setting the necessary parameters for the activity—timelines, expectations, and evaluation criteria—and on providing inspiration, guidance, and mentoring when appropriate.

In formal education at the higher levels, students spend much of their outside-of-class instructional time doing assigned readings and writing papers of various sorts. The analysis and synthesis work involved in writing makes this one of the most valuable of all academic activities.

Expression Defined

To express means to manifest one's ideas, opinions, or feelings in some patent, perceptible form, which may be ephemeral, physical, or virtual. Expression involving psychomotor actions—such as speech, dance, song/chant, musical-instrument playing, mime/skit, yogic *asanas*, tai chi movements, etc.—manifests in *ephemeral* form. Expression involving the creation of some physical artifact—such as a written document, painting, drawing, sculpture, etc.—manifests in *physical* form. Expression involving the creation of some electronic or virtual artifact—such as digital text, graphics, photographs, audio recordings, animation or video recordings, multimedia or hypermedia or social-media content, virtual environments such as simulations, walkthroughs, games, etc.—manifests in electronic or *virtual* form.

282 Expression

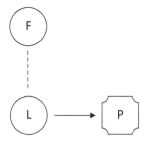

Figure 11.1 The Expression Communication Configuration. The P represents the tangible Product that is created by the Learner.

Expression: A Learner (L) creates some type of tangible Product (P) in order to process some new knowledge, skill, or attitude; the experience may be structured and/or monitored by a Facilitator (F), but the Learner controls what is created and how it is created (Figure 11.1).

Note that, like all configurations, Expression is an arrangement that may occupy the learner for only a brief period of time. They might well toggle back and forth between Expression and other configurations; for example, while preparing a research paper, a learner may go from Study—reading a library book, to Expression—writing notes on material from said book.

The product—the essay, the painting, the sculpture, the photograph, the video, the online discussion post, the website, the blog—itself is not the point. The point is using the process of creation to advance one's understanding of the concept or process being learned. Writing words on paper is simply practice of calligraphy or of plagiarism if those words do not represent the learner's own engagement with the content to be mastered. Painting a picture of a sunflower is just practicing a manual art unless the painter is consciously trying to implement a new skill (e.g., a technique for representing three-dimensionality) or to express an individual interpretation of a subject.

Writing, speaking, dancing, painting, carving, and building can be considered acts of Expression when they go beyond routine, repetitious practice. Creating a sculpture falls into the category of Expression if the learner is expressing his own ideas and feelings. Giving a public speech is Expression if the speaker is using her own words and opinions, not just reciting some borrowed text for practice in enunciation.

Formats Associated with Expression

In formal education, writing is the most common format for Expression. Expression can also take many other forms, such as artistic creations, audiovisual productions, or other constructed products.

Formats Focused on Text

- preparing a book report to present to a class
- writing a term paper
- writing a short reflection paper at the end of a class session
- preparing a report of findings of a small-group discussion
- writing a blog or memoir about one's experiences
- keeping a journal while taking a course, updating after each class meeting
- writing the script for a documentary about the historical period being studied
- generating a list of "pros" and "cons" on a controversial issue
- posting and responding to content on social media platforms
- generating Web 2.0 content such as blog and wiki entries
- participating in text-based online discussion forums and chats
- briefing an assigned case in a class on tort law.

Formats Focused on Symbolic Display

- drawing an "information map" showing relationships among concepts on a current topic
- drawing a schematic diagram of the life cycle of an insect
- using visualization software to create a flow chart of a process
- preparing a statistical analysis of data from an experiment
- completing an accounting spreadsheet as part of a business case study
- creating static 2D/3D visual models on paper
- creating "paper prototypes" of multimedia/hypermedia content.

Formats Focused on "Multimedia" Production

- producing a short video about the current topic in class
- producing a podcast
- producing a narrated slide set or other "multimedia" production, including hypermedia
- recording a personal performance and uploading it to a server (and thus transforming it from an ephemeral to an electronic entity)
- creating dynamic 3D models and simulations.

Formats Focused on Artistic Creation

- painting a picture with a new brush technique
- sculpting a memorial for a historical event
- weaving a basket in the style of a foreign culture

- creating needlework art
- designing and creating jewelry
- constructing a costume for a play.

Formats Focused on Performance

- Verbal presentations, such as speeches, poetry recitations, monologues, or skits
- performing modern or contemporary interpretive dance
- playing an instrument solo or in an ensemble/orchestra in a performance that involves improvisation
- singing a song of one's own composition
- performing yogic *asanas* or tai chi movements.

Formats Focused on Construction

- designing a set for a theatrical performance
- designing the plan of a building as an assigned problem in architecture class
- constructing a mock-up of a factory layout
- creating physical models of entities, phenomena, and processes.

Again, as stated above, the activity is a learning activity and one that fits into the Expression category only if it is done in pursuit of a learning goal. A plumber installing a dishwasher that he has done a hundred times is not engaged in a learning activity; he is practicing his profession. A sidewalk painter in Venice who is turning out the same watercolors every day to sell to tourists is not doing it to understand Venice better or to explore new techniques for expressing his feelings about Venice.

In the examples above, again, it is the *process* that matters. Preparing a book report requires remembering the main events of the story and your personal reactions to them. Writing down the results of that thought process is the Expression. Delivering the book report in front of class is a different activity, practicing public speaking, which is quite separate from the intellectual task of creating the report.

Expression in Distance Education

One of the challenges of distance education is to provide learners opportunities to express their thoughts about the subject matter and to get useful feedback about those thoughts. The very earliest versions of distance education, correspondence study, solved this problem by requiring students to submit some sort of written response—answers to study questions or essays—via postal mail, to be read and reacted to by a mentor. The forms of Expression were very limited and the feedback slow and often sparse. It required a great deal of perseverance to forge ahead and complete the course.

Much the same was true of the early versions of today's distance education. Courses mediated through radio or television tended to rely on the methods of correspondence study. Students completed written exercises of various types and submitted them to a central source or a regional study center. In the 1990s, computer conferencing enabled students to interact with the instructor and other students through the keyboard, but Expression was still limited to written form.

With the advent of Web-based distance learning, a much broader range of Expressions became feasible. Through the keyboard, students can debate ideas asynchronously through online discussion forums. Or they can enter a chatroom and discuss in real time, although still through the keyboard. They can also collaboratively brainstorm and share ideas through "wiki" applications. They can even write documents collaboratively, such as outlines for a term paper or project, through applications such as Google Docs.

However, most course management systems allow students to have live voice (or even voice and picture) discussions online, if the logistics of time zones and numbers of speakers can be managed. Students can also prepare how-to video clips or find video presentations and exchange them with classmates through video sharing applications, such as Vialogues.

Attitude Change through Expression

Although attitudes and feelings are considered difficult to address in the classroom, one way to approach them is through Expression. In a step-by-step way, learners can be asked to begin by expressing an idea or feeling or action that is slightly different from their original position and in the direction of the target objective (e.g., "Abstract art may be interesting for some people"). Any discomfort with this new position can be treated with information if the objection is cognitive ("The Museum of Modern Art has over three million visitors a year") or with emotional support if the objection is affective ("See, nobody is laughing at you"). Through repeated small steps of Expression, the learners can be moved toward the target (Kamradt and Kamradt 1999).

The special value of Expression for this purpose is that it makes the behavior or feeling visible, hence amenable to outside influence.

The Evolution of Expression

Writing to Learn

The writing of compositions as a means of learning core subjects was practiced in Scottish and American universities in the eighteenth and nineteenth centuries. But it was not until 1873, when Harvard began to require writing skill as an admission requirement, that composition began to be taught in high schools. Prior to that, writing meant penmanship (Freedman 2003). Composition skills became standardized in American high schools after the "Committee of Ten" report in 1894 proposed that one of the purposes of the study of English was "to enable the pupil...to give expression to thoughts of his own" (Committee of Ten 1894, 86). This was a watershed moment for the concept of "writing to learn."

Arts in the Historical Curriculum

Drawing to learn actually has a longer pedigree than writing to learn. Along with reading, writing, singing, and playing, it was part of the core elementary school curriculum in the eighteenth and nineteenth centuries. Drawing was deemed vital to skills such as nature study, geography, and manual arts and was, indeed, among the most popular subjects among schoolchildren. In the Industrial Age, drawing slowly gave way to the idea of making art for personal development rather than as a utilitarian tool (Walling 2003).

In the twenty-first century, making art is viewed as contributing to the development of several different sorts of basic skills. Using paint brushes and crayons helps young children learn fine motor skills. Making aesthetic choices while creating art carries over into problem-solving, critical thinking, and inventiveness in general. Self-expression through music, dance, and other performing arts has been ensconced in the curriculum, as well as in folk traditions, since early Western civilization. In the earliest days of Athenian civilization, young men of wealthy families were taught *gumnastike* (physical education) and *mousike*, encompassing the composing and playing of music, dance, and poetry. After the time of Socrates, the intellectual disciplines were emphasized, but *gumnastike* and *mousike* were retained. Curiously, although the Romans adopted most of the components of Greek education, they rejected *gumnastike* (except for military training) and *mousike* as irrelevant to their culture.

Colonial America followed the traditions of English and Scottish education to a great degree. Boys of wealthy families were taught at home; in addition to the traditional academic subjects, they learned fencing and music, if a suitable teacher could be found. Girls studied art, music, needlework, and weaving as core subjects. Both boys and girls were taught the latest dance steps by a dance master (Millar 1990). Meanwhile, enslaved boys and girls seldom received any formal education, beyond the Christian Bible and, rarely, literacy—which was officially outlawed. However, enslaved people, sometimes with the assistance of white sympathizers, managed to glean some literacy and other skills through "hidden education" processes. This included the transmission of knowledge and culture through such forms as dancing, singing, and storytelling, thus preserving some aspects of African culture and gaining some aspects of local American culture (Gundaker 2007). Indeed, African American music had a profound impact on the development of such American musical forms as ragtime, gospel, blues, and jazz. In addition to expressing their cultural heritage through music and dance, enslaved people also injected their own passion and emotions into the creation of craft objects such as wrought ironwork, baskets, jewelry, and quilts.

Self-Expression through Performing Arts

Written and oral communications, although they can have powerful emotional content, are generally considered as vehicles for advancing cognitive growth. Music, dance, singing, and acting, on the other hand, are seen as mediums for expressing internal impulses not necessarily translatable into words. A craving for creative expression is a universal human impulse. It is found in all cultures in every type of civilization.

Accomplishments in the creative arts are an end in themselves, providing personal fulfillment and more well-rounded personalities. Creative expressions tend to be of an emotional nature, which would place them in the affective domain of learning. However, expressions of the artist's feelings about himself and other people also constitute learning in the intra- and interpersonal domains. Further, arts such as dancing also develop kinesthetic and spatial learning abilities. In addition, cognitive science research shows that performing arts activities can complement and advance achievement in other areas of the curriculum, such as science, mathematics, and social studies.

Cognitive Science and Neuroscience behind Expression

Cognitive Psychology: How Oral and Written Expression Evolve

Before encountering schooling, most people express themselves mainly through ordinary oral conversation. Such conversations are directed to particular people, known to the speaker, for some purpose—to maintain a social relationship, to persuade, or to control their behavior in some way. The speakers (children and their families and friends) usually share a common background and a lot of common experience. The speaker gets constant feedback, enabling her to monitor the listener's reactions (Green and Morgan 1981).

In school, on the other hand, a good deal of the communication is received through written forms, especially textbooks. With textbooks, neither the author nor the reader knows anything about the other. The author is driven to a simple, impersonal description of facts, more or less what society accepts as known. When teachers speak, they tend to speak as mediators of the textbook, interpreting the material for an audience about which they know more than the textbook author, but which may be quite diverse. If the audience is small and quite well known to the teacher, the language may be less formal and impersonal than the textbook author's. If the audience is large and not well known, the language tends to sound more like the textbook (Olsen and Torrance 1981).

Schooling, then, entails learning to communicate in a new and different language. Children who are learning to write can get started by simply transforming their conversational language into written form. However, progress up the academic ladder requires mastery of a more impersonal style. In expository writing, the writer is preparing a message for an unknown reader, one who may not share his background or experience. The context and the presuppositions of the writer have to be made explicit if the message is to have its intended effect. Therefore, it is no surprise to know that written Expression requires extensive, protracted education (Olsen and Torrance 1981).

The Neuroscience behind Expression

Writing

To be clear, when we refer to writing as a form of Expression, we are referring to writing as a process of transforming semantic information into coherent verbal form, not "expressive writing," or writing as a means of emotional release.

Given that writing is dependent on (spoken) language comprehension, language production, and fine motor skills, it is not surprising that it entails cooperation from several regions of the brain, especially the left temporal lobe (Wernicke's area for receptive speech) and the left frontal lobe (Broca's region for expressive speech) and another area, known as *Exner's writing area*, named for Sigmund Exner who identified this area in 1881, which is located adjacent to Broca's region. Exner's area translates auditory images transferred from the language areas into the motor impulses that enable writing (Joseph, n.d.). It appears that there are at least two stages involved in writing: first, a linguistic stage for translating auditory and visual information into symbols for letters and numbers, and, second, a motor-expressive stage for activating the hand and finger movements of writing. Coordination requires extensive interconnections between Broca's region and Exner's area (Joseph, n.d.).

Note-Taking

Incidentally, we now know that handwritten notes are far more efficacious than simply transcribing what is heard via keyboard. If merely typing what the lecturer says, the typist is not signaling to the brain that the material is significant, so it will be quickly discarded from memory. On the other hand, judiciously recording main ideas by longhand engages the part of the brain associated with memory formation. The key is engagement—processing and reframing the information (Mueller and Oppenheimer 2014).

Music

Just as writing begins with language comprehension, music reception and production begin in the temporal lobes, especially the dorsal area that relates to the auditory reception of speech. Musicians have a significantly larger auditory cortex than non-musicians, depending on how much musical training they have had (Weinberger 2004). It appears that spoken language and music evolved evolutionarily from emotion-laden primate calls. The link between emotion and music has long been noted, both being right hemisphere activities (Trimble and Hesdorffer 2017).

While a playing an instrument, the motor cortex and the cerebellum—both involved in the planning and execution of precisely timed movements, are particularly active. Looking specifically at motor control of the fingers used to play an instrument, the brain regions involved in receiving sensory inputs from the specific fingers used to play a specific instrument are larger in musicians than in non-musicians. Since most instruments require both hands, the motor regions that coordinate the two sides of the body—the anterior corpus callosum—is enlarged, again, depending on the amount of music training (Weinberger 2004).

Visual Art

Compared with language comprehension and production, our understanding of the neuropsychology of visual art is scanty, aside from the mechanics of the visual-motor systems. The visual module, spread across several areas of the brain, controls visual tracking, picture naming, and brightness perception—for printed words as well as for visual images (Bertolero and Bassett 2019). We know that people with brain abnormalities that affect their semantic ability retain their ability to perceive and produce art. Further, obsessive-compulsive disorders are linked to increased disposition to create art; and dopamine production is linked to improved motor control in art production (Chatterjee 2015). However, direct observation of art *production* via neuroimaging has been limited by the mechanics of the fMRI process, retarding a fine-grained understanding of the process.

Dance

As with the production of visual art described above, our understanding of the neuropsychology of the production of dance is hindered by the limitation of fMRI neuroimaging to capture the brain at work during performance. What is clear, though, is that the physical training entailed in dance production affects the dancer's basic motor control, equilibrium, posture, complex movement execution, timing, motor memory, motor imagery, and spatial transformations in profound ways. Thus, when dancers dance, they are engaging numerous brain regions in complex ways (Calvo-Merino 2015).

Strengths and Limitations: Why Expression?

The simplest rationale for employing the Expression configuration is that it induces learners to make their thinking visible, so it can be examined and, if necessary, corrected. As the old adage goes, "How can I know what I think until I see what I say?"

A more sophisticated rationale for Expression is that speaking and writing can engage learners in higher-order cognitive processes that actually advance their ability to think clearly and productively. Schools and colleges claim that their ultimate goal is to produce graduates who think creatively as constructive participants in society. This implies a goal of inculcating learners with critical thinking and problem-solving skills. Speaking and writing encourage learners to wrestle with competing ideas, to reformulate their existing knowledge, and to extend their understanding of complex phenomena.

Strengths

The Expression configuration is especially well suited to later stages of the learning process, after new material has been presented, demonstrated, and practiced. Expression helps the learner consolidate the new knowledge into a coherent whole and integrate it into their existing conceptual schemata. By verbalizing their feelings or expressing them through some graphic or plastic artistic creation, learners gain conscious access to those emotions, clarifying them and making them amenable to some sort of evaluation. Receiving comments from peers or an instructor further aids that evaluation.

While Expression plays a major role in cognitive learning, especially at the higher levels, it is also valuable for affective learning objectives, as discussed above regarding attitude change and regarding performing arts. Performing arts such as dance, music, and acting also entail significant motor skill abilities, which are developed through Repetition and displayed in finished form in Expression.

Limitations

Because it is not a receptive configuration, Expression is not a configuration well suited to acquiring new knowledge. Rather, it serves to make visible and to consolidate that which is already known and felt by the learner. Other configurations, such as

Presentation, Demonstration, Repetition, and Study are needed to provide the inputs for the outputs of Expression. If the Expression has no valid content, it has little value. If it lacks the proficiency born of practice, it has little appeal to others.

Best Practices for Using Expression

Advice for the Facilitator

Writing to Learn

Cognitive skills develop when learners actively process the material they are trying to master. Writing their thoughts about the subject matter supports various levels of learning. For example, writing short responses to study questions in the textbook promotes retention of new, specific information. It focuses learners' attention on key facts but may not necessarily lead to deeper understanding or ability to use the new knowledge.

Writing summaries at the end of a chapter or a unit of study encourages a more comprehensive view of the material and can serve to consolidate the new knowledge into some context, but understanding may still be superficial. On the other hand, writing an essay in which the learner expresses and supports a claim about the subject matter while reformulating and extending the new knowledge requires a deeper processing, suitable for reaching higher-level objectives such as evaluation and application.

Writing and Talking to Learn

A frequent criticism at all educational levels is that students tend to lack higher-order thinking skills, or cognitive strategy skills. One way to make those thought processes visible is to encourage learners to talk and write about their thoughts about the subject matter. They can express their thoughts in brainstorming sessions and other types of small-group activities. Short reflection papers at the end of class can provide material for discussion in teacher–student conferences, which could be carried out face-to-face or through distance education formats.

Students can get feedback on their expressed thoughts by means of peer review or "writing buddies." Working through multiple drafts and postponing editing until the final draft gives writers a chance to improve their ability to make their ideas clear to other readers.

Whatever sorts of writing assignments are given, several attributes are common to successful assignments: (1) giving the learner *ownership* of the material, which starts with developing their own sense of purpose and seeking their own interpretation; (2) being *appropriately challenging*, a task that the learner cannot do unaided but can do with some support; and (3) offering *support* to meet the challenge, such as a formulaic outline for a paper or a list of questions to answer in daily journal entries (Langer and Applebee 1987).

Community of Writers

In an academic setting, Expression could actually be placed at the center of a course of studies, especially in courses of a philosophical nature, in which "learning how to think" is a major objective. Such a course would feature regular essay writing by all students, with all essays deposited in a repository where all students could retrieve and read them. For a given topic, students would write their essays, deposit them, and then read two other students' papers, sending a critique to the student with copies to the moderator and the data bank. The moderator briefly reviews all the critiques and sends his own evaluative commentary to each author.

In such a framework, students are encouraged to write to engage their peers, not just the instructor. They receive abundant feedback, including discovering whether their essay attracted the interest of other students. Hence, the writing is aimed more at affecting other readers' opinions, a more natural form of communication than writing just to be judged by an expert (Finkel 2000, 78–85).

Writing across the Curriculum

Writing across the Curriculum (WAC) is the name of a movement at the elementary, secondary, and postsecondary levels of formal education aimed at encouraging teachers of all disciplines, not just English, to promote expressive writing—writing for emotional release—as well as "transactional" writing—writing intended to inform or persuade.

The core idea of the movement is that writing helps learners to order and represent their own understandings, thus providing a pathway to shaping new meanings and reaching new levels of understanding. Rather than assigning only large essays and project reports, instructors in all subjects can engage learners in a wide variety of "low-stakes" writing activities:

- journals
- end-of-class reflections
- problem statements
- abstracts modeled on abstracts appearing in professional journals
- annotations of readings or lectures
- synthesis papers at the end of a unit
- analysis of a process that has been observed, e.g., after a simulation-game
- analysis of a case that has been studied

- letters, e.g., a letter explaining a difficult concept to one's parent or friend (McKeachie 1999; Pershing et al. 2000).

Art across the Curriculum

The self-expression experienced in the creative arts is an end in itself—capturing and expressing some personal meaning. But the creative arts can interact with the other elements of a school or college curriculum. They impel learners to organize their experiences, to construct meanings, and to share those meanings. Such expressions bridge thought and feeling in a way that other academic activities do not, for example, a poem written in reaction to study of the history of the Great Depression or a modern dance composition related to a play of Shakespeare's. Such amalgams of ideas and emotional responses exemplify the highest aspirations of formal education (Smith 1980).

Encouraging Artistic Expression

A few basic guidelines can serve for helping beginners grow in their self-expression: (1) offer activities that involve personally meaningful experiences; (2) allow free exploration of the visual and physical properties of different media; (3) encourage learners to relate their sensory experiences to other ideas and processes they have been exposed to; and (4) allow learners to make their own decisions about their artistic expressions. Early learners can come to rely too much on approval from the teacher rather than trusting their own decisions. They need to feel safe in playing around; to take risks and make mistakes are crucial aspects of the creative arts learning process.

Advice for the Learner

Writing projects such as term papers can seem to be a daunting task. They become more manageable when broken down into a series of simple steps: finding a topic, gathering source material, developing an outline, fleshing out the outline into a first draft, getting feedback on that draft, and rewriting as necessary.

At each stage of the writing process, the writer can be aided by metacognitive strategies—consciously thinking about the writing process. Successful expository writers revisit these questions during the prewriting stage, the writing stage, and the editing stage: (1) What purpose am I trying to achieve: to inform, to persuade, or to critique? (2) What do I already know about the subject and what do I need to research further? (3) What claims am I making (the points I want to get across)? (4) Have I gotten my message across clearly and concisely?

Methods Featuring the Expression Configuration

Tactical Level

Note-Taking (Presentation or Study + Expression)

As with taking notes while listening to lectures (see "Advice to the Learner" in Chapter 5), taking notes while doing assigned readings or library research (see "Methods in Chapter 10) is an effective method of processing new material—what is most important, what is most relevant to your objective, and what the text means, translated into your own words. By expressing your interpretation, you are gaining ownership of the material.

Research Paper, Book Report, Reflection Paper (Study + Expression)

Undoubtedly, the most valuable way of amplifying the impact of Study is to follow reading and reflection with Expression. Constructing a document written in your own words is one of the most productive paths to converting the verbal information that has been ingested into a meaningful component of your long-term memory. That is why teachers are so fond of assigning reports, essays, and term papers. They encourage the learner to construct a coherent argument, which can be examined by the teacher, providing the basis for constructive feedback. Teachers also know well that there is no better way to master a topic than to teach it to someone else.

"Writing Buddies," Community of Writers (Expression + Tutorial)

As discussed above, "writing to learn" often entails having writers pair up and exchange drafts for peer evaluation and critique. The back-and-forth between "writing buddies" can be a potent form of tutorial assistance.

Chapter Summary

Expression is a learner-controlled configuration characterized by the learner's production of some sort of tangible indication of what has been learned, which might be of a verbal or nonverbal nature. Like Study, and unlike most other configurations, it focuses on the solitary learner, who typically exercises control of the time, place, and sequence of the activity. The analysis and synthesis work involved in producing written or other tangible products makes this one of the most valuable of all academic activities.

Many different formats may constitute Expression. Some culminate in texts, such as research reports, essays, reflection papers, blogs, or journals. Some culminate in symbolic representations, such as maps, diagrams, flow charts, or spreadsheets. Audiovisual formats would include how-to videos, podcasts, or narrated slide sets. In the creative arts, formats could include paintings, sculptures, jewelry, or decorative objects. In the performing arts, formats include dance, instrumental music, or song. Projects in other fields may yield such constructed products as set designs, building blueprints, or mock-up of building layouts. Behavioral responses can also be considered as a format for Expression, such as oral or written statements of opinion following attitude-change processes. In Web-based learning, students can exchange ideas via discussion forums or chatrooms, hold live debates through voice applications, share ideas via "wiki" applications, or share written statements or video clips via file-sharing applications.

Physical education, dance, and music were core curricula in Classical Greek times (although not Roman) and in British upper-class private education. Elementary and secondary public schools did not emphasize English composition until it was mandated at the university level in the late 1800s, when it began to gradually displace drawing, dance, music, and other arts from the curriculum. In elementary education, one of the main curricular goals is to teach children to transfer their oral conversation skills into writing skills.

From a neuroscience perspective, the activities done in the Expression configuration, such as writing essays and creating original artistic works, call upon probably the most extensive network of neural functions of any configuration—not only processing language and auditory and visual signals for understanding but also creating linguistic, auditory, and visual representations out of those understandings, which entail psychomotor skills finely coordinated with verbal, visual, and auditory functions.

A number of frameworks have been created for facilitators to use in guiding students into developing higher-order thinking skills through generating written and other types of tangible products: Writing to Learn, Writing and Talking to Learn, Writing across the Curriculum, and a Community of Writers. Frameworks such as these can support learners in a wide range of outputs, from "low-stakes" splinters of writing (e.g., end-of-class reflections) to full-blown semester research projects. Through these means, learners can attain the sorts of metacognitive skills to make them successful adults and lifelong learners.

Finally, stepping back, we see that Expression can be combined with other configurations to constitute methods at the strategic level—such as the Oxbridge System, and at the tactical level—such as note-taking, research papers, "writing buddies," and study groups.

Works Cited

Bertolero, Maxwell A., and Danielle S. Bassett. 2019. "How Matter Becomes Mind." *Scientific American* 321 (1): 26–33.

Calvo-Merino, Beatriz. 2015. "Sensorimotor Aesthetics: Neural Correlates of Aesthetic Perception of Dance. " In *Art, Aesthetics, and the Brain*, edited by Joseph P. Huston, Marcos Nadal, Francisco Mora, Luigi F. Agnati, and Camilo José Cela Conde. Oxford: Oxford University Press. Accessed March 15, 2020. doi:10.1093/acprof:oso/9780199670000.003.0011.

Chatterjee, Anjan. 2015. "The Neuropsychology of Visual Art." In *Art, Aesthetics, and the Brain*, edited by Joseph P. Huston, Marcos Nadal, Francisco Mora, Luigi F. Agnati and Camilo José Cela Conde. Oxford: Oxford University Press. Accessed March 15, 2020. doi:10.1093/acprof:oso/9780199670000.003.0017.

Committee of Ten. 1894. *Report of the Committee of Ten on Secondary School Studies*. New York: American Book Company.

Finkel, Donald L. 2000. *Teaching with Your Mouth Shut*. Portsmouth, NH: Boynton/Cook, Heinemann.

Freedman, Sarah Warshauer. 2003. "The Teaching of Writing." In *Encyclopedia of Education*, 2nd ed., edited by James W. Guthrie, 26–93. New York: Macmillan Reference.

Green, Georgia M., and Jerry L. Morgan. 1981. "Writing Ability as a Function of the Appreciation of Differences Between Oral and Written Communication." In *Writing: The Nature, Development, and Teaching of Written Communication*, vol. 2, *Writing Process, Development, and Communication*, edited by Carl H. Fredericksen and Joseph F. Dominic, 177–188. Hillsdale, NJ: Lawrence Erlbaum Associates.

Gundaker, Grey. 2007. "Hidden Education Among African Americans During Slavery." *Teachers College Record* 109 (7): 1591–1612.

Joseph, Rhawn Gabriel. n.d. *Agraphia: Disorders of Writing*. Accessed January 25, 2020. http://brainmind.com/Agraphia.html.

Kamradt, Thomas F., and Elizabeth J. Kamradt. 1999. "Structured Design for Attitudinal Instruction." In *Instructional-Design Theories and Models*, vol. 2, *A New Paradigm of Instructional Theory*, edited by Charles M. Reigeluth, 563–590. Mahwah, NJ: Lawrence Erlbaum Associates.

Langer, Judith A., and Arthur N. Applebee. 1987. *How Writing Shapes Thinking: A Study of Teaching and Learning*. Urbana, IL: National Council of Teachers of English.

McKeachie, Wilbert J. 1999. *Teaching Tips: Strategies, Research, and Theory for College and University Teachers*. 10th ed. Boston, MA: Houghton-Mifflin.

Millar, John Fitzhugh. 1990. *Country Dances of Colonial America*. Williamsburg, VA: Thirteen Colonies Press.

Mueller, Pam A., and Daniel M. Oppenheimer. 2014. "The Pen is Mightier than the Keyboard: Advantages of Longhand over Laptop Note Taking." *Psychological Science* 25 (6): 1159–1168. Accessed March 14, 2020. doi:10.1177/0956797614524581.

Olsen, David R., and Nancy Torrance. 1981. "Learning to Meet the Requirements of Written Text: Language Development in the School Years." In *Writing: The Nature, Development, and Teaching of Written Communication*, vol. 2, *Writing: Process, Development and Communication*, edited by Carl H. Frederiksen and Joseph F. Dominic, 235–255. Hillsdale, NJ: Lawrence Erlbaum Associates.

Pershing, James A., Michael H. Molenda, Trena Paulus, Judy Har Lai, and Emily Hixon. 2000. "Letters Home: The Meaning of Instructional Technology." *TechTrends* 44 (1): 31–38.

Smith, Nancy R. 1980. "Classroom Practice: Creative Meaning in the Arts." In *Arts and the Schools*, edited by Jerome J. Hausman, 79–115. New York: McGraw-Hill.
Trimble, Michael, and Dale Hesdorffer. 2017. "Music and the Brain: The Neuroscience of Music and Music Appreciation." *BJPsych International* 14 (2): 28–31. Accessed March 1, 2020. doi:10.1192/S205647000001720.
Walling, Donovan R. 2003. "Art Education." In *Encyclopedia of Education*, 2nd ed., edited by James W. Guthrie, 118–120. New York: Macmillan Reference.
Weinberger, Norman M. 2004. "Music and the Brain." *Scientific American* 291 (5): 88–95.

Summary and Conclusions

12

Summary Observations

Humans are Still Humans

From its inception, this book has aimed to take a fresh look at pedagogy in the twenty-first century, at a time when rapid changes in technology have been making all of us wonder if there is any firm ground left on which educators might stand with any sense of orientation, confidence, and security. We have suggested that, on the contrary, the most important factors in pedagogy—the art and science of teaching—are actually quite stable. While technology may evolve rapidly, humans do not. Our species, *Homo sapiens*, is the product of millions of years of evolution, with "anatomically modern man" dating back about 196,000 years. When the frozen body of a man was found by hikers in the Ötztal Alps in 1991, they thought he might be a fellow hiker who had been caught in an avalanche. The body, now known as Ötzi, was found to be 5,300 years old (dating to before the oldest of the pyramids in Egypt), giving tangible testimony to the notion that human evolution is gradual. People who are just like us also had the ingenuity over 5,000 years ago to live robust lives in the Alps and to build pyramidal structures of formidable engineering prowess.

The neurological system that human beings function with today is the same as Ötzi's. The invention of radio, television, and computers has not altered that evolutionary fact. Aristotle's, or Comenius's, or Montaigne's, or Mark Twain's, or William James's observations about human nature are as apt as any made by today's philosopher. Likewise, the processes of human learning function as they have for millennia. Our scientific understanding is deeper; our vocabulary for describing the processes is richer and more precise; the number and types of tools for teaching are more bountiful, but the neurological processes are what they are and have been.

Overall Approach

We have taken as our starting point the learner and the human learning apparatus. We have added to that the arrangements, invented by humans over the centuries, for facilitating different sorts of learning objectives and for accommodating different stages in the learning process. These are the basic elements of instruction. We have proposed that a functional description of the teaching–learning process can proceed from observation of these visible, audible, and tangible conditions of instruction: Who is communicating what, to whom, through what channels, in what settings? This is what we have referred to in Chapter 1 as a "back to basics" approach.

All commentators speak from a particular perspective with particular biases, conscious or unconscious. Our perspective has been shaped by our long involvement with one sector of pedagogy, namely, educational technology; that is the literature about which we are most informed, although we have also striven to keep abreast of developments in educational psychology and pedagogy broadly. Our teaching experience has primarily been with adult learners at the postsecondary level—featuring K–12 educators (pre- and in-service teachers, technology coordinators, and administrators) as well as educational technologists focusing on the corporate and postsecondary education sectors. We have endeavored to avoid the (often subconscious) biases of technocentrism, technological advocacy, and technological determinism. We have embraced a systemic, holistic approach to instructed learning that is intensely cognizant of the impacts of the socioeconomic, cultural, and political environments on instructed learning—concerns that have chiefly been addressed in Chapter 2.

Our aim has principally been descriptive, not prescriptive. This book intends neither to give advice on instructional design nor to proclaim new principles of instruction. The one concession to prescriptive advice has been that within Chapters 5 through 11 we have included a section on "best practices." This was meant to capture conventional and evidence-based advice about how each configuration can be used in practice. We have not attempted to prescribe which configuration or method to use for any particular objective or any particular instructional setting. The advice is meant to be generic.

We remain wary about the issue of scholars and practitioners inappropriately deriving prescriptions from descriptive theories or schemata. In an earlier generation, audiovisual education advocate Edgar Dale devised a simple, cone-shaped visual schema to classify instructional resources along a concrete-to-abstract scale (Dale 1946). That schema was purely descriptive. However, in later editions of his textbook—in the 1950s and 1960s—he pointed out that there was a rough correlation between the learner's amount of prior experience and whether they could profit from using more concrete or more abstract material—hence the "cone of experience." Enthusiasts found this simple formula extremely attractive, and someone—in the late 1970s—overlaid a folkloric table of percentages, indicating the quantum of information that was supposedly retained following different instructional treatments, making the conflated "cone" even more attractive in terms of its perceived usefulness as a prescriptive guideline. A Google search will yield about 140,000 results. The sordid, cautionary tale of how an innocent descriptive schema metastasized into a misleading prescriptive monster is detailed in a special issue of *Educational Technology* (Subramony et al. 2014).

Finally, we agree with the several scholars who are arguing for the establishing of a common vocabulary as a prerequisite for building a sound knowledge base for pedagogy. Reigeluth and Carr-Chellman (2009), for example, deduce that "vague and inconsistent language is impeding such growth. Different theorists use the same term to refer to different things and different terms to refer to the same things. This is confusing for all of us" (5). We have started by identifying the basic elements involved in the instructed learning process—giving them names and definitions—and then continued building outward with other terms and their definitions. We have insisted that the names given to these constructs be words that already exist within the vocabulary of pedagogy—albeit with inconsistent meanings—as opposed to coining neologisms or buzzwords that would have to be explained and "sold" to the book's readers. Along the same line, we have endeavored to align our definitions of these constructs as closely as possible with conventional usage, with the addition of wording that clarifies the critical attributes of the construct and differentiates it from other related constructs. In lexicography, this is known as avoiding *stipulative* definitions and instead using *precising* definitions.

Status and Directions

We have made a number of claims throughout this book. Chapter 1 focused on some of the thorny, ill-conceived constructs that we believe have clouded our collective view of the underlying realities of where we are in our state of knowledge about pedagogy. Briefly:

- *Media* should refer to communication delivery channels, not to the products that flow through or emerge at the end of those channels.
- *Multimedia*, on the basis of its connotations as a psychedelic combination of voice, music, and multiple still and moving images, is a rather poor descriptor—the Construct Identity Fallacy—for mundane presentations that happen to include a picture in addition to a verbal message.
- *Educational technology* is the name of a field, a theory, or a profession (AECT Task Force on Definition and Terminology 1977) and not the name of any specific instructional intervention—another example of a Construct Identity Fallacy.
- *Emerging technologies* is a fashionable term for any technological innovations that are less than fully implemented; it also should not be used as though it referred to some specific set of interventions. To use one label to refer to

multiple different constructs is the "jingle" fallacy. If used that way, it will be but a nanosecond before someone attempts a meta-analysis comparing "emerging technologies" to "conventional instruction."
- *Social media* is a label that is firmly entrenched in popular vocabulary as a construction parallel to *mass media*. However, *social media* actually denotes a collection of Web applications for generating and sharing content and does not denote a new or different *medium*, as such.

In addition to critiquing some popular concepts within educational technology, we have introduced a number of novel constructs as contributions toward a more constructive conversation regarding pedagogical issues. The most central of these constructs is *instructed learning*, which we have proposed as the most appropriate label for the sorts of learning outcomes produced by instructional interventions. This term has been used for three decades within foreign-language teaching in recognition of the qualitative difference in outcomes between the natural learning of one's mother tongue and the contrived learning that results from planned doses of language instruction. *Instructed learning* is also a term of art within the field of neuroscience to distinguish *implicit learning* (occurs unconsciously through everyday transactions) from *explicit learning* (occurs as a result of conscious effort), since these two types of learning follow different neural pathways.

A Framework for the Instructed Learning Process

In Chapter 2, we presented the most significant claim of this book—a comprehensive framework developed to lay out the array of factors that influence the success of instructed learning. We are unaware of any other previously existent framework that is as inclusive, thorough, or substantiated with research evidence as ours is—which signifies that there has existed a giant hole within the nomological network of the field of pedagogy, considering how important it is in social science research that investigations be based on models or frameworks so that subsequent discoveries are able to add to a coherent body of knowledge. Another feature of our framework is that it explicitly acknowledges and details the role played by sociocultural factors within the complex process of instructed learning, along with the role of "media and methods." We believe that the achievement represented by our framework is unique in terms of a major work on pedagogy written from an educational technology perspective.

Our framework has been based primarily on a number of major meta-analyses of research on the factors affecting instructed learning, particularly Walberg (1984), *HPLI* (National Research Council 2000) and *HPLII* (National Academies of Sciences 2018), and Hattie (2009). Meanwhile, our visualization of this framework has been influenced by diagrams proposed previously by Walberg (1984) and Huitt (Huitt et al. 2009).

302 Summary and Conclusions

The purpose of our framework has been to serve as a map identifying the range of key factors influencing instructed learning and showing the myriad interconnections between these factors (Figure 12.1).

Our framework could be interpreted as a statement detailing the chain of influences that lead up to instructed learning, as follows:

> There are three factors that *directly* affect Instructed Learning—Aptitude, Effort, and Instruction; that is, Instructed Learning will be successful if the Learner (a) has the requisite Aptitude—including prerequisite skills, (b) is exposed to appropriately designed Instruction, and (c) expends Effort to respond to the Instruction.
>
> These three Proximal factors are influenced by several Distal factors. The Learner's Psychological Traits (self-efficacy, locus-of-control, maturational level, and personal interests) and the Learner's Psychological State (expectancies, valuations, situational interest, and motivation to learn) determine whether they will activate their Aptitude and expend Effort; the Facilitator determines the instructional methods and can influence the Learner's Psychological State (i.e., motivation to learn).
>
> Learners and Facilitators work within a Classroom Environment that determines or constrains what instructional choices are available and creates an atmosphere that may or may not be conducive to learning; the classroom

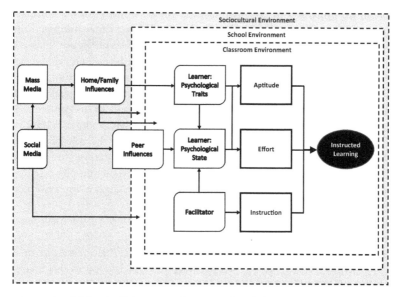

Figure 12.1 Molenda–Subramony Framework of the Forces That Impact Instructed Learning.

operates within a School Environment that may or may not support Learners' and Facilitators' efforts.

Among Second-Level Distal Factors, Peer Influences have considerable impact on individual Learners' Psychological State (expectancies, valuations, situational interest, and motivation to learn). Home/Family Influences impact the Classroom Environment, the School Environment, and their respective Learner's Psychological Traits (self-efficacy, locus-of-control, maturational level, and personal interests).

Finally, Mass Media influence the Home/Family and Peers, while Social Media impact the School Environment and Peers.

All these factors operate within a Sociocultural Environment; to give just one example, Home/Family values are largely determined by the ways in which Learners and their parents or relatives are shaped by their socioeconomic status (SES) and cultural identity.

Given the array of factors that influence success or failure in instructed learning, one must marvel that schooling is effective at all! Instructed learning is an enterprise of staggering complexity, but with a map such as our framework, pedagogical scholars and practitioners can locate their interests relative to the goal of instructed learning and make better predictions about what interventions might yield benefits—and at what point during the process.

We would like to highlight one of the research findings described in Chapter 9 that relates directly to one of the key factors in the framework—Aptitude—to underline the importance of inherited traits in attaining the ability to succeed at all sorts of learning goals. The studies of Hambrick (Hambrick et al. 2018), plus many twin studies, remind us that a great deal of the variance in instructional success or failure may be accounted for by heredity, perhaps outweighing the importance of instructional choices by a large margin. That is, Learners with a high aptitude for a given task, especially if they have high motivation to learn, will manage to successfully learn regardless of the Facilitator's qualifications and/or instructional choices.

Learning, Instruction, and the Elements of Instruction

We began Chapter 3 with a general survey of commonly recognized theories of— or perspectives on—the process of learning in order to establish a frame of reference for our later discussion of *instructed learning* and how it emerged from cognitive psychology and neuroscience research. This survey and the labels used in it have not been intended to serve as authoritative judgments about what is important or how it should be named; they have merely aimed to make our own perspective explicit. For example, one widely discussed contemporary perspective—constructivism—is discussed as a subset of cognitive theory, on the basis of our belief that virtually all of the prescriptions recommended by constructivists are compatible with and have already been widely discussed under the rubric of cognitive theory. In our survey, we have argued that these perspectives are not mutually contradictory, but rather that each is valid within its own limits. Taken together, they form a mosaic of descriptions covering the vast range of human learnings.

Another theme in our survey is that recent neuroscience research—particularly that made possible by a new ability to observe the functioning of the brain *in vivo*, using neuroimaging technologies—has verified many of the conclusions previously reached by research within the fields of behavioral and cognitive psychology. One somewhat unexpected finding of neuroscientific research is that there is a qualitative difference between the neural pathways for *implicit* learning (unconscious, naturally occurring) and those for *explicit* learning (conscious, guided by instruction). This distinction is congruent with the observations of Geary (2008), Paas and Sweller (2014), and others who refer to biologically *primary* learning and biologically *secondary* learnings. The latter include knowledge and skills that are needed for successful navigation of the cultural environment but are not an inborn part of neurological development. As Geake (2009, 53) puts it, "school learning relies on appropriating brain functions which originally evolved for other purposes."

This finding is in fact the basis of our decision to propose *instructed learning* as our label for the sorts of learning outcomes produced by instructional interventions—a primary subject of this book.

Another insight from Chapter 3 stems from what has been revealed in recent fMRI neuroimaging studies about the surprisingly complex overall level of neural activity in the human brain. Previously, it was common for researchers to draw sketches of the pathway for some type of learning—from sensory reception to engagement of some local area of the brain, to signals sent out to the muscularskeletal system. A simple line drawing could capture the action. But neuroimaging now shows us a brain that is simultaneously processing information all over the brain all the time. The *Scientific American* authors (Bertolero and Bassett 2019) use the analogy of an orchestra, with many sections playing at once, all operating on a harmonious level. Amidst this clamor there is considerable competition for attention, and it takes vigorous executive control to keep the orchestra playing together. This problem is reflected in Cognitive Load Theory (and perhaps there should be a Sensory Load Theory as well!), reminding designers of the challenges faced by learners in decoding busy "multimedia" productions—handling the sensory load of moving images, text, voice, and music as well as the cognitive load of the semantic content.

The remainder of Chapter 3 has been devoted to setting forth the terms and definitions that provide the foundation for the rest of this book, beginning with *instruction*: a deliberate effort to provide learners with conditions suitable for achieving specified learning objectives. Further, to be considered successful, instruction should be humane, effective, and efficient. Regarding *Learner* and *Facilitator*, we have made the important observation that it is Learners who produce learning; they are the "workers" in the classroom, not the teachers. Facilitators guide, and even coproduce, student learning, but they cannot cause it without the full cooperation of Learners.

We have argued for the substitution of the construct of *resources* for the more ambiguous term, *media*. We believe professional communication would be clearer if *media* were viewed as communication channels, not the things studied by learners. We have added one more element as a component of instructional events—a *setting*, the physical space and its furnishings. To have an event you must have an event space! Furthermore, the affordances offered by that space and its furnishing constrain the facilitator's instructional choices.

Communication Configurations and Methods

In Chapter 4, we have introduced yet another key original construct—the *communication configuration*—to add to the basic elements of instruction. We claim that the number of possible arrangements of people and resources for instructed learning is finite; in fact, our typology consists of eight categories, which capture all of the most common teaching–learning arrangements. This typology grew out of a long process of gestation, borrowing ideas from a dozen earlier classifications systems. Two typologies, by Berliner (1983) and Stodolsky (1988)—which were developed as operational definitions for research on classroom teaching—are most nearly comprehensive. However, a weakness of virtually all previous typologies has been that, while they capture what is happening in the classroom, they miss all the critical activities that take place elsewhere—such as Study in the library, Expression at one's desk at home, or Repetition outside on the athletic field or in the music studio.

The purpose of clustering like objects together is to reduce the complexity of choices faced by instructional planners. When the instructional designer is trying to choose "media and methods" to pursue a given instructional objective, our typology offers a decision tree with eight choices, not a grab-bag, random assortment of "flavors of the day." Each of the configurations offers affordances for different types of learning or different stages in the learning process, as follows:

- Presentation: new verbal or visual information reception
- Demonstration: behavior modeling, interpersonal and affective objectives
- Discussion: mental processing of new information
- Tutorial: deep learning of declarative knowledge
- Repetition: practice of mental and psychomotor skills
- Study: contemplation of verbal or visual information at one's own pace
- Expression: consolidation of declarative knowledge.

Placing different formats—such as lectures, film showings, panel discussions—under a common heading, Presentation, signals that these arrangements have similar pedagogical consequences. They may differ in logistical features—media delivery channels; cost of acquisition, installation, development of software, use and maintenance;

and local availability—but they are largely interchangeable alternatives for distributing new information.

Although different fields of study often have their own "signature pedagogies" (Shulman 2005), we contend that those "pedagogies" are composed of the same elements as those of other fields. That is, our configuration typology is comprehensive enough to describe teaching–learning arrangements in the broadest array of applications.

No Configuration Stands Alone

One of the major points we have made within Chapter 4 is that any single communication configuration is not intended to be viewed as encompassing the whole of any given lesson. As described in Chapter 4, each instructional event is but a "snapshot" taken from the "movie" of the live, flowing lesson, and each instructional event may well employ a different configuration. That is, any well-designed lesson will carry the Learner through a series of experiences suitable for each stage of the instructed learning process. Robert Gagné (1985), for example, proposed that a comprehensive lesson entails several stages (which he calls *events of instruction*):

- gaining attention
- informing learner of the objective and activating motivation
- stimulating recall of prior knowledge
- presenting the stimulus material
- providing learning guidance
- eliciting performance
- providing feedback and assessing performance
- and enhancing retention and transfer (304).

The second-grade science lesson described in Chapter 4 featured a rapid sequence of activities in different configurations, adding up to coverage of all of Gagné's *events*: Demonstration (to gain attention, inform about objectives, and motivate), Repetition (to elicit performance), Presentation (to present new stimulus material), Repetition (to elicit performance), Demonstration (to provide learning guidance), Repetition (more performance with feedback), Study (more performance, enhancing retention), and Expression (for assessment and enhancing transfer).

In Chapter 4, we have also proposed a formal definition for the construct of *method*, another construct that has been subjected to random abuse—both "jingle" and "jangle" fallacies. Probably no other term in pedagogy has endured greater indignities than *method*. We have made the claim that "methods" can be viewed as replicable templates of instructional activities composed of a number of configurations. That is, when any given "method" is applied, Learners move through a series of steps, typically toggling between two or more configurations. In Chapters 5–11, we enumerate the methods that are most closely associated with each configuration.

For example, the buzz group, the study group, and the collaborative learning group methods all revolve around Small-Group Discussion (Chapter 7), differing in how other configurations are added into the mix.

Like the construct of *configuration*, the construct of *method* can add order to the menu of choices of instructional designers. Indeed, across Chapters 5 through 11, we name nearly four dozen different specific methods, with around half being applicable at the strategic level and the other half being applicable at the tactical level.

Elaboration of the Communication Configurations

Chapters 5–11 comprise an overview of all of the communication configurations, the formats in which they are manifested, and the methods they animate. We have taken care to provide some historical context for each configuration, primarily to demonstrate that *all* of the configurations we use in today's technology-driven world have lengthy historical antecedents, believe it or not! Humans have always faced the necessity of teaching the same types of knowledge, skill, and attitude that we grapple with today. It should not be surprising to learn that our ancestors actualized the same sorts of solutions that we rely on today.

"Everything Old Is New Again" (from the musical, *All That Jazz*)

In Chapter 9, as we reviewed the formats and methods associated with Repetition, we have reminded the reader that different configurations fall into and out of fashion, just as different theories of learning move into and out of the spotlight. When the "cognitive revolution" displaced behaviorism as the dominant paradigm in the study of learning theories, it did *not* mean that the principles discovered by Pavlov and Skinner had somehow stopped operating. It simply meant that other aspects of the learning process (such as mental states) were deemed higher priority for researchers. The rediscovery of "clicker training" demonstrates the timelessness of behaviorist principles of learning—when applied to appropriate types of objectives, that is, not to those demanding the mastery of declarative knowledge. Behaviorist instructional principles have considerable relevance to motor skills, as in military training, sports and athletics, and routine on-the-job tasks.

Learner-Centered Configurations

Study and Expression, covered in Chapters 10 and 11, will probably be the least familiar configurations to readers coming from the field of educational technology, although they have certainly been manifested in technological formats—such as studying "multimedia" modules, and producing videos and podcasts as culminating activities. They are also typically neglected in courses and textbooks devoted to instructional methods, simply because they typically take place outside the classroom setting, and so outside the immediate awareness and primary control of the Facilitator. Nevertheless, they probably account for the largest quantum of the learning "take-aways" within most academic courses and training programs.

Concluding Thought

Although we have briefly touched on schema theory in Chapter 5, it might be worth our while to pause a little at this point and think a bit further about mental sets. Schema theory (Rumelhart 1980) is a well-accepted subset of cognitive theory, reminding us of the importance of mental sets—the frameworks, belief structures, and schemata we use to filter our incoming semantic inputs and to store our declarative knowledge. Mental sets are real, and they are in fact visibly central to neurological functioning. Neuroimaging research has revealed the density of "white matter," consisting of the myelin sheaths surrounding the axons that extend out from neurons, insulating the axons and enhancing their transmission of electrical impulses; the greater this density, the stronger the connections.

So how do mental sets manifest within and impact our common human experience? A vivid example of the durability of mental sets can be found in the study of the letters and diaries of the soldiers who fought on both sides during the American Civil War, by researchers such as Carmichael (2018). Having all grown up in a society thoroughly suffused with the moral philosophy of sentimentalism—a perspective nearly universally accepted around the mid-nineteenth century but quite alien to twenty-first century mentality—these soldiers viewed themselves as heroic Christian warriors whose individual actions would prevail over the enemy and instill a deeper moral character in themselves. This sentiment—powerfully manifested in the letters these men wrote to persuade their family members, as well as in the diaries they wrote to persuade themselves—collided abruptly against the reality of raucous military camp life and the incredibly gruesome toll of battle. But these soldiers, Carmichael insists, did not abandon their sentimental, Christian framework, even though they often expressed an inability to make it congruent with the sordid reality of their lives. The dogged durability of their mental set in spite of it being so hopelessly misaligned with their everyday experiences speaks to the power of such frameworks.

And yet, the literature of pedagogy tends to treat the incoming learner as a *tabula rasa*, ready to start storing up new facts, principles, and procedures. In reality, one of the first and largest barriers to instructed learning is preexisting mental sets. What are, to the Facilitator, "misconceptions" to be disabused, may be, to the Learner, understandings and belief structures that have guided her thinking and actions for all of her previous life. As Laurilhart (2002) puts it, "teaching is essentially a rhetorical activity, seeking to persuade students to change the way they experience the world through an understanding of the insights of others" (2002, 23). Recognizing the scale of this challenge and developing and disseminating powerful pedagogical solutions surely must be one of the great missions of the future.

Works Cited

AECT Task Force on Definition and Terminology. 1977. *Educational Technology: Definition and Glossary of Terms*. Vol. 1. Washington, DC: Association for Educational Communications and Technology.

Berliner, David C. 1983. "Developing Conceptions of Classroom Environments: Some Light on the T in Classroom Studies of ATI." *Educational Psychologist* 18 (1): 1–13.

Bertolero, Maxwell A., and Danielle S. Bassett. 2019. "How Matter Becomes Mind." *Scientific American* 321 (1): 26–33.

Carmichael, Peter. 2018. *The War for the Common Soldier: How Men Thought, Fought, and Survived in Civil War Armies*. Chapel Hill, NC: University of North Carolina Press.

Dale, Edgar. 1946. *Audio-Visual Methods in Teaching*. New York: The Dryden Press.

Gagné, Robert M. 1985. *The Conditions of Learning*. 4th ed. New York: Holt, Rinehart, and Winston.

Geake, John G. 2009. *The Brain at School: Educational Neuroscience in the Classroom*. Maidenhead: Open University Press/McGraw-Hill.

Geary, David C. 2008. "An Evolutionarily Informed Education Science." *Educational Psychologist* 43 (4): 179–195.

Hambrick, David Z., Alexander P. Burgoyne, Brooke N. Macnamara, and Fredrik Ullen. 2018. "Toward a Multifactorial Model of Expertise: Beyond Born Versus Made." *Annals of the New York Academy of Sciences* 1423 (1): 284–295. doi:10.1111/nyas.13586.

Hattie, John A. C. 2009. *Visible Learning: A Synthesis of over 800 Meta-Analyses Relating to Achievement*. New York: Routledge.

Huitt, William G., Marsha A. Huitt, David M. Monetti, and John H. Hummel. 2009. "A Systems-Based Synthesis of Research Related to Improving Students' Academic Performance." *Educational Psychology Interactive*. October 16–19. Accessed October 8, 2019. http://www.edpsycinteractive.org/papers/improving-school-achievement.pdf.

Laurillard, Diana. 2002. *Rethinking University Teaching: A Conversation Framework for the Effective Use of Learning Technologies*. 2nd ed. New York: Routledge Falmer.

National Academies of Sciences, Engineering, and Medicine. 2018. *How People Learn II: Learners, Contexts, and Cultures*. Washington, DC: The National Academies Press.

National Research Council. 2000. *How People Learn: Brain, Mind, Experience, and School*. Expanded Edition. Washington, DC: The National Academies Press. doi:https://doi.org/10.17226/9853.

Paas, Fred, and John Sweller. 2014. "Implications of Cognitive Load Theory for Multimedia Learning." In *The Cambridge Handbook of Multimedia Learning*, 2nd ed., edited by Richard E. Mayer, 27–42. New York: Cambridge University Press.

Reigeluth, Charles M., and Alison A. Carr-Chellman, eds. 2009. *Instructional-Design Theories and Models: Building a Common Knowledge Base*. Vol. 3. New York: Routledge.

Rumelhart, David E. 1980. "Schemata: The Building Blocks of Cognition." Chap. 2 in *Theoretical Issues in Reading Comprehension*, edited by Rand J. Spiro, Bertram C. Bruce and William F. Brewer, 33–58. Hillsdale, NJ: Lawrence Erlbaum Associates.

Shulman, Lee. 2005. "Signature Pedagogies in the Professions." *Daedalus* 134 (3): 52–59.
Stodolsky, Susan S. 1988. *The Subject Matters: Classroom Activities in Math and Social Studies*. Chicago, IL: University of Chicago Press.
Subramony, Deepak Prem, Michael Molenda, Anthony K. Betrus, and Will Thalheimer. 2014. "A Special Issue Examining the Mythical Retention Chart and Corrupted Dale's Cone." *Educational Technology*, November–December: 3–49. Accessed March 18, 2020. https://www-jstor-org.proxyiub.uits.iu.edu/stable/44430316?Search=yes&resultItemClick=true&searchText=subramony&searchText=mythical&searchText=retention&searchText=chart&searchUri=%2Faction%2FdoBasicSearch%3FQuery%3Dsubramony%2Bmythical%2Bretention%2Bchar.
Walberg, Herbert J. 1984. "Improving the Productivity of America's Schools." *Educational Leadership* 41 (8): 19–27.

Epilogue

The finalization of this book's manuscript has coincided with a proverbial "black swan"—an unforeseen event with extreme consequences—for educational systems around the globe. With the World Health Organization (WHO) designating the Coronavirus Disease 2019 (COVID-19) outbreak as a pandemic in March 2020, postsecondary institutions worldwide were forced to hastily render their physical campuses off-limits and—where even possible—to move all face-to-face (F2F) instruction to online delivery in a desperate attempt to help slow the disease's exponential spread. Within the United States, the University of Washington took the lead—canceling all in-person classes effective March 6, 2020—with other colleges and universities across the country rapidly following suit. During the subsequent weeks, postsecondary institutions and K–12 schools in nearly every country in the world closed temporarily, with a majority mandating that classes continue to meet through online technologies.

The virtually overnight switch from F2F to distance learning models was not easy on any of the numerous stakeholders of the world's educational systems. Of primary concern, of course, was the welfare of students. In the United States, the federal Department of Education's Office for Civil Rights (OCR) scrambled to release resources aimed at fostering Web accessibility for students and protecting the latter's civil rights as educational institutions moved to distance delivery. Their intent was to remind educational leaders of their legal obligations to ensure that all students—including those with disabilities and those with limited financial means—could equitably access online learning programs.

Unsurprisingly, instructors were deeply affected as well. As institutions scrambled to survive the pandemic, educators who had had pedagogical, logistical, or philosophical objections to distance learning were compelled to abandon those misgivings overnight and "get with the program." F2F instructors had to quickly adapt their carefully honed instructional endeavors for distance delivery *without* the benefit of the extensive training, consultation, and perhaps release time required to develop effective online instruction.

In short, educators across the globe were facing—with vastly heightened intensity—some of the very questions we discuss in this book: (a) What are my objectives? (b) What are the learning requirements for those objectives? (c) How can I fulfill those learning requirements at a distance? Some instructional activities such as lectures and demonstrations could be accomplished via telecommunications with relative ease, so long as all parties had access to the necessary technological tools, and so long as the thorny issue of intellectual property rights was set aside for the time being. Discussion, too, could be cobbled together through various Web-based applications. But other crucially important activities, such as practice, were immensely more difficult to arrange. One of this book's authors watched his spouse—a professor of piano performance—wrestle with figuring out how to effectively teach piano performance to students who now lacked access to a piano after being forced to leave behind the wealth of resources on campus.

It is hard to imagine that these drastic measures will not leave a lasting impression on how education is conducted in the future. One sobering prediction is that some of the instructional activities hastily shifted from F2F to online delivery will never revert to their former status—especially as those educational institutions that manage to survive the pandemic will struggle mightily to recover from the unimaginable financial blow they have been dealt. If the Great Recession of 2008 is any guide, we expect diminished state government support for public institutions, reduced philanthropic giving, and declines in the value of endowment funds. Corners that were cut during the emergency could remain cut. For example, videos or slide shows made as online substitutes for lectures might be retained and used instead of live lectures. F2F courses might become blended or totally online courses, potentially reducing the need for traditional faculty. Administrators might welcome the savings on classroom space, office space, and personnel costs. If the infrastructure costs of creating, delivering, and receiving instruction can be shifted from the institution to the teacher and student at home, why not continue to do so?

By the time this book reaches your hands, some postsecondary educational institutions will have closed their doors forever. Those that were struggling financially, those that were losing population due to the demographic cliff of the 2020s, and those that could not keep up with the technological tsunami— such institutions will have succumbed to the inevitable. Those that remain will live to carry on "the race between education and catastrophe," as H. G. Wells famously put it. For the survivors, it will be more important than ever to understand the elements of instruction so that they can succeed in helping people learn efficiently, effectively, and humanely. History offers no alternative.

Michael H. Molenda
Bloomington, Indiana, USA

Deepak Prem Subramony
Manhattan, Kansas, USA
March 28, 2020

Glossary

affective objective: A statement specifying the acquisition of particular attitudes, values, or feelings.
affordance: An opportunity offered by the setting to a learner.
AIME (amount of invested mental energy): The conscious application of mental elaborations by a learner to a unit of material.
aptitude: Innate capacity—mental, physical, or emotional—for learning, specifically: intelligence, prior academic achievement, and prior content knowledge.
asynchronous: Not occurring at the same time.
behavior modeling: According to social learning theory, the ability of people to learn by imitating the behavior of models—people they observe—just through observation, without trial-and-error practice.
behaviorism: In psychology, a systematic approach to understanding the behavior of humans and other animals; it assumes that behavior is either a reflex evoked by the pairing of certain antecedent stimuli in the environment or a consequence of that individual's history, including especially reinforcement and punishment contingencies.
behaviorist perspective: See **behaviorism**.
bimodal: Adj., the quality of involving two sensory modalities at a time.
biologically primary learning: A learning process developed by humans through evolution that includes such implicit skills as reflexive motor skills, reading human emotion in faces, listening to and speaking a mother tongue, and performing basic problem-solving; these skills are acquired quickly and easily, without conscious effort.
biologically secondary learning: A learning process developed by humans through evolution that relies on modules in the brain that evolved for other purposes; skills such as literacy and numeracy, along with many other skills related to human civilization, are learned through conscious effort.

brainstorming: A format of Small-Group or Whole-Class Discussion used for solving problems, stimulating creative thinking, or developing new ideas by unrestrained and spontaneous participation in discussion.

buzz group: A method of Discussion: a small group, formed spontaneously within a lecture; members share opinions and experiences on an assigned question. After brief discussion, the moderator gathers a sampling of responses from different groups.

case method: An instructional method in which learning is achieved chiefly on the basis of studying selected cases as primary authorities instead of from textbooks.

chavrusa: (Ashkenazic pronunciation of a Hebrew word, *khavrúta*). A pair of yeshiva students who study together, analyzing texts through discussion and debate.

classroom environment: The cohesiveness, satisfaction, goal direction, and related social-psychological properties or climate of the classroom group perceived by students.

clique: A small, exclusive group of individuals.

cognitive apprenticeship: In educational psychology, the teaching of complex skills by immersing the learner in a realistic context in order to ensure that the implicit processes are being learned along with the explicit processes; the learner receives guidance from a "knowledgeable other."

cognitive load theory: In psychology, a theory that due to the limitations of working memory, instructional design should pay special attention to the type (intrinsic, extraneous, or germane) and amount of cognitive load that is imposed on working memory.

cognitive objective: A statement specifying the acquisition of particular knowledge or information.

cognitivism: In psychology, an approach to understanding the mental processes involved in how information is received, processed, organized into an existing schema, and then retrieved upon recall.

cognitivist perspective: See **cognitivism**.

coherence principle: When narration accompanies a message in another modality, the relationship between the two messages must be strong and apparent.

collaborative group: Any small group formed to discuss a significant question or to carry out a project; may work face-to-face or via communications technology. See also **cooperative group**.

communication configuration: The pattern of the flow of information and control among learner, facilitator, and resources during an instructional event.

community of writers: A movement to encourage teachers at all levels to treat writing as a communal activity—establishing structures in the classroom to foster trust among students, e.g., by pairing up and exchanging drafts for peer evaluation and critique. The goal is to establish shared values about good writing, the work that writers do, and respect for others' work.

computer-assisted instruction: An instructional technique in which a learner interacts with a computer containing a stored instructional program designed to inform, guide, control, and test the student until a prescribed level of proficiency is reached.

computer-based: Adj., refers to any activity or function that depends on mediation by a computer system.

computer-based simulation: Computer programs that contain algorithmic, dynamic, simplified models of real-world or hypothetical phenomena that contain features that allow the manipulation of parameters, the testing of questions, and the observation of events.

concrete referent: In General Semantics, the real object or event being referred to in words.

conditions of learning: Conditions internal to the learner (e.g., aptitude, motivations, prior knowledge) and external (arrangement of instructional elements) that must be met for success in instructed learning. Also known as learning requirements.

constructivism: In educational psychology, an amorphous construct without a canonical definition; adherents derive instructional guidelines based on constructivist epistemology—a view that all knowledge is a human and social construction.

cooperative group: A small group formed for face-to-face structured learning activities, conducted as a team; members are individually accountable for their achievement, as is the group as a whole. See also **collaborative group**.

correspondence study: A program provided by an institution under which the institution provides instructional materials, by mail or electronic transmission, and conducts examinations to determine successful completion, to students who are separated from the instructor in space and time. Interaction between the instructor and student is limited, is not regular and substantive, and is primarily initiated by the student.

cultural capital: The general social assets influencing an individual's mobility across socioeconomic strata—such as cultural background, knowledge, disposition, and skills—that are passed on from one generation to the next.

deep learning: A term borrowed from machine programming. In pedagogy, the cognitive skills needed to succeed in the twenty-first century: critical thinking, problem-solving, communication, collaboration, and learning to learn.

deliberate practice: The process of systematically organizing practice to consciously focus on specific subskills.

Demonstration: A communication configuration in which a facilitator, or some instructional resource playing the role of facilitator, displays and explains an example of some concept, process, procedure, or other complex task to a number of learners; the facilitator controls the flow of communication.

depiction: A visual, symbolic, or graphic representation of a person, place, thing, or event.

description: A verbal representation of a person, place, thing, event, or idea.

digital divide: The gap between those who have access to the digital technologies vital to success within the current Information Age society and those who do not. Also, the gap between those who know how to effectively use these technologies to uplift themselves socioeconomically—and those who do not.

Direct Instruction (DI): A specific instructional method for group instruction in which a facilitator presents a small chunk of new material, prompts a choral response in unison, and gives appropriate feedback based on that response.

distal: Located further from the point of interest.

distance education: A program of some duration with specific learning goals, leading to formal recognition of achievement (such as course credit or professional certification), in which the learner is separated from the instructor and in which communication technologies facilitate frequent and substantive dialogue between the remote student(s) and the instructor and possibly among the students themselves.

drill-and-practice: An instructional method for psychomotor skills in which the learner repeats the essential movements in successive practice trials, discovering the kinesthetic cues that signal the difference between error and error-free performance. A similar process may be applied to the practice of cognitive skills.

dual-coding theory: In educational psychology, a theory that both visual and verbal information are processed differently along different neural pathways, creating separately coded representations; both visual and verbal codes can be used when recalling information.

dyad: A group of two people.

educational technology: The study and practice of applying psychological and communication technologies to the processes of teaching and learning.

effort: Exertion of a person's mental, physical, and emotional resources.

emerging technologies: Advanced applications of computer technology that are not yet well incorporated into conventional usage.

expectancy: The belief that one's effort will result in attainment of a desired performance goal.

explicit learning: A class of learning that requires conscious participation and is concerned with acquiring information about people, places, and things. Also known as declarative learning.

Expression: A communication configuration in which a learner creates some type of tangible product in order to process some new knowledge, skill, or attitude; the experience may be structured and/or monitored by a facilitator, but the learner controls what is created and how it is created.

F2F: Face-to-face; instructional settings involving participants present in the same space.

facilitator: A person or device that manages instructional events, selecting instructional objectives and methods, monitoring and guiding learner progress, and assessing achievement.

feedback: In psychology, knowledge of the results of any behavior, considered as influencing or modifying further performance.

fMRI: Functional magnetic resonance imaging; it creates a map of brain functions by creating images derived from nuclear magnetic resonance signals.

format: An example of a larger category of things (e.g., 16-mm film as a format of motion picture or Peer Instruction as a format of discussion) having a specific style or physical features.

frame factor: In systems theory, any of the features of a setting that serve as resources or constraints for actors in that setting.

frame game: A game that has a structure that is clear and robust enough that it can be adapted to deal with different content.

framework: An abstract representation of the concepts involved in a process and the possible connections among them.

game: See **instructional game** and **instructional simulation game**.

gamification: The process of modifying an activity, such as a task, a course, or a training program, to have some of the qualities of a game, such as having ludic elements, having a scoring system, striving toward a challenging goal, and recognition of achievement.

habitus: An individual's embodied intellectual dispositions—their system of internalized structures, schemes of perception, conception, and action—inculcated to them by their home/family influences.

homework: Learners work individually outside of school, typically using assigned reading, writing, and other Expression activities, to practice new material.

implicit learning: A class of learning that does not require conscious participation, usually in the form of habits, perceptual or motor strategies, and associative and nonassociative conditioning. Also known as procedural learning.

instructed learning: The acquisition of new—or the modification of existing—knowledge, skills, or attitudes resulting from the individual's participation in instructional events; learning that is mediated symbolically in planned interactions between facilitators and learners. Contrast with **natural learning**.

instruction: A deliberate effort to provide learners with conditions suitable for achieving specified learning objectives; success criteria include being humane, effective, and efficient.

instructional event: Any occasion during which one or more learners engage in purposive and controlled learning in some setting.

instructional game: A structured, ludic activity in which participants follow prescribed rules that differ from those of real life as they strive to attain a challenging goal, directed toward a specified learning outcome.

instructional method: A generalized pattern of activities that affords learners the opportunity to exercise the cognitive and/or motor and emotional processes necessary to achieve some instructed learning objective.

instructional resources: Materials or devices that carry information relevant to some instructional purpose. Also known as "resources by design."

instructional role-play: A learning activity in which participants act out or perform the part of a person or character.

instructional simulation: An experiential activity involving learners in realistic problems in settings that are scaled-down versions of reality, directed toward a specified learning outcome.

instructional simulation game: An experiential activity involving learners in settings that are modified versions of reality and in which participants follow prescribed rules that differ from those of real life as they strive to attain a challenging goal, directed toward a specified learning outcome.

intelligence: Capacity for learning, reasoning, understanding, and similar forms of mental activity.

intelligent tutoring: A computer-based process of tutoring that offers a semantically connected conceptualization of the content to be taught, a way of knowing what the learner does and does not understand, and a delivery method that adapts to individual performance.

interactive lecture: An oral presentation that is punctuated with audience interaction by means of switching to another configuration, such as Discussion or Repetition.

interpersonal objective: A statement specifying the acquisition of skills involved in the relations among people.

intersectionality: The interconnected nature of key social variables—race, ethnicity, language, class, gender, sexual orientation, gender identity, ability, etc.—applying to a given individual or group, resulting in the creation of overlapping, interdependent, and compounding systems of privilege or oppression.

interteaching: A method of Discussion; in a classroom setting, learners in dyads take turns asking and answering problem-oriented questions based on assigned readings; after discussion they complete a formulaic report of their answer, including unresolved issues. Also known as learning cell. See also **Peer Instruction**.

ism: A distinctive practice, system, or philosophy, typically a political ideology or an artistic movement.

knowledgeable other: Someone who has a better understanding or a higher ability level than the learner, with respect to a particular task, process, or concept.

laboratory: An instructional activity in which the learner is immersed in a problem space in which they are free to explore real-world resources and instructional resources, possibly in collaboration with other learners, making decisions and practicing skills that lead to attainment of some instructed learning goal. A facilitator may structure and/or monitor the experience, but learners are in control of the exploratory process. See also **Problem-Based Learning**.

learner: Anyone who voluntarily enters into an instructional setting and participates in teaching–learning activities.

learner-centered education: An approach based on the understanding that the learning of complex subject matter is an intentional process of constructing meaning from information and experience; therefore, learners exercise control over the nature and sequence of activities.

learning: See **natural learning** and **instructed learning**.

Learning for Mastery (LFM): An instructional method in which individual learners work through the units, getting individual corrective feedback and other sorts of learning guidance; they can advance to the next unit only upon successful completion of the current one. See also **Personalized System of Instruction (PSI)**.

locus-of-control: A personality trait: a person's judgment about how much control they have over their daily experiences.

ludic: Adj., refers to the quality of being fun or playful, not serious.

mass medium (*plural* **media**)**:** Any of the large-scale, industrialized means of communication, such as radio, television, or newspapers, that reach very large numbers of people simultaneously.

maturation: The process of progressing in natural growth and development, excluding changes caused by experience.

medium (*plural* **media**)**:** A communication channel through which signals are transmitted from senders to receivers.

mega-analysis: A statistical procedure for combining data from multiple meta-analyses in order to determine a common effect.

mentoring: A reciprocal and collaborative at-will relationship that most often occurs between a senior and junior employee for the purpose of the mentee's growth, learning, and career development.

meta-analysis: A statistical procedure for combining data from multiple studies; when the treatment effect (or effect size) is consistent from one study to the next, meta-analysis can be used to identify the common effect.
metacognition: Awareness and understanding of one's own thought processes.
method: See **instructional** method.
method, strategic level: An instructional method that is applied at the level of a whole course or whole curriculum, for example, problem-based learning (PBL).
method, tactical level: An instructional method that is applied within one instructional event for one learning phase in a lesson, for example, a simulation exercise in a sales training lesson.
mnemonic: Adj., pertaining to memory and techniques of memorization.
model: A conceptualization in the form of an equation, a physical device, a narrative, or a graphic analog representing a real-life situation either as it is or as it should be.
modified reality setting: A setting, such as a simulation, game, or case study, that has been intentionally designed to simplify or alter the rules of reality in order to focus learners on salient points.
MOOC: Massive Open Online Course; a Web-based course open to anyone and potentially having a huge number of enrolled participants, usually available at no cost.
motivation to learn: A condition that activates and sustains behavior toward a learning goal; it is an emergent phenomenon—it can grow and change over time.
multimedia: Adj., as used in educational psychology: something that includes two or more forms of representation, at least words and pictures. Adj., as used colloquially: a resource or event of dramatic character that includes several forms of representation, usually including music and moving images in addition to words and pictures.
multimodal: Adj., the quality of involving more than two sensory modalities at a time.
natural learning: The acquisition of new—or the modification of existing—knowledge, skills, or attitudes resulting from the individual's interaction with the environment without artificial intervention.
note-taking: During a presentation or during study activities, learners write brief, private notes to summarize their understanding of the material being presented.
overhead projector: An electrical device that projects an enlarged image of a transparency placed on it onto a screen by means of an overhead mirror.
peer influence: Social pressure by members of one's peer group to take a certain action, adopt certain values, or otherwise conform in order to be accepted.
Peer Instruction: A method of Discussion; after a short presentation, listeners are given a challenging conceptual question; after some reflection time, they write their response, which they discuss with nearby peers. After Whole-Class Discussion, the instructor explains the preferred answer and collects the responses. See also **interteaching**.
personal interest: A relatively enduring preference for certain topics, subject areas, or activities.

Personalized System of Instruction (PSI): An instructional method in which individual learners advance through self-paced modularized units of instruction, usually text-based; unit tests are given on each module; learners must score at least 90 percent to progress to the next module; may involve proctors as aides and lectures to supplement the text materials. Also known as the Keller Plan.

portrayal: In educational psychology, an external representation of some object, process, or event in visual, symbolic, or graphic form—not verbal. Also known as **depiction**.

Presentation: A communication configuration in which a facilitator, or some instructional resource playing the role of facilitator, conveys information one-way to a number of learners; the facilitator or instructional resource controls the flow of communication.

privilege: A special right, advantage, or immunity available to a particular individual or group, to which the latter is generally oblivious.

Problem-Based Learning (PBL): an instructional method in which real-world problems are used as the vehicle to promote learner discovery of concepts and principles as opposed to direct presentation of those concepts and principles. See also **laboratory**.

programmed instruction: A format for self-paced study of text material in the form of a book or a mechanical device that presents information in small steps, poses questions requiring a written or multiple-choice response, and provides immediate knowledge of results. Note: spelled as *programed instruction* from 1950s through 1970s.

proximal: Located closer to the point of interest.

psychological state: Transitory feelings and tendencies perceived at a given time; includes expectancies and valuations, situational interest, and motivation to learn.

psychological traits: Quasi-permanent psychological attributes of an individual; includes aspects of personality such as self-efficacy and locus-of-control.

psychomotor objective: A statement specifying the acquisition of some muscular or motor skill, some manipulation of objects, or some act that requires neuromuscular coordination.

real-world resources: People, objects, and events that exist for their own purposes but can be employed for instructional purposes. Also known as "resources by utilization."

recitation: An activity in which learners study independently, then are called upon by the teacher to display what they have learned by reciting or solving problems in front of the class.

reinforcement: A process in which some stimulus, presented immediately following a response, increases the rate at which the response is emitted or increases the probability that the response will recur when the situation recurs. See **reinforcer**.

reinforcer: A stimulus that is presented following a desired behavior that increases the likelihood that the behavior will occur in the future. See **reinforcement**.

Repetition: A communication configuration in which a learner performs repeatedly all or part of a specified skill in order to improve retention and proficiency.

resource: Any material or device that learners interact with during instructional events; they may be **instructional resources** or **real-world resources**.

role-play: See **instructional role-play**.

school environment: The overall circumstances of a school, including the physical plant, equipment, learning resources, demographics and socioeconomic status of parents, language of instruction, admission and graduation standards, staff composition and professional development, curriculum, and organization of instruction (e.g., self-contained classrooms, ability grouping, etc.).

seatwork: An instructional activity in which learners work individually in-class, typically using pencil-and-paper exercises, to practice using the new material.

self-directed learning: An instructional method in which individuals take the initiative in diagnosing their learning needs, formulating learning goals, identifying resources for learning, choosing and implementing appropriate learning strategies, and evaluating learning outcomes.

self-efficacy: A personality trait: a person's judgment about their ability to accomplish a given task.

self-identity: The global understanding a person has of themselves, particularly the recognition of their potential in relation to their social context.

sensory modality: In psychology, the various types of perceptions triggered by stimuli; often used interchangeably with **sense**; thus, the basic sensory modalities include light, sound, taste, temperature, pressure, and smell.

setting: The physical surroundings in which the learner, facilitator, and resources interact.

shiur: (Hebrew term). In a yeshiva, a lesson, typically an oral presentation by a teacher.

signature pedagogy: A characteristic way of teaching peculiar to a given field or profession.

simulation: See **instructional simulation** and **instructional simulation game**.

simulator, physical: A device that enables the user to experience, under realistic conditions, phenomena likely to occur in actual performance.

situational interest: A spontaneous, transitory, and environmentally activated preference for certain topics, subject areas, or activities.

Small-Group Discussion: A communication configuration in which two or more learners exchange information and opinions without the intermediation of a facilitator; a facilitator may set the agenda and control logistics, but learners control the flow of communication within the group.

social cognitive learning perspective: See **social learning theory**.

social learning theory: In psychology, a theory that learning is a cognitive process that takes place in a social context and can occur purely through observation or direct experience, even in the absence of motor reproduction or direct reinforcement. Also known as social cognitive learning theory.

social media: The use of mobile and web-based technologies to create highly interactive platforms through which individuals and communities share, cocreate, discuss, and modify user-generated content, and participate in social networking.

sociocultural environment: The matrix of beliefs, customs, practices, and behavior that exists within a given population's geographical and social setting. It includes the culture that the population was educated or lives in and the individuals and institutions with whom they interact.

socioeconomic status (SES): An individual's or group's position within a hierarchical social structure, which depends on a combination of variables, including occupation, education, income, wealth, and place of residence.

Study: A communication configuration in which a learner interacts with instructional resources, or with real-world resources, or with their own inner resources, without the direct supervision of a facilitator but often inspired or guided by someone playing the role of facilitator. The learner is in control of events, deciding exactly what to do and when to do it.

study group: Voluntary, self-organized groups of students convene outside of class to discuss class topics and support each other's understandings.

synchronous: Happening at the same time.

teacher-centered: Refers to instructional activities in which the facilitator controls the flow of information and makes decisions about the nature and sequence of activities.

teaching machine: Colloquial term for a device that mechanically, electrically, or electronically presents an instructional program at a rate controlled by the learner's response to questions that are posed. See also **programmed instruction**.

technocentrism: A way of thinking characterized by the uncritical acceptance of the proposition that all problems are amenable to technological solutions.

time on task: The amount of time learners spend engaged in instructional events related to specified learning objectives.

tutee: The person who is the learner in a Tutorial configuration.

tutor: The "knowledgeable other" who plays the role of facilitator in a Tutorial configuration.

Tutorial: A communication configuration in which a person or device playing the role of facilitator interacts, intensively and substantively, one-to-one with a learner (or small group of learners acting as one or taking turns); the facilitator (tutor) and learner (tutee) share control of two-way communication.

typology: A systematic classification of objects or events according to their characteristics.

valuation: The individual's perception of how important a task is to them.

Whole-Class Discussion: A communication configuration in which a facilitator engages the whole class in a conversation in which learners take turns sharing information and opinions, with the facilitator remaining at the center, setting the agenda and controlling the flow of communication.

Writing across the Curriculum (WAC): A movement at the elementary, secondary, and postsecondary levels of education aimed at encouraging teachers of all disciplines, not just English, to promote writing skills in their curricular area. See also **Writing to Learn**.

Writing to Learn: An instructional method in which teachers of all subjects assign short, impromptu or otherwise informal and low-stake writing tasks that help students think through key concepts or ideas presented in a course. See also **Writing across the Curriculum (WAC)**.

yeshiva: (Hebrew term). A Jewish educational institution that focuses on the study of traditional religious texts.

Index

ability 44, 53–55, 69–70, 88, 120, 160, 170, 180, 196–197, 204, 206, 247, 271, 289–291, 303–304, 314, 319, 322; average 225; cognitive 41, 63; comprehension 162; criterion 34; goal-scoring 256; grouping 50, 55, 322; high 50, 225, 319; infinite 97; inherent 92; initial 34; innate 124, 250, 262; learners' 104; low 50, 215, 225; native 247; physical 41; powerful 217; semantic 289
Acar, Adam 23–24
access 60, 103–104, 210, 219, 241–242, 272, 311–312, 316; conscious 290; equitable 20, 64, 69; lack of 104, 312; limiting 104; rights of 69; -to-content 20; to knowledge 92; to learning resources 53; to resources 134, 279; to teachers 270
achievement 47, 63, 68, 72–73, 136, 222, 287, 301, 314, 317; academic 33, 39, 40, 47, 51, 59–61, 63, 69, 72, 97; dominant 53; hierarchy 50; learners' 31, 73; learning 33, 35; levels of 262; motivation 204; prior 41, 53; recognition of 16, 134, 318; school 60; student 7, 45, 55–56, 69, 72–74; successful 68
activity 47, 83, 96–97, 112–114, 120, 122, 129, 154, 187, 201, 205, 236–237, 246, 249, 255, 262, 266, 281, 284, 316, 318, 321; communal 315; concluding the 255; conducting the 254; core 137, 149; culminating 279; game 233; electrical 195; experiential 111, 140, 205, 318; framing the 253; fun 238; heuristic 254; human 270; instructional 41, 92, 114, 118, 196, 201, 224, 249, 319, 322; inter- 24; introducing the 254; learner-centered 253; learning 99, 116, 133, 198, 284, 318; major 243; mental 40, 318; neural 304; objective of the 254; post- 260; presentation 159; rhetorical 308; segments 114; sequence of the 281, 295; shared 66; social 194; structures 112, 116; study 225; teacher-centered 253; voluntary 98; *see also* ludic
Adler, Mortimer J. 205
affective objective 155, 198, 305, 314
affordance 26, 33, 65, 111, 128, 130–131, 133–134, 305, 314; communication 130; of moving pictures 131; of pictorial information 131, 134; of verbal interaction 133; sensory 131; symbolic 134; technological 66
Alexander the Great 179, 269
American Civil War 149, 157, 308
American Educational Research Association (AERA) 24
amount of invested mental energy (AIME) 42, 224, 237, 314
analysis 72, 158, 187, 235, 254, 273, 281, 292, 295; critical 10, 220; deep 72; evidence-based 31; habits of 235;

Index

input 273; longitudinal 56; statistical 241, 283; systematic 239; systemic 38; *see also* mega-analysis; meta-analysis
Anderson, Lorin 43
Anderson, Terry 19
APA Task Force on Psychology in Education 86, 100
aptitude 31, 38–39, 40–41, 94, 112, 314, 316; high 303; intellectual 41; physical 41
Aristotle 162, 179, 269, 298
artificial intelligence 1, 217, 226
Aspinwall, William B. 243
Association for Educational Communications and Technology (AECT) 10–11, 18, 69, 93; Task Force on Definition and Terminology 18, 93, 300
Association for Supervision and Curriculum Development (ASCD) 42
asynchronous 14, 132, 175, 191–193, 200, 207, 216, 285, 314
attainment 46, 74, 93, 259, 317, 319; educational 60, 73
audiovisual 113, 143, 145, 169; content 22; education 299; educators 10; era 240; experience 7, 9; format 165, 295; material 217, 272; presentation 167; production staff 5; recordings 134, 145; researchers 153; resources 104, 279; showmanship 165; showing 169; shows 131; technologies 26; units 271; *see also* medium
auditory 85, 111, 145, 156; learning 150–152; processing 152–155, 169, 244, 288–289, 295; resources 7, 152
augmented reality 1, 20, 25
autism spectrum disorder (ASD) 87
autonomy 48, 67; individual 58; student 49
AutoTutor 217, 227

background 86, 96, 125, 169, 205, 229, 288; common 287; cultural 51, 316; diverse 198; family 61; marginalized 57–58; socioeconomic 59, 97, 192
Banas, John A. 49
Bandura, Albert 42, 45, 54, 88, 180, 185, 245
Barron, Ann E. 152
behavior 49, 61, 63, 67, 70, 84–85, 88, 123, 183, 202, 237, 248–249, 270, 285, 287, 314, 317, 320–322; change 191; complex 173, 176; conscious 84; democratic 198; desired 119, 123, 156, 216, 221, 237, 258–259, 261, 321; experiments 84–85; future 252; good 53; habitual 256; human 88, 93, 270, 314; learned 85; learning theory 209; maladaptive 84; modeling 55–57, 62, 64, 88, 118, 138, 156, 161, 173, 176–182, 184–185, 225, 234, 277, 305, 314; negative 200; new 122; observable 89, 185; observations 27; online 21; of organisms 83; of others 88; outward 83; patterns 244; principle 216; psychologists 83, 89, 304; reflex 83; reinforcing 83; repertoire 118, 181–182; responses 252, 295; right 178, 269; student 270; target 88, 180, 249; teacher 49, 54, 73; theorist 221; therapy 84; voting 24
behaviorism 83–84, 314; displaced 307; principles of 83; radical 83
behaviorist 88, 119; instructional principles 307; perspective 83, 123, 314; principles of learning 307; theory 84, 87
Belief-Expectancy-Control (BEC) framework 48
Belleza, Francis S. 165, 276
Berliner, David C. 34, 70, 112, 114, 116, 305
Bertolero, Max 40, 83, 98, 289, 304
Betrus, Anthony Karl 102, 268
Biech, Elaine 99
bimodal 149, 314; combinations 157; instructed learning 12; learning 11, 134, 156; presentation 132
biologically: determined 45; primary knowledge 125; primary learning 90, 304, 314; secondary communication skills 125; secondary knowledge 118; secondary learning 90–92, 304, 314
blockchain 1, 21
blogs 20, 22, 135, 204, 295
Bloom, Benjamin 217, 221
Bonk, Curtis J. 16, 216
Bourdieu, Pierre 51, 61–62
Bowers, C. A. 58
Bowles, Samuel 62
Boyce, Thomas E. 209
brainstorming 111, 169–170, 190, 192, 200–201, 206, 209, 291, 315
Broca, Pierre Paul 151, 154–155, 288
Brookfield, Stephen D. 194, 197–198, 206
Bruner, Jerome S. 84–85, 90, 98, 160, 178, 180
Brunsma, David L. 72
buzz group 111, 139, 167, 191, 206, 209, 307, 315

California Community Colleges Chancellor's Office 68
Campus Technology 17
Carmichael, Peter 308
Carnegie unit 68, 274
Carroll, John B. 70
case method 129, 235, 253, 255, 257, 315
chalk talk 145
chavrusa 148, 193, 315
civilization 240, 287; ancient 261; Athenian 286; human 314; Western 23, 286
Clark, Richard E. 6–7, 18, 48, 135–136, 248
Clark, Ruth Colvin 144, 159, 163–164, 247
classroom environment 38, *44*, 48, *59*, 61–62, 64–65, *302*, 302–303, 315
Classwide Peer Tutoring (CWPT) 215, 225, 227
clique, 50, *59*, 61, 315
coaching 139, 181, 183, 185, 214, 224, 245–246, 248, 260–262; athletic 214, 226, 260; executive 184; physical 260; *see also* cognitive
Code of Federal Regulations (CFR) 14–15
cognitive: ability 41, 63, 123–124; activities 40; angle 66; apprenticeship 139, 179–181, 185, 315; capabilities 274; capacity 86; coaching 226, 260; competition 164; complexity 255; components 98, 244, 246; comprehension 181; constructivist 66; development 45; disabilities 64; domain 10, 41, 124, 155, 162, 196–197, 249; equilibration 66; flexibility 220; function 40, 82; games 113; growth 287; information processing (CIP) 248; knowledge 197, 259; learning 40, 87, 98, 124–125, 152, 290, 322; load theory 86, 163–164, 246, 304, 315; neuroscience 153, 269; objection 285; objective 117, 133, 159, 167, 197–198, 241, 259, 315; operations 153; organization 6; overload 163, 165, 170; performance 40; practice 262; processes 6, 35, 48, 108, 126, 130, 136, 138, 140, 153, 169, 245, 272, 290, 318, 322; psychologists 11, 83–84, 89; psychology 85, 111, 153, 287, 303–304; research 85, 153, 244; revolution 191, 194, 272, 307; science 35, 84–85, 149–150, 153–154, 157, 169, 180–181, 185, 194, 219, 224, 244, 273, 275, 287; skills 45, 88, 98, 122–123, 134, 155, 183, 225, 229–230, 247, 250, 258–259, 261–262, 291, 295, 316–317; stage 181;
stimulation 87; strategy 138, 272, 275, 279, 291, 293; structure 163–164, 196, 223, 249; support 92, 118; systems 152; tasks 83, 246; theory 88, 221, 303–304, 308; underpinnings 279
cognitivism 315
cognitivist perspective 86, 119, 123, 315
Cohen, Elizabeth G. 50
coherence: condition 158, 273; principle 158, 273, 315
Cole Neurocognition Lab 95
Coleman, James S. 59
collaborative group 66, 315
Comenius, Johann Amos 148–149, 218, 236, 244, 272, 274, 298
Committee of Ten 286
communication: affordances 130; asynchronous 192; bias of 23; change 23; channels 22–23, 103, 110, 305, 319; clear 1, 3, 95, 195; configurations 2–3, 16, 26–27, 103–105, 108–109, 117, 126, 128–130, 135, 138, 141, 143, 147, 150, 169, 173, 190, 197, 209–210, 266, 281, 305–307, 315–317, 321–323; delivery channels 300; easy 198; everyday 64; face-to-face 62; flow 110, 117, 119–121, 141, 143, 169, 174, 187–189, 209, 316, 321–323; games 233; human 3, 110; interpersonal 233; landscape 22; learning-related 216; mass 7; media 109, 117, 159; mediated 215–216; one-to-one 216; one-way 112, 117, 134, 143, 204, 214; oral 109, 125, 287; patterns of 2, 82, 95, 103, 105, 108–111, 113–114, 116, 120, 129; peer-to-peer 216; person-to-person 195, 219; process 110; professional 3, 305; research 4; respectful 198; skills 125, 140; spoken 178; symbolic 95; technologies 11, 16, 134, 315, 317; theory of 110; two-way 122, 213, 323; voice 192; voluminous 214; wireless 14; written 125, 287
community of writers 292, 294–295, 315
competence 48; acquisition of 135; academic 45
comprehension 66, 154, 159, 189, 212, 232; deeper 134; language 151, 154, 169, 174, 181, 195, 219, 288–289; learner 162; reading 154; speech 154, 197; student 259; *see also* cognitive
computer 6, 11, 25, 85, 128, 134–135, 191–192, 208, 222, 227, 238–239, 257, 271–272, 279, 285, 298, 315; advocates 227;

animations 131; applications 21–22; delivery 261; games 238–239; gaming industry 58; -generated slideshow 117; hardware 101; interaction 20; media 131; -mediated 153, 192; model 85; operator 257; personal 13; programs 110, 123, 126, 230, 252, 316; projection 131; science 17; -scored exercises 17; simulation 173, 257; software 92, 252; technology 117, 219, 317
computer-assisted: instruction 216, 219, 226, 315; intelligent tutoring 137, 226
computer-based 316; distance education 192; drill-and-practice program 18; entertainment games 261; forms 63; games 102, 239; instruction 7; instructional games 238; instructional simulation 233, 240; intelligent tutoring 227; leisure games 238; lessons 217; media 63; physics simulation 18; process 318; program 183; simulation 139, 261, 316; word-processing software 125
concrete referent 155, 316
conditioning: classical 83; nonassociative 318; operant 83, 248, 253
conditions of learning 94, 316
Connell, James P. 60
constructivism 11, 86, 115, 272, 303, 316; social 66
control-based learning theory (COBALT) 244–245
Cooley, William W. 34
cooperation 49, 64, 154, 203, 288, 305
cooperative group 115–116, 315–316
correspondence study 8, 12–13, 17, 68, 134, 191, 268, 284–285, 316
Coursera 17
Craik, Kenneth 153
Crenshaw, Kimberle 52–53, 61–62
critical scholars 57
Crowder, Norman A. 216
Csikszentmihalyi, Mihaly 55, 161
Cuban, Larry 4–5, 24–25, 49, 223
cultural capital 47, 51–54, 57, 60–63, 316
curricula 5, 37, 91, 257, 271; challenging 55; core 295; education 239; training 136
curriculum 50, 60, 69, 71, 92, 136, 140, 205, 218, 235, 286–287, 295, 322; academic 238; art across the 293; choices 50; classical 149; college 219, 293; elementary school 239, 286; externally imposed 47; historical 286; plan 205; planners 70, 99; whole 136, 166, 320; writing across the (WAC) 292, 295, 323

Dale, Edgar 299
dance 103, 117, 125, 133, 146, 281, 286–287, 289–290, 295; composition 293; go-go 9; interpretive 284; master 286; partner 134; production of 289; routines 125
Davies, Ivor K. 111–112, 116, 167, 257
Dean, Ceri B. 42, 207
debriefing 111, 130, 139, 190, 205, 208–209, 254–255, 258, 260, 262
decision 50, 69, 117, 234, 237, 254, 259, 293, 304; crucial 111; difficult 235; final 201; making 154, 229, 234, 319, 323; mental 179; phase 201; process 130; rational 68; tree 305
deductive: approach 137, 258; concept teaching 137, 138, 170
deep learning 223–224, 305, 316
deliberate practice 247, 256, 316
demographics 23, 53, 312, 322; characteristics 74; data 240; descriptors 199; features 64
demonstration 2, 24, 27, 100, 104, 111, 113–116, 118–119, 126–127, 130–131, 137–138, 141, 143, 146, 148, 167–168, 173–174, 176–178, 180–185, 187, 197, 204, 212, 217–218, 225, 229, 236, 242, 256–257, 277, 291, 305–306, 312, 316; configuration 128, 131, 148, 174–178, 183, 185; dramatic 185; evolution of 178; experimental 174; functions 135; learning by 178; motor-skills 177, 185; power of 118; video 88, 132, 251
Department of Audio-Visual Instruction (DAVI) 10
Department of Education's Office for Civil Rights (OCR) 311
depiction 157, 181, 316, 321; visual 158
description 26–27, 100, 112, 117, 129, 157, 181, 189, 199, 248, 255, 257, 277, 304, 316; brief 114; functional 299; impersonal 287; learner-centered 100; verbal 235; visual 158; written 155
Dewey, John 42, 46, 194
digital 147; age typology 115; applications 23; audiovisual media 134; badges 21; data 85; devices 132, 134; divide 52–53, 316; forms of instruction 86; images 103; information 101; instructional resources 102; marketplace 21; media 134–135; natives 1; peers 124; phase 58; recordings 102; resources 102; slide presentation

146; storage 151; technologies 1, 26, 316; texts 103, 281
Direct Instruction (DI) 137, 221, 256, 262, 316, 322
discovery 114–116, 130, 137–138, 151, 168, 219, 237, 248, 258, 321
discussion 22, 197; *see also* small-group discussion; whole-class discussion
distal 37–38; causes 32, 71; factors 33, 36, 43, 59, 63–64, 66–67, 302–303, 316; influence 43
distance education 1, 12, 14–16, 27, 68, 103, 109, 115, 121, 124, 126, 134–135, 141, 144–147, 161, 175, 191–193, 200, 204, 206, 210, 216, 241, 252, 279, 284–285, 291, 317
drill-and-practice 18, 114, 139, 219, 237, 239–240, 259, 317
Driscoll, Marcy P. 86, 93–94, 96, 249
dual-coding theory 85, 153–154, 156, 317
Dudley-Marling, Curt 190, 194
Dusek, Val 3
dyad 190–191, 193, 208–210, 212–213, 317, 319

Edison, Thomas 5, 24
educational: activities 68, 91; adoption 25; areas 25; attainment 60; beliefs 57; benefits 13; consequences 59; disadvantaged 256; discourse 100; entities 14; evaluation 35; experience 16, 52; experimentation 21; films 24; games 239; goal 196, 251; innovations 26, 221–222; institutions 12, 47, 67, 68, 91–92, 97, 99, 125, 134, 219, 311–312, 323; intentions 16; leaders 69, 311; levels 41, 237, 275, 291; material 276; media 10; method 149, 227, 270; objectives 162, 249; opportunities 68, 91, 274; philosophy 98, 136; policy 50, 67; problem 24; processes 2; productivity 35; program 8, 12, 69, 136; psychology 11, 18, 82, 85, 90, 299, 315–317, 320–321; purposes 193, 210; reform 72; research 2, 7, 9, 11, 25, 31, 33, 35, 46, 67, 68, 190, 276; resources 16, 20; settings 49, 205, 248; shifts 215; standpoint 22; system 2, 51, 53, 62, 311; technology 1, 18–20, 24–27, 58, 100, 116, 208, 212, 299–301, 307, 317; television broadcasts 177; tool 236; value 189, 240
edX 17
effort 39, 42–47, 51, 58, 60–63, 65, 71, 74, 90, 93–94, 102, 105, 114, 136, 184, 196, 198, 214–215, 219, 221–222, 224, 229, 240, 254, 260, 268, 275, 302–303, 317–318; conscious 81, 85, 90, 93, 105, 153, 301, 314; individual 124; instructional 97; investing 81, 93, 100, 198; learner 42; major 35; mental 48, 164; national 222; notions of 70; periodic 6; reinforcing 42; serious 13; sustained 42; unifying 81
Egalite, Anna J. 60
e-learning 20
electroencephalography (EEG) 195
Elementary and Secondary Education Act (ESEA) (1965) 237, 295
Ellis, Rod 94
Ellson, Douglas G. 215, 221
emerging technologies xiv, 1, 4, 18–19, 21, 25, 27, 53, 58, 300–301, 317
energy poverty 104
Engelmann, Siegfried 221, 256
entertainment 4–5, 22, 63–64, 190, 237, 240, 261
Erasmus, Desiderius 270–271, 279
Ericsson, K. Anders 247
ethnic; identity 97; minority 50, 61
ethnicity 197, 204, 319
evaluation 201, 239, 254, 290–291; criteria 281; district-by-district 74; educational 35; end-of-course 128; peer 294, 315; self- 226, 275, 279; study 7
Exner, Sigmund 155, 288
expectancy 46, 54, 71, 317; -value theory 46; *see also* belief
explicit learning 84, 90, 93, 301, 304, 317
Expo 67 9
expression 2, 20, 27, 94, 104, 114–117, 123, 125–130, 133–135, 140–141, 148, 154, 167–168, 207, 209, 225, 242, 255, 257, 277–279, 281–282, 284–288, 290–295, 305–307, 317–318; artistic 91, 293; creative 287; facial 103; of affection 60; self- 119, 125, 286–287, 293

Facebook 21, 23, 64
face-to-face (F2F) 132, 145–147, 160, 210, 213–214, 261, 291, 311–312, 315–317; classroom 68, 101, 129, 192, 214, 242; communications 62; discussions 22; educational institution 134, 141, 146; instruction 15, 144, 147, 311; lectures 55; meetings 132; practice 242; programs 13; settings 271; tutorials 132, 213
facilitator 2, 5, 31, 33, 43, 47–50, 54–58, 66–67, 69, 81–82, 95–100, 103–105,

108–110, 116–126, 135, 140, 143–144, 147, 163, 167, 169, 174, 185, 187–190, 193, 198, 208–209, 212–214, 226–227, 229–230, 241, 253, 259, 267, 278, 281–282, 295, 302–305, 308, 315–319, 321–323

feedback 66, 110, 123–125, 139, 147–148, 159, 161, 184, 189, 191, 203, 212, 214, 217, 226, 230–233, 239, 241, 246, 248, 252–253, 269, 271, 274, 284, 291, 293, 306, 317; abundant 292; appropriate 135, 183, 217, 222, 224, 252, 256, 262, 316; conditions of 119; constant 94, 287; constructive 224, 278, 294; corrective 91, 196, 217, 221–222, 229–232, 250, 260, 277, 319; device-controlled 252; evaluative 12; expert 183, 242; explanatory 252; helpful 239; individualized 227; interpersonal 252; practice-and- 57, 249; precise 94; prerecorded 226; prompt 65; proprioceptive 245; quality 222; routine 259

Fleming, Malcolm 153, 157–158, 161

format 111, 116–117, 147, 155, 163, 203, 208, 212, 215–216, 225, 237–238, 295, 315, 317, 321; audiovisual 165; common 282; discussion 197; game 252; growing 103; ideal 149; lecture 253; media 147; mediated 99; obvious 144, 213; recitation 244; simulation-game 240; structured 200

frame 82, 160, 175, 258; conceptual 166; factor 33, 43, 56, 67, 70–71, 104, 317; game 238, 317; informational 216; numeral 175; of reference 96, 303

framework 1, 20, 26, 32–38, 41, 43, 61, 67, 71, 74, 81–82, 113, 136, 154, 167, 202, 227, 232, 238, 255, 292, 295, 301–303, 308, 317; Christian 308; competitive 238; comprehensive 34, 301; conceptual 3, 32, 34; corporate 34; evidenced-based 74; holistic 111; limitations of the 33; mental 154, 170; motivational 279; organizational 223; pedagogical 128; philosophical 2; practical 48; socioeconomic 53; structural 32; system-based 37; technological 57; verbal-visual 27, 31, 37, 74

Freeman, Andrew A. 160
Freire, Paulo 66
Frick, Theodore W. 2–3, 95–97, 99, 101, 104

functional magnetic resonance imaging (fMRI) 48, 82, 85, 151, 289, 304, 317
funding 67–68

Gagné, Robert M. 94, 96, 109–111, 113, 116, 147, 166, 259, 306
Gagnon, Monika Kin 9
Gaider, David 58
game 4, 20, 23, 111–112, 115, 123, 130, 133, 139, 160, 190, 208, 229, 231–233, 236–240, 255, 258, 260–262, 281, 317–318, 320; activity 233; algorithm 240; board 237; business 241; card 237; childhood 237; cognitive 113; communication 233; computer-based 102, 238–239, 261; context 205; designs 125, 238; educational 239; exer- 239; football 88; format 252; individual 239; learning 113; multimedia 133; multiplayer 219; parlor 238; play 208, 238–239, 260; recreational 238; serious 240, 260; simulation 4, 111, 130, 205, 232–233, 237, 240–241, 254–255, 292; traditional 233; video 233, 238, 240, 252; *see also* frame; instructional
gamification 239, 318
Gardner, Howard 40
Geake, John G. 87, 90, 304
Geary, David C. 90, 118, 125, 304
gender 51–52, 58, 63–64, 97, 197, 199, 204, 319
Giroux, Henry A. 53, 62–63
Gius, Mark 73
Gladwell, Malcolm 247
Glaser, Robert 135
Goldschmid, Marcel 191, 209
Goodale, Melvyn A. 153
great recession (2008) 312
Greenspan, Stanley I. 87
Greenwood, Charles 248
Guthrie, Edwin R. 248

habitus 47, 51, 53, 57, 60–62, 318
Hambrick, David Z. 247, 250, 303
Harkness Discussion 205
Harvard Law School 235
Hattie, John A. C. 36, *37*, 37–38, 47, 49, 54–56, 59, 61–63, 71, 73–74, 252–253, 301
Hayakawa, Samuel I. 155
health; education 8; good 70; professionals 235, 242; sciences 242; student 67, 70
Heinich, Robert 114, 233, 255
Hidi, Suzanne 46
Hoffer, Eric 271

330 Index

home: and family influences 38, 59–60; environment 46, 59–60, 125
homework 63, 70, 99, 104, 110–111, 133, 168, 231, 260, 271, 318; assignments 101, 193, 206, 267; supervised 60
Hovland, Carl I. 162
How People Learn II (*HPLII*) 35, 37, 47–49, 56, 59, 63, 67, 71, 301
Huitt, William G. 34, 37–38, *38*, 43, 301
Huizinga, Johan 237
Hutcheson, Francis 179

identity 52, 300; cultural 60, 303; ethnic 97; gender 319; group 203; problems 18, 22; *see also* self
implicit learning 83–84, 88, 301, 304, 318
Industrial Age 286
Industrial Revolution 58
Information Age 25, 52–53, 316
Ingle, Yolanda R. 71
Innis, Harold 23
innovations 50, 112, 191, 194, 227; educational 26, 221–222; effective 256; instructional 239; revolutionary 4; successful 215; systemic 222; technological 25, 175, 223, 300; tutoring 227
Instagram 64
institutions 55, 68–69, 92, 311, 322; academic 180; educational 12, 47, 67–68, 91–92, 97, 125, 219, 242, 311–312; federal aid 13; postsecondary 311; public 312
instruction: aspects of 26; classroom 5, 42, 135, 159, 209; computer-assisted 216, 219, 226, 315; computer-based 7; concept of 93, 136; conscious 118, 125; conventional 240, 301; cost-efficient 219; deliberate 11; designing 2, 302; direct 137, 221, 256, 262, 316, 322; domain of 105; effective 17, 95, 221; elements of 43, 74–75, 82, 95, 100, 103–104, 299, 303, 305, 313; events of 147, 306; face-to-face 144, 147, 311; field of 3, 100; improvement of 24; individualized 41, 98, 222, 225; individually prescribed 137; language 50, 301, 322; large-group 131, 223; live 15; methods of 6, 44, 130, 173, 194; modes of 109, 111, 159, 182; motivational 48; online 8, 14, 312; peer 54, 137, 191, 208–210, 317, 319–320; personalized system of 137, 277, 321; planned 32, 114; process of 27, 95, 105; programmed 110–112, 216, 221–222, 321, 323; purpose of 81, 93; quality of 42–43, 60, 74; science of 90; self- 110; teacher-centered 212, 227; televised 8; theory 1, 248; tutorial 12, 135, 218, 219, 221, 226; underpin 1; verbal 149; well-designed 17
instructional: activities 6, 34, 38–39, 42, 52, 54, 73, 92, 99, 113–114, 118, 131, 196, 201, 224, 249, 273, 306, 312, 319, 322–323; approaches 50, 129, 302–303, 305; choice 55, 104; conditions 31, 33, 94, 155, 158, 222; design 2, 13–14, 18, 26, 86, 93, 105, 111, 115, 135, 152, 159, 183, 299, 305, 307, 315; elements 94, 316; event 2, 11, 26, 34, 54, 55, 72, 82, 89, 95–97, 99, 101–105, 108, 114, 126, 136, 141, 147, 208, 229, 232, 305–306, 315, 317–318, 320–321, 323; format 111, 113, 116; game 140, 208, 232, 233, 237–238, 252, 258, 261, 318; implication 4; interventions 2, 87, 92, 94, 158, 300–301, 304; materials 14–15, 110, 146, 237, 271, 316; method 2, 18, 54–58, 69, 130, 133, 136, 141, 148, 194, 205, 218, 260, 262, 279, 302, 308, 315–323; mode 95, 101, 103; objectives 31, 117, 159, 181, 305, 317; planning 98, 105, 305; practices 69, 73; principles 26, 307; process 23, 27, 150; quality 14, 56; resources 101–102, 117–118, 124, 134, 143, 174, 258, 266–267, 273, 278–279, 299, 316, 318–319, 321, 323; role-play 318, 322; setting 33, 94, 97, 101, 299, 317, 319; simulation 140, 233, 240, 258, 318, 322; simulation game 240, 258, 261, 318, 322; strategies 12, 33, 57, 100, 129, 219; theorists 81, 109, 126; time 101, 112, 281; tools 64, 130, 151; treatments 50, 300; videos 18, 140, 231, 267 *see also* interaction
intelligence 33–34, 39–41, 163, 314, 318; artificial 1, 21, 217, 226; collective 207, 210; -gathering 205; verbal 40
intelligent tutoring 137, 217, 226–227, 318
interaction 15, 23, 35, 66, 69, 95–96, 103, 105, 109, 112, 128, 131, 133, 167, 192–193, 202, 204, 210, 213, 216, 274, 316; asynchronous 192; audience 318; central 38; combinations of 95; conceptual 207; human 234; human–computer 20; individual's 89, 105, 320; instructional 2; learner 17, 38; meaningful 192; pattern 110; peer 66, 119; person-to-person 131; planned 95, 318; players' 240; social

22, 52, 62, 88, 124, 164, 209, 270, 274; student 207; styles 64; substantive 12–14, 68; teaching–learning 33; teacher–student 177, 189; true 134; two-way 132; verbal 133; vicarious 204; visible 116; whole-class 190
interactive lecture 139, 167, 170, 204, 250, 262, 318
Internet Research Agency (IRA) 24
interpersonal objective 198, 242, 319
intersectionality 47, 51–53, 57, 61–62, 319
interteaching 139, 191, 208, 210, 319–320
intrinsic 9, 86, 164, 315; motivation 47–48

James, William 43, 85–86, 270, 298
Johnson, Sandra 195, 220
Johnson-Laird, Philip N. 153
Junco, Reynol 65

Kandel, Eric R. 82–84, 90
Kaplan, Andreas M. 22
Kavanagh, Sam 25
Keller, John M. 48, 251
Kennedy, John F. 73
Kietzmann, Jan H. 22, 64
kindergarten 99, 102, 236–237
Kindermann, Thomas A. 61
knowledge 6, 42, 51, 66, 81, 85, 88–90, 98, 105, 122, 159–160, 179, 196, 216, 236, 241, 248–249, 271–272, 276, 290–291, 300–301, 304, 307, 315–318, 320–321; access to 92; accumulation of 269; base 260, 300; cognitive 197, 259; construction 66, 100, 189; content-level 65; cultural 60; declarative 260, 273–274, 305, 307–308; development 66; dissemination 12, 25; expert 91; inert 42, 134; integration of 126; interpretation of 223; intuitive 260; lesson 167, 170; necessary 223; new 27, 35, 42, 55, 70, 98–99, 111, 119–120, 125–126, 133, 137, 160, 166–167, 170, 181, 183, 190, 196, 207, 224, 249, 260, 282; organized 2; primary 125; prior 39, 42, 47, 94, 97, 122, 133, 147, 196, 229, 257, 306, 314, 316; reproducing 223; secondary 118; secondhand 225; specified 43, 93, 259, 271; subject 41, 53; superior 99; target 119; transmission of 286; usable 195, 274; useful 134; working 180
knowledgeable other 105, 191, 212–213, 231, 315, 319, 323
Knowles, Malcolm S. 271

Koffka, Kurt 153
Köhler, Wolfgang 153
Konnikova, Maria 17
Korzybski, Alfred 155
Kozma, Robert B. 6, 135
Krakauer, John W. 245
Kraus, Nina 151–152
Kuh, George D. 56

laboratory 110, 115–116, 138, 149, 175, 189, 205, 242, 261, 274, 319
language 45, 84, 151–152, 197, 239, 288, 295, 319; areas 155, 288; body 103, 161, 213, 252; centers 154; comprehension 151, 154, 169, 174, 181, 195, 219, 289; conversational 288; fluency 60; foreign 152, 210, 231, 243, 247, 301; French 180; human 151; inconsistent 300; instruction 301, 322; laboratory 123, 138, 231; learning 102, 111, 191, 214; majority 50; minority 50, 61; native 90, 197, 243; natural 217; of cognitive psychology 111; of instruction 50; oral 269; production 151, 154, 195, 219, 288; programming 219; second- 31, 94–95; sign 151; spoken 90, 288–289; vocal 178; written 90, 148
Laurillard, Diana 308
Lazarsfeld, Paul F. 4
learner: achievement 31, 35, 73; aptitude 60, 94, 112, 230; attention 48, 55, 134, 152, 183, 271, 291; attributes 33; behavior 21, 123, 216; -centered education 86, 319; curiosity 47; distant 13, 38; expectancies 46, 61, 65, 302–303; guidance 13, 147–148, 248; habitus 47, 51, 61–62; interaction 17, 38; mental state 46, 307; motivation 49–51, 214, 252, 271, 316; performance 33, 135, 221–222, 241, 252; sense of self-efficacy 48, 54; sensory systems of 7; sociocultural environment 53, 60–61
learning: for mastery (LFM) 50, 137, 277, 279, 319; guidance 147–148, 277, 306, 319; interaction 33; management systems (LMS) 20, 146; objects 20
limitations 26, 33, 55, 111, 124, 129, 132, 136, 141, 159, 161, 169–170, 181–182, 195–196, 220, 222, 238, 248, 250, 273–274, 290, 315; potential 197; technical 25
Lincoln, Abraham 160
locus-of-control 45–46, 51, 302–303, 319, 321
ludic 112, 237, 258, 319; activity 140, 233, 258, 318; element 261, 318

Mace, Cecil Alec 270
Mager, Robert F. 42
mass media 4, 23, 46, 63, 303
Massive Open Online Courses (MOOCs) 1, 16–17, 20, 27, 145–147, 206–208, 210, 320
maturation 45, 319; level 34, 45–46, 51, 57, 302–303; processes 45; stage 45
Mayer, Richard E. 11, 156–157, 158, 252, 273
McCombs, Barbara L. 86
McIlrath, Deborah A. 34, 43
McIntosh, Peggy 52–53, 61–62
McKeachie, Wilbert J. 163, 194, 293
media, medium 4, 7, 12, 103, 135, 152, 287; audiovisual 85, 134, 170; different 301; expressive 161
mega-analysis 36–37, 49, 54, 73–74, 319
memorization 140, 231–232, 243, 260, 262, 320
mentoring 97, 122, 214, 224, 226–227, 281, 319
merit pay 72–73
Merrill, M. David 2–3, 6, 41, 93–96, 99–101, 103, 143, 145, 157, 183, 185, 246
meta-analysis 22, 35–36, 62, 68, 217, 221–222, 253, 301, 320
metacognition 183, 272, 279, 320
method 2, 111, 129–130, 135–136, 138, 141, 181, 189, 191, 198, 206–207, 209, 214, 235, 244, 248, 253, 257, 259, 273, 278, 299, 306–307, 315, 319–320; common 144; delivery 217, 318; discovery 130; educational 149, 166, 227; effective 168, 294; fishbowl 204; gallery walk 208; instructional 55, 130, 136, 173, 315–323; lecture 130, 148, 166–167, 170, 198, 216; Montessori 138; pedagogical 235; scientific 25; skills practice 184; stand-alone 225; strategic level 116, 166; structured 190, 209; supplementary 218; tactical level 320; think-pair-share 209; tutorial 176, 218; whole-class 219; see also instructional
Mitra, Sugata 208
mnemonic 124, 140, 165, 170, 268, 276, 278–279, 320
modality 158, 273, 315; principle 158; sensory 153, 155–156, 158, 322
model 12–13, 33–35, 48, 55–56, 70, 88, 118, 132, 151, 173, 175, 177, 179, 183, 202–203, 215, 234, 253, 269, 320; anatomical 175; behavior 173, 179–180; classroom 243; computer 85; Cooley-Lohnes 34; dynamic 176; information-processing 87; mechanical 173; mental 41; multifactorial 247; of reality 233; oversize 175; pedagogical 66; physical 175; process 32; recitation 243; role 170, 180, 214, 269; seminar 205; simplistic 35; static 175; study 13; verbal-visual 35, 37, 39, 56; visual mental 157; Walberg's 39; working 176, 181
modified reality 232–233, 257–258; activities 254; formats 261; conditions 258; setting 133, 320
Molenda, Michael 5, 14, 110–116, 216, 219; –Subramony Framework 32, 302
Montaigne, Michel de 270–271, 279, 298
Montessori, Maria 45, 222; movement 236; schools 237; see also method
Moore, Dudley 103
motion graphics 176
motivation to learn 44, 46–51, 54, 62, 302–303, 320–321
Multi-Image 10–11
multimedia 1, 8–12, 18, 27, 126, 133, 149, 156, 240, 273, 281, 283, 300, 304, 308, 320
multimodal 149–150, 156–157, 169, 273, 320

NASA 4
National Academies of Sciences, Engineering, and Medicine 35, 47–49, 67, 247, 301
National Assessment of Educational Progress 35
National Association of Elementary School Principals 54
National Education Association 70
National Institute of Information Technology (NIIT) 208
National Policy Board for Educational Administration (NPBEA) 69
National Research Council 35, 249, 301
natural learning 35, 83, 89, 94–95, 189, 301, 318–320
neural: activities 169, 304; channels 85; circuitry 84; connections 275; entrainment 195; fingerprint 98; functions 295; modules 152; networks 40, 83, 220; oscillations 195, 220; pathways 83, 95, 174, 195, 219, 301, 304, 317; processing 11, 154, 181, 185, 195, 219; synchronization 210

neurological 32, 157–158; bases 154; development 90, 304; functioning 308; imaging technology 261; pathways 89; processes 149, 152, 169, 298; system 298
neurons 82, 180, 244, 308; cortical 195; mirror 88, 180, 185
note-taking 140, 168, 170, 278, 288, 294–295, 320

Olson, David R. 6
open educational resources (OER) 16, 20
Open University (OU) 13
opportunity 34, 108, 120, 130, 132, 134, 136, 183–185, 195–196, 214, 221, 226, 230, 251, 274–275, 314, 318
oppression 52–53, 319
overhead projector 102, 128, 320
Oxbridge system 130, 137, 225, 277–279, 295
Oxhandler, Eugene K. 219

Paas, Fred 86, 90, 164, 304
Pacansky-Brock, Michelle 19
Paideia seminar 190, 205–206
Paivio, Allan 85, 153, 156
participation 196, 200, 232, 261; active 65, 122; audience 139; conscious 317–318; equalized 64; facilitator 214; individual's 89, 318; MOOC 207; non- 200; spontaneous 315; student 128; unlimited 16; veteran 13
peer influence 33, 49, 59, 61–62, 64, 303
personal interest 46–47, 51, 64, 302–303, 320
personal learning environments (PLE) 20
Personalized System of Instruction (PSI) 137, 277, 321
Petroski, Henry 100
phenomena 1, 18–22, 82, 87, 233, 266, 268, 284, 290, 316, 322
Piaget, Jean 45
Plato 179, 219, 269
portrayal 143, 145, 176, 178, 182, 185, 321
positron emission tomography (PET) 156
PowerPoint 134, 145, 267
presentation 2, 5, 10, 13, 17, 23, 27, 47, 94, 104, 112, 114–118, 122, 126–128, 130–132, 134, 138, 141, 143–145, 147–148, 150, 155–170, 173–174, 184–185, 187, 191, 193, 197, 199, 204, 206, 209, 212–213, 228, 229, 232, 236, 244, 256–257, 261, 266, 273, 279, 291, 294, 305–306, 320–321; activity 159; analog 101;

audiovisual 167; bimodal 132; concrete 145; course 269; direct 321; evolution of 148; explicit 137; external 156, 181, 321; information- 135, 147; internal 156, 181; media 165; mediated 112–113, 165, 185; multimedia 126; multiscreen 10; mundane 300; one-way 112–113; oral 117, 144, 148, 163, 165, 176, 225, 277, 318, 322; pictorial 158; realistic 111; recorded 55; short 209, 320; slide 102, 111–112, 146; symbolic 295; teacher-centered 100; two-way 112; verbal 155, 163, 185, 284; video 192, 206, 269, 285; visual 124, 155, 158, 273, 295
privilege 47, 51–53, 57–58, 61–62, 91, 95, 279, 319, 321
Problem-Based Learning (PBL) 116, 138, 258–259, 319–321
problem-solving 90, 114–115, 133, 233, 239, 286, 290, 314, 316
process-oriented guided inquiry learning (POGIL) 138, 248, 257, 262
programmed 99, 240; device 231, 277; teaching 25, 221; texts 227; tutoring 137, 215, 221, 225, 227; *see also* instruction
Protheroe, Nancy 54
proximal 37–38, 321; causal factors 39; cause 32, 42, 55, 71; determined 46; factors 33, 36, 38–39, 42, 302
psychological: state 39, 42–43, 46–48, 54, 61, 65, 71, 302–303, 321; traits 43–49, 51, 53, 60, 63, 71, 302–303, 321
psychomotor: objective 242, 321; structures 45

rapid instructed task learning (RITL) 95
real-world resources 101–103, 124, 134, 258, 266–268, 278, 319, 321, 323
recitation 109, 113–114, 127, 129, 140, 148, 189, 218, 232, 243–244, 259, 261–262, 284, 321
regular and substantive interaction (RSI) 12–15, 68
Reigeluth, Charles M. 3, 81, 94, 115, 136, 246, 261, 300
reinforcement 55, 88, 95, 180, 221, 224, 248, 314, 321–322
reinforcer 123, 216, 248, 250, 321
repetition 2, 27, 104, 116–117, 122–123, 126–127, 129–130, 133, 135, 139, 141, 148, 167–168, 182–185, 193, 196, 208, 214, 226, 229–233, 236–237, 239, 241–245, 247–250, 255–262, 275, 277, 279, 290–291, 305–307, 318, 321

resources 31, 43, 47–49, 53, 55–57, 60, 66–67, 71, 82, 92, 95, 100–104, 124–125, 143, 145, 175–178, 225, 235, 258, 266–268, 273, 277–279, 305, 318, 321, 323
retention 6, 42, 66, 123, 159–160, 166, 197, 245, 247, 291, 321; enhancing 148, 306; improving 159, 230; long-term 66, 119, 245, 247, 252, 261
Rocca, Kelly A. 196
role-play 112, 118, 131, 140, 146, 169, 184–185, 199, 233, 236, 242, 254, 258, 261, 318, 322
Rosenshine, Barak 118–119, 123–124, 126
Ross, Steven M. 18
Roulis, Eleni 197, 199
Russell, Thomas L. 6
Ryan, Richard M. 47–48

Saettler, Paul 5, 148, 218, 223, 244, 269
Salas, Eduardo 34, 46–47, 50, 57
Salomon, Gavriel 42, 136
schemata 154, 160, 165, 170, 196, 299, 308; conceptual 290; mental 118, 182, 276
Schiefele, Ulrich 46
Schnotz, Wolfgang 156–158, 181, 273
school environment 38, 49–51, 61–62, 303, 322
Schrader, Dawn E. 23, 64, 66
Schramm, Wilbur 7
Schroeder, Ray 17
seatwork 112–114, 132, 322
Select Committee on Intelligence, U.S. Senate 24
self: -directed learning 137, 271–272, 277, 322; -efficacy 44–51, 54, 62, 302–303, 321–322; -identity 47, 53, 57, 62, 322; -organized learning environments (SOLE) 208
seminar 111, 115, 138, 149, 190–191, 196, 205, 209, 212
sensory modality 153, 155–156, 158
Sesame Street 7, 146, 169
setting 31, 66–67, 70, 82, 95–97, 104, 108, 120, 124, 127, 129–131, 133–134, 140, 147, 159, 164, 187, 196, 214, 223–224, 229, 232, 234, 236, 248, 250–251, 253, 259, 261, 268, 271, 275, 277, 281, 299, 304–305, 314, 317–318, 322; academic 92, 102, 236, 238, 292; boundaries 4; classroom 64, 143, 209, 250, 308, 319; corporate 177, 271; distance education 134, 210; educational 49, 144, 200, 205, 248; experiential 141; group 145, 207, 259; instructional 33, 94, 97, 101, 299, 317, 319; large-group 131, 176–178; learning 130; lecture 139, 191, 226; modified reality 133; natural 133; noninstructional 97; physical 104; professional 65; realistic 133; real-life 11; real-world 92, 133, 231, 260; rehearsal 191; school 67; small-group 132; social 49, 322; teaching–learning 98
Shannon, Claude E. 110
shiur 148, 193, 322
show and tell 138, 182, 184–185
Shulman, Lee 128, 306
signature pedagogy 322
simulation 4, 23, 57, 102, 114–115, 133, 139, 141, 160, 190, 208, 229, 232–234, 237, 240, 252, 254–255, 257–258, 260–262, 281, 283, 292, 320, 322; animated 146, 185; computer 139, 173, 257, 261; data 257; exercises 234, 258, 320; features 232, 239; lifelike 132; online 96; physics 18; realistic 11, 234, 241; social 133, 135, 205, 232, 234, 258; technical 241; see also game; instructional
simulator 233, 242; advanced 242; flight 231, 233; physical 231, 233, 261, 322
situational interest 42, 47, 48, 51, 55, 302–303, 321–322
Skinner, B. F. 83, 216, 248, 307
Slavin, Robert E. 203–204
Smaldino, Sharon E. 115
small-group discussion 2, 27, 104, 112, 116, 120–121, 128–129, 132, 139, 141, 143, 187–188, 190, 196, 200–201, 204, 206–209, 213, 235, 250, 253, 257, 283, 307, 322
Smith, Lawrence A. 205
Smith-Woolley, Emily 40
Snapchat 64
social cognitive learning perspective 322
social learning theory 87–88, 180, 185, 245, 314, 322
social media 1, 20–24, 27, 46, 63–66, 132, 215, 281, 283, 301, 303, 322
social reproductionists 58
sociocultural environment 36, 51, 53, 57, 60, 62, 66–67, 303, 322
socioeconomic status (SES) 51–52, 59–63, 74, 197, 303, 322–323
Socrates 179, 269, 286
Sophist 148, 218
status 222, 300, 312; conferral 4–5; cultural 57–58; learning 217; publication 23; unequal 50; see also socioeconomic

Stodolsky, Susan S. 113–114, 116, 305
strengths 26, 122, 129, 141, 159, 169, 181, 195–196, 203, 220, 248–249, 273, 290
Student Teams-Achievement Divisions (STAD) 203–204
study 2, 27, 104, 116, 124, 126–130, 133, 140–141, 144, 146, 148, 159, 167, 175–178, 205–207, 209, 225–226, 242, 255, 257–258, 260, 266–275, 277–279, 281–282, 291, 294, 305–307, 315, 323; activities 134, 225, 320; classroom 101; correspondence 8, 12–13, 17, 134, 191, 268, 284–285, 316; evaluation 7; field of 13, 18, 127; group 129–130, 139, 191, 193, 206, 275, 295, 323; independent 110–111, 115, 124, 140, 194, 259, 270, 277, 279; large-scale 45; nonresidential 12; online 101, 146, 206; overseas 56; private 133, 269, 274, 279; programs 68, 192; research 18; scientific 25; self- 124, 158; skills 271, 274–275; strategies 274; textbook 133
Subramony, Deepak Prem. 8, 53, 58, 300
Suhrie, Ambrose L. 189
Sutton, Leah A. 204
synchronous 14, 132, 139, 144, 175, 191–192, 200, 206, 208, 214, 241, 323

Tadros, Marlyn 66
Tamim, Rana M. 18
Taylor, Mark 65–66
teacher-centered 323
teaching machine 25, 216, 219, 323
technocentrism 25–27, 299, 323
The Point 137–138, 258
Thiagarajan, Sivasailam. 167
TikTok 64
time on task 43, 65, 69, 220, 238, 275, 323
Titchener, Edward B. 272
training 1, 7, 26–27, 34, 42, 45–46, 49, 56–57, 61, 74, 92–94, 101–102, 121, 128, 144, 152, 164, 179, 196, 208, 218, 233–235, 243, 245, 248, 253, 259, 271, 276, 289, 312, 320; athletic 123, 176, 260; basic 230, 246; clicker 253, 307; contexts 99; corporate 17, 25, 31, 33, 42, 45–46, 49–50, 56–57, 68, 74, 112, 159, 169, 184, 192, 210, 223, 227, 234, 240–241, 261, 271; courses 17, 239; CPR 233; curricula 136; flight 152; in-service 73; institution 99; manuals 101–102, 275, 277; material 46; military 33, 243, 249, 286, 307; on-the-job 122, 177, 213; profession 25, 242; program 33, 42, 46, 49, 97, 271, 308, 318; residential 15; sales 184; self- 239; sensitivity 10, 191; sessions 8, 202; teacher 231; troops 194; videos 102; vocational 50; weapons 178
Tuckman, Bruce W. 202
Tumblr 23
tutee 96, 110, 122, 132, 212–213, 215, 220, 222, 224–225, 227, 232, 323
tutor 96, 99, 109–110, 122, 132, 176, 184, 212–213, 215, 218, 220, 222–225, 227, 232, 269, 278, 323; academic 223; knowledgeable 90; professional 122; skilled 221
tutorial 2, 18, 27, 104, 110–111, 114–116, 122–123, 126, 128, 131–132, 139, 141, 149, 149, 167, 184–185, 188, 195, 212–214, 217–223, 225–227, 232, 242, 250, 259–260, 269, 273–274, 277, 294, 305, 323; activities 130, 217, 220; arrangements 212; assistance 259, 294; education 218; evolution 217; face-to-face 132; guidance 91; help 257, 259; method 176, 220; mode 144, 183; relationship 193, 213, 223; sessions 225, 227, 229, 277; student-teacher 122; system 149, 193, 219; video 212; Web 102, 132, 212, 267; *see also* instruction
TutorIT 217, 227
Twain, Mark 298
Twitter 20–21, 23
Tyler, Ralph W. 35
typology 2, 26–27, 104, 108–109, 111–117, 129, 190, 266, 305–306, 323

Udacity 17
US Department of Education (ED) 15, 215, 222

valuation 46–48, 51, 54–55, 65, 71, 74, 128, 302–303, 321, 323
values 48, 51, 56, 61–62, 67, 69, 274, 314, 320; academic 62; cultural 58, 207; ecological 231; family 60, 303; personal 47; shared 315; task 46–47
Veletsianos, George 19
verbal-visual model 37, 39, 56
videoconference 144–145
virtual reality 25, 242, 261
visual art 102, 289
visualization 101, 176, 246, 283, 301

Walberg, Herbert J. 35–36, *36*, 38–39, 47, 48–49, 56, 59–61, 63, 68–69, 71, 221, 301
Weinstein, Rhona S. 50, 54–55
well-being 67, 70, 104
Weller, Martin 16, 20–21, 24–25
Wellington, Arthur M. 93
Wells, H. G. 312
Wentzel, Kathryn R. 61–62
Wertheimer, Max 153
whole-class discussion 2, 27, 104, 116, 119–121, 129, 131, 139, 141, 168–169, 187, 189, 193, 196, 198–200, 204–206, 208–209, 227, 253, 255, 257, 315, 320, 323
Wikis 20, 192
Willingham, Daniel B. 244–245, 261
Willingham, Daniel T. 40
Willis, Paul 53, 62
Winn, William 152, 158, 273
Witherspoon, John 180
World Health Organization (WHO) 311
World Wide Web 13, 219, 269, 272
Wouters, Pieter 260
Writing across the Curriculum (WAC) 292, 295, 323
Writing to Learn 140, 285, 291, 295, 323

Yelon, Stephen L. 176, 183, 185, 250–251
yeshiva 148, 193, 315, 322–323
Yeung, Ryan 73
YouTube 16, 18, 21, 64, 147, 177

ZOSMAT 217